DISKI

Dissertationen zur Künstlichen Intelligenz

Mit Unterstützung des Fachbereichs 1 „Künstliche Intelligenz" der Gesellschaft für Informatik e.V. herausgegeben von

Automated Deduction for Projection Elimination

Christoph Wernhard

AKA

Christoph Wernhard

Vom Promotionsausschuss des Fachbereichs: 4 Informatik
der Universität Koblenz-Landau
zur Verleihung des akademischen Grades
Doktor der Naturwissenschaften (Dr. rer. nat.)
genehmigte Dissertation.

Vorsitzender des Promotionsausschusses: Prof. Dr. Dietrich Paulus
Vorsitzender der Promotionskommission: Prof. Dr. Ralf Lämmel
Berichterstatter: Prof. Dr. Ulrich Furbach, Senior Lecturer Dr. Renate A. Schmidt

Tag der wissenschaftlichen Aussprache: 15. Februar 2008

Bibliographic information published by *Die Deutsche Bibliothek*
Die Deutsche Bibliothek lists this publication in the *Deutsche Nationalbibliografie*;
Detailed bibliographic data is available on the Internet at http://dnb.ddb.de.

Akademische Verlagsgesellschaft
AKA GmbH
Postfach 103305
69023 Heidelberg
Deutschland
Tel. +49 (0) 6221 21881
FAX +49 (0) 6221 167355
E-Mail: info@aka-verlag.de

Verlagsauslieferung
HEROLD Auslieferung & Service GmbH
Raiffeisenallee 10
82041 Oberhaching
Deutschland
Tel. +49 (0) 89 6138710
FAX +49 (0) 89 61387120
E-Mail: herold@herold-va.de

Co-publisher: IOS Press, Amsterdam

Reproduced from PDF supplied by the author
Printed in the Netherlands

ISSN 0941-5769
ISBN 978-3-89838-324-0 (AKA)
ISBN 978-1-58603-983-7 (IOS Press)

Acknowledgments

I am very grateful to Renate Schmidt and Uli Furbach. I had the luck to meet Renate from time to time during working on this thesis – occasions which became the key moments in its development. In Uli's research group I was enabled to transfer scientific ideas into results. I thank Peter Baumgartner for his support in the initial phase of the project during his time in Koblenz. Of course, the focus on tableau- or model-based methods in this thesis is inspired heavily by the work of Peter and Uli. I am also very obliged to Bernhard Beckert for some suggestions, technical and non-technical, that were essential to the progress of the thesis.

Special thanks go to Claudia Obermaier for her helpful feedback on drafts of the thesis and for the good collaboration on related topics. I also wish to thank the other members and guests of the Artificial Intelligence group at Koblenz University, in particular Adnan Yahya, Bernd Thomas, Björn Pelzer, Christoph Gladisch, Gerd Beuster, Jan Murray, Margret Groß-Hardt, Markus Maron, Oliver Obst and Vladimir Klebanov, who accompanied the different stages of the project at many meetings and supported me with suggestions, good questions, or by giving me their theses, which became motivating examples. The ideas for this thesis emerged while I was working with Ingo Dahn on semantic retrieval from a mathematical library, around ten years ago, where I was interested to make our somewhat ad-hoc methods more "semantic". I am further grateful to anonymous reviewers for their helpful comments on earlier versions of material in this thesis. Underlying research was funded in part by Deutsche Forschungsgemeinschaft with the project FU 263/10.

I thank Petra Gillert for sharing with me the personal aspects involved in thesis writing, spanning the decade since the first ideas. Many thanks also to Luc Döbereiner for his understanding and to Jana Kittelmann for her encouragement.

Contents

1 Introduction

The *projection* operator can extend logics used for knowledge representation. For propositional and first-order logic, it generalizes Boolean and second-order quantifiers, respectively, by allowing to specify the quantified items with a finer granularity: While a second-order quantifier can be considered as applying to all atoms with some predicate symbol, the projection operator can apply just to a subset of these atoms. Moreover, for formulas in negation normal form, it also can apply only to atoms in positive or negative literals.

The projection operator can be written as $\mathsf{project}(F, S)$, where F is a formula and S specifies the set of ground literals that are *not* "quantified". We call S the *scope* of the projection. The projection operator "projects" the formula F "onto the scope" S, meaning that $\mathsf{project}(F, S)$ is equivalent to F as far as literals in the scope S are concerned, but does not express anything about other literals.

In analogy to *second-order quantifier elimination*, we call the central computational operation to process the projection operator *projection elimination*. It means to compute for a given sentence in which the projection operator occurs an equivalent sentence in which it does not occur. The term *projection elimination* is derived from the idiom *quantifier elimination*, which, understood literally, expresses that occurrences of *quantifiers* – logic operators – are eliminated. Likewise, occurrences of the projection operator are eliminated. A second motivation for speaking of *projection elimination* is to indicate the close relationship to second-order quantifier elimination. Speaking of *projection elimination*, however, does not match with the alternate possible view of *predicate quantifier elimination* as elimination of the *quantified predicate variables*, since projection scopes are considered complementary: predicates not in the projection scope are, so to speak, eliminated, while those in the scope are retained.

In knowledge representation, projection provides a straightforward semantics-based account for tasks that involve the *removal* of knowledge about concepts in a given vocabulary, or – viewed dually – extracting the portion that concerns the vocabulary. Applications of quantifier and projection elimination (or closely related operations) described in the literature include synthesizing properties of accessibility relations from Hilbert axiomatizations of modal logics [GO92], computation of circumscription [GO92, DŁS97], forgetting about past states in agent knowledge bases [LR94], the specialization of knowledge compilation targets to given vocabularies [Dar01a], approximate reasoning [DS04], image computation to prove invariants of transition systems in model checking [McM05], and the modularization of ontologies with the notion of conservative theory extension [GLW06]. Unfolding in the partial evaluation of logic programs [Kom91] corresponds to projection elimination with respect to the (ground instances of) residual literals as scope. Further proposed applications of projection elimination are the removal of knowledge for security reasons, controlling vocabularies by which answers are expressed for human users or machine-to-machine information integration, and structuring of knowledge bases on the ground of implicit dependency relationships of predicates and functions [Wer04]. Many additional applications, in various fields such as complexity theory, correspondence theory and deductive databases, are described in [GSS08], the first monograph on second-order quantifier elimination, which has been released recently.

In the literature, works with different backgrounds and terminologies can be found that include characterizations of aspects of projection. Methods for second-order quantifier elimination and “forgetting” about a ground atom (projection, where the scope is the set of all ground literals except those with the given atom), basically for clausal first-order sentences, have been described in the early nineties, along with applications for various tasks in artificial intelligence [GO92, LR94]. Subsequently, methods have been developed that operate directly on formulas instead of clauses [Sza93, DŁS97]. These methods recently gained renewed interest, especially in the context of modal correspondence theory [CGV06, Sch08]. The previously cited monograph [GSS08] provides a comprehensive account of the different approaches to second-order quantifier elimination. In another line of research, concepts related to projection have been investigated just for propositional logic [KHM99, Dar01a, MR03, LLM03], reflecting the interest in propositional knowledge representation stimulated by the substantial advances in propositional satisfiability solving in the late nineties.

After fixing notation and technical preliminaries in Chapter 2, we develop in Chapter 3 a semantic concept related to projection, the *essential literal base* of a sentence. That is the set of ground literals “about which” the sentence expresses something. In Chapter 4 we then give a formal characterization of projection that applies to first-order logic. We also make precise the relationship of projection to second-order quantification. Chapter 5 presents a collection of properties of projection. Their application possibilities are outlined and formally proven statements are provided. Relationships between alternative characterizations of projection are shown. In Chapter 6 we review and compare works from the literature that include characterizations and properties of projection or similar concepts.

Our concept of projection covers sets of *literals*, in contrast to sets of atoms, as projection scopes, such that projection has different effects on positive and negative literals in formulas in negation normal form. For propositional logic, this has been considered in [LLM03]. However, properties of its interplay of with conjunction, which form a basis for projection elimination methods, have previously only been developed in a rudimentary way.

The semantic properties of projection suggest to apply techniques of automated deduction as *methods for projection elimination.* However, projection elimination cannot be straightforwardly expressed as a theorem proving task, but, like model generation, partial deduction and knowledge compilation, it can be considered as a special mode of reasoning that can be performed by adapted theorem provers. We consider two approaches, based on different approaches to theorem proving: resolvent generation and tableau construction. Our main focus is on the tableau approach. We explicitly consider one possibility to relate both approaches, the integration of special cases of methods based on resolvent generation as formula simplification operations into tableau methods.

SCAN [GO92, GHSV04] is an algorithm for the elimination of second-order quantifiers. Its core phase operates on a first-order clausal sentence. It proceeds by exhaustively adding all resolvents upon literals with predicate symbols corresponding to second-order variables, followed by deleting the clauses with such literals. SCAN uses a special kind of resolution, *C-resolution*, that has the effect that semantic equality, the possibility that an interpretation maps different terms to the same object, is implicitly taken into account.

> In Chapter 7 we develop a variant of the SCAN method, called replace-by-resolvents, that uses ordinary resolution and is independent of semantic equality. It thus can be used directly with semantics based on Herbrand models. We show a preprocessing technique that permits to apply replace-by-resolvents to projection elimination onto scopes that are characterized as the set of literals which fail to match a given pattern.

Many of the modern automated deduction systems that are successful in practical applications proceed by constructing a tree data structure that can be regarded as a tableau. This includes systems developed in different communities for different logics, such as theorem provers and model generators for first-order logic that implement calculi like hypertableau and model evolution [MB88, Wer03, BFT04], reasoners for modal and description logics [Hor98, HM01], propositional satisfiability solvers and model counters [MSS96, BS97, BP00], propositional knowledge compilers [Dar04], as well as answer set programming systems for non-monotonic propositional logics [NS97].

A branch in such a tableau represents a partial interpretation or model candidate of the input sentence. Some of the referenced systems utilize this for model computation. A whole tableau represents a sentence with a certain syntactic structure. For propositional sentences with specific such structures, projection elimination is a linear-time operation. Thus, projection elimination for arbitrary propositional sentences can be performed essentially by tableau construction. Also other operations, for example deciding whether a given clause is entailed, can be performed in linear time on tableaux meeting particular syntactic restrictions. This has been utilized for the specification of knowledge compilers explicitly as tableau construction procedures [MR03, HMR05] or as procedures that implicitly construct tableaux, which are made explicit as traces of procedure runs [Dar04, HD05].

Certain kinds of knowledge compilation, projection elimination and deciding propositional satisfiability can be considered as different instantiations of a single task: For knowledge compilation, a tableau is computed that represents a sentence which is equivalent to the input sentence. For projection elimination in a sentence $\mathsf{project}(F, S)$, where F is a conventional propositional sentence, it suffices to compute a tableau representing a sentence that is equivalent to F *just as far as the literals in the scope* S *are concerned.* The tableau then can be submitted as input to a linear-time projection elimination procedure. Deciding satisfiability corresponds to the special case of projection elimination in this way, where the scope S is the empty set. The resulting sentence is then either valid or unsatisfiable, which can be decided in linear time.

In Chapter 8 we make this general view on projection elimination, knowledge compilation and deciding satisfiability precise. We consider applications that combine knowledge compilation with projection elimination. We show that, under an assumption considered as very likely in complexity theory, the approach of performing projection elimination as a postprocessing step to equivalence preserving compilation [Dar01a, MR03] can be essentially improved by partially performing projection elimination already within the compilation phase.

Essential characteristics of the practically successful automated systems mentioned above are the use of tableau data structures with nodes labeled by literals in contrast to complex formulas, space efficiency by explicitly representing at any point of time just a single tableau branch in memory, and the flexible restructuring of search space by techniques of dependency directed backtracking. Such features can also be utilized in tableau construction methods for formula transformation tasks, like projection elimination and knowledge compilation. Efficient SAT solvers based on the Davis-Putnam-Logemann-Loveland (*DPLL*) procedure have, for example, been adapted for Boolean quantifier elimination [McM02] and knowledge compilation [Dar04, HD05].

Characteristics of efficient automated tableau construction methods transfer to tasks like projection elimination and knowledge compilation, independently of the particularities of these methods.

In Chapter 9 we take account of that by developing an abstract tableau framework for tasks such as projection elimination and knowledge compilation. The framework provides constraints that essentially relate child to parent nodes and can be verified as invariants for a concrete calculus by showing that they are preserved by its rules. Atomic cut, clausal expansion and variants of dependency directed backtracking with context unit lemmas are rules that comply with these constraints. Furthermore, these constraints permit techniques that implement the improvements suggested in Chapter 8 by partially performing projection elimination during compilation.

Variants of dependency directed backtracking for formula transformation can behave differently than for satisfiability testing. They can effect that in the tableau under construction a part is deleted that would be correct in the final output, but possibly can be replaced by a preferable sub-tableaux. This has already been remarked before [Dar04], but the effects are obscured there, due to the presentation by means of pseudocode.

In Chapter 10 we work out a variant of dependency directed backjumping with context unit lemmas that applies to various tableau methods. It is based on a recent abstract specification of backjumping in modern DPLL-based SAT solvers [NOT06]. We show the specific behavior for formula transformation tasks by means of several examples.

State-of-the-art systems for solving propositional satisfiability are based on DPLL. Such systems exemplify practically successful automated tableau systems, as considered here. They are relatively simple, since they are confined to propositional logic. As noted above, there are previous works where such systems have been adapted to Boolean quantifier elimination and knowledge compilation [McM02, Dar04, HD05].

In Chapters 11 and 12 we work out an adaption of DPLL for projection elimination and knowledge compilation as a prototypical instantiation of the framework developed in Chapters 9 and 10. The DPLL adaption is specified by means of tableau construction rules – in contrast to pseudocode, which is common in the literature on SAT solvers. It performs projection elimination partially during tableau construction, as suggested in Chapter 8, by the integration of appropriate formula simplification operations and by a special destructive tableau construction rule. In Chapter 11 the main focus is on semantic aspects of the method and the verification that it matches the framework. Efficiency aspects are discussed in Chapter 12.

As noted above, many tableau methods are space efficient because they represent at any point of time just a single tableau branch in memory. While this space efficiency is clearly beneficial for theorem proving tasks, where a yes/no answer is computed, it can also be utilized for formula transformation tasks if pieces of the overall output are delivered as soon as they are computed. Such an algorithm can be employed in applications in which output pieces by themselves are useful, output pieces can be piped to another program, or the first few output pieces are expected to provide a solution.

In Chapter 13 we show a variant of our DPLL adaption that utilizes space efficiency by delivering its output in a piecemeal fashion. Due to destructive tableau construction rules, the combined output pieces are not trivially identical to the implicitly constructed tableau.

In Chapter 14 we review and compare works related to our tableau methods. This includes the DPLL-based systems mentioned before [McM02, Dar04]. For a further proposed knowledge compilation method [MR03] that is based on a particular way of equivalence preserving rewriting of subformulas, we show formally that it can be simulated by our DPLL method.

2 Notation and Preliminaries

We use a formal framework in which interpretations are identified with sets of ground literals. This framework gives a semantic account to classical propositional logic, classical first-order logic, classical first-order logic in Skolemized clausal form and also to second-order constructs and other logics that can be considered as special cases of these. The framework can be seen as a notational variant of the framework of Herbrand interpretations, which is commonly used in the field of automated deduction in first-order logic. It allows to express many semantic properties conveniently as properties of sets of ground literals. There is no need for referencing to "external" entities, such as real-world objects, with functions and relations on them. The satisfaction relation only applies to sentences, that is, formulas without free variables, which however is sufficient for our purposes.

Syntax is specified in Sections 2.3–2.7, semantics in Sections 2.8–2.9. In Section 2.10 the relationship of our framework to first-order model theory and to Herbrand interpretations is made precise. In Section 2.11 the framework is adapted to sentences in clausal form.

2.1 Presentation of Proofs

Most of the proofs of theorems and propositions are presented formally by means of a table that shows numbered proof steps in symbolic form and is followed by verbal justifications.

2.2 Notational Conventions

If X_1, X_2 are sets, then $X_1 - X_2$ is the set difference of X_1 and X_2. If X is a set, then $|X|$ is its cardinality. A tuple, written $\langle X_1, \ldots, X_n \rangle$, combines a fixed number n of objects $X_1, \ldots, X_n$ that may have different types. A sequence with varying length whose elements have the same type is written as juxtaposition of elements and subsequences. If, for example, S_1 is the sequence of objects $X_1, \ldots, X_m$ and S_2 the sequence of objects $X_{m+2}, \ldots, X_n$, then the following are four different ways to express the sequence of objects $X_1, \ldots, X_n$: (1) $X_1 \ldots X_n$, (2) $S_1 X_{m+1} \ldots X_n$, (3) $X_1 \ldots X_m X_{m+1} S_2$, (4) $S_1 X_{m+1} S_2$. The symbol $\emptyset$ is used to denote the empty sequence as well as the empty set, depending on context.

2.3 Terms and Atoms

We use the notions *term* and *atom* with their standard meaning for first-order logic. Unless explicitly stated otherwise, we assume that all terms and atoms are constructed from a fixed "global" first-order *signature*, i. e., a finite or denumerable set of predicate symbols with arity ≥ 0, a nonempty, finite or denumerable set of constant symbols, and a finite or denumerable set of function symbols with arity ≥ 1. We also assume a denumerable set of *variables* x, y, z, also with subscripts.

Definition 1 (Term) *Terms* are precisely those expressions that can be obtained by a finite number of applications of the following rules:

1. A constant symbol is a term.
2. A variable is a term.
3. If f is an n-ary function symbol and $t_1, \ldots, t_n$ are terms, then $f(t_1, \ldots, t_n)$ is a term.

Definition 2 (Atom) *Atoms* are precisely the expressions obtained by the following rule: If p is an n-ary predicate symbol and $t_1, \ldots, t_n$ are terms, then $p(t_1, \ldots, t_n)$ is an atom.[1]

Definition 3 (Ground Term, Ground Atom) A term or atom is called *ground* if and only if it does not contain a variable.

Definition 4 (Special Sets of Terms and Atoms)

(i) GTERMS is the set of all ground terms.

(ii) GATOMS is the set of all ground atoms.

Definition 5 (Complement of a Set of Ground Atoms) If S is a set of ground atoms, then

$$\overline{S} \stackrel{\text{def}}{=} \mathsf{GATOMS} - S.$$

2.4 Formulas and Sentences

We consider first-order logic and several other logic formalisms that can be considered as restrictions of first-order logic.

Definition 6 (Formula) *Formulas* are precisely those expressions that can be obtained by a finite number of applications of the following rules:

1. An atom is a formula.
2. $\top$ and $\bot$ are formulas.
3. If F is a formula, then $\neg F$ is a formula.

[1] As a special case, if p is a predicate symbol with arity 0, then p is an atom.

4. If F_1 and F_2 are formulas, then $(F_1 \wedge F2)$, $(F_1 \vee F_2)$, $(F_1 \rightarrow F_2)$ and $(F_1 \leftrightarrow F_2)$ are formulas.
5. If F is a formula and x is a variable, then $\forall x F$ and $\exists x F$ are formulas.

Definition 7 (Further Notation for Formulas) The formulas $\top$ and $\bot$ are called *truth value constants*. A *conjunction* of formulas $F_1, \ldots, F_n$, where $n \geq 0$, is written as $\bigwedge_{i \in \{1,\ldots,n\}} F_i$ or $F_1 \wedge \ldots \wedge F_n$, where the $\wedge$ operator is understood as the binary connective, right-associative, with $\top$ as zero element. A *disjunction* of formulas is defined analogously for the $\vee$ connective, with $\bot$ as zero element.

Definition 8 (Free, Bound) An occurrence of a variable x in a formula F is *free* if it is not in the scope of a quantifier $\forall x$ or $\exists x$. If an occurrence of a variable x is free in a formula F, then this occurrence is *bound* in $\forall x F$ or $\exists x F$ by the displayed occurrence of the respective quantifier.

To avoid clumsy handling of quantifier scopes, we assume that in a formula all occurrences of the same variable are either free or are bound by an occurrence of a quantifier, and that no two quantifier occurrences bind occurrences of the same variable. Since any formula can be brought into such a form by a suitable variable renaming, this assumption is without loss of generality.

Definition 9 (Sentence) A formula without a free variable is called a *sentence.*

Definition 10 (Propositional) A formula or sentence that does not contain quantifiers and variables is called *propositional.*

Obviously, the notions of *propositional formula* and *propositional sentence* are equivalent. A propositional sentence can be viewed as a sentence of propositional logic, where ground atoms correspond to so-called propositional variables.

Definition 11 (Size of a Propositional Sentence) If F is a propositional sentence, then the *size* of F, in symbols $|F|$, is the number of occurrences of atoms and truth value constants in F.

2.5 Literals

Definition 12 (Literal, Positive, Negative) A *literal* is an atom A or a negated atom $\neg A$. We also write a literal A ($\neg A$, resp.) as $+A$ ($-A$, resp.). A literal of the form $+A$ ($-A$, resp.) is called *positive* (*negative*, resp.). The atom A is called *the atom of* the literal $+A$ ($-A$, resp.). The atom of a literal L is written in symbols as $\mathsf{atom}(L)$.

Definition 13 (Complement of a Literal) If L is a literal, $\widetilde{L}$, the *complement* of L is defined as follows: If A is an atom, then

$$\widetilde{+A} \stackrel{\text{def}}{=} -A;$$
$$\widetilde{-A} \stackrel{\text{def}}{=} +A.$$

Definition 14 (Ground Literal) A literal is called *ground* if and only if its atom is ground.

Definition 15 (Special Sets of Literals)

(i) GLITS is the set of ground literals.

(ii) GPOS is the set of positive ground literals.

(iii) GNEG is the set of negative ground literals.

(iv) If S is a set of atoms, then $+S \stackrel{\text{def}}{=} \{+A \mid A \in S\}$ and $-S \stackrel{\text{def}}{=} \{-A \mid A \in S\}$.

Definition 16 (Operations on Sets of Literals) If S is a set of literals, then

(i) $\widetilde{S} \stackrel{\text{def}}{=} \{\widetilde{L} \mid L \in S\}$;

(ii) $\mathsf{atoms}(S) \stackrel{\text{def}}{=} \{A \mid +A \in S\} \cup \{A \mid -A \in S\}$;

(iii) S is called *consistent* if and only if it does not contain a literal and its complement.

Definition 17 (Complement of a Set of Ground Literals) If S is a set of ground literals, then

$$\overline{S} \stackrel{\text{def}}{=} \mathsf{GLITS} - S.$$

Definition 17 for sets of ground literals is analogous to Definition 5 for sets of ground atoms.

2.6 Polarity and Literals Contained in a Formula

With a subformula occurrence, a *polarity* with respect to the containing formula can be associated, which indicates whether the subformula occurs in the scope of the $\leftrightarrow$ operator (polarity 0) or in the scope of an even or odd number of negation operators (polarity 1 or -1, respectively). Negation operators in this sense are the $\neg$ operator and, with respect to its left argument, the $\rightarrow$ connective. *Polarity* is made precise in Definition 18. An atom paired with polarity 1 or -1 is conveniently represented by a positive or negative, respectively, literal. We say that a *literal is contained in* a formula, if the atom of the literal occurs in the formula either with the polarity indicated by the literal sign or with polarity 0. This concept is specified in Definition 19.

We call a formula *polar* if none of its atomic subformulas has polarity 0. This is stated in Definition 20. Polar formulas are closely related to negation normal form: A polar formula can be converted into negation normal form with linear effort; a formula in negation normal form is polar. Thus, in the parameter specification of a proposition, the requirement for a formula to be *polar* is similar to the requirement of being in negation normal form, except that *polar* allows more "syntactic sugar", such as the use of the $\rightarrow$ connective and the $\neg$ operator with complex formulas as argument. A formula is polar if and only if it does not contain an atom occurrence in the scope of the $\leftrightarrow$ operator. For all formulas, it is possible to construct a polar equivalent by expanding the $\leftrightarrow$ operator, e. g. into a conjunction of two applications of $\rightarrow$. The effort of this transformation can however be exponential.

Polar formulas allow forms of systematic substitution of atom occurrences by truth values, with effects depending on the polarity of the respective occurrences. Two such kinds of substitution, *literal substitution* and *polar substitution*, are defined in Definitions 21 and 22. Literal substitution is applied for example in the proof of Theorem 1. Straightforward substitution of atoms by truth values will be defined in a subsequent section, in Definition 46.

Definition 18 (Polarity) If F is a formula, then the *polarity in* F of an occurrence of a subformula of F is

- 0 if and only if the subformula occurrence is within F in an argument of the $\leftrightarrow$ connective;
- 1, otherwise, if and only if the number of occurrences of negation operators in F in whose argument the subformula occurrence is (i. e., the total of the number of occurrences of $\neg$ in whose argument it is, and of $\rightarrow$ in whose left argument it is) is even.
- -1, otherwise.

Definition 19 (Literal Contained) If F is a formula and L is a literal, then L is a *literal contained in* F if and only if

- L is positive and the atom of L occurs with a polarity ≥ 0 in F, or
- L is negative and the atom of L occurs with a polarity ≤ 0 in F.

Example 1 (Literal Contained in a Formula) The set of literals contained in $(\mathsf{p} \rightarrow \mathsf{q})$ is $\{-\mathsf{p}, +\mathsf{q}\}$. The set of literals contained in $(\mathsf{p} \leftrightarrow \mathsf{q})$ is $\{+\mathsf{p}, -\mathsf{p}, +\mathsf{q}, -\mathsf{q}\}$. The set of literals contained in $\forall x(\mathsf{p}(x) \rightarrow \mathsf{p}(\mathsf{f}(x)))$ is $\{-\mathsf{p}(x), +\mathsf{p}(\mathsf{f}(x))\}$.

Definition 20 (Polar Formula) A formula is called *polar* if and only if it contains no atom occurrence with polarity 0.

Definition 21 (Literal Substitution) If F is a polar propositional formula, L is a ground literal with atom A and either $W = \top$ and $\widetilde{W} = \bot$, or $W = \bot$ and $\widetilde{W} = \top$, then if L is positive,

$$F[\![L \backslash W]\!]$$

stands for F with all occurrences of A with polarity 1 substituted by W; otherwise, if L is negative, it stands for F with all occurrences of A with polarity -1 substituted by $\widetilde{W}$.

Example 2 (Literal Substitution) Let $F \stackrel{\text{def}}{=} (\mathsf{p} \rightarrow \mathsf{q}) \wedge (\mathsf{p} \vee \mathsf{r})$.

$$F[\![+\mathsf{p} \backslash \top]\!] = (\mathsf{p} \rightarrow \mathsf{q}) \wedge (\top \vee \mathsf{r});$$
$$F[\![-\mathsf{p} \backslash \top]\!] = (\bot \rightarrow \mathsf{q}) \wedge (\mathsf{p} \vee \mathsf{r}).$$

Definition 22 (Polar Substitution) If F is a polar propositional formula, A is a ground atom, and either $W = \top$ and $\widetilde{W} = \bot$, or $W = \bot$ and $\widetilde{W} = \top$, then

$$F[\![A \backslash W]\!]$$

stands for F with all occurrences of A with polarity 1 substituted by W and with polarity -1 by $\widetilde{W}$.

Example 3 (Polar Substitution)

$$((\mathsf{p} \rightarrow \mathsf{q}) \wedge (\mathsf{p} \vee \mathsf{r}))[\![\mathsf{p} \backslash \top]\!] = (\bot \rightarrow \mathsf{q}) \wedge (\top \vee \mathsf{r}).$$

Polar substitution can be defined in terms of literal substitution: If F is a polar propositional formula, A is a ground atom and either $W = \top$ or $W = \bot$, then

$$F[\![A \backslash W]\!] = F[\![+A \backslash W]\!][\![-A \backslash W]\!].$$

2.7 Variable Substitutions

Definition 23 (Variable Substitution) A *variable substitution* is a mapping of variables to terms. If F is a term, atom, formula or literal, and σ is a variable substitution, then $F\sigma$ denotes F with all variables occurring in the domain of σ replaced by their image in σ. A variable substitution that maps for all $i \in \{1, \ldots, n\}$ the variable x_i to the term t_i is written $\{x_1 \mapsto t_1, \ldots, x_n \mapsto t_n\}$. The empty substitution is denoted by ϵ. Composition of variable substitutions is denoted by $\circ$, where the substitution on the left side is applied first.

Definition 24 (Instance) If F_1, F_2 are both terms, atoms or literals, then F_1 is an *instance* of F_2 if and only if there exists a variable substitution σ such that and $F_1 = F_2\sigma$.

Definition 25 (Unifiable, Weakly Unifiable, Most General Unifier) If F_1, F_2 are two terms, atoms, or literals, respectively, then

(i) A *unifier* of F_1 and F_2 is a substitution σ such that $F_1\sigma = F_2\sigma$;

(ii) F_1 and F_2 are *unifiable* if and only if there exists a unifier of F_1 and F_2;

(iii) F_1 and F_2 are *weakly unifiable* if and only if there exists a unifier of F_1 and F_2', where F_2' is F_2 with variables renamed such that it has no variables in common with F_1;

(iv) A *most general unifier* of F_1 and F_2 is a unifier σ such that for all unifiers τ of F_1 and F_2 there exists a substitution λ such that $\tau = \sigma \circ \lambda$;

(v) If F_1 and F_2 are unifiable, then $\mathsf{mgu}(F_1, F_2)$ denotes a most general unifier of F_1 and F_2.[2]

2.8 Interpretations

As a semantic basis, we use a notational variant of the framework of Herbrand interpretations, which is a common semantic framework for first-order logic in the field of automated deduction. We call interpretations and models in the sense of this framework simply *interpretations* and *models*. In Sections 2.10 and 4.10 we relate it to the common model theoretic framework for first-order and second-order logic.

Definition 26 (Interpretation) An interpretation is a set of ground literals that contains for all ground atoms A exactly one of $+A$ or $-A$.

Definition 27 (Operations on Interpretations) If I is an interpretation, A is a ground atom, L is a ground literal and S is a set of ground literals, then

(i) $I.A$ is defined as the literal with atom A that is contained in I;

(ii) I *assigns* to A the value $\top$, if $I.A$ is positive, otherwise the value $\bot$;

(iii) $I[L] \stackrel{\text{def}}{=} (I - \{\widetilde{L}\}) \cup \{L\}$;

(iv) $I[S] \stackrel{\text{def}}{=} (I - \widetilde{S}) \cup S$.

Proposition 1 *If I is an interpretation, then*

$$\widetilde{I} = \overline{I}.$$

Proof. Follows easily from the definition of *interpretation*. □

[2] Most general unifiers are unique up to variable renaming.

2.9 Satisfaction Relation

Definition 28 (Model) If I is an interpretation and F is a sentence, then the satisfaction relation *I is a model of F*, in symbols $I \models F$, is defined inductively as follows, where A is a ground atom, F_1 and F_2 are sentences, and F' is a formula such that x is the only variable that possibly occurs free in it:

$$
\begin{array}{lll}
I \models A & \text{iff}_{\text{def}} & +A \in I, \\
I \models \top, & & \\
I \not\models \bot, & & \\
I \models \neg F_1 & \text{iff}_{\text{def}} & I \not\models F_1, \\
I \models F_1 \wedge F_2 & \text{iff}_{\text{def}} & I \models F_1 \text{ and } I \models F_2, \\
I \models F_1 \vee F_2 & \text{iff}_{\text{def}} & I \models F_1 \text{ or } I \models F_2, \\
I \models F_1 \rightarrow F_2 & \text{iff}_{\text{def}} & I \not\models F_1 \text{ or } I \models F_2, \\
I \models F_1 \leftrightarrow F_2 & \text{iff}_{\text{def}} & I \models F_1 \text{ if and only if } I \models F_2, \\
I \models \forall x F' & \text{iff}_{\text{def}} & \text{for all } t \in \mathsf{GTERMS} \text{ it holds that } I \models F'\{x \mapsto t\}, \\
I \models \exists x F' & \text{iff}_{\text{def}} & \text{there exists a } t \in \mathsf{GTERMS} \text{ such that } I \models F'\{x \mapsto t\}.
\end{array}
$$

Definition 29 (Entailment, Equivalence) A sentence F_1 *entails* a sentence F_2, in symbols $F_1 \models F_2$, if and only if for all interpretations I it holds that if $I \models F_1$ then $I \models F_2$.[3] A sentence F_1 is *equivalent* to a sentence F_2, in symbols $F_1 \equiv F_2$, if and only if $F_1 \models F_2$ and $F_2 \models F_1$.

2.10 Relationship to First-order Model Theory

In this section we make precise the relationship of the semantic framework specified in Sections 2.8–2.9 to the common model theoretic framework for first-order logic. As a point of reference we use the presentation in the book by Ebbinghaus et al. [EFT96, Section III, pp. 29–62, and Section XI § 3, pp. 213–221]. To distinguish interpretations in the sense of this "standard" model theoretic framework, we call them *std-interpretations*, write them in a Gothic font, e. g. $\mathfrak{I}$, and use $\models_{std}$ as symbol for the satisfaction relation. The satisfaction relation for std-interpretations also applies to formulas with free variables, and not only to sentences.

We define std-interpretations and a satisfaction relation for them. Herbrand interpretations are then defined as a special case of std-interpretations, whose domain is a set of syntactic objects, the set of ground terms. A mapping from Herbrand interpretations to interpretations in the sense of our framework is defined (Definition 33). The correspondence of the satisfaction relation for Herbrand interpretations to the satisfaction relation for interpretations obtained by this mapping is then made precise in Proposition 3.

[3] As common in the literature, the symbol $\models$ is overloaded by two different meanings, entailment and the satisfaction relation. We use it for entailment with a single sentence as left and as right argument.

Definition 30 (Std-Interpretation and Related Concepts) A *structure* is a pair $\langle A, \mathfrak{a}\rangle$ of a nonempty set A, the *domain*, and a mapping $\mathfrak{a}$ of predicate and function symbols to relations and functions, respectively, on A and of constant symbols to elements of A. A *std-interpretation* is a pair $\langle \mathfrak{A}, \beta\rangle$ of a structure $\mathfrak{A} = \langle A, \mathfrak{a}\rangle$ and a *variable assignment* β, a mapping of the set of variables into A. If β is a variable assignment, then $\beta\frac{a}{x}$ denotes the variable assignment that maps the variable x to a and all other variables to the same values as β. If $\mathfrak{I} = \langle\langle A, \mathfrak{a}\rangle, \beta\rangle$ is a std-interpretation, then $\mathfrak{I}\frac{a}{x}$ stands for $\langle\langle A, \mathfrak{a}\rangle, \beta\frac{a}{x}\rangle$.

If $\mathfrak{I} = \langle\langle A, \mathfrak{a}\rangle, \beta\rangle$ is a std-interpretation, then a mapping, also named $\mathfrak{I}$, from the set of terms onto A is defined as follows: For a variable x let $\mathfrak{I}(x) = \beta(x)$, for a constant symbol c let $\mathfrak{I}(c) = \mathfrak{a}(c)$ and for an n-ary function symbol f and terms $t_1, \ldots, t_n$ let $\mathfrak{I}(f(t_1, \ldots, t_n)) = \mathfrak{a}(f)(\mathfrak{I}(t_1), \ldots, \mathfrak{I}(t_n))$.

Definition 31 (Std-Model) If $\mathfrak{I} = \langle\langle A, \mathfrak{a}\rangle, \beta\rangle$ is a std-interpretation and F is a formula, then the satisfaction relation $\mathfrak{I}$ *is a std-model of* F, in symbols $\mathfrak{I} \models_{std} F$, is defined inductively as follows, where p is a predicate symbol, $t_1, \ldots, t_n$ are terms and F' is a formula:

$\mathfrak{I} \models_{std} p(t_1, \ldots, t_n)$	iff$_{\text{def}}$	$\langle \mathfrak{I}(t_1), \ldots, \mathfrak{I}(t_n)\rangle \in \mathfrak{a}(p)$,[4]
$\mathfrak{I} \models_{std} \forall x F'$	iff$_{\text{def}}$	for all $a \in A$ it holds that $\mathfrak{I}\frac{a}{x} \models_{std} F'$,
$\mathfrak{I} \models_{std} \exists x F'$	iff$_{\text{def}}$	there exists an $a \in A$ such that $\mathfrak{I}\frac{a}{x} \models_{std} F'$.

Definition clauses for the other logic operators are analogously to Definition 28 and not displayed here.

Definition 32 (Herbrand Interpretation) A std-interpretation $\langle\langle A, \mathfrak{a}\rangle, \beta\rangle$ is called a *Herbrand interpretation* if and only if

1. $A = \mathsf{GTERMS}$;
2. For all constant symbols c it holds that $\mathfrak{a}(c) = c$;
3. For all n-ary function symbols f and ground terms $t_1, \ldots, t_n$ it holds that $\mathfrak{a}(f)(t_1, \ldots, t_n) = f(t_1, \ldots, t_n)$.

Proposition 2 *If F is a formula, x is a variable that does not occur bound in F, a is a ground term and $\mathfrak{I}$ is a Herbrand interpretation, then*

$$\mathfrak{I} \models_{std} F\{x \mapsto a\} \text{ if and only if } \mathfrak{I}\tfrac{a}{x} \models_{std} F.$$

Proof. The proposition can be proven by induction on formulas. We only show the base case of atomic formulas and the induction step for universally quantified formulas. The induction step for existentially quantified formulas can be shown analogously. Showing the proposition for $\top$ and $\bot$ and showing the induction step for the other logic operators is straightforward. The base case of atoms $p(t_1, \ldots, t_n)$ can be shown as follows:

[4] A relation with arity zero is either the empty set or the singleton set containing the empty tuple $\langle\rangle$.

(1)	$\mathfrak{I} \models_{std} p(t_1, \ldots, t_n)\{x \mapsto a\}$	iff
(2)	$\langle \mathfrak{I}(t_1\{x \mapsto a\}), \ldots, \mathfrak{I}(t_n\{x \mapsto a\})\rangle \in \mathfrak{a}(p)$	iff
(3)	$\langle \mathfrak{I}\frac{a}{x}(t_1), \ldots, \mathfrak{I}\frac{a}{x}(t_n)\rangle \in \mathfrak{a}(p)$	iff
(4)	$\mathfrak{I}\frac{a}{x} \models_{std} p(t_1, \ldots, t_n)$.	

Equivalence of (2) to (1) follows from the definition of $\models_{std}$. $x\{x \mapsto a\} = \mathfrak{I}\frac{a}{x}(x) = a$; hence it is easy to see that for $i \in \{1, \ldots, n\}$ it holds that $\mathfrak{I}(t_i\{x \mapsto a\}) = \mathfrak{I}\frac{a}{x}(t_i)$. Thus (3) is equivalent to (2). Equivalence of (4) to (3) follows from the definition of $\models_{std}$. The induction step for formulas of the form $\forall y F'$ can be shown as follows:

(1)	$\mathfrak{I} \models_{std} (\forall y F')\{x \mapsto a\}$	iff
(2)	$\mathfrak{I} \models_{std} (\forall y (F'\{x \mapsto a\})$	iff
(3)	For all $a \in \mathsf{GTERMS}$: $\mathfrak{I}\frac{a}{y} \models_{std} F'\{x \mapsto a\}$	iff
(4)	For all $a \in \mathsf{GTERMS}$: $\mathfrak{I}\frac{a}{y}\frac{a}{x} \models_{std} F'$	iff
(5)	For all $a \in \mathsf{GTERMS}$: $\mathfrak{I}\frac{a}{x}\frac{a}{y} \models_{std} F'$	iff
(6)	$\mathfrak{I}\frac{a}{x} \models_{std} \forall y F'$.	

Equivalence of (2) to (1) follows from the specification of x. Equivalence of (3) to (2) follows from the definition of $\models_{std}$. Equivalence of (4) to (3) follows from the induction assumption. y must be different from x, since y is not a free variable of $\forall y F'$. Hence (5) is equivalent to (4). Equivalence of (6) to (5) follows from the definition of $\models_{std}$.

□

The following definition specifies a mapping between Herbrand interpretations and interpretations represented as sets of literals according to Definition 26. With a Herbrand interpretation a unique such literal set representation is associated.

Definition 33 (Literal Set Representation) An interpretation I is called the *literal set representation* of a Herbrand interpretation $\langle\langle \mathsf{GTERMS}, \mathfrak{a}\rangle, \beta\rangle$ if and only if for all ground atoms $p(t_1, \ldots, t_n)$ it holds that

$$\langle t_1, \ldots, t_n\rangle \in \mathfrak{a}(p) \text{ if and only if } +p(t_1, \ldots, t_n) \in I.$$

Proposition 3 *If F is a sentence, $\mathfrak{I}$ is a Herbrand interpretation and I its literal set representation, then*

$$\mathfrak{I} \models_{std} F \textit{ if and only if } I \models F.$$

Proof. We show by induction on formulas the following property, from which the proposition immediately follows: If F is a formula, σ is a variable substitution with the set of free variables of F as domain and a set of ground terms as range, $\mathfrak{I} = \langle\langle \mathsf{GTERMS}, \mathfrak{a}\rangle, \beta\rangle$ is a Herbrand interpretation and I its literal set representation, then

$$\mathfrak{I} \models_{std} F\sigma \textit{ if and only if } I \models F\sigma.$$

As in the proof of Proposition 2, we only show the base case of atomic formulas and the induction step for universally quantified formulas. The base case of atoms $p(t_1, \ldots, t_n)$ can be shown as follows:

$$\begin{array}{lll}
(1) & \mathfrak{I} \models_{std} p(t_1, \ldots, t_n)\sigma & \text{iff} \\
(2) & \langle I(t_1\sigma), \ldots, I(t_n\sigma)\rangle \in \mathfrak{a}(p) & \text{iff} \\
(3) & \langle t_1\sigma, \ldots, t_n\sigma\rangle \in \mathfrak{a}(p) & \text{iff} \\
(4) & +p(t_1, \ldots, t_n)\sigma \in I & \text{iff} \\
(5) & I \models p(t_1, \ldots, t_n)\sigma. &
\end{array}$$

Equivalence of (2) to (1) follows from the definition of $\models_{std}$. For all $i \in \{1, \ldots, n\}$ it holds that $t_i\sigma$ is ground. Since $\mathfrak{I}$ is a Herbrand interpretation it follows that $I(t_i\sigma) = t_i\sigma$. Thus (3) is equivalent to (2). Equivalence of (4) to (3) follows from the specifications of $\mathfrak{I}$ and I. Equivalence of (5) to (4) follows from the definition of $\models$. The induction step for formulas of the form $\forall x F'$ can be shown as follows:

$$\begin{array}{lll}
(1) & \mathfrak{I} \models_{std} (\forall x F')\sigma & \text{iff} \\
(2) & \mathfrak{I} \models_{std} \forall x (F'\sigma) & \text{iff} \\
(3) & \text{For all } a \in \mathsf{GTERMS}\text{: } \mathfrak{I}\tfrac{a}{x} \models_{std} F'\sigma & \text{iff} \\
(4) & \text{For all } a \in \mathsf{GTERMS}\text{: } \mathfrak{I} \models_{std} F'\sigma\{x \mapsto a\} & \text{iff} \\
(5) & \text{For all } a \in \mathsf{GTERMS}\text{: } I \models F'\sigma\{x \mapsto a\} & \text{iff} \\
(6) & I \models \forall x (F'\sigma) & \text{iff} \\
(7) & I \models (\forall x F')\sigma. &
\end{array}$$

Equivalence of (2) to (1) follows from the specification of σ. Since $\mathfrak{I}$ is a Herbrand interpretation, its domain is the set of ground terms. Thus equivalence of (3) to (2) follows from the definition of $\models_{std}$. Equivalence of (4) to (3) follows from Proposition 2. x is the only variable that possibly occurs free in $F'\sigma$. Thus the equivalence of (5) to (4) follows from the induction assumption. Equivalence of (6) and (5) follows from the definition of $\models$. Equivalence of (7) to (6) follows from the specification of σ.

□

2.11 Clausal Sentences and Herbrand Expansion

The majority of automated deduction techniques for propositional and first-order logic has been developed for sentences in clause form. The Herbrand expansion of such a clausal sentence is a construct that links first-order logic to propositional logic by allowing to view a first-order sentence in clause form as an infinite propositional conjunction. If a first-order sentence is unsatisfiable, then a finite fragment of its Herbrand expansion is so. This justifies first-order theorem proving methods that interleave the construction of the Herbrand expansion of their input clauses with testing for propositional unsatisfiability.

For this work, we do not take clausal sentences as a basis. However, some of the properties and techniques that we will develop apply only to clausal sentences or are particularly straightforward for them. Thus, in this section we formally define *clausal sentence* and *Herbrand expansion*, and show how our semantic framework relates to them (Proposition 4).

Definition 34 (Conjunctive and Disjunctive Normal Form) A formula is in *conjunctive normal form* (CNF) if and only if it is a conjunction of disjunctions of atoms or negated atoms. A formula is in *disjunctive normal form* (DNF) if and only if it is a disjunction of conjunctions of atoms or negated atoms.

Definition 35 (Tautology-Free, Contradiction-Free) A sentence in CNF (DNF, resp.) in which no conjunct (disjunct, resp.) contains a literal and its complement is called *tautology-free* (*contradiction-free*, resp.).

Definition 36 (Clause, Clausal Sentence) A *clause* is a sentence of the form $\forall x_1 \ldots \forall x_k (L_1 \vee \ldots \vee L_n)$, where $L_1, \ldots, L_n$ are literals and $x_1, \ldots, x_k$ are the variables in these literals. A clause can be represented (modulo associativity, commutativity and idempotence of the $\vee$ operator, and permutations of the quantifier ordering) by the set of its literals. We use finite sets of literals to represent clauses in this way and write them as disjunctions $(L_1 \vee \ldots \vee L_n)$. The set representation of the empty clause is written as $\perp$.

A *clausal sentence* is a sentence of the form $\forall x_1 \ldots \forall x_k F$, where F is a formula in CNF and $x_1, \ldots, x_n$ are the variables in F. A clausal sentence $\forall x_1 \ldots \forall x_n F$ can be represented (modulo associativity, commutativity and idempotence of the $\wedge$ and $\vee$ operators, and equivalent ways of quantifier positioning) by a set of clauses, each representing a conjunct of F. We use finite sets of clauses to represent clausal sentences in this way.

Definition 37 (Tautological Clause, Subsumed Clause)

(i) A clause containing a literal and its complement is called *tautological*.

(ii) A clause C_1 is *subsumed* by a clause C_2 if and only if there exists a substitution σ such that $C_2\sigma \subseteq C_1$. A clause C is *subsumed* by a clausal sentence F if and only if C is subsumed by a clause of F.

Definition 38 (Herbrand Expansion) If F is a clausal sentence and Σ is a finite or denumerable set of constant and function symbols that includes those in F, then the *Herbrand expansion of F over Σ* is the set of all ground instances of clauses of F, obtained by instantiating with terms constructed from Σ.

Proposition 4 *If F is a clausal sentence, H is a Herbrand expansion of F over some set of constant and function symbols Σ that includes those in F and I is an interpretation (with respect to a signature that includes at least the symbols in F and Σ), then*

(i) $I \models F$ *if and only if for all clauses* $C \in H$ *it holds that* $I \models C$;
(ii) $I \models F$ *if and only if for all clauses* $C \in H$ *it holds that* $I \cap C \neq \emptyset$;
(iii) $I \not\models F$ *if and only if there exists a clause* $C \in H$ *such that* $\widetilde{C} \subseteq I$.

Proof. Follows easily from the definitions of *Herbrand expansion*, $\models$ and *interpretation* (Definitions 38, 28 and 26).

□

2.12 Semantically Determined Relations and Functions

We call a relation on sentences that is independent of syntactic properties *semantically determined*. Whenever such a relation holds for a tuple of sentences, it also holds for the tuple with one of the sentences replaced by an equivalent. A 1-ary such relation is called *semantically determined property*. Analogously, we call a function that maps sentences independently of their syntactic properties to values *semantically determined*. In the formal definitions that follow now, also additional arguments which are not sentences are considered.

Definition 39 (Semantically Determined Relation and Property) An n-ary relation R, where $n \geq 1$, whose arguments at places in $S \subseteq \{1, \ldots, n\}$ are those with type *sentence* is called a *semantically determined relation* if and only if for all $i \in S$, sentences F_1, F_2 and arbitrary objects $X_1, \ldots, X_{i-1}, X_{i+1}, \ldots X_n$ it holds that

$$\text{If } F_1 \equiv F_2, \text{ then} \quad R(X_1, \ldots, X_{i-1}, F_1, X_{i+1}, \ldots, X_n) \quad \text{if and only if} \quad R(X_1, \ldots, X_{i-1}, F_2, X_{i+1}, \ldots, X_n).$$

If $S = \{1\} = \{n\}$, then R is also called a *semantically determined property*.

Definition 40 (Semantically Determined Function) An n-ary function F, where $n \geq 1$, whose arguments at places in $S \subseteq \{1, \ldots, n\}$ are those with type *sentence* is called a *semantically determined function* if and only if for all $i \in S$, sentences F_1, F_2 and arbitrary objects $X_1, \ldots, X_{i-1}, X_{i+1}, \ldots, X_n$ it holds that

$$\text{If } F_1 \equiv F_2, \text{ then} \quad F(X_1, \ldots, X_{i-1}, F_1, X_{i+1}, \ldots, X_n) = F(X_1, \ldots, X_{i-1}, F_2, X_{i+1}, \ldots, X_n).$$

3 Essential Literal Base and Related Concepts

The set of non-logic symbols, or signature, of a knowledge base hints the objects, concepts and relations about which it expresses "knowledge". But the signature might be too large for this: For example, the sentence *KnowledgeBase* $= (\mathsf{p} \lor (\mathsf{q} \land \neg\mathsf{q}))$ is clearly equivalent to p. Thus *KnowledgeBase* does express something about p but not about q, although q is in its signature. One might argue that in practice such redundancies might be avoided by carefully engineering knowledge bases. But such redundancies may also arise by combining knowledge bases that are free of them. For example conjoining $(\mathsf{q} \rightarrow \mathsf{p})$ with $(\neg\mathsf{q} \rightarrow \mathsf{p})$ results in an equivalent to *KnowledgeBase*, which, as we have seen, does not express anything about q, although each of the conjuncts expresses something about q.

We call the set of atoms in a propositional formula its *atom base*. This concept can be generalized to first-order formulas, it then denotes the set of all ground instances of atoms in the formula. For a propositional formula the atom base is the same as its signature, but for first-order formulas both notions differ. The *essential atom base* of a sentence is the set of atoms "about which the sentence expresses something". For example, the essential atom base of *KnowledgeBase* is $\{\mathsf{p}\}$. *Literal base* and *essential literal base* are refinements of *atom base* and *essential atom base* in which also the polarity of atom occurrences is taken into account.

In Section 3.1 these four concepts are formally defined and some basic properties of them are stated. It is intuitively clear that for the satisfaction relation of an interpretation and a sentence only those values of the interpretation are relevant which are assigned to atoms in the atom base of the sentence. We formally show in Section 3.2 a related property, which states that from a given model of a sentence another model can be obtained by switching value assignments of any literals that are not in the literal base of the sentence. Based on this property, we then shown that the essential atom or literal base of a sentence is a subset of its atom base or literal base, respectively. An analog of the value assignment switching property for *essential* literal bases is discussed in Section 3.3. It is shown that this analog holds for a syntactically restricted class of sentences, which includes propositional sentences and clausal first-order sentences. In Section 3.4 further properties of the essential atom and literal base are shown for *propositional* formulas, for example that the essential literal base of a given sentence is the smallest set of literals from which an equivalent to the sentence can be constructed. Also, procedures for eliminating atoms and literals not in the essential base are given in this section.

3.1 Definitions

The concepts *literal base*, *atom base*, *essential literal base* and *essential atom base*, which have been discussed informally in the introduction of Chapter 3, are defined formally. The definitions are followed by some properties that can be derived from them. A characterization of *essential literal base*, which, in a sense, is dual to the definition (Definition 43) is given in Proposition 5. This proposition is applied in the proof of Theorem 1 for DNF sentences, while the proof for CNF sentences is based on the definition. As one would expect, the essential atom base of a sentence is just the set of atoms of the literals in the essential literal base. A corresponding characterization of the essential atom base in terms of the essential literal base is shown in Proposition 6. Essential literal base and essential atom base are semantically determined functions. Their value is independent of syntactic properties of argument sentences. This is stated formally in Propositions 7 and 8.

Definition 41 (Literal Base) The *literal base* of a formula F, in symbols $\mathcal{L}(F)$, is the set of ground instances of literals contained in F.

Definition 42 (Atom Base) The *atom base* of a formula F, in symbols $\mathcal{A}(F)$, is the set of ground instances of atoms occurring in F.

Definition 43 (Essential Literal Base) The *essential literal base* of a sentence F, in symbols $\mathcal{L}_{\mathcal{E}}(F)$, is defined as

$$\begin{aligned}\mathcal{L}_{\mathcal{E}}(F) \stackrel{\text{def}}{=} \{L \mid\ & L \text{ is a ground literal}\\ & \text{and there exist an interpretation } I \text{ such that}\\ & I \models F \text{ and } I[\widetilde{L}] \not\models F\}.\end{aligned}$$

Definition 44 (Essential Atom Base) The *essential atom base* of a sentence F, in symbols $\mathcal{A}_{\mathcal{E}}(F)$, is defined as

$$\begin{aligned}\mathcal{A}_{\mathcal{E}}(F) \stackrel{\text{def}}{=} \{A \mid\ & A \text{ is a ground atom}\\ & \text{and there exist an interpretation } I \text{ such that}\\ & \text{exactly one of } I[+A] \models F \text{ or } I[-A] \models F \text{ holds}\}.\end{aligned}$$

Example 4 ([Essential] Literal and Atom Base) Let $F \stackrel{\text{def}}{=} \mathsf{p} \lor (\mathsf{q} \land \neg\mathsf{q})$.

$$\begin{aligned}\mathcal{L}(F) &= \{+\mathsf{p}, +\mathsf{q}, -\mathsf{q}\};\\ \mathcal{A}(F) &= \{\mathsf{p}, \mathsf{q}\};\\ \mathcal{L}_{\mathcal{E}}(F) &= \{+\mathsf{p}\};\\ \mathcal{A}_{\mathcal{E}}(F) &= \{\mathsf{p}\}.\end{aligned}$$

Example 5 (Literal and Atom Base – First-Order) Let

$$
\begin{aligned}
F \stackrel{\text{def}}{=} \forall x((\mathsf{q}(x) \wedge \mathsf{p}(x)) \rightarrow \mathsf{p}(\mathsf{f}(x))) \wedge \\
((\neg\mathsf{q}(x) \wedge \mathsf{p}(x)) \rightarrow \mathsf{p}(\mathsf{f}(x))).
\end{aligned}
$$

$$
\begin{aligned}
\mathcal{L}(F) = {} & \{+\mathsf{p}(\mathsf{f}(t)) \mid t \in \mathsf{GTERMS}\} \cup \\
& \{-\mathsf{p}(t) \mid t \in \mathsf{GTERMS}\} \cup \\
& \{+\mathsf{q}(t) \mid t \in \mathsf{GTERMS}\} \cup \\
& \{-\mathsf{q}(t) \mid t \in \mathsf{GTERMS}\};
\end{aligned}
$$

$$
\begin{aligned}
\mathcal{A}(F) = {} & \{\mathsf{p}(t) \mid t \in \mathsf{GTERMS}\} \cup \\
& \{\mathsf{q}(t) \mid t \in \mathsf{GTERMS}\}.
\end{aligned}
$$

The values of $\mathcal{L}_{\mathcal{E}}(F)$ and $\mathcal{A}_{\mathcal{E}}(F)$ are shown in Example 6 (p. 27).

Proposition 5 *If F is a sentence, then*

$$
\begin{aligned}
\mathcal{L}_{\mathcal{E}}(F) = \{L \mid {} & L \textit{ is a ground literal} \\
& \textit{and there exist an interpretation } I \textit{ such that} \\
& I[L] \models F \textit{ and } I \not\models F\}.
\end{aligned}
$$

Proof.

(1) $I \models F$ and $I[\widetilde{L}] \not\models F$.
(2) $I = I[L]$.
(3) $J \stackrel{\text{def}}{=} I[\widetilde{L}]$.
(4) $J[L] = I[L]$.
(5) $J[L] \models F$ and $J \not\models F$.

We only show one direction of the equivalence of both characterizations, since the other direction follows from similar arguments with L and $\widetilde{L}$ switched in steps (2)–(4). Let L be a literal in $\mathcal{L}_{\mathcal{E}}(F)$. By the definition of $\mathcal{L}_{\mathcal{E}}$ there exists an interpretation I such that (1) holds. (2) follows from (1). Let J be an interpretation as defined in (3). (4) follows from (3). (5) follows from (1)–(4). Thus, with J there exists an interpretation that satisfies (5) and hence L satisfies the characterization stated in the proposition.

□

Proposition 6 *If F is a sentence, then*

$$\mathcal{A}_{\mathcal{E}}(F) = \{A \mid A \text{ is the atom of an element of } \mathcal{L}_{\mathcal{E}}(F)\}.$$

Proof. Follows easily from the definitions of $\mathcal{A}_{\mathcal{E}}$ and $\mathcal{L}_{\mathcal{E}}$.

□

Proposition 7 *$\mathcal{L}_{\mathcal{E}}$ is a semantically determined function, i. e., if F_1, F_2 are sentences, then*

$$\textit{if } F_1 \equiv F_2, \textit{ then } \mathcal{L}_{\mathcal{E}}(F_1) = \mathcal{L}_{\mathcal{E}}(F_2).$$

Proof. Follows easily from the definition of $\mathcal{L}_{\mathcal{E}}$.

□

Proposition 8 *$\mathcal{A}_{\mathcal{E}}$ is a semantically determined function, i. e., if F_1, F_2 are sentences, then*

$$\textit{if } F_1 \equiv F_2, \textit{ then } \mathcal{A}_{\mathcal{E}}(F_1) = \mathcal{A}_{\mathcal{E}}(F_2).$$

Proof. Follows easily from Propositions 7 and 6.

□

3.2 Switching Values Outside the Literal Base

From a given model of a sentence another model can be obtained by switching only literals not in the literal base of the sentence. This is stated in Proposition 9. One of the preconditions of this proposition, $S \cap \mathcal{L}(F) = \emptyset$, is equivalent to $\widetilde{S} \cap \widetilde{\mathcal{L}(F)} = \emptyset$. This suggests a second way to read the proposition: another model can be obtained by switching literals in a way such that none of the new values is complementary to an element of the literal base.

Only the values assigned by an interpretation to atoms in the atom base of a sentence are relevant for the satisfaction relation. This intuitively clear fact is an adaption of the *coincidence lemma* [EFT96, p. 39] to our semantic framework. It follows from Proposition 9 and is stated as Proposition 10.

The essential literal and atom base are subsets of the literal and atom base, respectively. Based on Proposition 9, this is proven in Propositions 11 and 12.

Proposition 9 *If I is an interpretation, F is a sentence and S is a consistent set of ground literals, then*

$$\textit{if } I \models F \textit{ and } S \cap \mathcal{L}(F) = \emptyset, \textit{ then } I[\widetilde{S}] \models F.$$

Proof. We show by induction on formulas the following property, from which the proposition immediately follows: If I is an interpretation, F is a formula, S is a consistent set of ground literals and σ is a variable substitution with the set of free variables of F as domain and a set of ground terms as range, then

$$\textit{if } I \models F\sigma \textit{ and } S \cap \mathcal{L}(F) = \emptyset, \textit{ then } I[\widetilde{S}] \models F\sigma.$$

We show the base case of atomic formulas and the induction step for the negation, conjunction and universal quantification operators. Showing the induction step for the other logic operators is analogous. Showing the proposition for $\top$ and $\bot$ is straightforward. The base case of atoms A can be shown as follows:

(1) $I \models A\sigma$.
(2) $S \cap \mathcal{L}(A) = \emptyset$.
(3) $A\sigma \in I$.
(4) $A\sigma \notin S$.
(5) $A\sigma \in I[\widetilde{S}]$.
(6) $I[\widetilde{S}] \models A\sigma$.

Assume (1) and (2). (3) follows from (1) and the definition of $\models$. (4) follows from (2). (5) follows from (4) and (3). (6) follows from (5) and the definition of $\models$. The induction step for formulas of the form $\neg F_1$ can be shown as follows:

(1) $I \models (\neg F_1)\sigma$.
(2) $S \cap \mathcal{L}(\neg F_1) = \emptyset$.
(3) $I \not\models F_1\sigma$.
(4) $J[I \cap S] \not\models F_1\sigma$.
(5) $S \cap \widetilde{\mathcal{L}(F_1)} = \emptyset$.
(6) $\widetilde{S} \cap \mathcal{L}(F_1) = \emptyset$.
(7) $\widetilde{I \cap S} \cap \mathcal{L}(F_1) = \emptyset$.
(8) $J \not\models F_1\sigma$.
(9) $I[\widetilde{S}] \not\models F_1\sigma$.

Assume (1) and (2). (3) follows from (1) and the definition of $\models$. Let $J \stackrel{\text{def}}{=} I[\widetilde{S}] = I[\widetilde{I \cap S}]$. Then $I = J[I \cap S]$. (4) then follows from (3). (5) follows from (2), since $\mathcal{L}(\neg F_1) = \widetilde{\mathcal{L}(F_1)}$. (6) follows from (5); (7) follows from (6). (8) follows from (7), (5) and the induction assumption

$$\textit{if } J \models F_1\sigma \textit{ and } \widetilde{I \cap S} \cap \mathcal{L}(F_1) = \emptyset, \textit{ then } J[I \cap S] \models F_1\sigma,$$

which is equivalent to

$$\textit{if } J[I \cap S] \not\models F_1\sigma \textit{ and } \widetilde{I \cap S} \cap \mathcal{L}(F_1) = \emptyset, \textit{ then } J \not\models F_1\sigma.$$

(9) follows from (8) and the definition of J. The induction step for formulas of the form $(F_1 \land F_2)$ can be shown as follows:

(1) $I \models (F_1 \land F_2)\sigma$.
(2) $S \cap \mathcal{L}(F_1 \land F_2) = \emptyset$.
(3) For $i \in \{1, 2\}$: $I \models F_i\sigma$.
(4) For $i \in \{1, 2\}$: $I \models F_i\sigma_i$.
(5) For $i \in \{1, 2\}$: $S \cap \mathcal{L}(F_i) = \emptyset$.
(6) For $i \in \{1, 2\}$: $I[\widetilde{S}] \models F_i\sigma_i$.
(7) For $i \in \{1, 2\}$: $I[\widetilde{S}] \models F_i\sigma$.
(8) $I[\widetilde{S}] \models (F_1 \land F_2)\sigma$.

Assume (1) and (2). (3) follows from (1) and the definition of $\models$. For $i \in \{1, 2\}$ let σ_i be the restriction of σ to the free variables of F_i. Evidently, for $i \in \{1, 2\}$ it holds that $F_i\sigma = F_i\sigma_i$. Hence (4) follows from (3). (5) follows from (2), since $\mathcal{L}(F_1 \wedge F_2) = \mathcal{L}(F_1) \cup \mathcal{L}(F_2)$. (6) follows from (5), (4) and the induction assumption. (7) follows from (6). (8) follows from (7) and the definition of $\models$. The induction step for formulas of the form $\forall x F_1$ can be shown as follows:

(1) $I \models (\forall x F_1)\sigma$.
(2) $S \cap \mathcal{L}(\forall x F_1) = \emptyset$.
(3) For all $t \in \mathsf{GTERMS}$: $I \models F_1\sigma\{x \mapsto t\}$.
(4) $S \cap \mathcal{L}(F_1) = \emptyset$.
(5) For all $t \in \mathsf{GTERMS}$: $I[\widetilde{S}] \models F_1\sigma\{x \mapsto t\}$.
(6) $I[\widetilde{S}] \models (\forall x F_1)\sigma$.

We quietly make use of the facts that x can not be in the domain of σ and that $(\forall x F_1)\sigma = \forall x(F_1\sigma)$. Assume (1) and (2). (3) follows from (1) by the definition of $\models$. (4) follows from (2), since $\mathcal{L}(\forall x F_1) = \mathcal{L}(F_1)$. (5) follows from (4), (3) and the induction assumption. (6) follows from (5) and the definition of $\models$.

□

Proposition 10 *If I_1, I_2 are interpretations and F is a sentence such that for all atoms A in $\mathcal{A}(F)$ it holds that $I_1.A = I_2.A$, then*

$$I_1 \models F \text{ if and only if } I_2 \models F.$$

Proof.

(1) $I_1 \cap (+\mathcal{A}(F) \cup -\mathcal{A}(F)) = I_2 \cap (+\mathcal{A}(F) \cup -\mathcal{A}(F))$.
(2) $I_1 \models F$.
(3) $I_1 \cap (\mathcal{L}(F) \cup \widetilde{\mathcal{L}(F)}) = I_2 \cap (\mathcal{L}(F) \cup \widetilde{\mathcal{L}(F)})$.
(4) $I_1 \cap \mathcal{L}(F) = I_2 \cap \mathcal{L}(F)$.
(5) $(I_2 - I_1) \cap \mathcal{L}(F) = \emptyset$.
(6) $I_1[I_2 - I_1] \models F$.
(7) $I_2 \models F$.

Assume (1) and (2). (3) follows from (1) by the definition of $\mathcal{L}$ and $\mathcal{A}$. (4) follows from (3) by the definition of *interpretation*. (5) follows from (4). (6) follows from (5), (2) and Proposition 9. (7) follows from (6).

□

Proposition 11 *If F is a sentence, then*

$$\mathcal{L}_{\mathcal{E}}(F) \subseteq \mathcal{L}(F).$$

Proof.

(1) $L \in \mathcal{L}_{\mathcal{E}}(F)$.
(2) $L \notin \mathcal{L}(F)$.
(3) $I \models F$.
(4) $I[\widetilde{L}] \not\models F$.
(5) $\{L\} \cap \mathcal{L}(F) = \emptyset$.
(6) $I[\widetilde{\{L\}}] \models F$.
(7) $\mathsf{contradiction}$.

Let L be a literal such that (1) and (2) holds. By the definition of $\mathcal{L}_{\mathcal{E}}$ there exists an interpretation I such that (3) and (4) hold. (5) follows from (2). (6) follows from (5), (3) and Proposition 9. (6) contradicts with (4), since $I[\widetilde{\{L\}}] = I[\widetilde{L}]$.

□

Proposition 12 *If F is a sentence, then*

$$\mathcal{A}_{\mathcal{E}}(F) \subseteq \mathcal{A}(F).$$

Proof. Follows easily from Propositions 11 and 6.

□

Example 6 (Essential Literal and Atom Base – First-Order) Let F be defined as in Example 5 (p. 23).

$$\mathcal{L}_{\mathcal{E}}(F) = \{+\mathsf{p}(\mathsf{f}(t)) \mid t \in \mathsf{GTERMS}\} \cup \{-\mathsf{p}(t) \mid t \in \mathsf{GTERMS}\};$$

$$\mathcal{A}_{\mathcal{E}}(F) = \{\mathsf{p}(t) \mid t \in \mathsf{GTERMS}\}.$$

Proof. We first show $\mathcal{L}_{\mathcal{E}}(F) \subseteq \{+\mathsf{p}(\mathsf{f}(t)) \mid t \in \mathsf{GTERMS}\} \cup \{-\mathsf{p}(t) \mid t \in \mathsf{GTERMS}\}$.

(1) $F' \stackrel{\text{def}}{=} \forall x(\mathsf{p}(x) \rightarrow \mathsf{p}(\mathsf{f}(x)))$.
(2) $F' \equiv F$.
(3) $\mathcal{L}_{\mathcal{E}}(F) \equiv \mathcal{L}_{\mathcal{E}}(F')$.
(4) $\mathcal{L}_{\mathcal{E}}(F) \subseteq \mathcal{L}(F')$.
(5) $\mathcal{L}(F') = \{+\mathsf{p}(\mathsf{f}(t)) \mid t \in \mathsf{GTERMS}\} \cup \{-\mathsf{p}(t) \mid t \in \mathsf{GTERMS}\}$.
(6) $\mathcal{L}_{\mathcal{E}}(F) \subseteq \{+\mathsf{p}(\mathsf{f}(t)) \mid t \in \mathsf{GTERMS}\} \cup \{-\mathsf{p}(t) \mid t \in \mathsf{GTERMS}\}$.

Let F' be a sentence as defined in (1). Clearly (2) follows from (1). (3) follows from (2) and Proposition 7. (4) follows from (3) and Proposition 11. (5) follows from (1) and the definition of $\mathcal{L}$. (6) follows from (5) and (4). We now show $\{+\mathsf{p}(\mathsf{f}(t)) \mid t \in \mathsf{GTERMS}\} \subseteq \mathcal{L}_{\mathcal{E}}(F)$.

(1) $+\mathsf{p}(\mathsf{f}(t)) \notin \mathcal{L}_{\mathcal{E}}(F)$.
(2) For all interpretations I such that $I \models F$: $I[-\mathsf{p}(\mathsf{f}(t))] \models F$.
(3) $\mathsf{GPOS} \models F$.
(4) $\mathsf{GPOS}[-\mathsf{p}(\mathsf{f}(t))] \not\models \mathsf{p}(t) \rightarrow \mathsf{p}(\mathsf{f}(t))$.
(5) $\mathsf{GPOS}[-\mathsf{p}(\mathsf{f}(t))] \not\models F$.
(6) contradiction.

Assume that there exists a ground term t such that (1) holds. (2) follows from (1) and the definition of $\mathcal{L}_{\mathcal{E}}$. (3) and (4) are easy to see (F is equivalent to $\forall x(\mathsf{p}(x) \rightarrow \mathsf{p}(\mathsf{f}(x))))$. (5) follows from (4). (5) and (3) contradict with (2). That $\{-\mathsf{p}(t) \mid t \in \mathsf{GTERMS}\} \subseteq \mathcal{L}_{\mathcal{E}}(F)$ can be shown analogously:

(1) $-\mathsf{p}(t) \notin \mathcal{L}_{\mathcal{E}}(F)$.
(2) For all interpretations I such that $I \models F$: $I[+\mathsf{p}(t)] \models F$.
(3) $\mathsf{GNEG} \models F$.
(4) $\mathsf{GNEG}[+\mathsf{p}(t)] \not\models \mathsf{p}(t) \rightarrow \mathsf{p}(\mathsf{f}(t))$.
(5) $\mathsf{GNEG}[+\mathsf{p}(t)] \not\models F$.
(6) contradiction.

Thus we have shown that $\mathcal{L}_{\mathcal{E}}(F) = \{+\mathsf{p}(\mathsf{f}(t)) \mid t \in \mathsf{GTERMS}\} \cup \{-\mathsf{p}(t) \mid t \in \mathsf{GTERMS}\}$. That $\mathcal{A}_{\mathcal{E}}(F) = \{\mathsf{p}(t) \mid t \in \mathsf{GTERMS}\}$ then follows from Proposition 6.

□

3.3 Switching Values Outside the Essential Literal Base

The subject of this section is the analog of Proposition 9 for *essential* literal bases: From a given model of a sentence another model can be obtained by switching only literals not in the *essential* literal base of the sentence. If only a single literal is switched, this property is an easy consequence of the definition of the essential literal base and stated as Proposition 13. We call sentences that also satisfy this property if arbitrary sets of literals are switched *$\mathcal{E}$-sentences*, formally defined in Definition 45. Being an $\mathcal{E}$-sentence is a semantically determined property, i. e., an equivalent to an $\mathcal{E}$-sentence is also an $\mathcal{E}$-sentence. This is stated in Proposition 14. An analog to Proposition 10 for essential literal bases is stated in Proposition 16.

Proposition 17 shows a compactness property which entails that a sentence is an $\mathcal{E}$-sentence. Propositional sentences and also clausal first-order sentences (and any sentences equivalent to such a sentence) satisfy this compactness property and thus are $\mathcal{E}$-sentences. This is shown in Proposition 18.

Some of the material in Chapter 5, for example in Section 5.3, is shown in two variants: one in which the literal base is used with proofs based on Proposition 9, and a second variant in which the essential literal base is used, with proofs based on Definition 45, and thus applying only to $\mathcal{E}$-sentences.

Proposition 13 *If I is an interpretation, F is a sentence and L is a ground literal, then*

$$\text{if } I \models F \text{ and } L \notin \mathcal{L}_{\mathcal{E}}(F), \text{ then } I[\widetilde{L}] \models F.$$

Proof. Follows immediately from Definition 43. □

Definition 45 ($\mathcal{E}$-Sentence) A sentence F is called *$\mathcal{E}$-sentence* if and only if for all interpretations I and consistent sets of ground literals S it holds that

$$\text{if } I \models F \text{ and } S \cap \mathcal{L}_{\mathcal{E}}(F) = \emptyset, \text{ then } I[\widetilde{S}] \models F.$$

Proposition 14 *Being an $\mathcal{E}$-sentence is a semantically determined property, i. e., if F_1, F_2 are sentences, then*

$$\text{if } F_1 \equiv F_2 \text{ and } F_1 \text{ is an } \mathcal{E}\text{-sentence, then } F_2 \text{ is an } \mathcal{E}\text{-sentence.}$$

Proof. Follows easily from the definition of $\mathcal{E}$-sentence and Proposition 7. □

Proposition 15 *If F is an $\mathcal{E}$-sentence, then*

$$\text{if } \mathcal{L}_{\mathcal{E}}(F) = \emptyset, \text{ then } F \equiv \top \text{ or } F \equiv \bot.$$

Proof. Assume $F \not\equiv \top$ and $F \not\equiv \bot$. Then there exist interpretations I_1, I_2 such that $I_1 \models F$ and $I_2 \not\models F$. There exists a literal scope S such that $I_2 = I_1[S]$. Since F is an $\mathcal{E}$-sentence it follows from Definition 45 that

$$\text{if } I_1 \models F \text{ and } I_1[S] \not\models F, \text{ then } \widetilde{S} \cap \mathcal{L}_{\mathcal{E}}(F) \neq \emptyset.$$

Thus $\mathcal{L}_{\mathcal{E}}(F) \neq \emptyset$. □

Proposition 16 *If I_1, I_2 are interpretations and F is an $\mathcal{E}$-sentence such that for all atoms A in $\mathcal{A}_{\mathcal{E}}(F)$ it holds that $I_1.A = I_2.A$, then*

$$I_1 \models F \text{ if and only if } I_2 \models F.$$

Proof. Can be shown in the same way as Proposition 10, with $\mathcal{A}_{\mathcal{E}}$ and $\mathcal{L}_{\mathcal{E}}$ in place of $\mathcal{A}$ and $\mathcal{L}$ and reference to the definition of $\mathcal{E}$-sentence instead of Proposition 9. □

Proposition 17 *If F is a sentence such that for all interpretations I and consistent sets of ground literals S it holds that*

$$\text{if } I \models F \text{ and } I[S] \not\models F, \text{ then}$$
$$\text{there exists a finite set } S' \subseteq S \text{ such that } I[S'] \not\models F,$$

then

$$F \text{ is an } \mathcal{E}\text{-sentence.}$$

Proof.

(1) $I \models F$.
(2) $S \cap \mathcal{L}_{\mathcal{E}}(F) = \emptyset$.
(3) $I[\widetilde{S}] \not\models F$.
(4) $I[S'] \not\models F$.
(5) $I[S'] \models F$.
(6) contradiction.

Assume the precondition of the proposition. Assume that F is not an $\mathcal{E}$-sentence. Hence there exists an interpretation I and a consistent set of ground literals S such that (1)–(3) hold. From the precondition of the proposition it follows that there exists a set $S' \subseteq \widetilde{S}$ such that (4) holds. Since S' is finite and for all $L \in S'$ it holds that $\widetilde{L} \notin \mathcal{L}_{\mathcal{E}}(F)$, (5) follows by induction on the cardinality of S' from (1) and Proposition 13. (5) contradicts with (4).

□

Proposition 18 *A sentence that is equivalent to a clausal sentence is an $\mathcal{E}$-sentence.*

Proof. Let F be a sentence. Assume – by Proposition 14 without loss of generality – that F is a clausal sentence. Let I be an interpretation and S be a consistent sets of ground literals such that $I \models F$ and $I[S] \not\models F$. By Proposition 4.iii then there exists a ground instance C of a clause of F such that $\widetilde{C} \subseteq I[S]$. Hence there exists a finite set $S' = S \cap \widetilde{C}$ such that $I[S'] \not\models F$. It then follows from Proposition 17 that F is an $\mathcal{E}$-sentence.

□

Obviously, propositional sentences and sentences that contain as quantifiers only $\forall$ occurring as outermost operator of subformulas with polarity 1 are equivalent to clausal sentences, and thus are $\mathcal{E}$-sentences.

3.4 Elimination of Inessential Literals in Propositional Sentences

On propositional sentences, the substitution of atoms or literals by truth values, which we call *atom substitution* (Definition 46) or *literal substitution* (Definition 21), respectively, can be used to eliminate atoms or literals that are not in the essential atom or literal base. *Eliminating* means here to compute for a given sentence an equivalent sentence that does not contain the respective atoms or literals. An atom not in the essential atom base of a propositional sentence can be eliminated with linear effort (Proposition 20). For sentences in conjunctive or disjunctive normal form, also a *literal* not in the essential literal base can be eliminated with linear effort (Theorem 1).

The essential literal base of a given sentence is the smallest set of literals from which an equivalent to the sentence can be constructed. Similarly, the essential atom base is the smallest set of atoms from which an equivalent can be constructed. This is shown, based on the elimination properties, in Proposition 21 and 22.

Definition 46 (Atom Substitution) If F is a propositional formula, A is a ground atom and W is either $\top$ or $\bot$ we write F with all occurrences of A substituted by W as

$$F[A \backslash W].$$

Example 7 (Atom Substitution)

$$((\mathsf{p} \rightarrow \mathsf{q}) \land (\mathsf{p} \lor \mathsf{r}))[\mathsf{p} \backslash \top] = (\top \rightarrow \mathsf{q}) \land (\top \lor \mathsf{r}).$$

For polar formulas F, atom substitution can be defined in terms of literal substitution:

$$F[A \backslash W] = F[\![+A \backslash W]\!][\![-A \backslash \widetilde{W}]\!],$$

where $\widetilde{W} = \bot$ $(\top, \mathit{resp.})$ if $W = \top$ $(\bot, \mathit{resp.})$.

Proposition 19 *If I is an interpretation, A is a ground atom and F is a propositional sentence, then*

$$I[+A] \models F \textit{ if and only if } I \models F[A \backslash \top],$$

and

$$I[-A] \models F \textit{ if and only if } I \models F[A \backslash \bot].$$

Proof. By induction on formulas. We only show the base case of atomic formulas A, since the remaining base cases and induction steps are straightforward. It holds that $I[+A] \models A$ if and only if $I \models A[A \backslash \top]$, since both sides of this equivalence are true. Analogously it holds that $I[-A] \models A$ if and only if $I \models A[A \backslash \bot]$, since both sides of that equivalence are false.

□

Proposition 20 *There exists an algorithm that constructs for a propositional sentence F and a ground atom $A \notin \mathcal{A}_{\mathcal{E}}(F)$ as inputs in time linear in $|F|$ a propositional sentence F' such that*

1. $F' \equiv F$,
2. $\mathcal{A}(F') \subseteq \mathcal{A}(F) - \{A\}$,
3. $|F'| \leq |F|$.

Proof. $F[A\backslash\top]$ is a suitable F'. It can be constructed from F by substituting A with $\top$. It is obvious that F' can be computed in time linear in $|F|$. Also items 2. and 3. are evident. We have to show item 1. Since $A \notin \mathcal{A}_{\mathcal{E}}(F)$ it follows from the definition of $\mathcal{A}_{\mathcal{E}}$ that $I[+A] \models F$ holds if and only if $I[-A] \models F$. Since either $I = I[+A]$ or $I = I[-A]$ it follows that $I \models F$ holds if and only if $I[+A] \models F$. From Proposition 19 it follows that $I \models F$ if and only if $I \models F[A\backslash\top]$, which concludes the proof.

□

$F[A\backslash\bot]$ is another sentence suitable as F' in Proposition 20. Based on this sentence, the proposition can be proven with help of the fact that $I \models F$ holds if and only if $I[-A] \models F$.

Theorem 1 (Elimination of Inessential Literals for CNF and DNF) *There exist algorithms that construct for a propositional sentence in tautology-free CNF (or contradiction-free DNF, resp.) and a ground literal $L \notin \mathcal{L}_{\mathcal{E}}(F)$ as inputs in time linear in $|F|$ a propositional sentence F' also in tautology-free CNF (or contradiction free DNF, resp.) such that*

1. $F' \equiv F$,
2. $\mathcal{L}(F') \subseteq \mathcal{L}(F) - \{L\}$,
3. $|F'| \leq |F|$.

Proof. We first show the theorem for sentences in CNF. $F[\![L\backslash\bot]\!]$ is a suitable F'. It (up to equivalence) can be computed by removing all occurrences of L from the clauses in F. It is obvious that F' can be computed in time linear in $|F|$. Also items 2. and 3. are evident. We have to show item 1. Since $A \notin \mathcal{L}_{\mathcal{E}}(F)$ it follows from the definition of $\mathcal{L}_{\mathcal{E}}$ that for all interpretations I it holds that if $I \models F$, then $I[\widetilde{L}] \models F$. Assume L is positive. Hence $L = +A$ for some atom A. From Proposition 19 it follows that if $I \models F$, then $I \models F[A\backslash\bot]$. Hence $F \models F[A\backslash\bot]$. Since F is in clausal form, $F[A\backslash\bot]$ is equivalent to the set of the clauses obtained from F by removing all clauses that contain $-A$ and removing all occurrences of $+A$ from their containing clauses. Since $F \models F[A\backslash\bot]$, the union of this clause set with F is equivalent to F. In this union each clause in F that contains $+A$ is subsumed by a clause that does not contain $+A$, but is otherwise identical. The clause set that results from removing clauses that are subsumed in this way is then identical to F with all occurrences of L removed from their containing clauses, i. e., F' constructed as described at the beginning of the proof. The same arguments, with $+A$ and $-A$ as well as $[A\backslash\top]$ and $[A\backslash\bot]$ switched, apply in the case of negative L.

For sentences in DNF, $F[\![L\backslash\top]\!]$ is a suitable F'. It (up to equivalence) can be computed by removing all occurrences of L from the clauses in F. The proof for sentences in CNF, read dually, applies: instead of the definition of $\mathcal{L}_\mathcal{E}$ the characterization of Proposition 5 is taken as a starting point. The role of the fact $F \models F[A\backslash\bot]$ is played by $F[A\backslash\top] \models F$, thus the union of F with the clausal representation of $F[A\backslash\top]$ is equivalent to F.

□

Proposition 21 *If F is a propositional sentence, then $\mathcal{L}_\mathcal{E}(F)$ is the unique smallest set of literals from which a propositional sentence that is equivalent to F can be constructed.*

Proof. Let F be a propositional sentence. We show that (a) any propositional sentence that is equivalent to F must contain all the literals in $\mathcal{L}_\mathcal{E}(F)$ and (b) there exists a propositional sentence that is equivalent to F and contains exactly the literals in $\mathcal{L}_\mathcal{E}(F)$.

(a) If F' is a propositional sentence that is equivalent to F, then it follows from Proposition 7 that $\mathcal{L}_\mathcal{E}(F') \equiv \mathcal{L}_\mathcal{E}(F)$. Since by Proposition 11 it holds that $\mathcal{L}_\mathcal{E}(F') \subseteq \mathcal{L}(F')$, it follows that $\mathcal{L}_\mathcal{E}(F) \subseteq \mathcal{L}(F')$.

(b) For all propositional sentences there exists an equivalent propositional sentence that is in CNF. Hence, from Theorem 1 and Proposition 7 it follows that there exists a propositional sentence F' such that F' is equivalent to F and $\mathcal{L}(F') \subseteq \mathcal{L}_\mathcal{E}(F)$. With (a) it follows that $\mathcal{L}(F') = \mathcal{L}_\mathcal{E}(F)$.

□

Proposition 22 *If F is a propositional sentence, then $\mathcal{A}_\mathcal{E}(F)$ is the unique smallest set of atoms from which a propositional sentence that is equivalent to F can be constructed.*

Proof. Follows from Propositions 8, 12 and 20, analogously as the proof of Proposition 21 from Propositions 7, 11 and Theorem 1. An alternate derivation from Propositions 21 and 6 is also possible.

3.5 Related Work

In [LLM03] Lang, Liberatore and Marquis investigate – for propositional logic only – the independence of the truth value of a sentence from the truth value of an atom. Especially polarity, corresponding to the essential *literal* base, is taken into consideration in this work. Our concepts $\mathcal{L}(F)$, $\mathcal{A}(F)$, $\mathcal{L}_\mathcal{E}(F)$, $\mathcal{A}_\mathcal{E}(F)$ are in the terminology of [LLM03] the sets of literals (atoms for $\mathcal{A}, \mathcal{A}_\mathcal{E}$, resp.) on which F is *syntactically* (*semantically* for $\mathcal{L}_\mathcal{E}, \mathcal{A}_\mathcal{E}$, resp.)

Lit-dependent (*Var-dependent* for $\mathcal{A}, \mathcal{A}_{\mathcal{E}}$, resp.).[1] Properties like our Propositions 7 and 11 are shown. Complexity results about determining whether a given literal is in the essential literal base of a given sentence and related problems are given.

A statement in [LLM03], which is related to our Theorem 1 however is an error: It is stated, at the end of Section 3.2, that (in our terminology) literals not in the essential literal base of a sentence in *negation normal form* can be eliminated by literal substitution with $\bot$. From this statement it is concluded in [LLM03] that the elimination of literals not in the essential literal base (this operation is called *Lit-simplifying* in [LLM03]) of a propositional sentence in negation normal form would be a polynomial operation. That the statement is false can be seen by the following simple example: Let $F \stackrel{\text{def}}{=} (\mathsf{p} \vee \neg\mathsf{p})$. The formula F is in negation normal form, $F \equiv \top$, $\mathcal{L}_{\mathcal{E}}(F) = \emptyset$, but $F[\![+\mathsf{p}\backslash\bot]\!][\![-\mathsf{p}\backslash\bot]\!] = (\bot \vee \bot) \equiv \bot \not\equiv F$. Also when only literals L are eliminated for which it holds that $\widetilde{L} \in \mathcal{L}_{\mathcal{E}}(F)$ (assuming that literals L with $L \notin \mathcal{L}_{\mathcal{E}}(F)$ and $\widetilde{L} \notin \mathcal{L}_{\mathcal{E}}(F)$ are eliminated according to Proposition 20) the purported statement is wrong, as the following example shows: Let $F' \stackrel{\text{def}}{=} ((\mathsf{p} \vee \mathsf{q}) \wedge (\mathsf{p} \vee \neg\mathsf{p}))$. The formula F' is in negation normal form, $F' \equiv (\mathsf{p}\vee\mathsf{q})$, $\mathcal{L}_{\mathcal{E}}(F') = \{+\mathsf{p}, +\mathsf{q}\}$, but $F'[\![-\mathsf{p}\backslash\bot]\!] = ((\mathsf{p}\vee\mathsf{q})\wedge(\mathsf{p}\vee\bot)) \equiv \mathsf{p} \not\equiv F'$.

[1] In an earlier work [Wer04] we investigated the essential *atom* base, unaware of [LLM03]. Our definition of essential *literal* base is an adaption of the semantic characterization of *Lit-independent* in [LLM03]. See also footnote 1 on p. 95.

4 Projection Characterized Semantically

Intuitively, the *projection* of a sentence F onto a set of ground atoms S is a sentence that is equivalent to F with respect to all the atoms in S, but does not express anything about other atoms. The projection of F onto the complement of S is called the *forgetting* about S in F. We extend the notion of formula by an operator $\mathsf{project\text{-}atoms}(F, S)$ that denotes the projection of formula F onto the set of ground atoms S.

We call a set of ground atoms in the role as parameter to projection *scope*. The polarity in which atoms occur in formulas can additionally be considered for projection. A scope is then instead of a set of ground atoms a set of ground literals. Thus we speak of *literal scopes* in contrast to *atom scopes*, and *literal projection* in contrast to *atom projection*. This terminology is used analogously for forgetting. Atom projection can be straightforwardly expressed as the literal projection to the union of the positive and negative literals whose atom is in an atom scope. Thus we use literal projection, with $\mathsf{project}$ as logic operator, as basis for developing formal material, although it is less intuitive than atom projection.

The following are key properties of projection, which are made precise in subsequent sections. Many further properties are shown in Chapter 5.

- The projection of a sentence can be regarded as the portion of the sentence which "is about" the scope of the projection: A sentence whose literal base is in the scope is entailed by the projection if and only if it is entailed by the original sentence. This is made precise in Section 5.6.
- Projection is a "semantic operation": Projection is formally characterized by the specification of the semantics of the $\mathsf{project}$ operator (Definition 52). Projection depends just on semantic properties of the argument sentence and not on its syntactic properties, as made precise in Proposition 32. A sentence that is equivalent to a projection is also a projection of the same sentence onto the same scope, as discussed in Section 5.15.
- The projection operator can be eliminated at low computational cost on sentences that satisfy certain syntactic criteria, which are related to knowledge compilation formats and tableau methods. This is made precise in Section 5.10 and is the foundation for applying tableau techniques to projection elimination, as developed starting with Chapter 8.

In Section 4.1 we formally extend syntax, as introduced in Section 2.4, with the projection operator. In Section 4.2 the semantic framework introduced in Sections 2.8–2.9 is used as a basis for the definition of a semantics for the projection operator, which is illustrated with examples in Section 4.3. As sketched in Section 4.4, most of the material from Chapters 2–3 straightforwardly transfers to sentences in the generalized sense with the projection operator. For Proposition 9, which is about switching value assignments of literals not in the literal base, we make this explicit. In Sections 4.5–4.8 variations of projection, such as forgetting and projection onto atom scopes are introduced. In Section 4.9 notation is introduced that allows to express special cases of projection in a concise way. Finally, in Section 4.10, we come back again to semantics: Based on the relationship of our semantic framework to the framework of first-order model theory, described in Section 2.10, it is shown that first-order logic with the projection operator is a generalization of second-order logic.

4.1 Extending Syntax by the Literal Projection Operator

We revise the definitions of *formula* and *sentence*, originally specified in Section 2.4, by introducing an additional logic operator that expresses literal projection. A formula or sentence in the original sense, i. e., without the projection operator, is then called *plain*.

Definition 47 (Literal Scope) A *literal scope* is a set of ground literals.

There are various kinds of expressions conceivable that could be used to specify literal scopes. For example, a list of ground literals can specify a finite literal scope, or a list of possibly non-ground literals can be considered as a list of patterns that denotes all ground instances of elements. We do not define here how literal scopes are specified syntactically and just speak of a *literal scope*, referring to the actual literal scope in a semantic context as well as some expression that denotes it in a syntactic context. In the context of algorithms for projection elimination, requirements on representations of literal scopes are stated, for example in Definitions 76 and 117.

Definition 48 (Formula – Definition 6 Generalized) A *formula* (in generalized sense) is defined as in Definition 6 with the following additional rule:

6. If F is a formula and S is a literal scope then $\mathsf{project}(F, S)$ is a formula.

   $\mathsf{project}(F, S)$ is called *the literal projection of F onto S.*

Definition 49 (Sentence – Definition 9 Generalized) A formula (in the generalized sense of Definition 48) without a free variable is called a *sentence*.

The syntactic notions of *subformula*, *polarity*, *literal contained in*, *literal base* ($\mathcal{L}$) and *atom base* ($\mathcal{A}$) generalize to formulas with the $\mathsf{project}$ operator in the following way: The formula F is a subformula of the formula $\mathsf{project}(F, S)$. The formulas F and $\mathsf{project}(F, S)$ have in all contexts the same polarity. It follows that the set of literals contained in $\mathsf{project}(F, S)$ is the set of the literals contained in F, and that

$$\mathcal{L}(\mathsf{project}(F, S)) = \mathcal{L}(F), \text{ and}$$
$$\mathcal{A}(\mathsf{project}(F, S)) = \mathcal{A}(F).$$

Definition 50 (Plain) A formula or sentence without the $\mathsf{project}$ operator, i. e., in the original sense of Definitions 6 and 9, is called *plain*.

The notions of *propositional formula*, *propositional sentence* (which is equivalent to *propositional formula*), *clausal sentence* and $\mathcal{E}$-*sentence*, retain their original meaning as defined in Chapter 2.

Definition 51 (Generalized Propositional) A formula or sentence (in the generalized sense of Definitions 48 and 49) that does not contain quantifiers and variables is called *generalized propositional formula* or *generalized propositional sentence* (both notions are equivalent).

4.2 Semantics of Literal Projection

We revise the satisfiability relation $\models$, originally specified in Definition 28, such that it takes the $\mathsf{project}$ operator into account. This provides a formal semantic characterization of projection.

Definition 52 (Model – Definition 28 Generalized) If I is an interpretation and F is a sentence, then the satisfaction relation $I \models F$ is defined by the clauses in Definition 28, extended with the following clause, where F_1 is a sentence and S is a literal scope specifier:

$$I \models \mathsf{project}(F_1, S) \quad \text{iff}_{\text{def}} \quad \begin{array}{l} \text{there exists an interpretation } J \\ \text{such that} \\ J \models F_1 \text{ and } J \cap S \subseteq I. \end{array}$$

4.3 Examples of Literal Projection

In this section the semantic definition of literal projection (Definition 52) is illustrated by examples. Further intuitions for understanding projection are shown in Section 5.15. First-order examples are given in Example 12 (p. 111).

Example 8 (Literal Projection: Forgetting a Negative Literal) Let $F \stackrel{\text{def}}{=} ((\mathsf{p} \rightarrow \mathsf{q}) \land (\mathsf{q} \rightarrow \mathsf{r}))$ and $S \stackrel{\text{def}}{=} \{+\mathsf{p}, -\mathsf{p}, +\mathsf{q}, +\mathsf{r}, -\mathsf{r}\}$. We now illustrate that $\mathsf{project}(F, S) \equiv ((\mathsf{p} \rightarrow \mathsf{q}) \land (\mathsf{p} \rightarrow \mathsf{r}))$. It is not hard to see that the models of F are exactly those interpretations which are a superset of at least one of $M_1, \ldots, M_4$, defined as follows:

$$\begin{aligned} M_1 &\stackrel{\text{def}}{=} \{+\mathsf{p}, +\mathsf{q}, +\mathsf{r}\}, \\ M_2 &\stackrel{\text{def}}{=} \{-\mathsf{p}, +\mathsf{q}, +\mathsf{r}\}, \\ M_3 &\stackrel{\text{def}}{=} \{-\mathsf{p}, -\mathsf{q}, +\mathsf{r}\}, \\ M_4 &\stackrel{\text{def}}{=} \{-\mathsf{p}, -\mathsf{q}, -\mathsf{r}\}. \end{aligned}$$

Thus

$$\begin{aligned} M_1 \cap S &= \{+\mathsf{p}, +\mathsf{q}, +\mathsf{r}\}, \\ M_2 \cap S &= \{-\mathsf{p}, +\mathsf{q}, +\mathsf{r}\}, \\ M_3 \cap S &= \{-\mathsf{p}, +\mathsf{r}\}, \\ M_4 \cap S &= \{-\mathsf{p}, -\mathsf{r}\}. \end{aligned}$$

By Definition 52, $\mathsf{project}(F, S)$ is a sentence whose models are exactly the interpretations which are a superset of at least one of the $M_i \cap S$, for $i \in \{1, \ldots, 4\}$. It is easy to see that this condition on interpretations, being a superset of at least one of the $M_i \cap S$, is equivalent to being a superset of M'_1 or M'_2, defined as follows:

$$\begin{aligned} M'_1 &\stackrel{\text{def}}{=} \{+\mathsf{p}, +\mathsf{q}, +\mathsf{r}\}, \\ M'_2 &\stackrel{\text{def}}{=} \{-\mathsf{p}\}. \end{aligned}$$

It is not hard to see that the models of $((\mathsf{p} \rightarrow \mathsf{q}) \land (\mathsf{p} \rightarrow \mathsf{r}))$ are exactly the interpretations that satisfy this condition.

Example 9 (Literal Projection: Forgetting a Positive Literal) Let F be defined as in Example 8 and $S \stackrel{\text{def}}{=} \{+\mathsf{p}, -\mathsf{p}, -\mathsf{q}, +\mathsf{r}, -\mathsf{r}\}$. Thus S is as in Example 8, except that it contains q negatively instead of positively. Analogously to Example 8, it can be shown that $\mathsf{project}(F, S) \equiv ((\mathsf{p} \rightarrow \mathsf{r}) \land (\mathsf{q} \rightarrow \mathsf{r}))$, where, if $M_1, \ldots, M_4$ are defined as in Example 8, it holds that

$$\begin{aligned} M_1 \cap S &= \{+\mathsf{p}, +\mathsf{r}\}, \\ M_2 \cap S &= \{-\mathsf{p}, +\mathsf{r}\}, \\ M_3 \cap S &= \{-\mathsf{p}, -\mathsf{q}, +\mathsf{r}\}, \\ M_4 \cap S &= \{-\mathsf{p}, -\mathsf{q}, -\mathsf{r}\}. \end{aligned}$$

Example 10 (Literal Projection: Forgetting an Atom) Let F be defined as in Example 8 and $S \stackrel{\text{def}}{=} \{+\mathsf{p}, -\mathsf{p}, +\mathsf{r}, -\mathsf{r}\}$. Thus S is as in Example 8 and 9, except that it does not contain a literal with atom q. Analogously to Example 8, it can be shown that $\mathsf{project}(F, S) \equiv (\mathsf{p} \rightarrow \mathsf{r})$, where, if $M_1, \ldots, M_4$ are defined as in Example 8, it holds that

$$\begin{aligned} M_1 \cap S &= \{+\mathsf{p}, +\mathsf{r}\}, \\ M_2 \cap S &= \{-\mathsf{p}, +\mathsf{r}\}, \\ M_3 \cap S &= \{-\mathsf{p}, +\mathsf{r}\}, \\ M_4 \cap S &= \{-\mathsf{p}, -\mathsf{r}\}. \end{aligned}$$

4.4 Generalization of Literal Base and Related Concepts

With exception of Proposition 9, which has been proven by induction on formulas, and the material in Section 2.10, it is evident that the definitions and propositions in Chapters 2 and 3 also apply to sentences and the satisfaction relationship in the generalized sense of Definitions 49 and 52. We defer revision of the material in Section 2.10 to Section 4.10 and show here, in Proposition 23, that Proposition 9 continues to hold with the generalized definitions.

The generalized Proposition 9 entails that propositions that have been proven by referencing to the original Proposition 9 also apply to the generalized notions. Notably these are Propositions 10, 11 and 12.

Proposition 23 (Proposition 9 Generalized) *Proposition 9 also applies to sentences F in the generalized sense of Definition 49. I. e., if I is an interpretation, F is a sentence and S is a consistent set of ground literals, then*

$$\text{if } I \models F \text{ and } S \cap \mathcal{L}(F) = \emptyset, \text{ then } I[\widetilde{S}] \models F.$$

Proof. The proof given for Proposition 9, which proceeds by induction on formulas, has to be extended by an induction step for formulas of the form $\mathsf{project}(F_1, S_1)$:

(1) $I \models \mathsf{project}(F_1, S_1)\sigma$.
(2) $S \cap \mathcal{L}(\mathsf{project}(F_1, S_1)) = \emptyset$.
(3) $J \models F_1\sigma$.
(4) $J \cap S_1 \subseteq I$.
(5) $S \cap \mathcal{L}(F_1) = \emptyset$.
(6) $J[\widetilde{S}] \models F_1\sigma$.
(7) $J[\widetilde{S}] \cap S_1 \subseteq I[\widetilde{S}]$.
(8) $I[\widetilde{S}] \models \mathsf{project}(F_1, S_1)\sigma$.

We quietly make use of the fact that $\mathsf{project}(F_1, S_1)\sigma = \mathsf{project}(F_1\sigma, S_1)$. Assume (1) and (2). Existence of an interpretation J that satisfies (3) and (4) follows from (1) and the definition of $\mathsf{project}$ (Definition 52). (5) follows from (2), since $\mathcal{L}(\mathsf{project}(F_1, S_1)) = \mathcal{L}(F_1)$. (6) follows from (5), (3) and the induction assumption. (7) follows from (4). (8), the induction conclusion, follows from (7) and the definition of $\mathsf{project}$.

□

4.5 Literal Forgetting

In some applications it is natural to consider projection onto all atoms or literals *with exception* of those in a given set. The concept of *forgetting* allows to express this conveniently. We introduce a logic operator forget for literal forgetting, similar to project. We define forget in terms of project such that it can be considered just as a shorthand for an expression with project and the notion of *formula* has not to be extended further beyond Definition 48.[1]

Definition 53 (Literal Forgetting) If F is a formula and S is a literal scope specifier, then

$$\mathsf{forget}(F, S) \stackrel{\text{def}}{=} \mathsf{project}(F, \overline{S}).$$

$\mathsf{forget}(F, S)$ is called *the literal forgetting in F about S.*

4.6 Variations in the Formulation of Literal Projection

The phrase $J \cap S \subseteq I$ in the definition of literal projection (Definition 52) is equivalent to a variety of other formulations, as shown in Proposition 24.i. Proposition 24.ii shows these equivalences adapted to literal forgetting.

Proposition 24 *If I, J are interpretations and S is a literal scope, then*

(i)

(1)	$J \cap S \subseteq I$	*iff*
(2)	$J \subseteq I \cup \overline{S}$	*iff*
(3)	$I \cap \widetilde{S} \subseteq J$	*iff*
(4)	*There exists a literal scope S' such that* $S' \cap S = \emptyset$ *and* $J = I[S']$	*iff*
(5)	*There exists a literal scope S' such that* $S' \cap \widetilde{S} = \emptyset$ *and* $I = J[S']$*;*	

(ii)

(1)	$J \cap \overline{S} \subseteq I$	*iff*
(2)	$J \subseteq I \cup S$	*iff*
(3)	$I \subseteq J \cup \widetilde{S}$	*iff*
(4)	*There exists a literal scope S' such that* $S' \subseteq S$ *and* $J = I[S']$	*iff*
(5)	*There exists a literal scope S' such that* $S' \subseteq \widetilde{S}$ *and* $I = J[S']$.	

Proof. (24.i) (2) is clearly equivalent to (1). (1) is clearly equivalent to $\widetilde{J} \cap \widetilde{S} \subseteq \widetilde{I}$, which by Proposition 1 is equivalent to $\overline{J} \cap \widetilde{S} \subseteq \overline{I}$ and thus equivalent to (3). That (1) entails (4) can be shown as follows: Let $S' \stackrel{\text{def}}{=} J - I$. (1) entails

[1] It would of course also be possible to define forget first and consider project as a shorthand for a forget expression.

$(J - I) \cap S = \emptyset$ and thus also entails $S' \cap S = \emptyset$. For all interpretations I', J' it holds that $J' = I'[J' - I']$; thus also $J = I[J - I]$; hence $J = I[S']$. That (4) entails (1) can be shown as follows: Assume (4). For all interpretations I' and scopes S'' it holds that $(I'[S''] - I') \subseteq S''$. Hence $(I[S'] - I) \subseteq S'$. From this and $S' \cap S = \emptyset$ follows $(I[S'] - I) \cap S = \emptyset$. With $J = I[S']$ then follows $(J - I) \cap S = \emptyset$, which is clearly equivalent to (1). Equivalence of (5) to (3) follows from the equivalence of (4) to (1). Both pairs are identical, except that I and J are switched and $\widetilde{S}$ has in (5) and (3) the place of S in (4) and (1).

(24.ii) (1), (2) and (4) are clearly instances of (1), (2) and (4), respectively, in Proposition 24.i, with $\overline{S}$ in place of S. (3) is clearly equivalent to $\widetilde{I} \subseteq \widetilde{J} \cup S$; hence equivalent to $\widetilde{I} \cap \overline{S} \subseteq \widetilde{J}$, which is clearly equivalent to (3) in Proposition 24.i with $\overline{S}$ in place of S. Equivalence of (5) to (3) follows, analogously to Proposition 24.i, from the equivalence of (4) to (1) (the syntactical forms of (3) and (1) are here different, but (3) is clearly equivalent to $I \cap \overline{\overline{\widetilde{S}}} \subseteq J$, which has the same form as (1)). □

4.7 Atom Projection and Atom Forgetting

Atom projection and atom forgetting can be both be defined in terms of literal projection. So we introduce logic operators project-atoms and forget-atoms, which, like the forget operator, can be considered just as shorthands for expressions with project.[2]

After defining atom projection in this way (Definition 55), we show in Proposition 25 another characterization of atom projection, which makes explicit that in the definitional expansion of the corresponding project expression interpretations J and I assign the same values to the elements of S.

We then define atom forgetting as atom projection onto the complement scope, analogously to the definition of literal forgetting (Definition 53). Proposition 26 shows that atom forgetting can also be characterized in terms of literal forgetting, analogously to the definition of atom projection (Definition 55).

Definition 54 (Atom Scope) An *atom scope* is a set of ground atoms.

Definition 55 (Atom Projection) If F is a formula and S is an atom scope specifier, then

$$\mathsf{project\text{-}atoms}(F, S) \stackrel{\text{def}}{=} \mathsf{project}(F, +S \cup -S).$$

[2] A converse characterization of literal forgetting in terms of atom forgetting results for propositional sentences from Proposition 66 (p. 62).

Proposition 25 *If I is an interpretation, F is a formula and S is an atom scope, then*

$$I \models \mathsf{project\text{-}atoms}(F, S) \text{ if and only if there exists an interpretation } J \text{ such that } J \models F \text{ and } J \cap {+S} = I \cap {+S}.$$

Proof. Follows easily from the definition of project-atoms and project with the fact that for all interpretations I, J and atom scopes S it holds that $J \cap {+S} = I \cap {+S}$ if and only if $J \cap ({+S} \cup {-S}) \subseteq I$, which is easy to see.

□

Definition 56 (Atom Forgetting) If F is a formula and S is an atom scope specifier, then

$$\mathsf{forget\text{-}atoms}(F, S) \stackrel{\text{def}}{=} \mathsf{project\text{-}atoms}(F, \overline{S}).$$

Proposition 26

$$\mathsf{forget\text{-}atoms}(F, S) \equiv \mathsf{forget}(F, {+S} \cup {-S}).$$

Proof. Follows easily from the definitions of forget-atoms, project-atoms and forget with the fact that $\overline{{+S} \cup {-S}} = {+\overline{S}} \cup {-\overline{S}}$, which is easy to see.

□

4.8 From Properties of Literal Projection to Atom Projection

Since atom projection can be defined in terms of literal projection, we consider literal projection as the more fundamental notion and use it as a basis to develop further material in subsequent sections. Propositions about atom projection can be derived in a straightforward way from propositions about literal projection, as we show here. Thus, if one is interested in atom projection instead of literal projection, one can read most of the material about literal projection just with *literal scope* replaced by *atom scope* and project replaced by project-atoms.

A literal scope S such that $S = \widetilde{S}$ can be considered as representation of an atom scope, as shown by the following proposition:

Proposition 27 *If F is a sentence and S is a literal scope, then*

$$\text{if } S = \widetilde{S}, \text{ then } \mathsf{project}(F, S) \equiv \mathsf{project\text{-}atoms}(F, \mathsf{atoms}(S)).$$

Proof. Follows easily from the definition of project-atoms.

□

By Proposition 27, if for all literal scopes S it holds that $\mathsf{project}(F, S)$ has some property, then for all literal scopes S such that $S = \widetilde{S}$ it holds that $\mathsf{project\text{-}atoms}(F, \mathsf{atoms}(S))$ has this property. From this in turn it follows that for all atom scopes S it holds that $\mathsf{project\text{-}atoms}(F, S)$ has this property.

As an example consider Proposition 32 below, which is about literal projection. It entails the corresponding assertion about atom projection: *If* F_1, F_2 *are sentences and* S *is an atom scope, then*

$$\textit{if } F_1 \equiv F_2, \textit{ then } \mathsf{project\text{-}atoms}(F_1, S) \equiv \mathsf{project\text{-}atoms}(F_2, S).$$

4.9 Entailment, Equivalence and Implication Relative to a Scope

Two relations and a logic operator are defined that allow concise notation for certain cases of projection. Various properties of them are summarized in Tables 5.1 and 5.2 (pp. 83f).

Definition 57 (Entailment Relative to a Scope) If F_1, F_2 are sentences and S is a literal scope, then F_1 *entails* F_2 *relative to* S, in symbols $F_1 \models_S F_2$, is defined as follows:

$$F_1 \models_S F_2 \ \text{iff}_{\text{def}} \ \mathsf{project}(F_1, S) \models \mathsf{project}(F_2, S).$$

Definition 58 (Equivalence Relative to a Scope) If F_1, F_2 are sentences and S is a literal scope, then F_1 *is equivalent to* F_2 *relative to* S, in symbols $F_1 \equiv_S F_2$, is defined as follows:

$$F_1 \equiv_S F_2 \ \text{iff}_{\text{def}} \ \mathsf{project}(F_1, S) \equiv \mathsf{project}(F_2, S).$$

Definition 59 (Implication Relative to a Scope) If F_1, F_2 are formulas and S is a literal scope, then F_1 *implies* F_2 *relative to* S, in symbols $F_1 \rightarrow_S F_2$, is defined as follows:

$$F_1 \rightarrow_S F_2 \ \stackrel{\text{def}}{=} \ \mathsf{project}(F_1, S) \rightarrow \mathsf{project}(F_2, S).$$

4.10 Second-Order Quantification as Special Case of Projection

Existential second-order quantification can be viewed as atom forgetting about all ground atoms with a given predicate. This is made precise in Proposition 29, which can be seen as a generalized version of Proposition 3 and expresses the correspondence of

- Second-order formulas with Herbrand models according to standard model theoretic semantics, extending the framework of Section 2.10, and
- First-order formulas that include the projection operator and are associated with a semantics based on literal sets as defined in Section 4.2, extending the framework of Sections 2.8–2.9.

Second-order logic extends first-order logic by the possibility of quantifying about predicates. A *second-order* formula is a formula (in the sense of Section 2.4) in which also *predicate variables* X, Y, Z, also with subscripts, may occur. The other variables are called *individual variables* to distinguish them. With a predicate variable an arity is associated, the predicate variable can occur in predicate position of atoms with this arity. A predicate variable can be bound by the $\exists$ quantifier. $\forall XF$ is shorthand for $\neg\exists X \neg F$.

As we have done for individual variables, we assume for predicate variables that there is a denumerable number of them and in a formula all occurrences of the same predicate variable are either free or are bound by an occurrence of a quantifier, and that no two quantifier occurrences bind occurrences of the same variable.

The framework of std-interpretations described in Section 2.10 can be extended to assign a semantics to formulas of second-order logic. As before, we use the book by Ebbinghaus et al. as a point of reference [EFT96, Section IX § 1, pp. 150–155].

A *second-order std-interpretation* is a pair $\langle\langle A, \mathfrak{a}\rangle, \gamma\rangle$, where $\langle A, \mathfrak{a}\rangle$ is a structure and γ is a *second-order variable assignment*, a mapping that assigns to each individual variable an element of A and to each predicate variable with arity n a subset of A^n.

The notion of *Herbrand interpretation* (Definition 32) applies to a second-order std-interpretation in the same way as to a std-interpretation. We call a second-order std-interpretation that is a Herbrand interpretation *second-order Herbrand interpretation.*

In analogy to the $\frac{a}{x}$ notation for individual variables, if γ is a second-order variable assignment, then $\gamma\frac{R}{X}$ denotes the second-order variable assignment that maps the predicate variable X to the relation R and all other variables to the same values as γ. If $\mathfrak{I} = \langle\langle A, \mathfrak{a}\rangle, \gamma\rangle$ is a second-order std-interpretation then $\mathfrak{I}\frac{R}{X}$ stands for $\langle\langle A, \mathfrak{a}\rangle, \gamma\frac{R}{X}\rangle$.

We now generalize the definition of the satisfaction relation $\models_{std}$ and Proposition 2 such that they apply to second-order formulas.

Definition 60 (Std-Model – Definition 31 Generalized) If $\mathfrak{I} = \langle\langle A, \mathfrak{a}\rangle, \gamma\rangle$ is a second-order std-interpretation and F is a second-order formula, the satisfaction relation $I \models_{std} F$ is inductively defined by the clauses in Definition 31, extended by the following two clauses, where F' is a formula, X is a predicate variable and $t_1, \ldots, t_n$ are terms:

$$\begin{array}{lll} \mathfrak{I} \models_{std} X(t_1, \ldots, t_n) & \text{iff}_{\text{def}} & \langle \mathfrak{I}(t_1), \ldots, \mathfrak{I}(t_n)\rangle \in \gamma(X), \\ \mathfrak{I} \models_{std} \exists X F' & \text{iff}_{\text{def}} & \text{there exists an } R \subseteq A^n \text{ such that } \mathfrak{I}\frac{R}{X} \models_{std} F'. \end{array}$$

Proposition 28 (Proposition 2 Generalized) *Proposition 2 also applies to second-order formulas F. I. e., if F is a second-order formula, x is an individual variable that does not occur bound in F, a is a ground term and $\mathfrak{I}$ is a second-order Herbrand interpretation, then*

$$\mathfrak{I} \models_{std} F\{x \mapsto a\} \text{ if and only if } \mathfrak{I}\tfrac{a}{x} \models_{std} F.$$

Proof. The proof given for Proposition 2, which proceeds by induction on formulas, has to be extended by the base case of atoms with a predicate variable and the induction step for existential quantification over a predicate variable. The base case of atoms $X(t_1, \ldots, t_n)$, where X is a predicate variable, can be shown in the same way as the base case of atoms $p(t_1, \ldots, t_n)$, where p is a predicate symbol, except that $\gamma(X)$ plays the role of $\mathfrak{a}(p)$. The induction step for formulas of the form $\exists Y F_1$, where Y is a predicate variable with arity n, can be shown as follows:

(1)	$\mathfrak{I} \models_{std} (\exists Y F_1)\{x \mapsto a\}$	iff
(2)	$\mathfrak{I} \models_{std} \exists Y(F_1\{x \mapsto a\})$	iff
(3)	There exists an $R \subseteq A^n$: $\mathfrak{I}\frac{R}{Y} \models_{std} F_1\{x \mapsto a\}$	iff
(4)	There exists an $R \subseteq A^n$: $\mathfrak{I}\frac{R}{Y}\frac{a}{x} \models_{std} F_1$	iff
(5)	There exists an $R \subseteq A^n$: $\mathfrak{I}\frac{a}{x}\frac{R}{Y} \models_{std} F_1$	iff
(6)	$\mathfrak{I}\frac{a}{x} \models_{std} \exists Y F_1$.	

(2) is clearly equivalent to (1). Equivalence of (4) to (3) follows from the induction assumption. (5) is clearly equivalent to (4). The other equivalences follow from the definition of $\models_{std}$.

□

We are now going to show Proposition 29. First we need to define concepts used in the proposition statement: Definitions 61 and 62 specify the syntactic mapping between second-order formulas and formulas with the projection operator. Definition 63 specifies a literal set representation for second-order std-interpretations, analogously to Definition 33 for first-order std-interpretations. Proposition 29 can be seen as a version of Proposition 3 that has been generalized to take second-order quantification and projection operators into account.

Definition 61 (Predicate Symbols for Predicate Variables) Define an injective mapping from the set of predicate variables to a subset of the predicate symbols. If X is a predicate variable, then p_X denotes the image of X in this mapping.

We quietly assume that if a second-order formula contains a predicate variable X, then it does not contain an atom with predicate p_X. By variable renaming, all second-order formulas can be brought into a form that satisfies this assumption; hence it is without loss of generality.

Definition 62 (Projection-Form of a Second-Order Formula) The *projection-form* of a second-order formula F, in symbols $\mathsf{pf}(F)$, is a formula (in the sense of Definition 48) defined inductively as follows, where X is a predicate variable, x is an individual variable, F_1, F_2 are second-order formulas and $t_1, \ldots, t_n$ are terms:

$$\begin{aligned}
\mathsf{pf}(X(t_1, \ldots, t_n)) &\stackrel{\text{def}}{=} p_X(t_1, \ldots, t_n), \\
\mathsf{pf}(\exists X F_1) &\stackrel{\text{def}}{=} \mathsf{forget\text{-}atoms}(\mathsf{pf}(F_1), S_{p_X}), \\
&\quad \text{where } S_{p_X} \text{ is an expression denoting the} \\
&\quad \text{set of ground atoms with predicate } p_X, \\
\mathsf{pf}(F_1 \circ F_2) &\stackrel{\text{def}}{=} \mathsf{pf}(F_1) \circ \mathsf{pf}(F_2) \\
&\quad \text{if } \circ \text{ is a binary connective,} \\
\mathsf{pf}(\neg F_1) &\stackrel{\text{def}}{=} \neg\mathsf{pf}(F_1), \\
\mathsf{pf}(QxF_1) &\stackrel{\text{def}}{=} Qx\ \mathsf{pf}(F_1) \\
&\quad \text{if } Q \text{ is a quantifier,} \\
\mathsf{pf}(F) &\stackrel{\text{def}}{=} F \\
&\quad \text{otherwise.}
\end{aligned}$$

In Definition 62 the forget-atoms operator is used. From the definitions of forget-atoms (Definition 56) and project-atoms (Definition 55) it follows that

$$\mathsf{forget\text{-}atoms}(\mathsf{pf}(F_1), S_{p_X})$$

is a shorthand for an expression with the project operator:

$$\mathsf{project}(\mathsf{pf}(F_1), \overline{+S_{p_X}} \cup \overline{-S_{p_X}}).$$

Thus a projection-form actually is a formula in the sense of Definition 48, i. e., a first-order formula that possibly contains the project operator.

Definition 63 (Second-Order Literal Set Representation) An interpretation I is called the *literal set representation* of a second-order Herbrand interpretation $\mathfrak{I} = \langle\langle \mathsf{GTERMS}, \mathfrak{a}\rangle, \gamma\rangle$ for a set of predicate variables $X_1, \ldots, X_r$ if and only if

1. For all ground atoms $p(t_1, \ldots, t_n)$ such that $p \notin \{p_{X_1}, \ldots, p_{X_r}\}$ it holds that

$$\langle t_1, \ldots, t_n\rangle \in \mathfrak{a}(p) \text{ if and only if } +p(t_1, \ldots, t_n) \in I, \text{ and}$$

2. For all ground atoms $p_{X_i}(t_1, \ldots, t_n)$, where $i \in \{1 \ldots r\}$, it holds that

$$\langle t_1, \ldots, t_n\rangle \in \gamma(X_i) \text{ if and only if } +p_{X_i}(t_1, \ldots, t_n) \in I.$$

Proposition 29 *If F is a second-order sentence, $\mathfrak{I}$ is a second-order Herbrand interpretation and I is the second-order literal set representation of $\mathfrak{I}$ for the empty set of predicate variables (or equivalently the first-order literal set representation, according to Definition 33), then*

$$\mathfrak{I} \models_{std} F \textit{ if and only if } I \models \mathsf{pf}(F).$$

Proof. We show by induction on formulas the following property, from which the proposition immediately follows: If F is a second-order formula, σ is a variable substitution with the set of free individual variables of F as domain and a set of ground terms as range, $\mathfrak{I} = \langle\langle \mathsf{GTERMS}, \mathfrak{a}\rangle, \gamma\rangle$ is a second-order Herbrand interpretation, and I is the second-order literal set representation of $\mathfrak{I}$ for the predicate variables free in F, then

$$\mathfrak{I} \models_{std} F\sigma \text{ \textit{if and only if} } I \models \mathsf{pf}(F)\sigma.$$

The proof given for Proposition 3, which proceeds by induction on formulas, has to be extended by the base case of atoms with a predicate variable and by the induction step for existential quantification over a predicate variable. The base case, of atoms $X(t_1, \ldots, t_n)$, where X is a predicate variable, can be shown as follows:

$$\begin{array}{lll}
(1) & \mathfrak{I} \models_{std} X(t_1, \ldots, t_n)\sigma & \text{iff} \\
(2) & \langle \mathfrak{I}(t_1\sigma), \ldots, \mathfrak{I}(t_n\sigma)\rangle \in \gamma(X) & \text{iff} \\
(3) & \langle t_1\sigma, \ldots, t_n\sigma\rangle \in \gamma(X) & \text{iff} \\
(4) & +p_X(t_1, \ldots, t_n)\sigma \in I & \text{iff} \\
(5) & I \models p_X(t_1, \ldots, t_n)\sigma & \text{iff} \\
(6) & I \models \mathsf{pf}(X(t_1, \ldots, t_n))\sigma & \text{iff}
\end{array}$$

Equivalence of (2) to (1) follows from the definition of $\models_{std}$. For all $i \in \{1, \ldots, n\}$ it holds that $t_i\sigma$ is ground. Since $\mathfrak{I}$ is a Herbrand interpretation it follows that $I(t_i\sigma) = t_i\sigma$. Thus (3) is equivalent to (2). Equivalence of (4) to (3) follows from the definitions of $\mathfrak{I}$ and I. Equivalence of (5) to (4) follows from the definition of $\models$. Equivalence of (6) to (5) follows from the definition of pf. The induction step for formulas of the form $\exists X F_1$, where X is a predicate variable, can be shown as follows:

$$\begin{array}{lll}
(1) & \mathfrak{I} \models_{std} (\exists X F_1)\sigma & \text{iff} \\
(2) & \mathfrak{I} \models_{std} \exists X (F_1\sigma) & \text{iff} \\
(3) & \text{There exists an } R \subseteq A^n\text{: } \mathfrak{I}^{R}_{X} \models_{std} F_1\sigma & \text{iff} \\
(4) & \text{There exists a second-order Herbrand interpretation } \mathfrak{J}\text{:} & \\
 & \mathfrak{J} \models_{std} F_1\sigma \text{ and} & \\
 & \mathfrak{J} \text{ is identical to } \mathfrak{I} \text{ except that their predicate variable} & \\
 & \text{assignments possibly map } X \text{ to different relations} & \text{iff} \\
(5) & \text{There exists an interpretation } J\text{:} & \\
 & J \models \mathsf{pf}(F_1)\sigma \text{ and} & \\
 & J \cap \widetilde{+S_{p_X}} = I \cap \widetilde{+S_{p_X}} & \text{iff} \\
(6) & I \models \mathsf{forget\text{-}atoms}(\mathsf{pf}(F_1)\sigma, S_{p_X}) & \text{iff} \\
(7) & I \models \mathsf{forget\text{-}atoms}(\mathsf{pf}(F_1), S_{p_X})\sigma, & \text{iff} \\
(8) & I \models \mathsf{pf}(\exists X F_1)\sigma. &
\end{array}$$

Equivalence of (2) to (1) is easy to see. Let n be the arity of X. Equivalence of (3) to (2) follows from the definition of $\models_{std}$. Equivalence of (4) to (3) is not hard to see. Let S_{p_X} denote the set of all ground atoms with predicate p_X. Equivalence of (5) to (4) follows from the induction assumption with the definition of I. Equivalence of (6) to (5) follows from the definition of $\models$. The remaining equivalences are easy to see.

□

5 Properties of Projection

This chapter collects properties of literal projection that underlie applications, clarify intuitions, are the basis for procedures to compute projection or are useful as lemmas for referencing in proofs. The properties concern projection, its interplay with the literal base and the essential literal base, its interplay with various logic operators, and elementary methods for projection elimination in propositional logic.

Most of the properties are stated as propositions which are proven straightforwardly on the basis of the semantic framework developed in Chapters 2–4. More complex proofs are required to show properties that concern the interplay of projection with conjunction, in particular for *literal* projection. These properties are stated as Theorems 2–4. They refer to a certain syntactic restriction on formulas, being *linkless*, which is introduced in the context of their presentation. Linkless formulas permit projection elimination in linear time, which follows from one of the theorems and is stated as Proposition 87. Since tableau methods can be used to construct linkless formulas, this proposition justifies the application of tableau methods for projection elimination – which will be elaborated in subsequent chapters.

Several of the shown properties of projection arise in two variants: either based on Proposition 9, applying to sentences in general but referring to their *literal base*, a syntactic property; or based on Definition 45, referring to the semantic concept of *essential literal base*, but applying only to $\mathcal{E}$-sentences. This is discussed further in Section 5.3.

This chapter also provides an alignment of alternate views on projection: If appropriate, properties are expressed not only in terms of projection but also by forgetting and entailment and equivalence relative to a scope. Different characterizations of projection and closely related concepts, some of which can be found in the literature, are made precise and related formally in Section 5.15.

The material is grouped into 15 sections of related properties, which are formally stated and proven. Each section is introduced by an informal presentation of key properties and an outline of the roles and interdependencies of further properties stated in the section. If useful, a proposition is presented as a bundle of several notational variations, which in addition to the $\mathsf{project}$ operator include the forget operator and the $\models_S$ and $\equiv_S$ relations. Equivalence of these variations easily follows from the definition of the respective construct and is not made explicit in proofs. It is further possible to read the propositions about literal projection also as propositions about *atom* projection, as has been outlined in Section 4.8. Properties that can be expressed with the $\models_S$ and $\equiv_S$ relations are additionally summarized in tabular form (pp. 83f).

Most of the shown properties apply to sentences in the sense of Definition 49, i. e., to sentences of first-order logic with the extension that they can contain the projection operator. Some properties are, however, just shown for a restricted class of sentences, such as propositional sentences or $\mathcal{E}$-sentences (Definition 45). The latter class includes propositional sentences and clausal first-order sentences.[1]

5.1 Basic Properties

Projection has the following basic properties:

- A sentence entails its projections (Proposition 30).
- If a sentence entails another sentence, then the projection of the first sentence entails the projection of the second sentence onto the same scope (Proposition 31).
- Projection is "semantically determined" in the sense that projections of equivalent sentences onto the same scope are equivalent (Proposition 32).
- A projection entails a projection of the same sentence onto a subset scope; a forgetting entails a forgetting in the same sentence about a superset scope (Proposition 33).

Proposition 30 *If F is a sentence and S is a literal scope, then*

$$F \models \mathsf{project}(F, S).$$
$$F \models \mathsf{forget}(F, S).$$

Proof.

(1) $I \models F$.
(2) $I \cap S \subseteq I$.
(3) $I \models \mathsf{project}(F, S)$.

Let I be an interpretation such that (1) holds. (2) is trivially true. (3) follows from (1), (2) and the definition of project.

□

[1] In this work no effort has been made to show that such properties *can not* be shown for larger classes of sentences.

Proposition 31 *If F_1, F_2 are sentences and S is a literal scope, then*

$$\text{if } F_1 \models F_2, \text{ then } \mathsf{project}(F_1, S) \models \mathsf{project}(F_2, S).$$
$$\text{if } F_1 \models F_2, \text{ then } \mathsf{forget}(F_1, S) \models \mathsf{forget}(F_2, S).$$
$$\text{if } F_1 \models F_2, \text{ then } F_1 \models_S F_2.$$

Proof.

(1) $F_1 \models F_2$.
(2) $I \models \mathsf{project}(F_1, S)$.
(3) There exists an interpretation J: $J \models F_1$ and $J \cap S \subseteq I$.
(4) There exists an interpretation J: $J \models F_2$ and $J \cap S \subseteq I$.
(5) $I \models \mathsf{project}(F_2, S)$.

Assume (1). Let I be an interpretation such that (2) holds. (3) follows from (2) and the definition of project. (4) follows from (3) and (1). (5) follows from (4) and the definition of project.

□

Proposition 32 *If F_1, F_2 are sentences and S is a literal scope, then*

$$\text{if } F_1 \equiv F_2, \text{ then } \mathsf{project}(F_1, S) \equiv \mathsf{project}(F_2, S).$$
$$\text{if } F_1 \equiv F_2, \text{ then } \mathsf{forget}(F_1, S) \equiv \mathsf{forget}(F_2, S).$$
$$\text{if } F_1 \equiv F_2, \text{ then } F_1 \equiv_S F_2.$$

Proof. Follows immediately from Proposition 31.

□

Proposition 33 *If F is a sentence and S_1, S_2 are literal scopes, then*

$$\text{if } S_1 \supseteq S_2, \text{ then } \mathsf{project}(F, S_1) \models \mathsf{project}(F, S_2).$$
$$\text{if } S_1 \subseteq S_2, \text{ then } \mathsf{forget}(F, S_1) \models \mathsf{forget}(F, S_2).$$

Proof.

(1) $S_1 \supseteq S_2$.
(2) $I \models \mathsf{project}(F, S_1)$.
(3) There exists an interpretation J: $J \models F$ and $J \cap S_1 \subseteq I$.
(4) There exists an interpretation J: $J \models F$ and $J \cap S_2 \subseteq I$.
(5) $I \models \mathsf{project}(F, S_2)$.

Assume (1) and let I be an interpretation such that (2) holds. (3) follows from (2) and the definition of project. (4) follows from (3) and (1). (5) follows from (4) and the definition of project.

□

5.2 Nested Projection

The projection of a projection is equivalent to the projection onto the intersection of the scopes of the two projections; the forgetting in a forgetting is equivalent to the forgetting about the union of the scopes of the two forgettings (Proposition 34). A corollary of this proposition is that a nested projection onto the same scope collapses into a single projection onto that scope (Proposition 35). Propositions 36 and 37 depend on this corollary and are useful for referencing in proofs.

Proposition 34 *If F is a sentence and S_1, S_2 are literal scopes, then*

$$\mathsf{project}(\mathsf{project}(F, S_1), S_2) \equiv \mathsf{project}(F, S_1 \cap S_2).$$
$$\mathsf{forget}(\mathsf{forget}(F, S_1), S_2) \equiv \mathsf{forget}(F, S_1 \cup S_2).$$

Proof.

(1) $I \models \mathsf{project}(\mathsf{project}(F, S_1), S_2)$ iff
(2) there exists an interpretation J_1:
$J_1 \models \mathsf{project}(F, S_1)$ and $J_1 \cap S_2 \subseteq I$ iff
(3) there exist interpretations J_1 and J_2:
$J_2 \models F$ and $J_2 \cap S_1 \subseteq J_1$ and $J_1 \cap S_2 \subseteq I$ iff
(4) there exists an interpretation J_2:
$J_2 \models F$ and $J_2 \cap S_1 \cap S_2 \subseteq I$ iff
(5) $I \models \mathsf{project}(F, S_1 \cap S_2)$.

Let I be an interpretation. (3) implies (4), since if $J_2 \cap S_1 \subseteq J_1$ and $J_1 \cap S_2 \subseteq I$, then $J_2 \cap S_1 \cap S_2 \subseteq I$. (4) implies (3), since if $J_2 \cap S_1 \cap S_2 \subseteq I$, then there exists a J_1, namely $J_2 \cap S_1$, such that $J_2 \cap S_1 \subseteq J_1$ and $J_1 \cap S_2 \subseteq I$. The remaining equivalences follow from the definition of project.

□

Proposition 35 *If F is a sentence and S is a literal scope, then*

$$\mathsf{project}(\mathsf{project}(F, S), S) \equiv \mathsf{project}(F, S).$$
$$\mathsf{forget}(\mathsf{forget}(F, S), S) \equiv \mathsf{forget}(F, S).$$
$$\mathsf{project}(F, S) \equiv_S F.$$

Proof. Follows immediately from Proposition 34.

□

Proposition 36 *If F_1, F_2 are sentences and S is a literal scope, then*

if $F_1 \models \mathsf{project}(F_2, S)$, *then* $\mathsf{project}(F_1, S) \models \mathsf{project}(F_2, S)$.
if $F_1 \models \mathsf{forget}(F_2, S)$, *then* $\mathsf{forget}(F_1, S) \models \mathsf{forget}(F_2, S)$.
if $F_1 \models \mathsf{project}(F_2, S)$, *then* $F_1 \models_S F_2$.

Proof.

(1) $F_1 \models \mathsf{project}(F_2, S)$.
(2) $\mathsf{project}(F_1, S) \models \mathsf{project}(\mathsf{project}(F_2, S), S)$.
(3) $\mathsf{project}(F_1, S) \models \mathsf{project}(F_2, S)$.

Assume (1). (2) follows from (1) and Proposition 31. (3) follows from (2) and Proposition 35.

□

Proposition 37 *If F_1, F_2 are sentences and S is a literal scope, then*

$F_1 \models \mathsf{project}(F_2, S)$ *if and only if* $\mathsf{project}(F_1, S) \models \mathsf{project}(F_2, S)$.
$F_1 \models \mathsf{forget}(F_2, S)$ *if and only if* $\mathsf{forget}(F_1, S) \models \mathsf{forget}(F_2, S)$.
$F_1 \models \mathsf{project}(F_2, S)$ *if and only if* $F_1 \models_S F_2$.

Proof. Left to right is stated as Proposition 36. Right to left follows from Proposition 30.

□

5.3 Projecting to the Base and to the Essential Base

The projection of a sentence onto its [essential] literal base entails the original sentence (Propositions 38 and 39). Both of these propositions are similar, but Proposition 38 is based on Proposition 9, while Proposition 39 is based on Definition 45 instead. There is a trade-off: Proposition 38 applies to sentences in general, but relies on the notion of *literal base* ($\mathcal{L}$), which is dependent on syntactic properties; Proposition 39 uses the semantic concept of *essential literal base* ($\mathcal{L}_\mathcal{E}$) instead, but does only apply to $\mathcal{E}$-sentences. This branching into two possibilities also appears in later sections, when propositions are proven by referencing Proposition 38 or 39, for example in Sections 5.5 and 5.6, and with Propositions that are proven by referencing the underlying Propositions 9 or 45, for example in Section 5.10.

Propositions 40–43 depend on Proposition 38 or 39 and are useful for referencing in proofs. A further such consequence is that the projection onto the set of all ground literals and the forgetting about the empty set are both equivalent the original formula (Proposition 44).

Proposition 38 *If F is a sentence, then*

$$\mathsf{project}(F, \mathcal{L}(F)) \models F.$$
$$\mathsf{forget}(F, \overline{\mathcal{L}(F)}) \models F.$$

Proof.

(1) $I \models \mathsf{project}(F, \mathcal{L}(F))$.
(2) $J \models F$.
(3) $J \cap \mathcal{L}(F) \subseteq I$.
(4) $I \cap \widetilde{\mathcal{L}(F)} \subseteq J$.
(5) $(I - J) \cap \widetilde{\mathcal{L}(F)} = \emptyset$.
(6) $\widetilde{I - J} \cap \mathcal{L}(F) = \emptyset$.
(7) $J[I - J] \models F$.
(8) $I \models F$.

Let I be an interpretation such that (1) holds. By the definition of project it follows from (1) that there exists an interpretation J such that (2) and (3) hold. (4) follows from (3) by clauses (1) and (3) of Proposition 24.i. (5) follows from (4). (6) follows from (5). (7) follows from (6), (2) and Proposition 9. (8) follows from (7).

□

Proposition 39 *If F is an $\mathcal{E}$-sentence, then*

$$\mathsf{project}(F, \mathcal{L}_{\mathcal{E}}(F)) \models F.$$
$$\mathsf{forget}(F, \overline{\mathcal{L}_{\mathcal{E}}(F)}) \models F.$$

Proof. Can be shown in the same way as Proposition 38, with $\mathcal{L}_{\mathcal{E}}$ in place of $\mathcal{L}$. (7) follows from (6), (2) and Definition 45, since F is an $\mathcal{E}$-sentence.

□

Proposition 40 *If F is a sentence and S is a literal scope, then*

if $\mathcal{L}(F) \subseteq S$, *then* $\mathsf{project}(F, S) \models F$.
if $\mathcal{L}(F) \cap S = \emptyset$, *then* $\mathsf{forget}(F, S) \models F$.

Proof. Follows from Propositions 38 and 33.

□

Proposition 41 *If F is a sentence and S is a literal scope, then*

if $\mathcal{L}(F) \subseteq S$, *then* $\mathsf{project}(F, S) \equiv F$.
if $\mathcal{L}(F) \cap S = \emptyset$, *then* $\mathsf{forget}(F, S) \equiv F$.

Proof. Follows from Propositions 40 and 30.

□

Proposition 42 *If F is an $\mathcal{E}$-sentence and S is a literal scope, then*

if $\mathcal{L}_{\mathcal{E}}(F) \subseteq S$, *then* $\mathsf{project}(F, S) \models F$.
if $\mathcal{L}_{\mathcal{E}}(F) \cap S = \emptyset$, *then* $\mathsf{forget}(F, S) \models F$.

Proof. Follows from Proposition 39 (since F is an $\mathcal{E}$-sentence) and 33.

□

Proposition 43 *If F is an $\mathcal{E}$-sentence and S is a literal scope, then*

$$\text{if } \mathcal{L}_{\mathcal{E}}(F) \subseteq S, \text{ then } \mathsf{project}(F, S) \equiv F.$$
$$\text{if } \mathcal{L}_{\mathcal{E}}(F) \cap S = \emptyset, \text{ then } \mathsf{forget}(F, S) \equiv F.$$

Proof. Follows from Proposition 42 (since F is an $\mathcal{E}$-sentence) and 30.

□

Proposition 44 *If F is a sentence, then*

$$\mathsf{project}(F, \mathsf{GLITS}) \equiv F.$$
$$\mathsf{forget}(F, \emptyset) \equiv F.$$

Proof. Follows from Proposition 41.

□

Proposition 45 *If F is a sentence and S is a literal scope, then*

$$\mathsf{project}(\top, S) \equiv \top.$$
$$\mathsf{forget}(\top, S) \equiv \top.$$

Proof. Follows from Proposition 41, since $\mathcal{L}(\top) = \emptyset$.

□

Proposition 46 *If F is a sentence and S is a literal scope, then*

$$\mathsf{project}(\bot, S) \equiv \bot.$$
$$\mathsf{forget}(\bot, S) \equiv \bot.$$

Proof. Follows from Proposition 41, since $\mathcal{L}(\bot) = \emptyset$.

□

5.4 The Essential Base of a Projection

The essential literal base of a projection is a subset of its scope and also a subset of the essential literal base of its argument sentence (Propositions 47 and 48). Propositions 49–51 depend on Proposition 47 and are useful for referencing in proofs. Proposition 51 additionally depends on the fact that the projection of an $\mathcal{E}$-sentence to its essential base entails the original sentence, as shown in Section 5.3. It can be considered as providing a characterization of the essential base in terms of projection: The essential literal base of a sentence is a subset of a scope if and only if the projection of the sentence onto that scope is equivalent to the sentence.

Proposition 47 *If F is a sentence and S is a literal scope, then*

$$\mathcal{L}_{\mathcal{E}}(\mathsf{project}(F,S)) \subseteq S.$$
$$\mathcal{L}_{\mathcal{E}}(\mathsf{forget}(F,S)) \cap S = \emptyset.$$

Proof.

(1) $L \in \mathcal{L}_{\mathcal{E}}(\mathsf{project}(F,S))$.
(2) $I \models \mathsf{project}(F,S)$.
(3) $I[\widetilde{L}] \not\models \mathsf{project}(F,S)$.
(4) $J \models F$.
(5) $J \cap S \subseteq I$.
(6) For all interpretations K: if $K \models F$, then $K \cap S \not\subseteq I[\widetilde{L}]$.
(7) $J \cap S \not\subseteq I[\widetilde{L}]$.
(8) $L \in S$.

Let L be a literal such that (1) holds. By the definition of $\mathcal{L}_{\mathcal{E}}$ then there exists an interpretation I such that (2) and (3) hold. For (2) follows with the definition of project that there exists an interpretation J such that (4) and (5) hold. (6) follows from (3) and the definition of project. (7) follows from (6) and (4). (8) follows from (7) and (5).

□

Proposition 48 *If F is a sentence and S is a literal scope, then*

$$\mathcal{L}_{\mathcal{E}}(\mathsf{project}(F,S)) \subseteq \mathcal{L}_{\mathcal{E}}(F).$$
$$\mathcal{L}_{\mathcal{E}}(\mathsf{forget}(F,S)) \subseteq \mathcal{L}_{\mathcal{E}}(F).$$

Proof.

(6) For all interpretations K: If $K\cap \subseteq I[\widetilde{L}]$, then $K \not\models F$.
(7) $J[\widetilde{L}] \cap S \subseteq I[\widetilde{L}]$.
(8) $J[\widetilde{L}] \not\models F$.
(11) $L \in \mathcal{L}_{\mathcal{E}}(F)$.

Let steps (1)-(5) be those of the proof of Proposition 47. (6) follows from (3) and the definition of project. (7) follows from (5): Let $S_1 \stackrel{\text{def}}{=} J[\widetilde{L}]\cap S = ((J - \{L\}) \cup \{\widetilde{L}\}) \cap S = ((J \cap S) - \{L\}) \cup (\{\widetilde{L}\} \cap S)$ and let $S_2 = I[\widetilde{L}] = (I - \{L\}) \cup \{\widetilde{L}\}$; It is easy to see that if $J \cap S \subseteq I$, then $S_1 \subseteq S_2$. (8) follows from (7) and (6). (9) follows from (8), (4) and the definition of $\mathcal{L}_{\mathcal{E}}$.

□

Proposition 49 *If F is a sentence and S is a literal scope, then*

if $\mathsf{project}(F,S) \equiv F$, *then* $\mathcal{L}_{\mathcal{E}}(F) \subseteq S$.
if $\mathsf{forget}(F,S) \equiv F$, *then* $\mathcal{L}_{\mathcal{E}}(F) \cap S = \emptyset$.

Proof. Follows from Propositions 47 and 7.

□

Proposition 50 *If F is a sentence and S is a literal scope, then*

$$\textit{if } \mathsf{project}(F,S) \models F, \textit{ then } \mathcal{L}_{\mathcal{E}}(F) \subseteq S.$$
$$\textit{if } \mathsf{forget}(F,S) \models F, \textit{ then } \mathcal{L}_{\mathcal{E}}(F) \cap S = \emptyset.$$

Proof. Follows from Propositions 49 and 30.

□

Proposition 51 *If F is an $\mathcal{E}$-sentence and S is a literal scope, then*

$$\mathcal{L}_{\mathcal{E}}(F) \subseteq S \textit{ if and only if } \mathsf{project}(F,S) \equiv F.$$
$$\mathcal{L}_{\mathcal{E}}(F) \cap S = \emptyset \textit{ if and only if } \mathsf{forget}(F,S) \equiv F.$$

Proof. Left to right is stated for $\mathcal{E}$-sentences as Proposition 43, right to left for sentences in general as Proposition 49.

□

5.5 Restriction of Scopes to the Base and to the Essential Base

Only the intersection of the given scope with the [essential] literal base of the argument sentence is relevant for projection and forgetting (Propositions 52–55). This justifies, for example, that algorithms to eliminate projection in propositional logic can be without loss of generality restricted to inputs where the scope of projection or forgetting operators are just finite subsets of the literal bases of their formula arguments.

These four propositions come in two pairs, which depend on Proposition 38 and 39, respectively, and thus are distinguished by applying to sentences in general and the literal base ($\mathcal{L}$) on one hand and applying to $\mathcal{E}$-sentences and the essential literal base ($\mathcal{L}_{\mathcal{E}}$) on the other hand.

Proposition 52 *If F is a sentence and S is a literal scope, then*

$$\mathsf{project}(F,S) \equiv \mathsf{project}(F,\mathcal{L}(F) \cap S).$$
$$\mathsf{forget}(F,S) \equiv \mathsf{project}(F,\mathcal{L}(F) - S).$$

Proof. Left to right follows from Proposition 33. Right to left:

(1) $\mathsf{project}(F,\mathcal{L}(F)) \models F.$
(2) $\mathsf{project}(\mathsf{project}(F,\mathcal{L}(F)),S) \models \mathsf{project}(F,S).$
(3) $\mathsf{project}(F,\mathcal{L}(F) \cap S) \models \mathsf{project}(F,S).$

(1) follows from Proposition 38. (2) follows from (1) and Proposition 31. (3) follows from (2) and Proposition 34.

□

Proposition 53 *If F is an $\mathcal{E}$-sentence and S is a literal scope, then*

$$\begin{aligned}\mathsf{project}(F, S) &\equiv \mathsf{project}(F, \mathcal{L}_{\mathcal{E}}(F) \cap S).\\ \mathsf{forget}(F, S) &\equiv \mathsf{project}(F, \mathcal{L}_{\mathcal{E}}(F) - S).\end{aligned}$$

Proof. Can be shown in the same way as Proposition 52 with $\mathcal{L}_{\mathcal{E}}$ in place of $\mathcal{L}$. (1) follows from Proposition 39, since F is an $\mathcal{E}$-sentence.

□

Proposition 54 *If F is a sentence and S is a literal scope, then*

$$\begin{aligned}\mathsf{forget}(F, S) &\equiv \mathsf{forget}(F, \mathcal{L}(F) \cap S).\\ \mathsf{project}(F, S) &\equiv \mathsf{forget}(F, \mathcal{L}(F) - S).\end{aligned}$$

Proof.

$$\begin{array}{lll}(1) & \mathsf{forget}(F, S) & \equiv\\ (2) & \mathsf{project}(F, \overline{S}) & \equiv\\ (3) & \mathsf{project}(F, \mathcal{L}(F) \cap \overline{S}) & \equiv\\ (4) & \mathsf{project}(F, \mathcal{L}(F) \cap \overline{\mathcal{L}(F) \cap S}) & \equiv\\ (5) & \mathsf{project}(F, \overline{\mathcal{L}(F) \cap S}) & \equiv\\ (6) & \mathsf{forget}(F, \mathcal{L}(F) \cap S). & \end{array}$$

Equivalence of (2) to (1) and of (6) to (5) follows from the definition of forget. Equivalence of (3) to (2) and of (5) to (4) follows from Proposition 52. Equivalence of (4) to (3) follows from set equivalence of the literal scopes.

□

Proposition 55 *If F is an $\mathcal{E}$-sentence and S is a literal scope, then*

$$\begin{aligned}\mathsf{forget}(F, S) &\equiv \mathsf{forget}(F, \mathcal{L}_{\mathcal{E}}(F) \cap S).\\ \mathsf{project}(F, S) &\equiv \mathsf{forget}(F, \mathcal{L}_{\mathcal{E}}(F) - S).\end{aligned}$$

Proof. Can be shown in the same way as Proposition 54 with $\mathcal{L}_{\mathcal{E}}$ in place of $\mathcal{L}$. Equivalence of (3) to (2) and of (5) to (4) follows from Proposition 53, since F is an $\mathcal{E}$-sentence.

□

5.6 Projection and Relevancy

The property of projection that motivates the elimination of projection in knowledge-based applications is that a sentence *Theorem* whose literal scope is contained in the scope of a projection of a sentence *KnowledgeBase* is entailed by the projection if and only if it is entailed by *KnowledgeBase*. Thus the projection of *KnowledgeBase* can be regarded as precisely the portion of *KnowledgeBase* which "is about" the scope of the projection. This property is made precise as Proposition 62.

If a sentence *KnowledgeBase* entails a second sentence *Theorem*, then the projection of *KnowledgeBase* onto the literal base of *Theorem* also entails *Theorem* (Proposition 56). Proposition 57 is similar, but based on Proposition 39 instead of Proposition 38 and thus applies to $\mathcal{E}$-sentences and the essential literal base ($\mathcal{L}_{\mathcal{E}}$) instead of sentences in general and the literal base ($\mathcal{L}$). Propositions 58 and 59 complete Propositions 56 and 57, respectively, by their converse.

Propositions 60–63 are straightforward generalizations of Propositions 56–59 that are useful for referencing in proofs. One of these, Proposition 62, directly corresponds to the intuition behind some applications of projection in knowledge processing, as outlined above.

Proposition 56 *If* F_1, F_2 *are sentences, then*

$$\text{if } F_1 \models F_2, \text{ then } \mathsf{project}(F_1, \mathcal{L}(F_2)) \models F_2.$$
$$\text{if } F_1 \models F_2, \text{ then } \mathsf{forget}(F_1, \overline{\mathcal{L}(F_2)}) \models F_2.$$

Proof.

(1) $F_1 \models F_2$
(2) $\mathsf{project}(F_1, \mathcal{L}(F_2)) \models \mathsf{project}(F_2, \mathcal{L}(F_2))$.
(3) $\mathsf{project}(F_1, \mathcal{L}(F_2)) \models F_2$.

Assume (1). (2) follows from (1) and Proposition 31. (3) follows from (2) and Proposition 38.

□

Proposition 57 *If* F_1 *is a sentence and* F_2 *is an* $\mathcal{E}$*-sentence, then*

$$\text{if } F_1 \models F_2, \text{ then } \mathsf{project}(F_1, \mathcal{L}_{\mathcal{E}}(F_2)) \models F_2.$$
$$\text{if } F_1 \models F_2, \text{ then } \mathsf{forget}(F_1, \overline{\mathcal{L}_{\mathcal{E}}(F_2)}) \models F_2.$$

Proof. Can be shown in the same way as Proposition 56, with $\mathcal{L}_{\mathcal{E}}$ in place of $\mathcal{L}$. (3) follows from (2) and Proposition 39, since F_2 is an $\mathcal{E}$-sentence.

□

Proposition 58 *If* F_1, F_2 *are sentences, then*

$$F_1 \models F_2 \text{ if and only if } \mathsf{project}(F_1, \mathcal{L}(F_2)) \models F_2.$$
$$F_1 \models F_2 \text{ if and only if } \mathsf{forget}(F_1, \overline{\mathcal{L}(F_2)}) \models F_2.$$

Proof. Left to right is stated as Proposition 56. Right to left follows from Proposition 30.

□

Proposition 59 *If F_1 is a sentence and F_2 is an $\mathcal{E}$-sentence, then*

$$F_1 \models F_2 \textit{ if and only if } \mathsf{project}(F_1, \overline{\mathcal{L}_{\mathcal{E}}(F_2)}) \models F_2.$$
$$F_1 \models F_2 \textit{ if and only if } \mathsf{forget}(F_1, \overline{\mathcal{L}_{\mathcal{E}}(F_2)}) \models F_2.$$

Proof. Left to right is stated as Proposition 57. Right to left follows from Proposition 30.

□

Proposition 60 *If F_1, F_2 are sentences and S is a literal scope, then*

$$\textit{if } \mathcal{L}(F_2) \subseteq S \textit{ and } F_1 \models F_2, \textit{ then } \mathsf{project}(F_1, S) \models F_2.$$
$$\textit{if } \mathcal{L}(F_2) \cap S = \emptyset \textit{ and } F_1 \models F_2, \textit{ then } \mathsf{forget}(F_1, S) \models F_2.$$

Proof. Follows from Propositions 56 and 33.

□

Proposition 61 *If F_1 is a sentence, F_2 is an $\mathcal{E}$-sentence and S is a literal scope, then*

$$\textit{if } \mathcal{L}_{\mathcal{E}}(F_2) \subseteq S \textit{ and } F_1 \models F_2, \textit{ then } \mathsf{project}(F_1, S) \models F_2.$$
$$\textit{if } \mathcal{L}_{\mathcal{E}}(F_2) \cap S = \emptyset \textit{ and } F_1 \models F_2, \textit{ then } \mathsf{forget}(F_1, S) \models F_2.$$

Proof. Follows from Propositions 57 and 33.

□

Proposition 62 *If F_1, F_2 are sentences and S is a literal scope, then*

$$\textit{if } \mathcal{L}(F_2) \subseteq S, \textit{ then}$$
$$F_1 \models F_2 \textit{ if and only if } \mathsf{project}(F_1, S) \models F_2.$$
$$\textit{if } \mathcal{L}(F_2) \cap S = \emptyset, \textit{ then}$$
$$F_1 \models F_2 \textit{ if and only if } \mathsf{forget}(F_1, S) \models F_2.$$

Proof. Left to right is stated as Proposition 60. Right to left follows from Proposition 30.

□

Proposition 63 *If F_1 is a sentence, F_2 is an $\mathcal{E}$-sentence and S is a literal scope, then*

$$\textit{if } \mathcal{L}_{\mathcal{E}}(F_2) \subseteq S, \textit{ then}$$
$$F_1 \models F_2 \textit{ if and only if } \mathsf{project}(F_1, S) \models F_2.$$
$$\textit{if } \mathcal{L}_{\mathcal{E}}(F_2) \cap S = \emptyset, \textit{ then}$$
$$F_1 \models F_2 \textit{ if and only if } \mathsf{forget}(F_1, S) \models F_2.$$

Proof. Left to right is stated as Proposition 61. Right to left follows from Proposition 30.

□

5.7 Projection Elimination in Propositional Formulas

The forgetting about a single ground literal is equivalent to a certain formula expansion (Proposition 64). For atom forgetting, instead of applying this expansion successively on the positive and negative literals, a more succinct expansion is possible (Proposition 65). It is similar to the Shannon expansion, which is expressed by the following equivalence: *For all propositional formulas F and ground atoms A it holds that*

$$F \equiv (A \land F[A\backslash\top]) \lor (\neg A \land F[A\backslash\bot]).$$

As shown in Proposition 26, atom forgetting can be expressed in terms of literal forgetting. In Proposition 66 we show, based on the formula expansions, that for propositional sentences also, vice versa, literal forgetting can be expressed in terms of atom forgetting.

Based on the formula expansion of Proposition 64, we then show that in propositional logic the projection operator can be "eliminated", which means that for all *generalized* propositional sentences (i. e., possibly with occurrences of the projection operator) there exists an equivalent propositional sentence without the projection operator (Proposition 68, with Proposition 67 as a lemma).

Later on, we show certain properties of projection just for sentences that meet one of two types of restrictions. We show here that generalized propositional sentences satisfy both of these types: In Proposition 69 for the type of restriction used in Propositions 100, 102, 110, 111 and 115, and in Proposition 70 for the type of restriction used in Propositions 73, 101, 103, 113, 114 and 116.

Proposition 64 *If F is a propositional sentence and A is a ground atom, then*

$$\mathsf{forget}(F, \{+A\}) \equiv F[A\backslash\top] \lor (\neg A \land F)$$

and

$$\mathsf{forget}(F, \{-A\}) \equiv F[A\backslash\bot] \lor (A \land F).$$

Proof.

(1)	$I \models \mathsf{forget}(F, \{+A\})$	iff
(2)	There exists an interpretation J: $J \models F$ and $J \cap \overline{\{+A\}} \subseteq I$	iff
(3)	$I[+A] \models F$ or $(I = I[-A]$ and $I \models F)$	iff
(4)	$I[+A] \models F$ or $(I \models \neg A$ and $I \models F)$	iff
(5)	$I \models F[A\backslash\top]$ or $(I \models \neg A$ and $I \models F)$	iff
(6)	$I \models F[A\backslash\top] \lor (\neg A \land F)$	.

We show the first statement, the second one can be shown analogously. Let I be an interpretation. Equivalence of (2) to (1) follows from the definition of forget. $J \cap \overline{\{+A\}} \subseteq I$ holds if and only if J and I contain the same literals for all atoms with exception of A and furthermore, if $-A \in J$, then $-A \in I$. Hence, $J \cap \overline{\{+A\}} \subseteq I$ holds if and only if $J = I[+A]$ holds or $J = I[-A]$ and $I = I[-A]$ hold. Thus (3) is equivalent to (2). Equivalence of (4) to (3) follows from the definition of $\models$. Equivalence of (5) to (4) follows from Proposition 19. Equivalence of (6) to (5) follows from the definition of $\models$.

□

Proposition 65 *If F is a propositional sentence and A is a ground atom, then*

$$\mathsf{forget\text{-}atoms}(F, \{A\}) \equiv F[A\backslash\top] \vee F[A\backslash\bot].$$

Proof.

(1)	$I \models \mathsf{forget\text{-}atoms}(F, \{A\})$	iff
(2)	$I \models \mathsf{forget}(F, \{+A, -A\})$	iff
(3)	There exists an interpretation J:	
	$J \models F$ and $J \cap \overline{\{+A, -A\}} \subseteq I$	iff
(4)	$I[+A] \models F$ or $I[-A] \models F)$	iff
(5)	$I \models F[A\backslash\top]$ or $I \models F[A\backslash\bot]$	iff
(6)	$I \models F[A\backslash\top] \vee F[A\backslash\bot]$.	

Let I be an interpretation. Equivalence of (2) to (1) follows from Proposition 26. Equivalence of (3) to (2) follows from the definition of forget. $J \cap \overline{\{+A, -A\}} \subseteq I$ holds if and only if J and I contain the same literals for all atoms with exception of A. Hence, $J \cap \overline{\{+A, -A\}} \subseteq I$ holds if and only if $J = I[+A]$ or $J = I[-A]$ hold. Thus (4) is equivalent to (3). Equivalence of (5) to (4) follows from Proposition 19. Equivalence of (6) to (5) follows from the definition of $\models$.

□

Proposition 66 *If F is a propositional sentence and A is a ground atom, then*

$$\mathsf{forget}(F, \{+A\}) \equiv \mathsf{forget\text{-}atoms}(A \wedge F, \{A\}) \vee (\neg A \wedge F)$$

and

$$\mathsf{forget}(F, \{-A\}) \equiv \mathsf{forget\text{-}atoms}(\neg A \wedge F, \{A\}) \vee (A \wedge F).$$

Proof.

(1)	$\mathsf{forget}(F, \{+A\})$	iff
(2)	$F[A\backslash\top] \vee (\neg A \wedge F)$	iff
(3)	$((A \wedge F)[A\backslash\top] \vee (A \wedge F)[A\backslash\bot]) \vee (\neg A \wedge F)$	iff
(4)	$\mathsf{forget\text{-}atoms}(A \wedge F, \{A\}) \vee (\neg A \wedge F)$.	

We show the first statement, the second one can be shown analogously. Equivalence of (2) to (1) follows from Proposition 64. Equivalence of (3) to (2) is easy to see. Equivalence of (4) to (3) follows from Proposition 65.

□

Proposition 67 *If F is a propositional sentence and S is a literal scope, then there exists a propositional sentence H such that*

$$H \equiv \mathsf{project}(F, S).$$

Proof. Can be shown by induction on the cardinality of $S' \stackrel{\text{def}}{=} \mathcal{L}(F) - S$. By Proposition 54 it holds that $\mathsf{project}(F, S) \equiv \mathsf{forget}(F, S')$. S' is finite, since $\mathcal{L}(F)$ is finite. By Proposition 44 it holds that $\mathsf{forget}(F, \emptyset) \equiv F$. By Proposition 34 for all literals L and literal scopes S'' it holds that $\mathsf{forget}(F, \{L\} \cup S'') \equiv \mathsf{forget}(\mathsf{forget}(F, \{L\}), S'')$. Hence the induction step follows from Proposition 65.

□

Proposition 68 *If F is a generalized propositional sentence and S is a literal scope, then there exists a propositional sentence H such that*

$$H \equiv F.$$

Proof. Can be shown by induction on formulas. The induction step for formulas of the form $\mathsf{project}(F', S')$ follows from Proposition 67. The base cases and induction steps for the remaining logic operators are easy to see.

□

Proposition 69 *If F is a generalized propositional sentence and S is a literal scope, then there exists a propositional sentence H such that*

1. *$H \equiv \mathsf{project}(F, S)$ and*
2. *$\mathcal{L}(H) \subseteq S$.*

Proof. By Proposition 68 there exists a propositional sentence H' such that $H' \equiv \mathsf{project}(F, S)$. Every propositional sentence has an equivalent propositional sentence in tautology-free CNF. Let H'' be a propositional sentence in tautology-free CNF that is equivalent to H'. By Propositions 47 and 7 it holds that $\mathcal{L}_{\mathcal{E}}(H'') \subseteq S$. $\mathcal{L}(H'')$ is finite, thus $S' \stackrel{\text{def}}{=} \mathcal{L}(H') - S$ is a finite set of ground literals not in $\mathcal{L}_{\mathcal{E}}(H'')$. By induction on the cardinality of S' it then follows from Theorem 1 that there exists a propositional sentence H which meets conditions (1.) and (2.).

□

The proof of Proposition 69 can also be based on DNF. If S represents an atom scope, i. e., $S = \widetilde{S}$, a proof based on Proposition 20 can be given that does not involve CNF or DNF equivalents.

Proposition 70 *If F is a generalized propositional sentence and S is a literal scope, then*

$$\mathsf{project}(F, S) \textit{ is an } \mathcal{E}\textit{-sentence.}$$

Proof. By Proposition 68 there exists a propositional sentence H such that $H \equiv \mathsf{project}(F, S)$. That H is an $\mathcal{E}$-sentence follows from Proposition 18. That $\mathsf{project}(F, S)$ is an $\mathcal{E}$-sentence then follows from Proposition 14.

□

5.8 Projection and Satisfiability

Projection preserves satisfiability as well as unsatisfiability: A projection is satisfiable if and only if its argument formula is satisfiable (Proposition 72, with Proposition 71 as a lemma that states preservation of unsatisfiability).

Proposition 73 can be used to show that for propositional sentences a program that computes the projection to the empty scope is a decision procedure: If F is a propositional sentence, then from Proposition 70 it follows that $\mathsf{project}(F, \emptyset)$ is an $\mathcal{E}$-sentence, thus by Proposition 73, depending on whether F is satisfiable, $\mathsf{project}(F, \emptyset)$ is either equivalent to $\top$ or to $\bot$. Let F' be the output of a procedure that computes an equivalent to $\mathsf{project}(F, \emptyset)$ which does not contain the projection operator. It follows from Proposition 20 that F' can be simplified in time linear in $|F'|$ to either $\top$ or $\bot$, respectively.

Proposition 71 *If F is a sentence and S is a literal scope, then*

if $\mathsf{project}(F, S)$ *is satisfiable, then* F *is satisfiable.*
if $\mathsf{forget}(F, S)$ *is satisfiable, then* F *is satisfiable.*

Proof.

(1) $I \models \mathsf{project}(F, S)$.
(2) There exists an interpretation J: $J \models F$.

Assume that there exists an interpretation I such that (1) holds. (2) follows from (1) and the definition of $\mathsf{project}$.

□

Proposition 72 *If F is a sentence and S is a literal scope, then*

F *is satisfiable if and only if* $\mathsf{project}(F, S)$ *is satisfiable.*
F *is satisfiable if and only if* $\mathsf{forget}(F, S)$ *is satisfiable.*

Proof. Left to right follows from Proposition 30. Right to left is stated as Proposition 71.

□

Proposition 73 *If F is a sentence such that* $\mathsf{project}(F, \emptyset)$ *is an $\mathcal{E}$-sentence, then*

F *is satisfiable if and only if* $\mathsf{project}(F, \emptyset) \equiv \top$.
F *is satisfiable if and only if* $\mathsf{forget}(F, \mathsf{GLITS}) \equiv \top$.

Proof. By Proposition 47 it holds that $\mathcal{L}_{\mathcal{E}}(\mathsf{project}(F, \emptyset)) = \emptyset$. Since $\mathsf{project}(F, \emptyset)$ is an $\mathcal{E}$-sentence, from Proposition 15 it follows that either $\mathsf{project}(F, \emptyset) \equiv \top$ or $\mathsf{project}(F, \emptyset) \equiv \bot$. The proposition then follows from Proposition 72.

□

5.9 Projection and Disjunction

Projection straightforwardly distributes over disjunction (Proposition 74). Propositions 75 and 76 are corollaries of Proposition 74 that are useful for referencing in proofs.

Proposition 74 *If* F_1, F_2 *are sentences and* S *is a literal scope, then*

$$\mathsf{project}(F_1 \lor F_2, S) \equiv \mathsf{project}(F_1, S) \lor \mathsf{project}(F_2, S).$$
$$\mathsf{forget}(F_1 \lor F_2, S) \equiv \mathsf{forget}(F_1, S) \lor \mathsf{forget}(F_2, S).$$

Proof.

(1) $I \models \mathsf{project}(F_1 \lor F_2, S)$ iff
(2) There exists an interpretation J: $J \models F_1 \lor F_2$ and $J \cap S \subseteq I$ iff
(3) There exists an interpretation J: $(J \models F_1$ or $J \models F_2)$ and $J \cap S \subseteq I$ iff
(4) There exists an interpretation J: $J \models F_1$ and $J \cap S \subseteq I$ or there exists an interpretation J: $J \models F_2$ and $J \cap S \subseteq I$ iff
(5) $I \models \mathsf{project}(F_1, S)$ or $I \models \mathsf{project}(F_2, S)$ iff
(6) $I \models \mathsf{project}(F_1, S) \lor \mathsf{project}(F_2, S)$.

Let I be an interpretation. Equivalence of (2) to (1) and of (5) to (4) follows from the definition of project. Equivalence of (3) to (2) and of (6) to (5) follows from the definition of $\models$. (4) and (3) are logically equivalent. □

Proposition 75 *If* F_1, F_2 *are sentences and* S *is a literal scope, then*

$$\mathsf{project}(F_1, S) \models \mathsf{project}(F_1 \lor F_2, S).$$
$$\mathsf{forget}(F_1, S) \models \mathsf{forget}(F_1 \lor F_2, S).$$
$$F_1 \models_S F_1 \lor F_2.$$

Proof. Follows from Proposition 74. □

Proposition 76 *If* F_1, F_2, F_3 *are sentences and* S *is a literal scope, then*

$$\mathsf{project}(F_1 \lor F_2, S) \models \mathsf{project}(F_3, S) \textit{ if and only if } \mathsf{project}(F_1, S) \models \mathsf{project}(F_3, S) \textit{ and } \mathsf{project}(F_2, S) \models \mathsf{project}(F_3, S).$$
$$\mathsf{forget}(F_1 \lor F_2, S) \models \mathsf{forget}(F_3, S) \textit{ if and only if } \mathsf{forget}(F_1, S) \models \mathsf{forget}(F_3, S) \textit{ and } \mathsf{forget}(F_2, S) \models \mathsf{forget}(F_3, S).$$
$$F_1 \lor F_2 \models_S F_3 \textit{ if and only if } F_1 \models_S F_3 \textit{ and } F_2 \models_S F_3.$$

Proof. Follows from Proposition 74. □

5.10 Projection, Conjunction and Linklessness

Projection does not distribute over conjunction in such a straightforward way as over disjunction. The analog to Proposition 75 holds: The projection of a conjunction entails the projections of the conjunct (Proposition 77). The converse, however, does not hold in general, but if the pair of conjuncts has a certain property, namely, if it is *linkless outside* the scope of the projection. This property is based on the notion of *link* as a pair of complementary literals, each in a different conjunct of a conjunction. The terminology, *link* and *linkless*, has its origins in the graph-based formula view of [MR93].

We use several variants of *linkless* properties. The basic notions are just defined for pairs of formulas, not taking into account the context in which these occur: A pair of formulas is *fully linkless* if there is no pair of complementary literals, each in the literal base of a different component of the pair of formulas. The property *linkless outside* is a variant of *fully linkless* that is weakened with respect to a literal scope: *Linkless outside* is defined like *fully linkless*, except that literals are permitted to occur complementary in the literal bases of the two pair components if they and their complements are both members of the literal scope. For example, the pair of formulas $\langle(p \lor q),\ (\neg p \lor q)\rangle$ is not fully linkless, but linkless outside the literal scope $\{+p, -p\}$. The property *linkless inside* is like *linkless outside*, except that the literal scope is considered complementary, corresponding to forgetting instead of projection.

As indicated above, projection distributes over a conjunction if the pair of its conjuncts is linkless outside the scope of the projection. Consequently, if for *all conjunctive subformulas* of a polar formula it holds that the pair of conjuncts is linkless outside some literal scope, then the projection operator for this scope can be distributed inwards, immediately in front of literals, where, in the propositional case, the result of elimination is either just the literal itself or $\top$. This will be explicated in Section 5.12 below, where corresponding *linkless* properties of *formulas* are defined, based on the *linkless* properties of *pairs* of formulas defined in this section.

The *linkless* properties considered so far are defined in terms of the *literal bases* of the formulas in the pair (Definition 64). We also consider analogous properties which are defined in terms of the *essential* literal bases instead: *Fully essentially linkless*, *essentially linkless outside* and *essentially linkless inside* (Definition 65). The plain *linkless* properties are stronger than their *essentially linkless* variants (Proposition 78). Since the essential literal base of a sentence is independent of syntactic properties, the *essentially* variants of the *linkless* properties are also independent of syntactic properties of the pair components (Proposition 79).

Corresponding to the plain and *essentially* variants of the *linkless* properties, there are two alternative sufficient preconditions under which the converse of Proposition 77 holds, which is missing for distribution of projection over conjunction. That is, under which the conjunction of two projections entails the projection of the conjunction. One alternative precondition is that the pair of the two argument formulas of projection on the left side is linkless outside the literal scope of the projection (Theorem 2). The other alternative is that the pair is *essentially* linkless outside the scope of the projection (Theorem 3). The latter precondition is weaker than the former. It is independent of syntactic properties which on one hand makes semantic handling easier, but on the other hand might be harder to verify by a program. It further applies only to $\mathcal{E}$-sentences, analogously to Proposition 39 in contrast to Proposition 38. The proofs of the theorems stating the alternative preconditions are based on Proposition 9 and Definition 45, respectively.

This section concludes with some derived propositions: Propositions 80 and 81 combine these theorems with Proposition 77 to equivalences, in analogy to Proposition 74 for disjunction. Propositions 82 and 83 are corollaries of Proposition 80 and 81, respectively, which are useful for referencing in proofs, analogously to Proposition 76 for disjunction.

Proposition 77 *If F_1, F_2 are sentences and S is a literal scope, then*

$$\begin{array}{l}\mathsf{project}(F_1 \land F_2, S) \models \mathsf{project}(F_1, S).\\ \mathsf{forget}(F_1 \land F_2, S) \models \mathsf{forget}(F_1, S).\\ F_1 \land F_2 \models_S F_1.\end{array}$$

Proof.

(1) $I \models \mathsf{project}(F_1 \land F_2, S)$.
(2) There exists an interpretation J: $I \models F_1 \land F_2$ and $J \cap S \subseteq I$.
(3) There exists an interpretation J: $I \models F_1$ and $J \cap S \subseteq I$.
(4) $I \models \mathsf{project}(F_1, S)$.

Let I be an interpretation such that (1) holds. (2) follows from (1) and the definition of project. (3) follows from (2) and the definition of $\models$. (4) follows from (3) and the definition of project.

□

Definition 64 (Linkless Pair of Formulas) If F_1, F_2 are formulas and S is a literal scope, then

(i) $\langle F_1, F_2\rangle$ is *linkless outside* S if and only if

$$\mathcal{L}(F_1) \cap \widetilde{\mathcal{L}(F_2)} \subseteq S \cap \widetilde{S};$$

(ii) $\langle F_1, F_2\rangle$ is *linkless inside* S if and only if

$$\langle F_1, F_2\rangle \text{ is linkless outside } \overline{S};$$

(iii) $\langle F_1, F_2\rangle$ is *fully linkless* if and only if

$$\langle F_1, F_2\rangle \text{ is linkless outside } \emptyset.$$

Definition 65 (Essentially Linkless Pair of Sentences) If F_1, F_2 are sentences and S is a literal scope, then

(i) $\langle F_1, F_2 \rangle$ is *essentially linkless outside* S if and only if

$$\mathcal{L}_{\mathcal{E}}(F_1) \cap \widetilde{\mathcal{L}_{\mathcal{E}}(F_2)} \subseteq S \cap \widetilde{S};$$

(ii) $\langle F_1, F_2 \rangle$ is *essentially linkless inside* S if and only if

$$\langle F_1, F_2 \rangle \text{ is essentially linkless outside } \overline{S};$$

(iii) $\langle F_1, F_2 \rangle$ is *fully essentially linkless* if and only if

$$\langle F_1, F_2 \rangle \text{ is essentially linkless outside } \emptyset.$$

Example 11 ([Essentially] Linkless Pair) Let S be the set of literals $\{+\mathsf{p}, -\mathsf{p}\}$. The pair of formulas $\langle (\mathsf{p} \lor \mathsf{q}), (\neg\mathsf{p} \lor \mathsf{q}) \rangle$ is then linkless outside S. The pair $\langle (\mathsf{p} \lor (\mathsf{q} \land \neg\mathsf{q})), (\neg\mathsf{p} \lor \mathsf{q}) \rangle$ is not linkless outside S, but it is essentially linkless outside S.

All of the *linkless* properties are symmetric with respect to the components of their pair argument. I.e., if *linkless for* is one of the properties *linkless outside*, *linkless inside*, *essentially linkless inside*, or *essentially linkless outside*, F_1 and F_2 are formulas (sentences, in case *linkless for* is one of the *essentially* properties, resp.) and S is a literal scope, then

$$\text{if } \langle F_1, F_2 \rangle \text{ is linkless for } S, \text{ then } \langle F_2, F_1 \rangle \text{ is linkless for } S.$$

For the literal scope argument of the *linkless* properties, it is only relevant whether an atom is included positively as well as negatively, is included not at all, or is included in just a single literal – where it makes no difference if this literal is positive or negative. This can be formally expressed as follows, where *linkless for*, F_1, F_2 and S are as just defined for the symmetry property, and S' is a literal scope:

If

$$S \cap \widetilde{S} = S' \cap \widetilde{S'},$$
$$\mathsf{atoms}(S) = \mathsf{atoms}(S'), \text{ and}$$
$$\langle F_1, F_2 \rangle \text{ is linkless for } S,$$

then

$$\langle F_1, F_2 \rangle \text{ is linkless for } S'.$$

The *linkless inside* property can, aside from their definition in terms of *linkless outside*, also be characterized in the following way: If F_1 and F_2 are formulas and S is a literal scope, then

$\langle F_1, F_2 \rangle$ is linkless inside S if and only if

$$\mathcal{L}(F_1) \cap \widetilde{\mathcal{L}(F_2)} \cap (S \cup \widetilde{S}) = \emptyset.$$

Equivalence of this characterization to the definition follows since $\overline{\overline{S} \cap \overline{\widetilde{S}}} = S \cup \widetilde{S}$. Of course, the *essentially linkless inside* property can be characterized analogously: If F_1 and F_2 are sentences and S is a literal scope, then

$\langle F_1, F_2 \rangle$ is essentially linkless inside S if and only if

$$\mathcal{L}_{\mathcal{E}}(F_1) \cap \widetilde{\mathcal{L}_{\mathcal{E}}(F_2)} \cap (S \cup \widetilde{S}) = \emptyset.$$

Proposition 78 *If F_1, F_2 are sentences and S is a literal scope, then*

if $\langle F_1, F_2 \rangle$ is linkless outside (inside, resp.) S, then
$\langle F_1, F_2 \rangle$ is essentially linkless outside (inside, resp.) S.

Proof. Follows from Proposition 11 and the definitions of *linkless outside* and *essentially linkless outside* (along with the definitions of *linkless inside* and *essentially linkless inside*, resp.).

□

Proposition 79 Essentially linkless outside (inside, resp.) *is a semantically determined relation, i. e., if F_1, F_2, F_1', F_2' are sentences and S is a literal scope, then*

if $\langle F_1, F_2 \rangle$ is essentially linkless outside (inside, resp.) S,
$F_1 \equiv F_1'$ and $F_2 \equiv F_2'$, then
$\langle F_1', F_2' \rangle$ is essentially linkless outside (inside, resp.) S.

Proof. Follows from the fact that $\mathcal{L}_{\mathcal{E}}$ is a semantically determined function, which has been shown in Proposition 7, and the definition of *essentially linkless outside* (along with the definition of *essentially linkless inside*, resp.).

□

Theorem 2 (Projection and Linkless Conjunction) *If F_1, F_2 are sentences and S is a literal scope, then*

if $\langle F_1, F_2 \rangle$ *is linkless outside* S, *then*
$$\mathsf{project}(F_1, S) \land \mathsf{project}(F_2, S) \models \mathsf{project}(F_1 \land F_2, S).$$
if $\langle F_1, F_2 \rangle$ *is linkless inside* S, *then*
$$\mathsf{forget}(F_1, S) \land \mathsf{forget}(F_2, S) \models \mathsf{forget}(F_1 \land F_2, S).$$

Proof. [2]

(1) $\langle F_1, F_2 \rangle$ is linkless outside S.
(2) $I \models \mathsf{project}(F_1, S)$.
(3) $I \models \mathsf{project}(F_2, S)$.
(4) $J_1 \models F_1$.
(5) $J_1 \cap S \subseteq I$.
(6) $J_2 \models F_2$.
(7) $J_2 \cap S \subseteq I$.
(8) $J'_1 \models F_1$.
(9) $J'_2 \models F_2$.
(10) $J'_1 \cap S \subseteq I$.
(11) $J'_1 = J'_2$.
(12) $J'_1 \models F_1 \land F_2$.
(13) $I \models \mathsf{project}(F_1 \land F_2, S)$.

Assume (1) and let I be an interpretation such that (2) and (3) hold. Let J_1, J_2 be interpretations satisfying (4)–(7). The existence of such interpretations follows from (2) and (3), respectively, with the definition of project. In the following we show the construction of interpretations J'_1 and J'_2 that satisfy (8), (9), (10) and are actually equal, which is expressed by (11). (12) follows from (11), (9) and (8). (13), which concludes the proof, follows from (12) and (10) with the definition of project.

(14) If $J_X.A \neq J_Y.A$ and 1
$J_X.A \notin \mathcal{L}(F_X)$ and 2
$(\widetilde{J_X.A} \in \mathcal{L}(F_Y)$ or $J_X.A \neq I.A)$, 3
then
$$J'_X.A \overset{\text{def}}{=} \widetilde{J_X.A}, \quad 4$$
else
$$J'_X.A \overset{\text{def}}{=} J_X.A. \quad 5$$

For all $X, Y \in \{1, 2\}$ with $X \neq Y$ let J'_X be the interpretation such that (14) holds for all ground atoms A.

[2] A variation of this proof is given with the proof of Theorem 4.

Subproof of (8) and (9). Let $M \stackrel{\text{def}}{=} \{J_1.A \mid J'_1.A = \widetilde{J_1.A}\}$. Then $J'_1 = J_1[\widetilde{M}]$. If A is a ground atom such that $J'_1.A = \widetilde{J_1.A}$, then the condition of line 2 in (14) for $X = 1$ must be true, thus $J_1.A \notin \mathcal{L}(F_1)$. Hence $M \cap \mathcal{L}(F_1) = \emptyset$. (8) then follows from (4) and Proposition 9. (9) follows by the same arguments with subscripts 1 and 2 switched.

Subproof of (10). For all ground atoms A it holds that if $J'_1.A \neq J_1.A$. Then the condition of line 1 in (14) for $X = 1$ must be true; hence $J_1.A = \widetilde{J_2.A}$; hence $J'_1.A = J_2.A$. Thus $J'_1 \subseteq J_1 \cup J_2$. (10) then follows from (5) and (7).

Subproof of (11). For all ground atoms A it holds that if $J_1.A = J_2.A$, then the condition of line 1 in (14) fails for $X = 1$ as well as for $X = 2$; hence $J'_1.A = J_1.A = J_2.A = J'_2.A$.

Otherwise $J_1.A \neq J_2.A$. We show that in this case the condition of (14) (i. e., lines 1–3) is satisfied exactly in one of the cases of $X = 1$ or $X = 2$. This implies (11): Assume lines 1-3 of (14) are satisfied for $X = 1$ but not for $X = 2$. From (14) then follows for $X = 1$ that $J'_1.A = \widetilde{J_1.A} = J_2.A$ and for $X = 2$ that $J'_2.A = J_2.A$. Thus $J'_1.A = J'_2.A$. The same argument also applies to switched subscripts 1 and 2.

(15) $J_1.A \neq J_2.A$.
(16) $J_1.A \notin (S \cap \widetilde{S})$.
(17) If $\widetilde{J_1.A} \in \mathcal{L}(F_2)$, then $J_1.A \notin \mathcal{L}(F_1)$.

Assume (15). (16) follows from (15), (5) and (7). (17) from (16) and (1).

(18) $\mathsf{cond}(1, 2, A)$ iff
(19) $J_1.A \notin \mathcal{L}(F_1)$ and $(\widetilde{J_1.A} \in \mathcal{L}(F_2)$ or $J_1.A \neq I.A)$ iff
(20) $(\widetilde{J_1.A} \in \mathcal{L}(F_2)$ and $J_1.A \notin \mathcal{L}(F_1))$ or
$(J_1.A \neq I.A$ and $J_1.A \notin \mathcal{L}(F_1))$ iff
(21) $\widetilde{J_1.A} \in \mathcal{L}(F_2)$ or $(J_1.A \neq I.A$ and $J_1.A \notin \mathcal{L}(F_1))$ iff
(22) $J_2.A \in \mathcal{L}(F_2)$ or $(J_2.A = I.A$ and $\widetilde{J_2.A} \notin \mathcal{L}(F_1))$ iff
(23) $\neg\mathsf{cond}(2, 1, A)$.

Define $\mathsf{cond}(X, Y, A)$ as abbreviation for the condition of (14) under the assumption (15). For instance, $\mathsf{cond}(1, 2, A)$ is

$$J_1.A \notin \mathcal{L}(F_1) \textit{ and } (J_1.A \neq I.A \textit{ or } \widetilde{J_1.A} \in \mathcal{L}(F_2)).$$

For all ground atoms A it holds that (18)–(23) are equivalent to each other: Equivalence of (19) to (18) follows by unfolding cond. (20) is logically equivalent to (19). Equivalence of (21) to (20) follows from (17). (22) is equivalent to (21), since by (15) it holds that $J_1.A = \widetilde{J_2.A}$. (23) is equivalent to (22) by folding into cond. Thus we have shown that under assumption (15) (and the initial assumptions (1)–(3)) the condition of (14) is satisfied exactly in one of the cases of $X = 1$ or $X = 2$, which implies (11).

□

Theorem 3 (Projection and Essentially Linkless Conjunction) *If* F_1, F_2 *are* $\mathcal{E}$*-sentences and* S *is a literal scope, then*

if $\langle F_1, F_2 \rangle$ *is essentially linkless outside* S, *then*
$\mathsf{project}(F_1, S) \land \mathsf{project}(F_2, S) \models \mathsf{project}(F_1 \land F_2, S)$.
if $\langle F_1, F_2 \rangle$ *is essentially linkless inside* S, *then*
$\mathsf{forget}(F_1, S) \land \mathsf{forget}(F_2, S) \models \mathsf{forget}(F_1 \land F_2, S)$.

Proof. Can be shown in the same way as Theorem 3, with $\mathcal{L}_{\mathcal{E}}$ in place of $\mathcal{L}$. Steps (8) and (9) follow from Definition 45 instead of Proposition 9, since F_1 and F_2 are $\mathcal{E}$-sentences.

□

Proposition 80 *If* F_1, F_2 *are sentences and* S *is a literal scope, then*

if $\langle F_1, F_2 \rangle$ *is linkless outside* S, *then*
$\mathsf{project}(F_1 \land F_2, S) \equiv \mathsf{project}(F_1, S) \land \mathsf{project}(F_2, S)$.
if $\langle F_1, F_2 \rangle$ *is linkless inside* S, *then*
$\mathsf{forget}(F_1 \land F_2, S) \equiv \mathsf{forget}(F_1, S) \land \mathsf{forget}(F_2, S)$.

Proof. Left to right follows from Proposition 77. Right to left is stated as Theorem 2.

□

Proposition 81 *If* F_1, F_2 *are* $\mathcal{E}$*-sentences and* S *is a literal scope, then*

if $\langle F_1, F_2 \rangle$ *is essentially linkless outside* S, *then*
$\mathsf{project}(F_1 \land F_2, S) \equiv \mathsf{project}(F_1, S) \land \mathsf{project}(F_2, S)$.
if $\langle F_1, F_2 \rangle$ *is essentially linkless inside* S, *then*
$\mathsf{forget}(F_1 \land F_2, S) \equiv \mathsf{forget}(F_1, S) \land \mathsf{forget}(F_2, S)$.

Proof. Left to right follows from Proposition 77. Right to left is stated as Theorem 3.

□

Proposition 82 *If* F_1, F_2, F_3 *are sentences and* S *is a literal scope, then*

if $\langle F_1, F_2 \rangle$ *is linkless outside* S, *then*
$\mathsf{project}(F_3, S) \models \mathsf{project}(F_1 \land F_2, S)$ *if and only if*
$\mathsf{project}(F_3, S) \models \mathsf{project}(F_1, S)$ *and*
$\mathsf{project}(F_3, S) \models \mathsf{project}(F_2, S)$.
if $\langle F_1, F_2 \rangle$ *is linkless inside* S, *then*
$\mathsf{forget}(F_3, S) \models \mathsf{forget}(F_1 \land F_2, S)$ *if and only if*
$\mathsf{forget}(F_3, S) \models \mathsf{forget}(F_1, S)$ *and*
$\mathsf{forget}(F_3, S) \models \mathsf{forget}(F_2, S)$.
if $\langle F_1, F_2 \rangle$ *is linkless outside* S, *then*
$F_3 \models_S F_1 \land F_2$ *if and only if* $F_3 \models_S F_1$ *and* $F_3 \models_S F_2$.

Proof. Follows from Proposition 80.

□

Proposition 83 *If F_1, F_2 are $\mathcal{E}$-sentences, F_3 is a sentence and S is a literal scope, then*

if $\langle F_1, F_2\rangle$ is essentially linkless outside S, then
$\mathsf{project}(F_3, S) \models \mathsf{project}(F_1 \wedge F_2, S)$ *if and only if*
$\mathsf{project}(F_3, S) \models \mathsf{project}(F_1, S)$ *and*
$\mathsf{project}(F_3, S) \models \mathsf{project}(F_2, S)$.
if $\langle F_1, F_2\rangle$ is essentially linkless inside S, then
$\mathsf{forget}(F_3, S) \models \mathsf{forget}(F_1 \wedge F_2, S)$ *if and only if*
$\mathsf{forget}(F_3, S) \models \mathsf{forget}(F_1, S)$ *and*
$\mathsf{forget}(F_3, S) \models \mathsf{forget}(F_2, S)$.
if $\langle F_1, F_2\rangle$ is essentially linkless outside S, then
$F \models_S F_1 \wedge F_2$ *if and only if* $F \models_S F_1$ *and* $F \models_S F_2$.

Proof. Follows from Proposition 81.

□

5.11 Projection and First-Order Quantification

The interplay of projection with disjunction and conjunction, as shown in Sections 5.9 and 5.10, can be transferred to existential and universal first-order quantification, respectively. Analogous to Propositions 74 and 77, Proposition 84 for existential and Proposition 85 for universal quantification easily follow from the definition of literal projection. However, analogously to Theorem 2, Theorem 4 is more involved to prove.

Proposition 84 *If F is a formula such that x is the only variable that possibly occurs free in F and S is a literal scope, then*

$$\mathsf{project}(\exists x F, S) \equiv \exists x\ \mathsf{project}(F, S).$$
$$\mathsf{forget}(\exists x F, S) \equiv \exists x\ \mathsf{forget}(F, S).$$

Proof.

(1) $I \models \mathsf{project}(\exists x F, S)$ iff
(2) There exists an interpretation J: $J \models \exists x\ F$ and $J \cap S \subseteq I$ iff
(3) There exists an interpretation J and a $t \in \mathsf{GTERMS}$: $J \models F\{x \mapsto t\}$ and $J \cap S \subseteq I$ iff
(4) There exists a $t \in \mathsf{GTERMS}$ and an interpretation J: $J \models F\{x \mapsto t\}$ and $J \cap S \subseteq I$ iff
(5) There exists a $t \in \mathsf{GTERMS}$: $I \models \mathsf{project}(F\{x \mapsto t\}, S)$ iff
(6) $I \models \exists x\ \mathsf{project}(F, S)$.

Let I be an interpretation. Equivalence of (2) to (1) and of (5) to (4) follows from the definition of project. Equivalence of (3) to (2) and of (6) to (5) follows from the definition of $\models$. (4) and (3) are logically equivalent.

□

Proposition 85 *If F is a formula such that x is the only variable that possibly occurs free in F and S is a literal scope, then*

$$\mathsf{project}(\forall x F, S) \models \forall x\ \mathsf{project}(F, S).$$
$$\mathsf{forget}(\forall x F, S) \models \forall x\ \mathsf{forget}(F, S).$$

Proof.

(1) $I \models \mathsf{project}(\forall x F, S)$.
(2) There exists an interpretation J: $J \models \forall x F$ and $J \cap S \subseteq I$.
(3) There exists an interpretation J such that for all $t \in \mathsf{GTERMS}$: $J \models F\{x \mapsto t\}$ and $J \cap S \subseteq I$.
(4) For all $t \in \mathsf{GTERMS}$ there exists an interpretation J: $J \models F\{x \mapsto t\}$ and $J \cap S \subseteq I$.
(5) For all $t \in \mathsf{GTERMS}$: $I \models \mathsf{project}(F\{x \mapsto t\}, S)$.
(6) $I \models \forall x\ \mathsf{project}(F, S)$.

Let I be an interpretation. (2) follows from (1) and the definition of project. (3) follows from (2) and the definition of $\models$. (4) follows logically from (3). (5) follows from (4) by the definition of project. (6) follows from (5) by the definition of $\models$.

□

Theorem 4 (Projection and Linkless Universal Quantification) *If F is a formula such that x is the only variable that possibly occurs free in F and S is a literal scope, then*

if for all $t, u \in \mathsf{GTERMS}$ such that $t \neq u$ it holds that $\langle F\{x \mapsto t\}, F\{x \mapsto u\}\rangle$ is linkless outside S, then
$$\forall x\ \mathsf{project}(F, S) \models \mathsf{project}(\forall x F, S).$$
if for all $t, u \in \mathsf{GTERMS}$ such that $t \neq u$ it holds that $\langle F\{x \mapsto t\}, F\{x \mapsto u\}\rangle$ is linkless inside S, then
$$\forall x\ \mathsf{forget}(F, S) \models \mathsf{forget}(\forall x F, S).$$

Proof. The proof is a variation of the proof of Theorem 2.

(1) For all $t, u \in \mathsf{GTERMS}$ such that $t \neq u$: $\langle F_t, F_u\rangle$ is linkless outside S.
(2) $I \models \forall x\ \mathsf{project}(F, S)$.
(3) For all $t \in \mathsf{GTERMS}$: $I \models \mathsf{project}(F_t, S)$.
(4) For all $t \in \mathsf{GTERMS}$: $J_t \models F_t$.
(5) For all $t \in \mathsf{GTERMS}$: $J_t \cap S \subseteq I$.
(6) For all $t \in \mathsf{GTERMS}$: $J \models F_t$.
(7) $J \cap S \subseteq I$.
(8) $J \models \forall x F$.
(9) $I \models \mathsf{project}(\forall x F, S)$.

Define F_t as shorthand for $F\{x \mapsto t\}$. Assume (1) and let I be an interpretation such that (2) holds. (3) follows from (2). For all $t \in \mathsf{GTERMS}$ let J_t be an interpretation such that $J_t \models F_t$ and $J_t \cap S \subseteq I$. (4) and (5) are then immediate. The existence of such interpretations J_t follows from (3) and the definition of project. In the following we show the construction of an interpretation J that satisfies (6) and (7). (8) follows from (6). (9), which concludes the proof, follows from (8), (7) and the definition of project.

Construction of J. The construction of J is based on two auxiliary sets of literals associated with each ground atom. If A is a ground atom, then $\mathcal{L}^{+A}$ and $\mathcal{L}^{-A}$ are defined as:

$$\mathcal{L}^{+A} \stackrel{\text{def}}{=} \bigcup_{J_t.A = +A,\ t \in \mathsf{GTERMS}} \mathcal{L}(F_t)$$

and

$$\mathcal{L}^{-A} \stackrel{\text{def}}{=} \bigcup_{J_t.A = -A,\ t \in \mathsf{GTERMS}} \mathcal{L}(F_t).$$

Now the interpretation J is defined as follows:

If $+A \notin \mathcal{L}^{+A}$ and	J1
$(-A \in \mathcal{L}^{-A}$ or $I.A = -A)$,	J2
then	
$J.A \stackrel{\text{def}}{=} -A$	J3
else	
$J.A \stackrel{\text{def}}{=} +A.$	J4

Subproof of (6). Let t be an element of GTERMS and let $M \stackrel{\text{def}}{=} \{J_t.A \mid J_t.A = \widetilde{J.A}\}$. Then $J = J_t[\widetilde{M}]$. (6) then follows from (4), Proposition 9 and the following fact, which we now show:

$$M \cap \mathcal{L}(F_t) = \emptyset.$$

(10) $J_t.A = \widetilde{J.A}$.
(11) $J_t.A \in \mathcal{L}(F_t)$.

Assume $M \cap \mathcal{L}(F_t) \neq \emptyset$, i.e., that there exists an atom A such that (10) and (11) hold. We show with some case distinctions that this assumption leads to a contradiction.

(12) *Case* $J_t.A = +A$:

(13) $+A \in \mathcal{L}(F_t)$.
(14) $+A \in \mathcal{L}^{+A}$.
(15) $J.A = +A$.

(13) follows from (12) and (11). (14) follows from (13), (12) and the definition of $\mathcal{L}^{+A}$. (15) follows from (14) and the definition of J: The condition of line J1 fails by (14), thus line J4 applies. (15), (12) and (10) contradict.

(16) *Case* $J_t.A = -A$:

(17) $-A \in \mathcal{L}(F_t)$.
(18) $-A \in \mathcal{L}^{-A}$.

(17) follows from (16) and (11). (18) follows from (17), (16) and the definition of $\mathcal{L}^{-A}$.

(19) *Case* $+A \notin \mathcal{L}^{+A}$:

(20) $J.A = -A$.

(20) follows from (19), (18) and the definition of J: The condition of line J1 is satisfied by (19), line J2 by (18), thus line J3 applies. (20), (16) and (10) contradict.

(21) *Case* $+A \in \mathcal{L}^{+A}$:

(22) *Case* $+A \notin S \cap \widetilde{S}$:

(23) $J_u.A = +A$.
(24) $+A \in \mathcal{L}(F_u)$.
(25) $u \neq t$.

From (21) and the definition of $\mathcal{L}^{+A}$ it follows that there exists an $u \in \mathsf{GTERMS}$ such that (23) and (24) hold. (25) follows from (23) and (16). (25), (24), (22), (17) and (1) contradict.

(26) *Case* $+A \in S \cap \widetilde{S}$:

(27) $I.A = -A$.
(28) For all $u \in \mathsf{GTERMS}$: $J_u.A = -A$.
(29) $\mathcal{L}^{+A} = \emptyset$.

(27) follows from (26), (16) and (5). (28) follows from (27) and (5). (29) follows from (28) and the definition of $\mathcal{L}^{+A}$. (29) contradicts with (21).

Subproof of (7). (7) follows from (5) and the following fact, which we now show:

$$J \subseteq \bigcup_{t \in \mathsf{GTERMS}} J_t \cup I.$$

Assume that A is an atom such that $+A \in J$, or equivalently $J.A = +A$. The if-condition in the definition of J must then be false for A, i. e., it must hold that

$$+A \in \mathcal{L}^{+A} \text{ or } (-A \notin \mathcal{L}^{-A} \text{ and } I.A = +A).$$

It follows easily from the definition of $\mathcal{L}^{+A}$ that if $+A \in \mathcal{L}^{+A}$, then there exists a $t \in \mathsf{GTERMS}$ such that $J_t.A = +A$, or equivalently $+A \in J_t$. Since $I.A = +A$ is equivalent to $+A \in I$ it follows that $+A \in \bigcup_{t \in \mathsf{GTERMS}} J_t \cup I$.

Assume, otherwise, that A is an atom such that $-A \in J$, or equivalently $J.A = -A$. The if-condition in the definition of J must then be true for A, i. e., it must hold that

$$+A \notin \mathcal{L}^{+A} \text{ and } (-A \in \mathcal{L}^{-A} \text{ or } I.A = -A).$$

With arguments analogous to the case $+A \in J$, it follows from the second conjunct of this condition that $-A \in \bigcup_{t \in \mathsf{GTERMS}} J_t \cup I$.

□

5.12 Projection Elimination in Linkless Propositional Formulas

A way to eliminate the projection operator when it is applied to a propositional formula has been shown in Section 5.7. This was based on the formula expansion of Proposition 64. As can be seen in the proof of Proposition 67, the expansion has to be successively applied for each literal to be forgotten, leading potentially to an exponential blow up of the size of the formula. Here we show that on formulas that satisfy a certain syntactic property, projection can be eliminated by literal substitution in time linear in the formula size (Proposition 87, which is based on Proposition 86). This syntactic property is that the *formula* is *linkless outside* (Definition 67) the scope of the projection, which means roughly that for all of its conjunctive subformulas it holds that the *pair* of conjuncts is linkless outside the scope, *linkless* as defined above in Section 5.10, Definition 64.

Certain knowledge compilation and tableau methods compute propositional formulas that are linkless – and thus allow linear projection elimination. We will work out such methods starting from Chapter 8. The main result of this section, Proposition 87, provides the basis of an abstract characterization of such methods (Proposition 121 in Section 8.1). Construction of tableaux that represent linkless formulas is abstractly specified in Section 9.2.1. Most of the work in the literature on projection for propositional logic has been developed in the context of investigating syntactic restrictions similar to *linkless* properties, as we will summarize in Section 6.2.

Definition 66 (Pairs of Conjuncts) If F is a plain polar formula, then the *pairs of conjuncts* in F is the following set:

$$\begin{array}{lll}
\{\langle F_1, F_2\rangle & \mid (F_1 \land F_2) \text{ occurs with polarity } 1 \text{ in } F\} & \cup \\
\{\langle \neg F_1, \neg F_2\rangle & \mid (F_1 \lor F_2) \text{ occurs with polarity } -1 \text{ in } F\} & \cup \\
\{\langle F_1, \neg F_2\rangle & \mid (F_1 \rightarrow F_2) \text{ occurs with polarity } -1 \text{ in } F\} & \cup \\
\{\langle F_1, F_1\rangle & \mid \forall x F_1 \text{ occurs with polarity } 1 \text{ in } F\} & \cup \\
\{\langle \neg F_1, \neg F_1\rangle & \mid \exists x F_1 \text{ occurs with polarity } -1 \text{ in } F\}. &
\end{array}$$

Definition 67 (Linkless Formula) A plain polar formula F is called *linkless outside* (*inside*, resp.) a literal scope S if and only if for all elements $\langle F_1, F_2 \rangle$ of the pairs of conjuncts of F it holds that $\langle F_1, F_2 \rangle$ is linkless outside (inside, resp.) S.

A plain polar formula that is linkless outside $\emptyset$ is called *fully linkless.*

Proposition 86 *If F is a polar propositional sentence that is linkless inside a literal scope $\{L\}$, then*

$$\mathsf{forget}(F, \{L\}) \equiv F[\![L \backslash \top]\!].^3$$

Proof. By induction on formulas it can be shown that for subformula occurrences F' of F with polarity 1 it holds that $F'[\![L \backslash \top]\!] \equiv \mathsf{forget}(F', \{L\})$ and with polarity -1 $(\neg F')[\![L \backslash \top]\!] \equiv \mathsf{forget}(\neg F', \{L\})$.

The four base cases of occurrences of $\top$, $\bot$, atoms with polarity 1 and atoms with polarity -1 can be easily verified with Proposition 64. The induction steps for formula occurrences with polarity 1 (-1, resp.) and $\vee, \rightarrow$ ($\wedge$, resp.) as outermost connective follow from Proposition 74. The induction steps for formula occurrences with polarity 1 (-1, resp.) and $\wedge$ ($\vee$, $\rightarrow$, resp.) as outermost connective follow from Proposition 80, since F is linkless inside $\{L\}$.

The induction step for formula occurrences $F' = \neg F_1$ can be shown as follows: If the polarity of the occurrence of F' is 1, the induction conclusion $F'[\![L \backslash \top]\!] \equiv \mathsf{forget}(F', \{L\})$ is an immediate consequence of the induction assumption $(\neg F_1)[\![L \backslash \top]\!] \equiv \mathsf{forget}(\neg F_1, \{L\})$. If the polarity is -1, the induction assumption is $F_1[\![L \backslash \top]\!] \equiv \mathsf{forget}(F_1, \{L\})$; hence $\neg\neg(F_1[\![L \backslash \top]\!]) \equiv \mathsf{forget}(\neg\neg F_1, \{L\})$; hence $(\neg\neg F_1)[\![L \backslash \top]\!] \equiv \mathsf{forget}(\neg\neg F_1, \{L\})$; hence the induction conclusion $(\neg F')[\![L \backslash \top]\!] \equiv \mathsf{forget}(\neg F', \{L\})$. □

Proposition 87 *If F is a polar propositional sentence that is linkless inside a literal scope $\{L_1, \ldots, L_n\}$, then*

$$\mathsf{forget}(F, \{L_1, \ldots, L_n\}) \equiv F[\![L_1 \backslash \top]\!] \ldots [\![L_n \backslash \top]\!].$$

Proof. It is easy to see that if a formula is linkless inside a literal scope, it still has this property after literal substitution by a truth value. Hence the proposition follows from Proposition 86 along with Propositions 44 and 34 by induction on the cardinality of $\{L_1, \ldots, L_n\}$, similar to the proof of Proposition 67. □

[3] This proposition can be strengthened by replacing the precondition that F is polar with the weaker requirement that just each occurrence of the atom of L in F has polarity 1 or -1, in contrast to 0.

For a polar propositional sentence F that is fully linkless, satisfiability and clausal entailment can be decided in linear time: F is satisfiable if and only if the result of simplifying truth value constants away is the constant $\bot$. If $C = (A_1 \lor \ldots \lor A_m \lor \neg A_{m+1} \lor \ldots \lor \neg A_n)$ is a non-tautological propositional clause, then $F \models C$ if and only if $(F \land \neg C)$ is unsatisfiable. Let

$$\begin{aligned} F' \stackrel{\text{def}}{=} \; & F[A_1 \backslash \bot] \ldots [A_m \backslash \bot][A_{m+1} \backslash \top] \ldots [A_n \backslash \top] \land \\ & \neg A_1 \land \ldots \land \neg A_m \land A_{m+1} \land \ldots \land A_n. \end{aligned}$$

The conjunction $(F \land \neg C)$ is clearly equivalent to F'. If F is fully linkless, then F' is so, and the linear satisfiability test can be applied to F'. Such properties of fully linkless propositional sentences are further discussed in [MR03, Section 3.2].

5.13 Properties of Entailment and Equivalence Relative to a Scope

Tables 5.1 and 5.2 (pp. 83f) summarize the properties of entailment and equivalence relative to a scope, which have been shown before at different places. The tables are preceded by additional propositions that show further properties of entailment relative to a scope and are useful for referencing in proofs.

Proposition 88 *If F_1, F_2 are sentences and S_1, S_2 are literal scopes, then*

$$\textit{if } S_1 \supseteq S_2 \textit{ and } F_1 \models_{S_1} F_2, \textit{ then } F_1 \models_{S_2} F_2.$$

Proof.

(1) $S_1 \supseteq S_2$.
(2) $\mathsf{project}(F_1, S_1) \models \mathsf{project}(F_2, S_1)$.
(3) $\mathsf{project}(F_1, S_1) \models \mathsf{project}(F_2, S_2)$.
(4) $\mathsf{project}(\mathsf{project}(F_1, S_1), S_2) \models \mathsf{project}(F_2, S_2)$.
(5) $\mathsf{project}(F_1, S_2) \models \mathsf{project}(F_2, S_2)$.

Assume (1) and (2). (3) follows from (2), (1) and Proposition 33. (4) follows from (3) and Proposition 36. (5) follows from (4), (1) and Proposition 34. □

Proposition 89 *If F_1, F_2 are sentences and S_1, S_2 are literal scopes, then*

$$\textit{if } S_1 \supseteq S_2 \textit{ and } F_1 \equiv_{S_1} F_2, \textit{ then } F_1 \equiv_{S_2} F_2.$$

Proof. Follows immediately from Proposition 88. □

Proposition 90 *If F_1, F_2 are sentences and S is a literal scope, then*

$$\text{if } \mathcal{L}(F_2) \subseteq S, \text{ then } F_1 \models F_2 \text{ if and only if } F_1 \models_S F_2.$$

Proof.

(1) $\mathcal{L}(F_2) \subseteq S$.
(2) $\mathsf{project}(F_1, S) \models \mathsf{project}(F_2, S)$.
(3) $\mathsf{project}(F_2, S) \equiv F_2$.
(4) $\mathsf{project}(F_1, S) \models F_2$.
(5) $F_1 \models F_2$.

Left to right follows immediately from Proposition 31. Right to left: Assume (1) and (2). (3) follows from (1) and Proposition 41. (4) follows from (3) and (2). (5) follows from (4) and Proposition 30.

□

Proposition 91 *If F_1 is a sentence, F_2 is an $\mathcal{E}$-sentence and S is a literal scope, then*

$$\text{if } \mathcal{L}_{\mathcal{E}}(F_2) \subseteq S, \text{ then } F_1 \models F_2 \text{ if and only if } F_1 \models_S F_2.$$

Proof. Can be shown in the same way as Proposition 90 with $\mathcal{L}_{\mathcal{E}}$ in place of $\mathcal{L}$. Step (3) follows from Proposition 43 (since F_2 is an $\mathcal{E}$-sentence).

□

Proposition 92 *If F_1, F_2 are sentences and S is a literal scope such that $\mathsf{project}(F_2, S)$ is an $\mathcal{E}$-sentence, then*

$$F_1 \models_S F_2 \text{ if and only if } F_1 \models_{\mathcal{L}(F_2) \cap S} F_2.$$

Proof.

(1) $\mathsf{project}(F_1, S) \models \mathsf{project}(F_2, S)$ iff
(2) $\mathsf{project}(F_1, S) \models \mathsf{project}(F_2, \mathcal{L}(F_2) \cap S)$ iff
(3) $\mathsf{project}(\mathsf{project}(F_1, S), \mathcal{L}(F_2) \cap S) \models \mathsf{project}(F_2, \mathcal{L}(F_2) \cap S)$ iff
(4) $\mathsf{project}(F_1, \mathcal{L}(F_2) \cap S) \models \mathsf{project}(F_2, \mathcal{L}(F_2) \cap S)$.

Equivalence of (2) to (1) follows from Proposition 52. Equivalence of (3) to (2) follows from Proposition 63. That the preconditions of Proposition 63 are satisfied can be shown as follows: By Proposition 52 it holds that $\mathsf{project}(F_2, S) \equiv \mathsf{project}(F_2, \mathcal{L}(F_2) \cap S)$. Since $\mathsf{project}(F_2, S)$ is an $\mathcal{E}$-sentence, it then follows from Proposition 14 that $\mathsf{project}(F_2, \mathcal{L}(F_2) \cap S)$ is also an $\mathcal{E}$-sentence. From Proposition 47 follows $\mathcal{L}_{\mathcal{E}}(\mathsf{project}(F_2, \mathcal{L}(F_2) \cap S)) \subseteq \mathcal{L}(F_2) \cap S$. Equivalence of (4) to (3) follows from Proposition 34.

□

Proposition 93 *If F_1 is a sentence, F_2 is an $\mathcal{E}$-sentence and S is a literal scope such that* $\mathsf{project}(F_2, S)$ *is an $\mathcal{E}$-sentence, then*

$$F_1 \models_S F_2 \text{ if and only if } F_1 \models_{\mathcal{L}_{\mathcal{E}}(F_2)\cap S} F_2.$$

Proof.

(1) $\mathsf{project}(F_1, S) \models \mathsf{project}(F_2, S)$ iff
(2) $\mathsf{project}(F_1, S) \models \mathsf{project}(F_2, \mathcal{L}_{\mathcal{E}}(F_2) \cap S)$ iff
(3) $\mathsf{project}(\mathsf{project}(F_1, S), \mathcal{L}_{\mathcal{E}}(F_2) \cap S) \models \mathsf{project}(F_2, \mathcal{L}_{\mathcal{E}}(F_2) \cap S)$ iff
(4) $\mathsf{project}(F_1, \mathcal{L}_{\mathcal{E}}(F_2) \cap S) \models \mathsf{project}(F_2, \mathcal{L}_{\mathcal{E}}(F_2) \cap S)$.

Can be shown in the same way as Proposition 93 with $\mathcal{L}_{\mathcal{E}}$ in place of $\mathcal{L}$. Equivalence of (2) to (1) follows from Proposition 53, since F_2 is an $\mathcal{E}$-sentence. A step in establishing the preconditions of Proposition 63 is $\mathsf{project}(F_2, S) \equiv \mathsf{project}(F_2, \mathcal{L}_{\mathcal{E}}(F_2) \cap S)$. This follows from Proposition 53 since F_2 is an $\mathcal{E}$-sentence.

□

Proposition 94 *If F_1, F_2, F_3 are sentences and S is a literal scope, then*

$$\text{if } F_1 \models_S F_2 \text{ and } F_2 \models_S F_3, \text{ then } F_1 \models_S F_3.$$

Proof. Easy to see.

□

Proposition 95 *If F_1, F_2 are sentences and S is a literal scope, then*

$$\text{if } F_1 \models (F_2 \rightarrow_S F_3), \text{ then } F_1 \land F_2 \models_S F_3.$$

Proof.

(1) $F_1 \models (\mathsf{project}(F_2, S) \rightarrow \mathsf{project}(F_3, S))$.
(2) $F_1 \land \mathsf{project}(F_2, S) \models \mathsf{project}(F_3, S)$.
(3) $F_1 \land F_2 \models \mathsf{project}(F_3, S)$.
(4) $\mathsf{project}(F_1 \land F_2, S) \models \mathsf{project}(F_3, S)$.

Assume (1). (2) follows from (1). (3) follows from (2) and Proposition 30. (4) follows from (3) and Proposition 36.

□

Proposition 96 *If F_1, F_2 are sentences and S is a literal scope, then*

if $\langle F_1, F_2 \rangle$ is linkless outside S, then

$$F_1 \models (F_2 \rightarrow_S F_3) \text{ if and only if } F_1 \land F_2 \models_S F_3.$$

Proof. Left to right follows from Proposition 95. Right to left:

(1) $\langle F_1, F_2 \rangle$ is linkless outside S.
(2) $\mathsf{project}(F_1 \land F_2, S) \models \mathsf{project}(F_3, S)$.
(3) $\mathsf{project}(F_1, S) \land \mathsf{project}(F_2, S) \models \mathsf{project}(F_3, S)$.
(4) $F_1 \land \mathsf{project}(F_2, S) \models \mathsf{project}(F_3, S)$.

Assume (1) and (2). (3) follows from (2), (1) and Theorem 2. (4) follows from (3) and Proposition 30.

□

Proposition 97 *If F_1, F_2 are $\mathcal{E}$-sentences and S is a literal scope, then*

$$\text{if } \langle F_1, F_2\rangle \text{ is essentially linkless outside } S, \text{ then}$$
$$F_1 \models (F_2 \rightarrow_S F_3) \text{ if and only if } F_1 \land F_2 \models_S F_3.$$

Proof. Can be shown in the same way as Proposition 96 with *essentially linkless* in place of *linkless*. Step (3) follows from Theorem 3 instead of 2, since $\langle F_1, F_2\rangle$ is by (1) essentially linkless outside S.

□

5.14 Entailment Relative to a Scope and Consequences

It is easy to see that a sentence entails another one if and only if each consequence of the second sentence is also a consequence of the first one: *If F_1, F_2 are sentences, then*

$$F_1 \models F_2$$

if and only if for all sentences G it holds that

$$\text{if } F_2 \models G, \text{ then } F_1 \models G.$$

Hence, two sentences are equivalent if and only if they have the same consequences:

$$F_1 \equiv F_2$$

if and only if for all sentences G it holds that

$$F_1 \models G \text{ if and only if } F_2 \models G.$$

Analogs of these obvious relationships for entailment and equivalence *relative to a scope* are not fully obvious. Hence we show them in this section in some detail. In Section 5.15 they are applied to show different characterizations of projection.

Propositions 98 and 99 show the direction from entailment relative to a scope to consequences whose [essential] literal base is included in the scope. Propositions 100 and 101 are their converses, but they require certain preconditions, which, as shown in Propositions 69 and 70, at least hold for propositional sentences. Propositions 102 and 103 combine Proposition 98 with 100 and 99 with 101, respectively, to equivalences. Propositions 104–106 then state properties of equivalence relative to a scope, which follow from Propositions 102 and 103.

If F_1, F_2, F_3 *are sentences and* S, S_1, S_2 *are literal scopes, then*	
If $F_1 \models F_2$, *then* $F_1 \models_S F_2$	(Prop. 31)
If $F_1 \models \mathsf{project}(F_2, S)$, *then* $F_1 \models_S F_2$	(Prop. 36)
$F_1 \models \mathsf{project}(F_2, S)$ *if and only if* $F_1 \models_S F_2$	(Prop. 37)
$F_1 \models_S F_1 \vee F_2$	(Prop. 75)
$F_1 \vee F_2 \models_S F_3$ *if and only if* $F_1 \models_S F_3$ *and* $F_2 \models_S F$	(Prop. 76)
$F_1 \wedge F_2 \models_S F_1$	(Prop. 77)
If $\langle F_1, F_2 \rangle$ *is linkless outside* S, *then* $F_3 \models_S F_1 \wedge F_2$ *if and only if* $F_3 \models_S F_1$ *and* $F_3 \models_S F_2$	(Prop. 82)
If F_1 *and* F_2 *are* $\mathcal{E}$*-sentences* *and* $\langle F_1, F_2 \rangle$ *is essentially linkless outside* S, *then* $F_3 \models_S F_1 \wedge F_2$ *if and only if* $F_3 \models_S F_1$ *and* $F_3 \models_S F_2$	(Prop. 83)
If $S_1 \supseteq S_2$ *and* $F_1 \models_{S_1} F_2$, *then* $F_1 \models_{S_2} F_2$	(Prop. 88)
If $\mathcal{L}(F_2) \subseteq S$, *then* $F_1 \models F_2$ *if and only if* $F_1 \models_S F_2$	(Prop. 90)
If F_2 *is an* $\mathcal{E}$*-sentence and* $\mathcal{L}_{\mathcal{E}}(F_2) \subseteq S$, *then* $F_1 \models F_2$ *if and only if* $F_1 \models_S F_2$	(Prop. 91)
If $\mathsf{project}(F_2, S)$ *is an* $\mathcal{E}$*-sentence, then* $F_1 \models_S F_2$ *if and only if* $F_1 \models_{\mathcal{L}(F_2) \cap S} F_2$	(Prop. 92)
If F_2 *and* $\mathsf{project}(F_2, S)$ *are* $\mathcal{E}$*-sentences, then* $F_1 \models_S F_2$ *if and only if* $F_1 \models_{\mathcal{L}_{\mathcal{E}}(F_2) \cap S} F_2$	(Prop. 93)
If $F_1 \models_S F_2$ *and* $F_2 \models_S F_3$, *then* $F_1 \models_S F_3$	(Prop. 94)
If $F_1 \models (F_2 \rightarrow_S F_3)$, *then* $F_1 \wedge F_2 \models_S F_3$	(Prop. 95)
If $\langle F_1, F_2 \rangle$ *is linkless outside* S, *then* $F_1 \models (F_2 \rightarrow_S F_3)$ *if and only if* $F_1 \wedge F_2 \models_S F_3$	(Prop. 96)
If F_1 *and* F_2 *are* $\mathcal{E}$*-sentences* *and* $\langle F_1, F_2 \rangle$ *is essentially linkless outside* S, *then* $F_1 \models (F_2 \rightarrow_S F_3)$ *if and only if* $F_1 \wedge F_2 \models_S F_3$	(Prop. 97)

Table 5.1. Summary of Properties of $\models_S$

If F, F_1, F_2 are sentences and S, S_1, S_2 are literal scopes, then	
If $F_1 \equiv F_2$, then $F_1 \equiv_S F_2$	(Prop. 32)
$\mathsf{project}(F, S) \equiv_S F$	(Prop. 35)
If $S_1 \supseteq S_2$ and $F_1 \equiv_{S_1} F_2$, then $F_1 \equiv_{S_2} F_2$	(Prop. 89)

Table 5.2. Summary of Properties of $\equiv_S$

Proposition 98 *If F_1, F_2 are sentences and S is a literal scope such that*

$$F_1 \models_S F_2,$$

then for all sentences G such that $\mathcal{L}(G) \subseteq S$ it holds that

$$\textit{if } F_2 \models G, \textit{ then } F_1 \models G.$$

Proof.

(1) $F_1 \models_S F_2$.
(2) $\mathsf{project}(F_1, S) \models \mathsf{project}(F_2, S)$.
(3) $\mathcal{L}(G) \subseteq S$.
(4) $F_2 \models G$.
(5) $\mathsf{project}(F_2, S) \models G$.
(6) $\mathsf{project}(F_1, S) \models G$.
(7) $F_1 \models G$.

Assume (1), which by the definition of $\models_S$ is equivalent to (2). Let G be a sentence such that (3) and (4) hold. (5) follows from (4), (3) and Proposition 60. (6) follows from (5) and (2). (7) follows from (6) and Proposition 30. □

Proposition 99 *If F_1, F_2 are sentences and S is a literal scope such that*

$$F_1 \models_S F_2,$$

then for all $\mathcal{E}$-sentences G such that $\mathcal{L}_{\mathcal{E}}(G) \subseteq S$ it holds that

$$\textit{if } F_2 \models G, \textit{ then } F_1 \models G.$$

Proof. Can be shown in the same way as Proposition 98 with $\mathcal{L}_{\mathcal{E}}$ in place of $\mathcal{L}$. Let G be an $\mathcal{E}$-sentence (instead of a sentence in general) such that (3) and (4) hold. (5) follows from (4), (3) and Proposition 61, since G is an $\mathcal{E}$-sentence.

□

Proposition 100 *If F_1, F_2 are sentences, S is a literal scope and there exists a sentence H such that $H \equiv \mathsf{project}(F_2, S)$ and $\mathcal{L}(H) \subseteq S$ and for all G such that $\mathcal{L}(G) \subseteq S$ it holds that*

$$\textit{if } F_2 \models G, \ \textit{then } F_1 \models G,$$

then

$$F_1 \models_S F_2.$$

Proof.

(1) For all sentences G such that $\mathcal{L}(G) \subseteq S$: if $F_2 \models G$, then $F_1 \models G$.
(2) $H \equiv \mathsf{project}(F_2, S)$.
(3) $\mathcal{L}(H) \subseteq S$.
(4) $F_2 \models H$.
(5) $F_1 \models H$.
(6) $F_1 \models \mathsf{project}(F_2, S)$.
(6) $\mathsf{project}(F_1, S) \models \mathsf{project}(F_2, S)$.
(7) $F_1 \models_S F_2$.

Assume (1), (2) and (3). (4) follows from (2) and Proposition 30. (5) follows from (4), (3) and (1). (6) follows from (5) and (2). (7) follows from (6) and Proposition 36. (8) follows from (7) and the definition of $\models_S$.

□

Proposition 101 *If F_1, F_2 are sentences and S is a literal scope such that $\mathsf{project}(F_2, S)$ is an $\mathcal{E}$-sentence and for all $\mathcal{E}$-sentences G such that $\mathcal{L}_{\mathcal{E}}(G) \subseteq S$ it holds that*

$$\textit{if } F_2 \models G, \ \textit{then } F_1 \models G,$$

then

$$F_1 \models_S F_2.$$

Proof.

(1) For all $\mathcal{E}$-sentences G such that $\mathcal{L}_{\mathcal{E}}(G) \subseteq S$: if $F_2 \models G$, then $F_1 \models G$.
(2) $\mathcal{L}_{\mathcal{E}}(\mathsf{project}(F_2, S)) \subseteq S$.
(3) $F_2 \models \mathsf{project}(F_2, S)$.
(4) $F_1 \models \mathsf{project}(F_2, S)$.
(5) $\mathsf{project}(F_1, S) \models \mathsf{project}(F_2, S)$.
(6) $F_1 \models_S F_2$.

Assume (1). (2) holds by Proposition 47. (3) holds by Proposition 30. (4) follows from (3), (2) and (1), since $\mathsf{project}(F_2, S)$ is an $\mathcal{E}$-sentence. (5) follows from (4) and Proposition 36. (6) follows from (5) and the definition of $\models_S$.

□

Proposition 102 *If F_1, F_2 are sentences, S is a literal scope and there exists a sentence H such that $H \equiv \mathsf{project}(F_2, S)$ and $\mathcal{L}(H) \subseteq S$, then*

$$F_1 \models_S F_2$$

if and only if for all sentences G such that $\mathcal{L}(G) \subseteq S$ it holds that

$$\text{if } F_2 \models G, \text{ then } F_1 \models G.$$

Proof. Left to right follows immediately from Proposition 98. Right to left is stated as Proposition 100.

□

Proposition 103 *If F_1, F_2 are sentences and S is a literal scope such that $\mathsf{project}(F_2, S)$ is an $\mathcal{E}$-sentence, then*

$$F_1 \models_S F_2$$

if and only if for all $\mathcal{E}$-sentences G such that $\mathcal{L}_{\mathcal{E}}(G) \subseteq S$ it holds that

$$\text{if } F_2 \models G, \text{ then } F_1 \models G.$$

Proof. Left to right follows immediately from Proposition 99. Right to left is stated as Proposition 101.

□

Proposition 104 *If F_1, F_2 are sentences, S is a literal scope and there exist sentences H_1, H_2 such that $H_1 \equiv \mathsf{project}(F_1, S)$, $H_2 \equiv \mathsf{project}(F_2, S)$, $\mathcal{L}(H_1) \subseteq S$ and $\mathcal{L}(H_2) \subseteq S$, then*

$$F_1 \equiv_S F_2$$

if and only if for all sentences G such that $\mathcal{L}(G) \subseteq S$ it holds that

$$F_1 \models G \text{ if and only if } F_2 \models G.$$

Proof. Follows immediately from Proposition 102.

□

Proposition 105 *If F_1, F_2 are sentences and S is a literal scope such that $\mathsf{project}(F_1, S)$ and $\mathsf{project}(F_2, S)$ are $\mathcal{E}$-sentences, then*

$$F_1 \equiv_S F_2$$

if and only if for all $\mathcal{E}$-sentences G such that $\mathcal{L}_{\mathcal{E}}(G) \subseteq S$ it holds that

$$F_1 \models G \text{ if and only if } F_2 \models G.$$

Proof. Follows immediately from Proposition 103.

□

Proposition 106 *If F_1, F_2 are sentences, S is a literal scope, $\mathcal{L}(F_2) \subseteq S$ and there exists a sentence H such that $H \equiv \mathsf{project}(F_1, S)$ and $\mathcal{L}(H) \subseteq S$, then*

$$F_1 \equiv_S F_2$$

if and only if

1. $F_1 \models F_2$ *and*
2. *for all sentences G such that $\mathcal{L}(G) \subseteq S$ it holds that*
   If $F_1 \models G$, then $F_2 \models G$.

Proof. Given that $\mathcal{L}(F_2) \subseteq S$, equivalence of $F_1 \models_S F_2$ to condition (1.) follows from Proposition 90. Equivalence of $F_2 \models_S F_1$ to condition (2.) follows immediately from Proposition 102.

□

Proposition 107 *If F_1 is a sentence, F_2 is an $\mathcal{E}$-sentence, S is a literal scope, $\mathcal{L}_{\mathcal{E}}(F_2) \subseteq S$ and $\mathsf{project}(F_1)$ is an $\mathcal{E}$-sentence, then*

$$F_1 \equiv_S F_2$$

if and only if

1. $F_1 \models F_2$ *and*
2. *for all $\mathcal{E}$-sentences G such that $\mathcal{L}_{\mathcal{E}}(G) \subseteq S$ it holds that*
   If $F_1 \models G$, then $F_2 \models G$.

Proof. Given that $\mathcal{L}_{\mathcal{E}}(F_2) \subseteq S$, equivalence of $F_1 \models_S F_2$ to condition (1.) follows from Proposition 91 (since F_2 is an $\mathcal{E}$-sentence). Equivalence of $F_2 \models_S F_1$ to condition (2.) follows immediately from Proposition 103.

□

5.15 Alternate Characterizations of Projection

Projection has been defined by a semantic characterization in Definition 52. It can be characterized in further ways that show different intuitions and relate to definitions from the literature. A first such possibility to characterize projection is the following:

(i) The projection of a sentence F onto a literal scope S is the weakest sentence that is equivalent to F relative to S (Proposition 108).

Three further possibilities come in two varieties, making a total of six more characterizations: (ii)–(iv) are based on the notion of literal base ($\mathcal{L}$) and involve syntactical conditions. Characterizations (v)–(vii) are analogous to (ii)–(iv), respectively, but based on the notion of essential literal base ($\mathcal{L}_{\mathcal{E}}$). They are purely semantic, but require certain formulas to be $\mathcal{E}$-sentences. In Propositions 109–114 the proofs of both varieties are given independently of each other, despite some duplication, to show exactly where the respective restriction of each characterization is required.

Let the relation $\mathsf{R}_{\mathsf{project}\text{-}\mathcal{B}}$ be defined as

$$\mathsf{R}_{\mathsf{project}\text{-}\mathcal{B}}(F, S, F') \stackrel{\text{def}}{=} F' \equiv \mathsf{project}(F, S) \textit{ and } \mathcal{L}(F') \subseteq S.$$

That is, F' is equivalent to the projection of F onto S, and the literal base of F' is contained in S. The relation $\mathsf{R}_{\mathsf{project}\text{-}\mathcal{B}}$ is not semantically determined, since it involves a constraint on the *literal base* of F'. Alternate characterizations of $\mathsf{R}_{\mathsf{project}\text{-}\mathcal{B}}(F, S, F')$ are:

(ii) The literal base of F' is in S and F' is equivalent to F relative to S (Proposition 109);

(iii) The literal base of F' is in S and F' has the same consequences with literal base in S as F (Proposition 110);

(iv) F' is the strongest consequence of F whose literal base is in S (Proposition 111).

Characterizations (iii) and (iv) require the additional precondition that there exists a sentence H such that $H \equiv \mathsf{project}(F, S)$ and $\mathcal{L}(H) \subseteq S$. If F is a generalized propositional sentence, this condition holds by Proposition 69.

The following three characterizations of projection are analogous to characterizations (ii)–(iv), but are based on the notion of *essential* literal base ($\mathcal{L}_{\mathcal{E}}$) instead of literal base ($\mathcal{L}$). Let the relation $\mathsf{R}_{\mathsf{project}}$ be defined as

$$\mathsf{R}_{\mathsf{project}}(F, S, F') \stackrel{\text{def}}{=} F' \equiv \mathsf{project}(F, S).$$

This relation is clearly semantically determined. The following are alternate characterizations of $\mathsf{R}_{\mathsf{project}}(F, S, F')$, where F' is constrained to be an $\mathcal{E}$-sentence:

(v) The essential literal base of F' is in S and F' is equivalent to F relative to S (Proposition 112);

(vi) The essential literal base of F' is in S and F' has the same consequences with essential literal base in S as F (Proposition 113);

(vii) F' is the strongest consequence of F whose essential literal base is in S (Proposition 114).

Characterizations (vi) and (vii) require the additional precondition that $\mathsf{project}(F, S)$ is an $\mathcal{E}$-sentence. If F is a generalized propositional sentence, this condition holds by Proposition 70.

Some of these characterizations of projection involve the notion of equivalence relative to a scope ($\equiv_S$), which is defined in terms of projection (Definition 58). This does not, however, cause a circular definitional dependency, since the two occurrences of $\mathsf{project}$ in Definition 58 could be expanded according to Definition 52, yielding a definition of $\equiv_S$ that is independent of $\mathsf{project}$.

Proposition 108 *If F, F' are sentences and S is a literal scope, then*

$F' \equiv \mathsf{project}(F, S)$ *if and only if*
1. *for all sentences G such that $G \equiv_S F$ it holds that $G \models F'$ and*
2. *$F' \equiv_S F$.*

$F' \equiv \mathsf{forget}(F, S)$ *if and only if*
1. *for all sentences G such that $G \equiv_{\overline{S}} F$ it holds that $G \models F'$ and*
2. *$F' \equiv_{\overline{S}} F$.*

Proof. Left to right:

(1) $G \equiv_S F$.
(2) $\mathsf{project}(G, S) \models \mathsf{project}(F, S)$.
(3) $G \models \mathsf{project}(F, S)$.
(4) $\mathsf{project}(F, S) \equiv_S F$.

We show that conditions (1.) and (2.) are satisfied with $\mathsf{project}(F, S)$ in the role of F'. Let G be a sentence such that (1) holds. (2) follows from (1) and the definition of $\equiv_S$. (3) – which shows condition (1.) – follows from (2) and Proposition 30. (4) – i. e., condition (2.) – holds by Proposition 35. Right to left:

(1) For all sentences G: If $G \equiv_S F$, then $G \models F'$.
(2) $F' \equiv_S F$.
(3) $\mathsf{project}(F, S) \equiv_S F$.
(4) $\mathsf{project}(F, S) \models F'$.
(5) $F' \models \mathsf{project}(F, S)$.
(6) $F' \equiv \mathsf{project}(F, S)$.

Assume (1) and (2). (3) holds by Proposition 35. (4) follows from (3) and (1). (5) follows from (2) by Proposition 30 and the definition of $\equiv_S$. (6) follows from (5) and (4).

□

Proposition 109 *If F, F' are sentences and S is a literal scope, then*

($F' \equiv \mathsf{project}(F, S)$ *and* $\mathcal{L}(F') \subseteq S$) *if and only if*
1. *$\mathcal{L}(F') \subseteq S$ and*
2. *$F' \equiv_S F$.*

($F' \equiv \mathsf{forget}(F, S)$ *and* $\mathcal{L}(F') \cap S = \emptyset$) *if and only if*
1. *$\mathcal{L}(F') \cap S = \emptyset$ and*
2. *$F' \equiv_{\overline{S}} F$.*

Proof. Assume $\mathcal{L}(F') \subseteq S$. Then $\mathsf{project}(F', S) \equiv F'$ follows from Proposition 41. Hence $F' \equiv \mathsf{project}(F, S)$ if and only if $\mathsf{project}(F', S) \equiv \mathsf{project}(F, S)$ if and only if $F' \equiv_S F$.

□

Proposition 110 *If F, F' are sentences, S is a literal scope and there exists a sentence H such that $H \equiv \mathsf{project}(F, S)$ and $\mathcal{L}(H) \subseteq S$, then*

$(F' \equiv \mathsf{project}(F, S)$ *and* $\mathcal{L}(F') \subseteq S)$ *if and only if*
1. $\mathcal{L}(F') \subseteq S$ *and*
2. *for all sentences G such that $\mathcal{L}(G) \subseteq S$ it holds that $F' \models G$ if and only if $F \models G$.*

$(F' \equiv \mathsf{forget}(F, S)$ *and* $\mathcal{L}(F') \cap S = \emptyset)$ *if and only if*
1. $\mathcal{L}(F') \cap S = \emptyset$ *and*
2. *for all sentences G such that $\mathcal{L}(G) \cap S = \emptyset$ it holds that $F' \models G$ if and only if $F \models G$.*

Proof. Assume condition (1.), which is identical to condition (1.) of Proposition 109. From Proposition 41 follows that $\mathsf{project}(F', S) \equiv F'$. Hence there exists a sentence H' such that $H' \equiv \mathsf{project}(F', S)$ and $\mathcal{L}(H') \subseteq S$. It then follows from Proposition 104 that condition (2.) here is equivalent to condition (2.) of Proposition 109.

□

Proposition 111 *If F, F' are sentences, S is a literal scope and there exists a sentence H such that $H \equiv \mathsf{project}(F, S)$ and $\mathcal{L}(H) \subseteq S$, then*

$(F' \equiv \mathsf{project}(F, S)$ *and* $\mathcal{L}(F') \subseteq S)$ *if and only if*
1. $\mathcal{L}(F') \subseteq S$ *and*
2. $F \models F'$ *and*
3. *for all sentences G such that $\mathcal{L}(G) \subseteq S$ it holds that if $F \models G$, then $F' \models G$.*

$(F' \equiv \mathsf{forget}(F, S)$ *and* $\mathcal{L}(F') \cap S = \emptyset)$ *if and only if*
1. $\mathcal{L}(F') \cap S = \emptyset$ *and*
2. $F \models F'$ *and*
3. *for all sentences G such that $\mathcal{L}(G) \cap S = \emptyset$ it holds that if $F \models G$, then $F' \models G$.*

Proof. Assume condition (1.), which is identical to condition (1.) of Proposition 109. From Proposition 106 it follows that the conjunction of conditions (2.) and (3.) is equivalent to condition (2.) of Proposition 109.

□

Proposition 112 *If F is a sentence, F' is an $\mathcal{E}$-sentence and S is a literal scope, then*

$F' \equiv \mathsf{project}(F, S)$ *if and only if*
1. $\mathcal{L}_{\mathcal{E}}(F') \subseteq S$ *and*
2. $F' \equiv_S F$.

$F' \equiv \mathsf{forget}(F, S)$ *if and only if*
1. $\mathcal{L}_{\mathcal{E}}(F') \cap S = \emptyset$ *and*
2. $F' \equiv_{\overline{S}} F$.

Proof. Assume $\mathcal{L}_{\mathcal{E}}(F') \subseteq S$. For the left-to-right direction, this assumption follows from $F' \equiv \mathsf{project}(F, S)$, Propositions 47 and 7; for the right-to-left direction, it is explicitly stated as condition (1.). From Proposition 43 (since F' is an $\mathcal{E}$-sentence) then follows $\mathsf{project}(F', S) \equiv F'$. Hence $F' \equiv \mathsf{project}(F, S)$ if and only if $\mathsf{project}(F', S) \equiv \mathsf{project}(F, S)$ if and only if $F' \equiv_S F$.

□

Proposition 113 *If F is a sentence, F' is an $\mathcal{E}$-sentence and S is a literal scope such that* $\mathsf{project}(F, S)$ *is an $\mathcal{E}$-sentence, then*

$F' \equiv \mathsf{project}(F, S)$ *if and only if*
1. $\mathcal{L}_{\mathcal{E}}(F') \subseteq S$ *and*
2. *for all $\mathcal{E}$-sentences G such that $\mathcal{L}_{\mathcal{E}}(G) \subseteq S$ it holds that $F' \models G$ if and only if $F \models G$.*

$F' \equiv \mathsf{forget}(F, S)$ *if and only if*
1. $\mathcal{L}_{\mathcal{E}}(F') \cap S = \emptyset$ *and*
2. *for all $\mathcal{E}$-sentences G such that $\mathcal{L}_{\mathcal{E}}(G) \cap S = \emptyset$ it holds that $F' \models G$ if and only if $F \models G$.*

Proof. Assume condition (1.), which is identical to condition (1.) of Proposition 112. From Proposition 43 it follows that $\mathsf{project}(F', S) \equiv F'$ (since F' is an $\mathcal{E}$-sentence); hence from Proposition 14 it follows that $\mathsf{project}(F', S)$ is also an $\mathcal{E}$-sentence. It then follows from Proposition 105 that condition (2.) here is equivalent to condition (2.) of Proposition 112.

□

Proposition 114 *If F is a sentence, F' is an $\mathcal{E}$-sentence and S is a literal scope such that* $\mathsf{project}(F, S)$ *is an $\mathcal{E}$-sentence, then*

$F' \equiv \mathsf{project}(F, S)$ *if and only if*
1. $\mathcal{L}_{\mathcal{E}}(F') \subseteq S$ *and*
2. $F \models F'$ *and*
3. *for all $\mathcal{E}$-sentences G such that $\mathcal{L}_{\mathcal{E}}(G) \subseteq S$ it holds that if $F \models G$, then $F' \models G$.*

$F' \equiv \mathsf{forget}(F, S)$ *if and only if*
1. $\mathcal{L}_{\mathcal{E}}(F') \cap S = \emptyset$ *and*
2. $F \models F'$ *and*
3. *for all $\mathcal{E}$-sentences G such that $\mathcal{L}_{\mathcal{E}}(G) \cap S = \emptyset$ it holds that if $F \models G$, then $F' \models G$.*

Proof. Assume condition (1.), which is identical to condition (1.) of Proposition 112. From Proposition 107 it follows that the conjunction of conditions (2.) and (3.) is equivalent to condition (2.) of Proposition 112.

□

6 Related Work on Projection

There are several works, with different backgrounds, that are concerned with characterizations and properties of projection and related notions. Aside from the works discussed in this chapter, projection is also related to interpolation properties, which we discuss in Section 14.2.3.

6.1 Projection for First-Order Logic

Much of the recent material on forgetting, projection and related operations is confined to propositional logic, although some of the earlier work was in the context of knowledge representation with first-order logic. For example, Lin and Reiter [LR94] introduced the term *forgetting*. They describe in standard model theoretic terms the semantics of forgetting about a ground atom and about a relation. Forgetting about a relation is in our terminology the forgetting about all ground atoms with a given predicate. As noted by Lin and Reiter, this corresponds to second-order quantification.

Gabbay and Ohlbach [GO92] investigated automated elimination of second-order quantifiers. The focus of that work is computation of quantifier elimination and its applications. We discuss it in Section 7.3. Gabbay, Schmidt and Szałas comprehensively describe the foundations of second-order quantifier elimination in their recent monograph [GSS08].

6.2 Projection and Propositional Knowledge Compilation

In Proposition 87 it has been shown that on propositional sentences that satisfy certain syntactic restrictions, projection can be eliminated just by literal substitution, an operation that is linear in the size of the sentence. There are several such restrictions on formulas for which the elimination of projection is an operation with low complexity. Hence projection and forgetting is often discussed in the context of such "normal forms", as these restrictions are often called. They are studied under the label *knowledge compilation*, referring to knowledge processing in two stages – in the "compilation phase" a knowledge base is transformed into a data structure (or *normal form*) which allows in the "run time phase" that certain operations can be performed with low complexity.

These normal forms include formula representations as graphs with shared subexpressions, such as ordered binary decision diagrams, for which atom forgetting has been described by Bryant [Bry92].

Both, atom projection and atom forgetting are discussed by Darwiche [Dar01a] in the context of decomposable negation normal form (DNNF), which can be defined as follows:

Definition 68 (Decomposable Negation Normal Form) A propositional formula is in *decomposable negation normal form* (DNNF) if and only if it is in negation normal form (only $\vee$ and $\wedge$ as binary connectives, only atoms, $\top$ and $\bot$ as arguments of $\neg$) and for all elements $\langle F_1, F_2 \rangle$ of the pairs of conjuncts of F it holds that $\mathcal{A}(F_1) \cap \mathcal{A}(F_2) = \emptyset$.

It seems that the term *projection* has been introduced in [Dar01a]. Projection is defined there as a ternary relation, identical our $\mathsf{R}_{\mathsf{project}\text{-}\mathcal{B}}(F', F, S)$ (see p. 88), except that S is an atom scope, i. e.,

$$F' \equiv \mathsf{project\text{-}atoms}(F, S) \text{ and } \mathcal{A}(F') \subseteq S.$$

This relation is characterized in [Dar01a] as follows (using our terminology): *A projection of a propositional sentence F on a set of atoms S is another propositional sentence F', which satisfies the following properties: (1) $\mathcal{A}(F) \subseteq S$; (2) For all propositional sentences G such that $\mathcal{A}(G) \subseteq S$ it holds that $F' \models G$ if and only if $F \models G$.* This characterization corresponds to our Proposition 110. In [Dar01a] it is further proven that if F is a propositional formula and S is a finite atom scope, then an F' such that this relation holds can be computed by polar substitution. Since a formula in DNNF clearly is polar and fully linkless, our Proposition 87 generalizes this. The notion *decomposable except on* a set of atoms in [Dar01a] is the analog for DNNF to our notion of linkless *outside* a literal scope. Methods for efficient clausal entailment on such formulas are shown. However, in contrast to our Proposition 87, the notion of *decomposable except on* is not incorporated into the methods for the elimination of projection. Murray and Rosenthal [MR03] generalize some of the material of [Dar01a] to formulas that are fully linkless (called just *linkless* in [MR03]). Projection is considered as the syntactic operation of – in our terminology – applying polar substitution by $\top$ to the atoms to be forgotten. Theorem 2 in [MR03] is rephrased in our terminology as: *For all sentences F_1, F_2 and atom scopes $\{A_1, \ldots, A_n\}$ it holds that if F_1 is linkless and $\mathcal{A}(F_2) \subseteq \{A_1, \ldots, A_n\}$, then*

$$F_1[\![A_1 \backslash \top]\!] \ldots [\![A_n \backslash \top]\!] \models F_2 \textit{ if and only if } F_1 \models F_2.$$

This is a consequence of our Propositions 87 and 62. From the proof of this theorem, in [MR03] a corollary is derived that is independent of the linklessness restriction: *If F_1 is in negation normal form and $\mathcal{A}(F_2) \subseteq \{A_1, \ldots, A_n\}$, then*

$$\textit{if } F_1[\![A_1 \backslash \top]\!] \ldots [\![A_n \backslash \top]\!] \models F_2, \textit{ then } F_1 \models F_2.$$

This corollary also follows from the fact that for all formulas F in negation normal form (and, slightly more general, polar formulas) and atoms A it holds that

$$F \models F[\![A \backslash \top]\!].$$

Further possibilities of utilizing polar substitution also with formulas that are not fully linkless are sketched informally, but a notion like *linkless outside* is not defined.

6.3 Literal Projection and Propositional Relevancy

Lang, Liberatore and Marquis [LLM03] describe and investigate *literal* forgetting for propositional logic in the context of exploring relevancy. Our definition of *literal* projection is an adaption of the semantic characterization given in that paper.[1] Literal forgetting is defined in [LLM03] as a function between propositional formulas by the syntactic construction that we use in the proof of Proposition 67. Semantic characterizations are provided as propositions: Proposition 14 shows two characterizations for singleton scopes. They correspond essentially to our Definition 52, applied to singleton scopes and with $J \cap \widetilde{S} \subseteq I$ expressed according to items (5.) and (4.), respectively, of Proposition 24.ii.[2] Proposition 15 generalizes the second characterization to arbitrary literal scopes. Proposition 16 is a further characterization that corresponds to our Proposition 114 (for forgetting instead of projection). Properties of literal projection are shown: Corollary 2 corresponds to our Propositions 30, 31 and 33; Corollaries 3 and 4 to our Propositions 51 and 63; Proposition 17 to our Proposition 74.

An analog to our Proposition 81 or Theorem 2 or 3, however, can not be found in [LLM03], apart from its Proposition 18, which can be seen as a rather restricted variant of our Proposition 81 that applies only to linkless conjunctions of atoms and negations of atoms (i. e., DNF-clauses).

Proposition 19 of [LLM03] shows a linear method for computing forgetting in a set of prime implicates, which can be considered as a special case of the replace-by-resolvents method discussed in Chapter 7. In [LLM03] also atom forgetting is defined (called *variable forgetting*) and some properties of it are shown, for example that atom forgetting can be defined in terms of literal forgetting. That also literal projection can be defined in terms of atom projection, as shown in our Proposition 66, is not noted.

---

1 In an earlier work [Wer04], we investigated *atom* projection and conjectured, unaware of the work of Lang, Liberatore and Marquis [LLM03], and motivated by the Lyndon interpolation theorem [Lyn59] that *literal* projection is possible.

2 Seemingly there is a bug in [LLM03]: the second characterization of Proposition 14 should probably be $Mod(\Sigma) \cup \{\omega \mid Force(\omega, l) \models \Sigma\}$ instead of just $\{\omega \mid Force(\omega, l) \models \Sigma\}$.

Further, complexity properties for computing forgetting and deciding equivalence relative to a scope given in [LLM03]. It is stated as Proposition 23 that (rephrased in our terminology) if F is a propositional sentence and S is a finite literal scope, then in the general case, there is no propositional sentence F' equivalent to $\mathsf{forget}(F, S)$ such that the size of F' is polynomially bounded in the sum of $|F| + |S|$, unless $\mathsf{NP} \cap \mathsf{co\text{-}NP} \subseteq \mathsf{P/poly}$.[3] The proof essentially refers to the property that the size of Craig interpolants (see Section 14.2.3, p. 217) of propositional sentences is not polynomially bounded, under the assumption $\mathsf{NP} \cap \mathsf{co\text{-}NP} \subseteq \mathsf{P/poly}$.[4]

6.4 Information Algebras and Propositional Information Systems

Kohlas et al. [Koh03, KS96] investigate so-called *information algebras*, algebraic structures composed of a set of "pieces of information" that can be manipulated by two operations: a *combination* operation to aggregate pieces of information and a *focusing* operation to extract the part of information related to a certain domain. These algebraic structures have been developed as abstractions of a method for the propagation of probability values, *local computation* [LS88], and its generalization to the *local computation framework* [SS90]. Applications of this framework to the processing of propositional formulas are developed in [KHM99], applications to deduction in various other logics, including first-order logic, are shown in [WM97]. In [Koh03, KS96] it is shown for a large number of further knowledge representation mechanisms and processing techniques that they can be considered as instances of information algebras and local computation.

Central to the application of the local computation framework to the processing of propositional formulas in [KHM99] is a so-called *marginalization* operation, which is closely related to projection. Thus [KHM99], of which a preliminary version was published in 1996 as technical report [KM96], precedes other works that investigate projection in the specific context of propositional knowledge representation [Dar01a, MR03, LLM03], an area that gained broadened interest stimulated by the substantial progress in SAT solving in the late nineties.

The *marginalization relation* defined in [KHM99, Section 2.1] is similar to our $\mathsf{R}_{\mathsf{project}}$ (see p. 88). We transfer it into our notation for precise comparison and call it $\mathsf{R}_{\mathsf{margin}}$. We understand *$G$ is expressible with symbols in S* as $\mathcal{A}_{\mathcal{E}}(G) \subseteq S$. Accordingly, $\mathsf{R}_{\mathsf{margin}}(F, S, F')$ is defined as holding exactly for those F, S, F' which satisfy conditions (2.) and (3.) of Proposition 114 (for

[3] See footnote 4 on p. 124 for information about the complexity class $\mathsf{P/poly}$.

[4] No proper source for this property is given in [LLM03]. For related material, see [Mun84, ST07].

atom scopes instead of literal scopes). Thus $\mathsf{R}_{\mathsf{margin}}$ is, like $\mathsf{R}_{\mathsf{project}}$, a semantically determined relation. However, since condition (1.) is not present, it is weaker than $\mathsf{R}_{\mathsf{project}}$. Probably this condition is implicitly presupposed, otherwise a formula would be a marginalization of itself with respect to any atom scope, making a main subject of [KHM99], the computation of marginalization, a void endeavor.

In Propositions 115 and 116 we make an interface between logic with the projection operation and information algebras explicit: We show on the basis of the propositions developed in Chapter 5 that logic sentences modulo equivalence with conjunction and projection as operations satisfy in a straightforward way the axioms of *domain free information algebras*, one of the variants of information algebras investigated in [Koh03]. We show this with two alternative restrictions on sentences, similar to the restrictions made in Propositions 100 and 101. Propositional logic meets both of these restrictions, as shown by Propositions 69 and 70, respectively.

The *combination* property shown in the proofs of Propositions 115 and 116 states – like Proposition 81 – a condition that allows to push the projection operator inwards into conjunctions. This property is the basis for the local computation techniques for projection elimination described in [KHM99].

Proposition 115 *Assume that for all sentences F and atom scopes S there exists a sentence H such that $H \equiv \mathsf{project}(F, S)$ and $\mathcal{L}(H) \subseteq S$.*

Then the set of equivalence classes of sentences as set of elements Ψ and the powerset of the set of ground atoms as lattice D of domains with conjunction as combination operation and atom projection as focusing operation is a domain free information algebra, as defined in [Koh03, pp. 162f].

Proof. We show for each of the axioms characterizing a domain free information algebra that it is satisfied. Numbering and naming of the axioms corresponds to [Koh03, pp. 162f]. A sentence represents its equivalence class. Equivalence $\equiv$ corresponds to equality on elements of Ψ.

We actually show the proposition for literal projection as focusing operator with the restriction that if S is the scope of a literal projection then $S = \widetilde{S}$. This allows to base the proof directly on propositions about literal projection in Chapter 5. The proposition for atom projection follows since $\mathsf{project\text{-}atoms}(F, S)$ is defined as $\mathsf{project}(F, +S \cup -S)$.

1. *Semigroup:* Conjunction is associative and commutative. $\top$ is a suitable neutral element: for all sentences F it holds that $F \land \top \equiv \top \land F \equiv F$.

2. *Transitivity:* If F is a sentence and S_1, S_2 are literal scopes, then

$$\mathsf{project}(\mathsf{project}(F, S_1), S_2) \equiv \mathsf{project}(F, S_1 \cap S_2).$$

   This follows from Proposition 34.

3. *Combination:* If F_1, F_2 are sentences and S is a literal scope such that

   – $S = \widetilde{S}$, and
   – There exists a sentence H such that $H \equiv \mathsf{project}(F_1, S)$ and $\mathcal{L}(H) \subseteq S$,

   then

$$\mathsf{project}(\mathsf{project}(F_1, S) \land F_2, S) \equiv \mathsf{project}(F_1, S) \land \mathsf{project}(F_2, S).$$

$$\begin{array}{lll}
(1) & \mathsf{project}(\mathsf{project}(F_1, S) \land F_2, S) & \equiv \\
(2) & \mathsf{project}(H \land F_2, S) & \equiv \\
(3) & \mathsf{project}(H, S) \land \mathsf{project}(F_2, S) & \equiv \\
(4) & \mathsf{project}(\mathsf{project}(F_1, S), S) \land \mathsf{project}(F_2, S) & \equiv \\
(5) & \mathsf{project}(F_1, S) \land \mathsf{project}(F_2, S). &
\end{array}$$

   Equivalence of (2) to (1) follows from Proposition 32. Since $\mathcal{L}(H) \subseteq S$ and $S = \widetilde{S}$ it holds that $\langle H, F_2 \rangle$ is linkless outside S. Thus equivalence of (3) to (2) follows from Proposition 80. Equivalence of (4) to (3) follows from Proposition 32. Equivalence of (5) to (4) follows from Proposition 35.

4. *Support:* If F is a sentence, then there exists a literal scope S such that $S = \widetilde{S}$ and

$$\mathsf{project}(F, S) \equiv F.$$

   GLITS is a suitable such S, which follows from Proposition 44.

5. *Idempotency:* If F is a sentence and S is a literal scope, then

$$F \land \mathsf{project}(F, S) \equiv F.$$

   This follows from Proposition 30.

□

Proposition 116 *Assume that for all $\mathcal{E}$-sentences F and atom scopes S it holds that* $\mathsf{project}(F, S)$ *is an $\mathcal{E}$-sentence.*

Then the set of equivalence classes of $\mathcal{E}$-sentences as set of elements Ψ and the powerset of the set of ground atoms as lattice D of domains with conjunction as combination operation and atom projection as focusing operation is a domain free information algebra, as defined in [Koh03, pp. 162f].

Proof. Satisfaction of all axioms with exception of *combination* can be shown in the same way as for Proposition 115, except that *$\mathcal{E}$-sentence* is used in place of *sentence* as type of the F parameters. *Combination* can be shown as follows:

If F_1, F_2 are sentences and S is a literal scope such that

- $S = \widetilde{S}$,
- F_2 is an $\mathcal{E}$-sentence and
- $\mathsf{project}(F_1, S)$ is an $\mathcal{E}$-sentence,

then

$$\mathsf{project}(\mathsf{project}(F_1, S) \land F_2, S) \equiv \mathsf{project}(F_1, S) \land \mathsf{project}(F_2, S).$$

$$\begin{array}{lll} (1) & \mathsf{project}(\mathsf{project}(F_1, S) \land F_2, S) & \equiv \\ (2) & \mathsf{project}(\mathsf{project}(F_1, S), S) \land \mathsf{project}(F_2, S) & \equiv \\ (3) & \mathsf{project}(F_1, S) \land \mathsf{project}(F_2, S). & \end{array}$$

By Proposition 47 it holds that $\mathcal{L}_{\mathcal{E}}(\mathsf{project}(F, S)) \subseteq S$. From this and the fact that $S = \widetilde{S}$ it follows that $\langle \mathsf{project}(F_1, S), F_2 \rangle$ is essentially linkless outside S. Thus equivalence of (2) to (1) follows from Proposition 81, since $\mathsf{project}(F_1, S)$ and F_2 are $\mathcal{E}$-sentences. Equivalence of (3) to (2) follows from Proposition 35.

□

7 Projection Elimination with Resolvent Generation

Let F be a propositional sentence in tautology-free CNF and A be a ground atom. A refinement of the expansion according to Proposition 65 can then be used to eliminate the forget-atoms operator in forget-atoms$(F, \{A\})$. It works as follows:

> Return the union of the set of all binary resolvents of clauses of F upon A with the set of clauses in F that do not contain A.

Let F_{+A}, F_{-A}, F_0 be the sets of clauses of F that contain $+A$, $-A$, or no literal with atom A, respectively. The following equivalences then show correctness of this method:

$$
\begin{array}{lll}
(1) & \mathsf{forget\text{-}atoms}(F, \{A\}) & \equiv \\
(2) & F[A\backslash\top] \lor F[A\backslash\bot] & \equiv \\
(3) & (F_{+A} \land F_{-A} \land F_0)[A\backslash\top] \lor (F_{+A} \land F_{-A} \land F_0)[A\backslash\bot] & \equiv \\
(4) & (F_{-A}[A\backslash\top] \land F_0) \lor (F_{+A}[A\backslash\bot] \land F_0) & \equiv \\
(5) & (F_{-A}[A\backslash\top] \lor F_{+A}[A\backslash\bot]) \land F_0. &
\end{array}
$$

Equivalence of (2) to (1) follows from Proposition 65. Formula (4) is equivalent to (3), since $F_{+A}[A\backslash\top] \equiv \top$ and analogously $F_{-A}[A\backslash\bot] \equiv \top$. The first conjunct of (5), that is $(F_{-A}[A\backslash\top] \lor F_{+A}[A\backslash\bot])$, is equivalent to the set of all binary resolvents of clauses of F upon A.

When performed in succession for all atoms A in F, interleaved with certain additional operations to simplify clause sets, this method corresponds to the original Davis-Putnam procedure [DP60] for propositional inputs.

In Section 7.1 a generalization of this method, replace-by-resolvents, is shown that also applies to first-order clausal sentences and to literal scopes. Its correctness is proven in Section 7.2. The method can be considered as a variant of the SCAN algorithm [GO92] for the elimination of second-order quantifiers, both methods are compared in Section 7.3. As shown in Section 7.4, certain special cases of replace-by-resolvents correspond to well-known simplifications employed for theorem proving. Also other simplifications that preserve equivalence relative to the scope of a projection can be integrated into replace-by-resolvents, which is discussed in Section 7.5. In Section 7.6 a preprocessing technique is shown that allows to apply replace-by-resolvents to "pattern forgetting", projection elimination for an atom scope that is characterized as the set of ground atoms that are not instances of a given first-order atom.

Remark on Notation. In this chapter we use the project operator explicitly and also implicitly via the $\equiv_S$ relation, but in a way that these uses can also be understood just as convenient meta-level notation for semantic relationships corresponding to the semantic definition of project (Definition 52).

7.1 The Replace-by-Resolvents Algorithm

We define the replace-by-resolvents algorithm, which is based on the auxiliary procedure replace-clause-by-resolvents. First we make precise the notion of *resolvent* that we use for the algorithm. Following the presentation by Chang and Lee [CL73], we understand a *resolvent* basically as obtained by optional factoring and binary resolution from the parent clauses. We additionally transfer the notion of *literals resolved upon* from binary resolvents to *resolvent* (for just one of the parent clauses) and incorporate standardizing apart of variables of the parent clauses.

Definition 69 (Resolvent)

(i) If two or more literals (with the same sign) of a clause C have a most general unifier σ, then $C\sigma$ is called a *factor* of F.

(ii) Let C_1 and C_2 be two clauses with no variables in common. Let L_1 and L_2 be two literals in C_1 and C_2, respectively. If L_1 and $\widetilde{L2}$ have a most general unifier σ, then the clause $((C_1\sigma - L_1\sigma) \cup (C_2\sigma - L_2\sigma))$ is called a *binary resolvent* of C_1 and C_2. The literals L_1 and L_2 are called the *literals resolved upon*.

(iii) A *resolvent* of clauses C_1 and C_2 *upon* a literal L_1 of C_1 is one of the following binary resolvents, where C_2' is C_2 with variables renamed such that it has no variables in common with C_1:

1. A binary resolvent of C_1 and C_2' upon L_1,
2. A binary resolvent of C_1 and a factor of C_2' upon L_1,
3. A binary resolvent of a factor $C_1\sigma$ of C_1 and C_2' upon $L_1\sigma$,
4. A binary resolvent of a factor of $C_1\sigma$ of C_1 and a factor of C_2' upon $L_1\sigma$.

Definition 70 (Algorithm Replace-by-Resolvents)

INPUT: A clausal sentence F and a representation of a literal scope S such that for all literals L in F it holds that either all or no ground instances of L are in S.

OUTPUT: If the algorithm terminates, a clausal sentence F' such that $\mathcal{L}(F') \subseteq S$ and $F' \equiv \mathsf{project}(F, S)$.

METHOD: While there is a clause $(C \lor L)$ in F such that no ground instance of L is in S, assign to F the result of applying replace-clause-by-resolvents to $F - (C \lor L)$, $C - L$ and L, optionally followed by simplifications that preserve equivalence relative to S. Output F.

Definition 71 (Auxiliary Procedure Replace-Clause-by-Resolvents)
INPUT: A clausal sentence F, a clause C and a literal L that is not in C.

OUTPUT: If the algorithm terminates, a clausal sentence $(F \wedge F')$ such that there does not exist a resolvent of $(C \vee L)$ and a clause of $(F \wedge (C \vee L) \wedge F')$ upon L that is not tautological and not subsumed by $(F \wedge F')$. It holds that $(F \wedge F') \equiv_S (F \wedge (C \vee L))$.

METHOD: While a resolvent D of $(C \vee L)$ and a clause of $(F \wedge (C \vee L))$ upon L exists, such that D is not tautological and not subsumed by F, add D to F. Output F.

7.2 Correctness of Replace-by-Resolvents

Theorem 5 states the correctness of replace-by-resolvents. It essentially follows from a correctness property of the auxiliary procedure replace-clause-by-resolvents, which is stated first as Proposition 119. Before we come to this proposition, we give further, mostly standard, material from clausal theorem proving that is used in its proof.

The following proposition is a variant of the lifting lemma as presented in [CL73] that is slightly strengthened in two respects: First we additionally consider a *literal resolved upon*. A proof of the lifting lemma where this is taken into account can be obtained as a corollary from the proof in [CL73]. Second, we include the fact that the property of being not tautological and not subsumed by a given clausal sentence "lifts" from the resolvent of the instances, which is easy to see.

Proposition 117 (Lifting Lemma) *If the clauses $(C_1' \vee L_1')$ and C_2' are instances of $(C_1 \vee L_1)$ and C_2, respectively, such that the literal L_1' is an instance of L_1 and if C' is a resolvent of $(C_1' \vee L_1')$ and C_2' upon L_1', then there is a resolvent C of $(C_1 \vee L_1)$ and C_2 upon L_1 such that C' is an instance of C.*

Moreover, if C' is not tautological and not subsumed by a clausal sentence F, then also C is not tautological and not subsumed by F.

So far we have assumed that sentences are constructed from a *finite* number of applications of logic operators. To transfer properties from the propositional to the first-order level, we additionally consider possibly infinite syntactic objects, sets of clauses, along with the notion of *satisfiable set of clauses* and Herbrand's theorem. For a proof of Herbrand's Theorem see e. g. [CL73].

Definition 72 (Satisfiable Set of Clauses) A set of clauses M is called *satisfiable* if and only if there exists an interpretation I such that for all $C \in M$ it holds that $I \models C$.

Proposition 118 (Herbrand's Theorem) *A set of clauses M is satisfiable if and only if every finite subset of ground instances of clauses in M is satisfiable.*

Proposition 119 *If F' is the output of* replace-clause-by-resolvents *applied to F, C and L, then it holds that*

$$F' \equiv_S F \wedge (C \vee L),$$

where S is the set of all ground literals that are not instances of L.

Proof. We show the following property, from which the proposition follows: If F is a clausal sentence, C is a clause, L is a literal not in C and if each resolvent of $(C \vee L)$ and a clause of $(F \wedge (C \vee L))$ upon L is tautological or subsumed by F, then

$$F \equiv_S F \wedge (C \vee L),$$

where S is the set of all ground literals that are not instances of L.

The proof proceeds in two parts. The first part applies to the case where $(C \vee L)$ is ground, making use of essentially propositional properties of literals, clauses and interpretations. The second part lifts this to the case where $(C \vee L)$ is non-ground, by means of an induction argument over an enumeration of ground instances of $(C \vee L)$ and a variant of the compactness property of first-order logic, which is shown to hold also in combination with projection.

Part 1 – The Proposition for the Case that $(C \vee L)$ is Ground.

(1) $F \not\equiv_S F \wedge (C \vee L)$.
(2) $F \wedge (C \vee L) \models_S F$.
(3) $F \not\models_S F \wedge (C \vee L)$.
(4) $F \not\models \mathsf{project}(F \wedge (C \vee L), S)$.
(5) $I \models F$.
(6) For all interpretations J: if $J \cap S \subseteq I$, then $J \not\models F \wedge (C \vee L)$.
(7) $I[L] \models (C \vee L)$.
(8) $I[L] \cap S \subseteq I$.
(9) $I[L] \not\models F$.
(10) $I[L] \not\models (D \vee \widetilde{L})$.
(11) $I \not\models (C \vee L)$.

Consider the proposition expressed in contrapositive form. We show that (1) implies the existence of a resolvent of $(C \vee L)$ and a clause of F upon L that is neither tautological or subsumed by F. Assume (1). (2) follows from (1) and Proposition 31. (3) follows from (2) and (1). (4) follows from (3) and Proposition 37. From (4) it follows that there exists an interpretation I such that (5) and (6) hold. (7) holds trivially. (8) holds, since $\{L\} \cap S = \emptyset$. (9) follows from (8), (7) and (6). From (9) and (5) it follows that there exists a clause $(D \vee \widetilde{L})$ which is a ground instance of a clause of F such that $\widetilde{L}$ is not in D and that (10) holds. We now show that $(C \vee D)$ is neither tautological nor subsumed by F. For this, we make use of (11), which follows from (6) and (5).

Assume $(C \vee D)$ is tautological. Then there exists a ground literal K such that both K and $\widetilde{K}$ are in $(C \vee D)$. Assume without loss of generality that K (instead of $\widetilde{K}$) is in I. In case K is in C it holds that $I \models C$, contradicting (11). In case K is in D, since $\widetilde{L}$ is not in D, it must hold that $K \neq \widetilde{L}$. It then follows that $I[L] \models D$, contradicting (10).

Assume $(C \vee D)$ is subsumed by F. It then follows from (5) that there exists a ground literal K in I which is in a ground instance of a clause of F and also in $(C \vee D)$. By the same arguments as for the case of the assumption that $(C \vee D)$ is tautological, this leads to a contradiction with (11) or (10).

Thus $(C \vee D)$ is a resolvent of $(C \vee L)$ and a ground instance of a clause in F upon L. Furthermore $(C \vee D)$ is not tautological and also not subsumed by F. It then follows from the lifting lemma (Proposition 117) that there exists a resolvent of $(C \vee L)$ and a clause of F upon L that is not tautological and not subsumed by F.

Part 2 – Extension for the Case that $(C \vee L)$ is Non-Ground. Assume the preconditions of the proposition. Each resolvent of $(C \vee L)$ and a clause of $(F \wedge (C \vee L))$ upon L is then tautological or subsumed by F. For all $i \geq 0$ let $(C_i \vee L_i)$ denote the i-th element in some enumeration of the ground instances of $(C \vee L)$ and for $n \geq 0$ define the clausal sentence G_n by:

$$G_n \stackrel{\text{def}}{=} (C_1 \vee L_1) \wedge \ldots \wedge (C_n \vee L_n).$$

For all $n \geq 0$ it holds that there does not exist a resolvent of $(C_n \vee L_n)$ and a clause of $(F \wedge G_{n-1})$ upon L_n that is not tautological and not subsumed by $(F \wedge G_{n-1})$. If such a resolvent would exist, by the lifting lemma, there also would exist a resolvent of $(C \vee L)$ and a clause of $(F \wedge (C \vee L))$ upon L that is not tautological and not subsumed F, which contradicts the assumed preconditions of the proposition.

Thus, the special case of the proposition shown in part 1 of the proof can be applied to conclude

(i) $$F \wedge G_{n-1} \equiv_S F \wedge G_{n-1} \wedge (C_n \vee L_n).$$

By straightforward induction then follows:

(ii) For all $n \geq 0$ it holds that $F \equiv_S F \wedge G_n$.

We now show that Herbrand's theorem can be applied to derive $F \wedge (C \vee L) \equiv_S F$ from (ii).

(1) For all conjunctions G of ground instances of $(C \vee L)$ it holds that $F \equiv_S F \wedge G$.
(2) For all conjunctions G of ground instances of $(C \vee L)$ it holds that $F \models \mathsf{project}(F \wedge G, S)$.
(3) For all conjunctions G of ground instances of $(C \vee L)$ and for all interpretations I it holds that if $I \models F$, then $((I \cap \widetilde{S}) \cup F \cup G)$ is satisfiable.
(4) For all interpretations I it holds that if $I \models F$, then $((I \cap \widetilde{S}) \cup F \cup \{(C \vee L)\})$ is satisfiable.
(5) $F \models \mathsf{project}(F \wedge (C \vee L), S)$.
(6) $F \equiv_S F \wedge (C \vee L)$.

Since a *conjunction* is understood as being composed of a *finite* number of conjuncts, (1) follows from (ii). (2) follows from (1) and Proposition 37. In Proposition 24.i it is shown that the condition $J \cap S \subseteq I$ in the definition of project (Definition 52) is equivalent to $I \cap \widetilde{S} \subseteq J$, and thus holds if and only if J is a model of all literals in $(I \cap \widetilde{S})$. From this it follows that if I is an interpretation, H is a clausal sentence and S is a literal scope, then

(iii) $I \models \mathsf{project}(H, S)$ holds if and only if $(I \cap \widetilde{S}) \cup H$ is satisfiable,

where $(I \cap \widetilde{S})$ is understood as a set of unit clauses. Thus (3) follows from (iii) and (2). (4) follows from (3) and Herbrand's theorem (Proposition 118). (5) follows from (4) and (iii). (6) follows from (5) with Propositions 37 and 31. □

Theorem 5 (Correctness of Replace-by-Resolvents) *Algorithm* replace-by-resolvents *is correct, that is, if* replace-by-resolvent *terminates with output F' for a clausal sentence F and a representation of a literal scope S such that for all literals L in F it holds that either all or no ground instances of L are in S, then it holds that*

1. $\mathcal{L}(F') \subseteq S$ and
2. $F' \equiv \mathsf{project}(F, S)$.

Proof. Condition (1.) follows immediately from the loop condition of the algorithm. Condition (2.) holds, since from Proposition 119 it follows that if F_2 is the result on an invocation of replace-clause-by-resolvents in the loop body on inputs $F_1 - (C_1 \vee L_1)$, $C_1 - L_1$ and L_1, then $F_2 \equiv_S F_1$.

□

7.3 Relation of **Replace-by-Resolvents** to **SCAN**

SCAN [GO92, GHSV04] is an algorithm for the elimination of the second-order quantifiers in sentences of the form $\exists X_1 \ldots \exists X_n F$, where F is a first-order formula. The core phase of SCAN operates on a clausal sentence, and, like replace-by-resolvents, replaces clauses that contain literals with a predicate symbol that represents a second-order variable by their resolvents upon such literals. Additional pre- and postprocessing steps handle the conversion from and to non-clausal sentences by means of clausal transformation, Skolemization and reverse Skolemization.

As shown in [GO92], the method in essence goes back to Ackermann [Ack35], where, not only *Ackermann's lemma*, the basis for *direct* second-order quantifier elimination methods [Sza93, GSS08], has been introduced, but also a second method that is a restricted variant of SCAN. A completeness property of SCAN, along with new a presentation of the algorithm that differs slightly from [GO92] has been recently given in [GHSV04]. The development of SCAN was motivated by applications in correspondence theory for modal logics. Also interpolant computation and the computing of circumscription are mentioned as applications in [GO92].

SCAN uses a special kind on resolution, *C-resolution*, where variables are not instantiated and equality constraints are added to the resolvents. A C-resolvent of $(\mathsf{p}(\mathsf{a}) \lor C)$ and $(\neg\mathsf{p}(\mathsf{b}) \lor D)$, for example, is $(\mathsf{a} \not\approx \mathsf{b} \lor C \lor D)$. C-resolution can simulate "standard" resolution (as specified in Definition 69): A standard resolvent can be obtained by C-resolution (possibly preceded by *C-factoring*) followed by an application of the *constraint elimination* rule, which is included in the variant of SCAN described in [GHSV04].

Vice versa, a C-resolvent can be obtained by standard resolution if the clausal sentence used for standard resolution is extended by a fragment of an equality axiomatization, namely for each n-ary predicate p of literals to be resolved upon a substitutivity axiom

$$\neg\mathsf{p}(x_1, \ldots, x_n) \lor x_1 \not\approx y_1 \lor \ldots \lor x_n \not\approx y_n \lor \mathsf{p}(y_1, \ldots, y_n).$$

A C-resolution step corresponds to a binary resolution step with such a clause, followed by a second binary resolution step, both steps upon literals with predicate p. A C-factoring step can similarly be modeled as a binary resolution step followed by standard factoring. As an example, consider the clauses $(\mathsf{p}(\mathsf{a}) \lor C)$ and $(\neg\mathsf{p}(\mathsf{b}) \lor D)$, of which $(\mathsf{a} \not\approx \mathsf{b} \lor C \lor D)$ is a C-resolvent. A binary resolvent of the first clause $(\mathsf{p}(\mathsf{a}) \lor C)$ and the substitutivity axiom $(\neg\mathsf{p}(x) \lor x \not\approx y \lor \mathsf{p}(y))$ is $(\mathsf{a} \not\approx y \lor \mathsf{p}(y) \lor C)$. A second binary resolution step with this resolvent and $(\neg\mathsf{p}(\mathsf{b}) \lor D)$ as parents yields $(\mathsf{a} \not\approx \mathsf{b} \lor C \lor D)$, that is, the C-resolvent.

Thus, all C-resolvents computed by SCAN can also be computed by replace-by-resolvents if predicate substitutivity axioms are added to the input. However, in presence of the substitutivity axioms, with standard resolution additional clauses can be derived, such as $(\mathsf{a} \not\approx y \lor \mathsf{p}(y) \lor C)$ in the example. These additional clauses can prevent termination of replace-by-resolvents with inputs for which SCAN terminates, since these clauses contain literals to be forgotten and are in general neither tautological nor subsumed by other clauses computed so far. Possibly their computation can be restricted by other redundancy criteria, but the investigation of this remains future work.

Replace-by-resolvents can be considered as a variant of SCAN that corresponds to Herbrand semantics, with the unique names assumption, and is independent of equality reasoning, which is "built-in" into SCAN. Consider for example the elimination of all literals with predicate p from the clausal sentence $\{\mathsf{p}(\mathsf{a}), \neg\mathsf{p}(\mathsf{b})\}$. SCAN returns $\{\mathsf{a} \not\approx \mathsf{b}\}$, the set of clauses containing just the C-resolvent of the two input clauses. Replace-by-resolvents returns the empty set of clauses, corresponding to $\top$, since the two input clauses have no standard resolvent. With the replace-by-resolvents algorithm it is made apparent that the basic predicate quantifier elimination method of SCAN – replacing clauses that contain literals to eliminate by resolvents – is in essence not dependent on equality and also not on the mechanism of C-resolution, in contrast to standard resolution. And thus directly available for the many knowledge representation techniques that use Herbrand semantics.

Replace-by-resolvents extends on SCAN by taking into account projection elimination not just for atom scopes that include either all or no literals with a predicate (corresponding to second-order quantification), but more generally, also projection elimination for literal scopes and, for example, scopes characterized as instances of a pattern, as shown below in Section 7.6.

A weakness of replace-by-resolvents as described here, compared to SCAN, is that in SCAN only C-resolutions of two *different* clauses are performed, where in replace-by-resolvents also resolvents with the same clause in the role of both parents are permitted. Investigation how replace-by-resolvents and the underlying Proposition 119 can be adapted accordingly remains future work.

7.4 Cases of **Replace-by-Resolvents** that are Simplifications

In the context of theorem proving, operations that can be performed fast (typically in linear time), can be applied only a number of times that is polynomial (typically linear) in the size of the formula and reduce the refutation task in some sense while preserving satisfiability are known as *simplifications* or *reductions* [BE93]. Certain special cases of replace-by-resolvents correspond to well known simplifications for propositional clausal sentences. That they can be described as special cases of replace-by-resolvents shows that they in fact do not just preserve satisfiability, but, moreover, equivalence relative to the set of all literals with exception of the literals upon which resolution is performed. This justifies to apply these simplifications in tasks like model computation and knowledge compilation, where equivalence with respect to a certain scope has to be preserved. And, of course, also to embed them in any other procedures for projection elimination, as shown for tableau-based procedures in Section 12.2.2. We outline these simplification operations in their basic form for propositional clausal sentences and indicate ways to generalize them for first-order clausal sentences.

7.4.1 Purity Simplification

Purity simplification effects that a clause containing a literal L is deleted from a sentence in which $\widetilde{L}$ does not occur. Purity simplification is also known as the *pure literal rule* or *affirmative-negative rule* of the Davis-Putnam procedure. Eliminating a clause in this way corresponds to an application of replace-clause-by-resolvents to (propositional) arguments F, C and L, where $\widetilde{L}$ does not occur in $(F \wedge (C \vee L))$. Replace-clause-by-resolvents then just returns F.

A straightforward generalization for first-order clausal sentences is, to use the condition that no literal which is *weakly unifiable* with $\widetilde{L}$ occurs in the sentence, instead of the condition that $\widetilde{L}$ does not occur in the sentence.

7.4.2 Isol and Isol* Simplification

The *isol** simplification [Bib92] effects that if a sentence contains just a single occurrence of literal L, then the clause containing L as well as the clauses containing $\widetilde{L}$ are replaced by their binary resolvents upon L and $\widetilde{L}$. The *isol* simplification is the special case of *isol** where it is also required that there is just a single occurrence of $\widetilde{L}$ in the sentence. *Isol* strictly reduces the number of literal occurrences as well as the number of clauses of the sentence, while *isol** just strictly reduces the number of clauses. This is further discussed in Section 12.2.2.

The *isol** and *isol* simplifications can be described as a succession of applications of replace-clause-by-resolvents. First replace-clause-by-resolvents is applied to (propositional) arguments F, C and L, where L does not occur in F. The result does not contain L. Each clause that contains $\neg L$ is then eliminated by an application of replace-clause-by-resolvents corresponding to purity simplification. Since the *isol* and *isol** simplifications involve applications of replace-clause-by-resolvents with L as well as $\widetilde{L}$ as literal arguments, they preserve equivalence relative to the set of all literals except of L and $\widetilde{L}$.

*Isol** can, like *purity*, be generalized to first-order sentences by using weak unifiability instead of identity as criterion, with the additional requirement that L and a literal weakly unifiable with $\widetilde{L}$ do not occur in the same clause. Since *isol** encompasses the application of unifiers, the size of terms in its output is not polynomially bounded. Thus, the first-order variant of *isol** is not strictly a simplification.

7.5 Simplifications Preserving Equivalence Relative to a Scope

Algorithm replace-by-resolvents maintains a clausal sentence that, in between the calls to replace-clause-by-resolvents, can be simplified by operations that preserve equivalence relative to the scope of the projection. This includes, of course, simplification operations that preserve equivalence "in full", such as *removal of tautological clauses*, *removal of subsumed clauses*, *subsumption resolution* and *condensation*. With *purity*, *isol* and *isol**, we already have shown Section 7.4 some simplifications that do not preserve equivalence "in full", but with respect to a certain scope. The following are further simplification operations that preserve equivalence relative to a scope, which can not straightforwardly be described as special cases of replace-by-resolvents.

7.5.1 Extended Purity

An *extended purity reduction rule* for first-order clausal sentences is given in [Sza93]: If the sentence does not contain two clauses such that literals with a predicate p occur only positively in one and only negatively in the other, then all clauses containing a literal with predicate p are deleted. This simplification preserves equivalence relative to the set of all literals with a predicate other than p.

7.5.2 Deletion of an Isolated Satisfiable Clause Group

A further simplification for first-order clausal sentences is the *deletion of an isolated satisfiable clause group*: If the clausal sentence can be split into two disjoint subsets F_1 and F_2 such that there are no weakly unifiable literals L_1 and L_2 with L_1 in F_1 and $\widetilde{L_2}$ in F_2, then if F_1 is satisfiable, the clauses of F_1 are deleted. The result sentence preserves equivalence relative to the set of all ground literals that are not instances of a literal in F_1.

7.6 Pattern Forgetting

Diff-expansion is a preprocessing procedure for replace-by-resolvents that allows to perform *pattern forgetting*, "forgetting about" the atoms that are instances of a given pattern, or more precisely, to perform projection elimination for sentences of the form

(iv) $\mathsf{project}(F, \{L \in \mathsf{GLITS} \mid \mathsf{atom}(L) \text{ is not an instance of } P\})$,

where F is a clausal sentence and P is an atom. The inputs of diff-expansion are F, P and a finite set Σ of constant and function symbols, which is assumed to include all such symbols that are considered in the application.

Diff-expansion outputs a clausal sentence that ensures the condition on the input sentence of replace-by-resolvents that either all or no ground instances of any literal in the sentence are in the scope of the projection. If the scope is characterized as in (iv) above – the set of ground literals whose atoms are not instances of an atom P – then this condition is implied by the following output condition of diff-expansion: For all literals L in the output sentence it holds that the atom of L is either an instance of P or is not unifiable with P. The output of diff-expansion also satisfies a second condition: it is equivalent to the input sentence in the sense that both sentences have the same Herbrand expansions over Σ. The pattern atoms P are required to be *linear*[1] since only then there always exists a *finite* clause set that meets both output conditions, which is explicated further in Example 16 below.

Pattern forgetting can be accomplished by applying replace-by-resolvents to the result of diff-expansion. We illustrate pattern forgetting with the following Example 12 and then discuss the diff-expansion procedure in detail.

Example 12 (Pattern Forgetting) Consider the clausal sentence

$$\begin{aligned} F = \{\ & \mathsf{p}(\mathsf{a}), \\ & \neg\mathsf{p}(x) \lor \mathsf{q}(x), \\ & \neg\mathsf{q}(x) \lor \mathsf{r}(x)\ \} \end{aligned}$$

and the set of constant symbols $\Sigma = \{\mathsf{a}, \mathsf{b}, \mathsf{c}\}$. Results F' of pattern forgetting applied to F, P, and Σ are shown for different patterns P:

$$\begin{aligned} P &= \mathsf{q}(y), \\ F' &= \{\ \mathsf{p}(\mathsf{a}), \\ &\quad \neg\mathsf{p}(x) \lor \mathsf{r}(x)\ \}. \end{aligned}$$

$$\begin{aligned} P &= \mathsf{p}(\mathsf{a}), \\ F' &= \{\ \mathsf{q}(\mathsf{a}), \\ &\quad \neg\mathsf{p}(\mathsf{b}) \lor \mathsf{q}(\mathsf{b}), \\ &\quad \neg\mathsf{p}(\mathsf{c}) \lor \mathsf{q}(\mathsf{c}), \\ &\quad \neg\mathsf{q}(x) \lor \mathsf{r}(x)\ \}. \end{aligned}$$

$$\begin{aligned} P &= \mathsf{r}(\mathsf{a}), \\ F' &= \{\ \mathsf{p}(\mathsf{a}), \\ &\quad \neg\mathsf{p}(x) \lor \mathsf{q}(x), \\ &\quad \neg\mathsf{q}(\mathsf{b}) \lor \mathsf{r}(\mathsf{b}), \\ &\quad \neg\mathsf{q}(\mathsf{c}) \lor \mathsf{r}(\mathsf{c})\ \}. \end{aligned}$$

$$\begin{aligned} P &= \mathsf{q}(\mathsf{a}), \\ F' &= \{\ \mathsf{p}(\mathsf{a}), \\ &\quad \neg\mathsf{p}(\mathsf{a}) \lor \mathsf{r}(\mathsf{a}), \\ &\quad \neg\mathsf{p}(\mathsf{b}) \lor \mathsf{q}(\mathsf{b}), \\ &\quad \neg\mathsf{p}(\mathsf{c}) \lor \mathsf{q}(\mathsf{c}), \\ &\quad \neg\mathsf{q}(\mathsf{b}) \lor \mathsf{r}(\mathsf{b}), \\ &\quad \neg\mathsf{q}(\mathsf{c}) \lor \mathsf{r}(\mathsf{c})\ \}. \end{aligned}$$

$$\begin{aligned} P &= \mathsf{p}(\mathsf{b}), \\ F' &= \{\ \mathsf{p}(\mathsf{a}), \\ &\quad \neg\mathsf{p}(\mathsf{a}) \lor \mathsf{q}(\mathsf{a}), \\ &\quad \neg\mathsf{p}(\mathsf{c}) \lor \mathsf{q}(\mathsf{c}), \\ &\quad \neg\mathsf{q}(x) \lor \mathsf{r}(x)\ \}. \end{aligned}$$

Diff-expansion outputs a sentence whose clauses are instances of clauses of the input sentence. These instances are in general not ground, but instantiate the input clauses as far as needed to ensure the two output conditions. Diff-expansion operates by exhaustively replacing some clause that contains a literal L whose atom is unifiable with P but not an instance of P with a number of instances of the clause in which the corresponding instantiations

[1] An atom is *linear* if and only if it does not contain multiple occurrences of the same variable.

of L no longer have this property. The substitutions to obtain these clause instances are computed by an auxiliary procedure, diff-substitutions, which maintains a set of substitutions that is initialized with the empty substitution as sole element. Diff-substitutions exhaustively replaces in this set some substitution σ such that $L\sigma$ contains a variable that would be bound under the most general unifier of $L\sigma$ and P by a number of extensions of σ, one for each symbol in Σ, extending σ by mapping the variable to a "template" for the symbol, a term with the symbol as operator and fresh variables as arguments.

Definition 73 (Algorithm Diff-Expansion)

INPUT: A first-order clausal sentence F, a linear atom P that does not have variables in common with F and a finite set Σ of constant and function symbols that includes those in F and P.

OUTPUT: A finite set of instances of clauses of F that

1. Has the same Herbrand expansion as F over Σ, and
2. Does not contain a literal L such that the atom A of L is unifiable with P and A is not an instance of P.

METHOD: While F contains a clause C with a literal L such that the atom A of L is unifiable with P and A is not an instance of P, replace C in F by $C\sigma$, for all substitutions σ in the result of diff-substitutions applied to A, P, and Σ. Output F.

Definition 74 (Auxiliary Procedure Diff-Substitutions)

INPUT: An atom A, a linear atom P that does not have variables in common with A and is unifiable with A and a finite set Σ of constant and function symbols that includes those in F and A.

OUTPUT: A set of substitutions S such that

1. For all clauses C that contain only constant and function symbols from Σ it holds that the Herbrand expansions of C and of $\{C\sigma \mid \sigma \in S\}$ over Σ are identical, and
2. There is no $\sigma \in S$ such that $A\sigma$ is unifiable with P and $A\sigma$ is not an instance of P.

METHOD: Let S be a set of substitutions initialized to $\{\epsilon\}$.

While S contains a substitution σ such that $A\sigma$ is unifiable with P and $A\sigma$ is not an instance of P, do the following steps:

- Choose a variable u in $A\sigma$ such that $(u)\mathsf{mgu}(A\sigma, P)$ is not a variable. (The existence of such a variable u follows from the while condition.)
- Remove σ from S.
- For each constant and function symbol f in Σ add $\sigma \circ \{u \mapsto f(u_1, \ldots, u_n)\}$ to S, where n is the arity of f and $u_1, \ldots, u_n$ are fresh variables.

Output S.

Example 13 (Diff-Expansion) The following clausal sentence is a possible output of diff-expansion applied to $F = \{\mathsf{p}(x, y)\}$, $P = \mathsf{p}(\mathsf{f}(z), \mathsf{a})$ and $\Sigma = \{\mathsf{a},\ \mathsf{b},\ \mathsf{f}\}$, where the a, b are constant symbols and f is a one-place function symbol:

$$\begin{aligned}\{\ &\mathsf{p}(\mathsf{a}, x),\\ &\mathsf{p}(\mathsf{b}, x),\\ &\mathsf{p}(\mathsf{f}(x), \mathsf{a}),\\ &\mathsf{p}(\mathsf{f}(x), \mathsf{b}),\\ &\mathsf{p}(\mathsf{f}(x), \mathsf{f}(y))\ \}.\end{aligned}$$ [2]

The cardinality of the output of diff-substitutions applied to A, P and Σ is linearly bounded by the product of the cardinality of Σ and the size of P. A precise calculation of the cardinality is given in the following Proposition 120. Since the atom P is linear, the value of the sum expression in that proposition must be less than or equal to the size of P.

Proposition 120 *The cardinality of the result of* diff-expansion *applied to inputs A, P and Σ is*

$$1 + (|\Sigma| - 1) * \sum_{v \text{ is a variable in } A} |\mathsf{ocfs}((v)\mathsf{mgu}(A, P))|,$$

where $|\mathsf{ocfs}(T)|$ is the number of occurrences of constant and function symbols in term T.

Proof. Let $|rounds|$ be the number of rounds, i.e. invocations of the body of the while loop, performed by the algorithm for inputs A, P and Σ. The cardinality of the result is obviously $1 + (|\Sigma| - 1) * |rounds|$: Initially one element is in S, in each round one element is removed and $|\Sigma|$ elements are added. We now show that $|rounds|$ equals to the value of the sum expression in the proposition. We number the rounds, starting from 1.

In each round i, where $i \geq 1$, when the loop body left, there is exactly one element τ_i in S for which it holds that $A\tau_i$ is unifiable with P. This can be shown by an inductive argument. We additionally define $\tau_0 \stackrel{\text{def}}{=} \epsilon$, the sole initial element of S. The unifiability of $A\tau_0 = A\epsilon = A$ with P is a condition for valid input arguments. Assume that S contains a single τ_i, where $i \geq 0$, such that $A\tau_i$ is unifiable with P. In the body of the loop τ_i is removed from S. The algorithm chooses a variable u occurring in $A\tau_i$ for which $(u)\mathsf{mgu}(A\tau_i, P)$ is a term with some constant or function symbol g as outermost functor. Let $\tau_{i+1} \stackrel{\text{def}}{=} \tau_i \circ \{u \mapsto g(u_1, \ldots, u_m)\}$, where m is the arity of g. Of all the substitutions σ that are added to S by the algorithm, only for

[2] Variables are standardized in the result to x and y for the first and second variable in each clause, respectively.

$\sigma = \tau_{i+1}$ it holds that $A\sigma$ is unifiable with P, since the other substitutions map u to a term with an outermost functor different from g.

Now, if round n is the last in a run of the algorithm, a one-to-one mapping between all occurrences of constant and function symbols in $(v)\mathsf{mgu}(A, P)$ for variables v in A, and the τ_i for $i \in \{1, \ldots, n\}$ can be established: If $\tau_i = \tau_{i-1} \circ \{u \mapsto g(u_1, \ldots, u_m)\}$, then u is a variable with a single occurrence in $v\tau_{i-1}$ for some variable v in A. (u is either identical to v or is a variable that has been freshly introduced as argument of some of the function symbol templates to which variables are bound in τ_{i-1}. Thus u can not occur in $v'\tau_{i-1}$ for a variable v' in A other than v.) τ_i can then be associated with the occurrence of g in $(v)\mathsf{mgu}(A, P)$ that is on the position of u in $v\tau_{i-1}$. Vice versa, if g is an occurrence of a constant or function symbol in $(v)\mathsf{mgu}(A, P)$ that is not associated with some τ_j for $j \in \{1, \ldots, i\}$, then there must be a variable u in A_{τ_i} such that $(u)\mathsf{mgu}(A\tau_i, P)$ is not a variable. The while condition of the algorithm then succeeds and round i can not be the last one.

□

Example 14 (A Run of Diff-Substitutions) Diff-substitutions applied to $A = \mathsf{p}(x, y, x)$, $P = \mathsf{p}(\mathsf{f}(\mathsf{g}(z)), \mathsf{a}, w)$ and $\Sigma = \{\mathsf{a},\ \mathsf{f},\ \mathsf{g}\}$, where a is a constant symbol and f, g are one-place function symbols, outputs a set of substitutions that, when applied to A, yield the following instances:

$$
\begin{aligned}
&\mathsf{p}(\mathsf{a}, y, \mathsf{a}),\\
&\mathsf{p}(\mathsf{f}(\mathsf{a}), y, \mathsf{f}(\mathsf{a})),\\
&\mathsf{p}(\mathsf{f}(\mathsf{f}(u_2)), y, \mathsf{f}(\mathsf{f}(u_2))),\\
&\mathsf{p}(\mathsf{f}(\mathsf{g}(u_3)), \mathsf{a}, \mathsf{f}(\mathsf{g}(u_3))),\\
&\mathsf{p}(\mathsf{f}(\mathsf{g}(u_3)), \mathsf{f}(u_4), \mathsf{f}(\mathsf{g}(u_3))),\\
&\mathsf{p}(\mathsf{f}(\mathsf{g}(u_3)), \mathsf{g}(u_5), \mathsf{f}(\mathsf{g}(u_3))),\\
&\mathsf{p}(\mathsf{g}(u_6), y, \mathsf{g}(u_6)).
\end{aligned}
$$

A sequence of $A\tau_i$, as used in the proof of Proposition 120, is

$$
\begin{aligned}
A\tau_0 &= \mathsf{p}(x, y, x),\\
A\tau_1 &= \mathsf{p}(\mathsf{f}(u_1), y, \mathsf{f}(u_1)),\\
A\tau_2 &= \mathsf{p}(\mathsf{f}(\mathsf{g}(u_3)), y, \mathsf{f}(\mathsf{g}(u_3))),\\
A\tau_3 &= \mathsf{p}(\mathsf{f}(\mathsf{g}(u_3)), \mathsf{a}, \mathsf{f}(\mathsf{g}(u_3))).
\end{aligned}
$$

The variables in A are x and y. Since $(A)\mathsf{mgu}(A, P) = \mathsf{p}(\mathsf{f}(\mathsf{g}(z)), \mathsf{a}, \mathsf{f}(\mathsf{g}(z)))$, it holds that $(x)\mathsf{mgu}(A, P) = \mathsf{f}(\mathsf{g}(z))$ and $(y)\mathsf{mgu}(A, P) = \mathsf{a}$. The algorithm performs three rounds, since $(x)\mathsf{mgu}(A, P)$ contains two occurrences of constant and function symbols, and $(y)\mathsf{mgu}(A, P)$ a single one.

Example 15 (Choices in Algorithm Diff-Substitutions) The result of diff-substitutions can vary, depending on the choice of variable u from $A\sigma$ in each round. Consider Example 13. If y is chosen before x from the variables in $p(x, y)$, the following result is obtained:

$$\{ \ \mathsf{p}(\mathsf{a}, \mathsf{a}), \\ \mathsf{p}(\mathsf{b}, \mathsf{a}), \\ \mathsf{p}(\mathsf{f}(x), \mathsf{a}), \\ \mathsf{p}(x, \mathsf{b}), \\ \mathsf{p}(x, \mathsf{f}(y)) \ \}.$$

Example 16 (Non-Linear Patterns) If P is a non-linear pattern and Σ is a set of constant and function symbols that contains a function symbol, then a *finite* set of substitutions that satisfies the two output conditions of diff-substitutions might not exist. Consider for example $A = \mathsf{p}(x, y)$, $P = \mathsf{p}(z, z)$, and $\Sigma = \{\mathsf{a}, \mathsf{f}\}$, where a is a constant symbol and f is a one-place function symbol. A substitution σ in a set of substitutions satisfying the second output condition of diff-substitutions – that is, if $\mathsf{p}(x, y)\sigma$ is unifiable with $\mathsf{p}(z, z)$ then $\mathsf{p}(x, y)\sigma$ is an instance of $\mathsf{p}(z, z)$ – must have one of the four following forms:

(1) $\{x \mapsto \mathsf{f}^n(u),\ y \mapsto \mathsf{f}^m(u)\}$, where $m, n \geq 0$;
(2) $\{x \mapsto \mathsf{f}^n(\mathsf{a}),\ y \mapsto \mathsf{f}^m(\mathsf{a})\}$, where $m, n \geq 0$;
(3) $\{x \mapsto \mathsf{f}^n(\mathsf{a}),\ y \mapsto \mathsf{f}^m(u)\}$, where $m > n \geq 0$;
(4) $\{x \mapsto \mathsf{f}^n(u),\ y \mapsto \mathsf{f}^m(\mathsf{a})\}$, where $n > m \geq 0$.

Let S be a set of such substitutions. With each of them the exponent n in the value of x as shown in the table can be associated. Assume S is finite. If S is nonempty, then let n_{max} be the largest exponent n of all members of S; if S is empty, then let n_{max} be 0. It is easy to verify that then S can not have a member σ such that the atom

$$\mathsf{p}(\mathsf{f}^{n_{max}+1}(\mathsf{a}), \mathsf{a})$$

is an instance of $\mathsf{p}(x, y)\sigma$. Since, however, this atom is a member of the Herbrand expansion of $\{\mathsf{p}(x, y)\}$ over Σ, the first output condition of diff-substitutions is not satisfied by S.

Example 17 (Exponential Cases of Diff-Expansion) The number of instances of a clause returned by diff-expansion can be exponential in the number of its literals that are unifiable with P but are not an instance of P. If, for example, diff-expansion is applied to

$$F = \{\mathsf{p}(x) \vee \mathsf{p}(y) \vee \mathsf{p}(z) \vee \mathsf{q}(x, y, z)\},$$

$P = \mathsf{p}(\mathsf{a})$ and $\Sigma = \{\mathsf{a},\ \mathsf{b}\}$, where a, b are constant symbols, then the output of diff-expansion contains the 2^3 instances of the clause in F with x, y, z instantiated to a or b.

Theorem 6 (Correctness of Diff-Expansion) *Algorithm* diff-expansion *terminates for all eligible inputs F, P, Σ with a correct output, that is, a finite set of instances of clauses of F that*

1. *Has the same Herbrand expansion as F over Σ, and*
2. *Does not contain a literal L such that the atom A of L is unifiable with P and A is not an instance of P.*

Proof. We first show termination of diff-expansion. The auxiliary procedure diff-substitutions returns finite sets of substitutions, as shown Proposition 120. Termination of diff-substitutions follows straightforwardly as a corollary from the proof of that proposition. Termination of diff-expansion then follows, since in each round of diff-expansion a clause C is replaced by a finite set of instances $C\sigma$, and each of these instances contains strictly less literals than C whose atom is unifiable with P and is not an instance of P.

Items (1.) and (2.) follow immediately from the correctness of the auxiliary procedure diff-substitutions. Thus, it remains to show that diff-substitutions satisfies its two output conditions. Let S be the output from an application of diff-substitutions to arguments A, P, Σ.

1. *For all clauses C that contain only constant and function symbols from Σ it holds that the Herbrand expansions of C and of $\{C\sigma \mid \sigma \in S\}$ over Σ are identical.*

   This can be shown by induction on the structure of S as constructed by diff-substitutions. If D is a clause, let D^{Σ} denote the Herbrand expansion of $\{D\}$ over Σ. Let C be a clause that contains only constant and function symbols from Σ. The base case, where $S = \{\epsilon\}$, holds, since $C^{\Sigma} = \bigcup_{\sigma \in \{\epsilon\}} C\sigma^{\Sigma}$. The induction step follows from the fact that for all variables $u, u_1, u_2, \ldots$ such that none of $u_1, u_2, \ldots$ is in C it holds that

$$C^{\Sigma} = \bigcup_{\sigma \in \{u \mapsto f(u_1, \ldots, u_n) \mid f \text{ with arity } n \text{ is in } \Sigma\}} C\sigma^{\Sigma}.$$

2. *There is no $\sigma \in S$ such that $A\sigma$ is unifiable with P and $A\sigma$ is not an instance of P.*

   This condition follows, since if a contradicting σ is in the set of substitutions maintained by diff-substitutions, the while condition succeeds.

□

An alternative to preprocessing by diff-expansion would be the use of disequality constraints, which we do not pursue here, since it has two features that we want to avoid: First, constant and function symbols that are meant to be "forgotten" are retained "negatively" in the constraints. Second, the framework of pure first-order logic is left. On the other hand, through diff-expansion, a result of pattern forgetting incorporates the set of constant and function symbols supplied as argument to diff-expansion. The result thus is possibly not usable in a context where the existence of further constant and function symbols is assumed.

8 Projection Elimination and Knowledge Compilation

Knowledge compilation [KS91] is an approach to overcome that computational costs are potentially too high for applications if reasoning tasks are specified in expressive logics. The idea is to shift costly operations into an "off-line" compilation phase such that reasoning tasks can then be efficiently performed at "run time" on the compilation result. More than a dozen target languages for knowledge compilation of propositional logic have been investigated in recent years [DM02, HMR05]. Typically these are characterized as syntactic restrictions of formulas. There is a twofold relationship between projection elimination and knowledge compilation:

1. In some applications of knowledge compilation, only the knowledge about a subset of the vocabulary of the input knowledge base is to be retained in the compilation target, which then can be substantially smaller. Projection elimination is the operation to restrict knowledge bases accordingly.
2. Projection elimination is for certain knowledge compilation target languages, in particular *fully linkless* propositional sentences, a linear operation.

An application of knowledge compilation in combination with projection elimination, as described in point (1.), is model-based diagnosis as presented in [Dar01a], where only atoms are retained that represent observed in- and outputs of the diagnosed system or the health of its components. Procedures that combine knowledge compilation with projection elimination are used to construct such restricted compilation targets. A straightforward way to realize such a procedure is suggested with point (2.): Compilation into fully linkless form, followed by linear projection elimination on the compilation target.

This approach has been described in [Dar01a, DM02, MR03]. It involves the construction of an intermediate sentence in the compilation target format that is equivalent to the input sentence. When the *efficiency of the compilation procedure* is taken into consideration, however, this construction of an intermediate equivalent is an unnecessary step, which can be avoided by performing projection elimination in part already at the compilation phase. This "weaving" of knowledge compilation with projection elimination can effect superpolynomial savings in time and space requirements, which is shown formally in Section 8.3 by giving a family of classes of sentences for which polynomial time methods exist that perform compilation into a fully linkless equivalent to a projection and, on the other hand, the size of an equivalent compilation target is not polynomially bounded, under an assumption that is considered as very likely in complexity theory.

Concrete methods that realize this efficient combination of knowledge compilation and projection elimination are developed in Chapter 11 for variants of the Davis-Putnam-Logemann-Loveland method (*DPLL*), with the inclusion of particular simplifications as described in Section 12.2.3, and a special rule, True-Up, described in Section 11.2.6.

We base the abstract considerations on a relation, defined in the following Section 8.1, that subsumes the input-output relations of different tasks such as certain kinds of knowledge compilation, projection elimination, their combination, and satisfiability testing, which is shown in Section 8.2.

8.1 The LP Relation: Generalizing Projection and Compilation

The LP relation, defined in the following, covers in different instantiations the relationships between in- and outputs of projection elimination, compilation to linkless formulas, and combinations of these. The name LP suggests the combination of a syntactic requirement related to *L*inklessness with semantic conditions related to *P*rojection.

We use this relation in Section 8.3 to show a certain aspect of the interaction of projection elimination and knowledge compilation abstractly, without referring to some particular computation method. The LP relation then serves as basis for the design and analysis of methods for projection elimination in Chapter 11 and subsequent chapters.

The LP relation has four places, where the first three represent inputs: A plain sentence and two literal scopes, "link scope" and "projection scope", where the former is a subset of or equal to the latter. The fourth place represents the output, a plain sentence. The relation constrains output sentences syntactically with respect to the link scope, and semantically with respect to the input sentence and the projection scope: An output sentence must be *linkless outside the link scope*, entail the input sentence *relative to the projection scope*, and be entailed by the input sentence.

Instantiations of LP for different application tasks are discussed in Section 8.2. A key property of LP is that if F is the input sentence, S_l is the link scope, S_p is the projection scope, and S is a literal scope such that $S_l \subseteq S \subseteq S_p$, then from any output sentence the result of eliminating the projection operator in $\mathsf{project}(F, S)$ can be linearly constructed. The LP relation can express knowledge compilation to fully linkless equivalents: If the link scope is empty and the projection scope is the set of all literals, then the output sentence is fully linkless and equivalent to the input sentence.

The LP relation is formally specified in terms of three separate conditions, *LP-L*, *LP-U* and *LP-D*, which can be investigated independently for a given formula transformation method, as for example in Section 11.3 and Chapter 13 below, resembling the independent investigation of soundness and completeness of satisfiability solving methods. Condition LP-L states that the output sentence is *L*inkless outside the link scope, condition LP-U states that the it entails the input sentence relative to the projection scope (U suggesting *upward*, since LP-U corresponds in tableau construction methods to requirements that formulas associated with lower nodes entail formulas associated with higher nodes), and condition LP-D states that it is entailed by the input sentence (D for *downward*).

Definition 75 (The LP Relation) For plain sentences F, F' and literal scopes S_l, S_p such that $S_l \subseteq S_p$ the relation LP is defined as

$$\begin{array}{ll} \mathsf{LP}(F, S_l, S_p, F') \stackrel{\text{def}}{=} & \\ \quad \text{(LP-L)} & F' \text{ is polar and linkless outside } S_l, \\ \quad \text{(LP-U)} & F' \models_{S_p} F, \text{ and} \\ \quad \text{(LP-D)} & F \models F'. \end{array}$$

The LP relation justifies a way to eliminate the project operator in a given sentence of the form $\mathsf{project}(F, S)$ where F is a propositional sentence and S is a literal scope: The input sentence F is first transformed into sentence F' such that $\mathsf{LP}(F, S, S, F')$ holds. The output sentence is then obtained from F' by replacing all literals that are not in S with $\top$. This is formally stated in the following proposition:

Proposition 121 *If F, F' are propositional sentences and S is a literal scope, then*

$$\textit{if } \mathsf{LP}(F, S, S, F'), \textit{ then } \mathsf{project}(F, S) \equiv F'[\![L_1 \backslash \top]\!] \ldots [\![L_n \backslash \top]\!],$$

where $\{L_1, \ldots, L_n\} \stackrel{\text{def}}{=} \mathcal{L}(F') - S$.

Proof.

$$\begin{array}{lll} (1) & \mathsf{project}(F, S) & \equiv \\ (2) & \mathsf{project}(F', S) & \equiv \\ (3) & \mathsf{forget}(F', \mathcal{L}(F') - S) & \equiv \\ (4) & F'[\![L_1 \backslash \top]\!] \ldots [\![L_n \backslash \top]\!]. & \end{array}$$

Assume $\mathsf{LP}(F, S, S, F')$. From conditions LP-U and LP-D, along with Proposition 31, follows $F' \equiv_S F$, i. e., equivalence of (2) to (1). Equivalence of (3) to (2) follows from Proposition 54. From condition LP-L and the definition of *linkless* (Definitions 67 and 64) it follows that F' is polar and linkless inside $\mathcal{L}(F') - S$. Hence equivalence of (4) to (3) follows from Proposition 87. □

As the following proposition states, the LP relationship is preserved if the link scope S_l is enlarged, and also if the projection scope S_p is made smaller.

Proposition 122 *If F, F' are plain sentences and S_l, S'_l, S_p, S'_p are literal scopes, then*

$$\text{if } S_l \subseteq S'_l \subseteq S'_p \subseteq S_p \text{ and } \mathsf{LP}(F, S_l, S_p, F'), \text{ then } \mathsf{LP}(F, S'_l, S'_p, F').$$

Proof. Follows easily from the definitions of LP and the underlying relations *linkless outside* and $\models_S$.

□

In condition LP-U, the use of entailment *relative to* S_p instead of plain entailment is essential, as will be shown in Section 8.3. Condition LP-D, in contrast, involves plain entailment, which makes LP-D simpler to handle, for example in Section 9.4, since projection has not to be taken into account. For LP-D this use of plain entailment is no disadvantage in the following sense: If a sentence F' satisfies LP-L, LP-U and the condition $F \models_{S_p} F'$ (which is like LP-D, except that it uses entailment relative to S_p instead of plain entailment, and is thus weaker than LP-D), then there exists a sentence F'' which satisfies LP (and thus also LP-D) and is not larger than F'. This is made precise in the following proposition:

Proposition 123 *If F, F' are propositional sentences and S_l, S_p are literal scopes such that $S_l \subseteq S_p$, then*

if
1. *F' is polar and linkless outside S_l,*
2. *$F' \models_{S_p} F$, and*
3. *$F \models_{S_p} F'$,*

then

there exists a propositional sentence F'' such that $\mathsf{LP}(F, S_l, S_p, F'')$ and $|F''| \leq |F'|$.

Proof. Assume that F, F', S_l and S_p satisfy the preconditions of the proposition. Let F'' be defined as follows:

$$F'' \stackrel{\text{def}}{=} F'[\![L_1\backslash\top]\!]\ldots[\![L_n\backslash\top]\!], \text{ where } \{L_1, \ldots, L_n\} = \mathcal{L}(F') - S_p.$$

Clearly $|F''| \leq |F'|$. We show that also $\mathsf{LP}(F, S_l, S_p, F'')$ holds, by proving each of the conditions LP-L, LP-U and LP-D for the respective parameters. Condition LP-L, that F'' is polar and linkless outside S_l, is easy to see. Since $S_l \subseteq S_p$, it follows from precondition (1.) that F' is also linkless outside S_p, which implies $\mathsf{LP}(F', S_p, S_p, F')$. From Proposition 121 then follows $\mathsf{project}(F', S_p) \equiv F''$. By precondition (2.) it then holds that $F'' \models \mathsf{project}(F, S_p)$, from which condition LP-U (i. e. $F'' \models_{S_p} F$) follows by Proposition 36. By precondition (3.) it then holds that $\mathsf{project}(F, S_p) \models F''$, from which condition LP-D (i. e. $F \models F''$) follows by Proposition 30.

□

8.2 Tasks Expressed in Terms of LP

Consider a program that computes for inputs F, S_l, S_p, where F is a propositional sentence and S_l, S_p are representations of literal scopes such that $S_l \subseteq S_p$, an output sentence F' such that $\mathsf{LP}(F, S_l, S_p, F')$ is satisfied. The program can be applied to solve the following different tasks, distinguished by the values of S_l and S_p:

- *Projection Elimination.* If S_l and S_p are identical, then the project operator in $\mathsf{project}(F, S_p)$ can be eliminated by substituting in F' all literals that are not in S_p with $\top$, as stated in Proposition 121. Assuming that the substitution is performed linearly in the size of F', the essential work for projection elimination is done by computing F'.

- *Compilation to an equivalent sentence that is linkless outside a given literal scope.* If S_p is the set of all literals, then Condition LP-U states that F' is equivalent to F. If S_l is the given set of literals, then Condition LP-L states that F' is linkless outside the given set.

- *Compilation to a fully linkless equivalent sentence.* This specializes the task described in the previous item by requiring S_l to be the empty set. As before, S_p is the set of all literals.

- *Deciding satisfiability.* If S_l is the empty set, then F' is fully linkless and its satisfiability can be checked in a linear time postprocessing step as outlined on p. 79. Since projection preserves equi-satisfiability (Proposition 72), an arbitrary set of literals can be taken as S_p. However, the empty set as S_p is preferable, since it least constrains LP.

The instantiation patterns of the LP relation for these tasks are summarized in the following table:

Task	*Instantiation of* LP
Elimination of the projection operator in $\mathsf{project}(F, S)$	$\mathsf{LP}(F, S, S, F')$
Compilation to an equivalent linkless outside a scope S	$\mathsf{LP}(F, S, \mathsf{GLITS}, F')$
Compilation to a fully linkless equivalent	$\mathsf{LP}(F, \emptyset, \mathsf{GLITS}, F')$
Deciding satisfiability	$\mathsf{LP}(F, \emptyset, \emptyset, F')$

Table 8.1. Instantiation Patterns of LP for Various Tasks

8.3 Weaving Projection Elimination and Compilation

In this section we consider the task of computing for a propositional sentence F and literal scope S as inputs a propositional sentence that is *fully linkless* and *equivalent to* $\mathsf{project}(F, S)$. An application of this task is model-based diagnosis with knowledge compilation, as described in [Dar01a].[1] A propositional sentence describing the device to be diagnosed is projected onto the union of *assumables*, special atoms representing the health of the system, and *observables*, the atoms whose truth value is going to be measured.The input-output relationships of algorithms that compute the considered task can be characterized by means of the LP relation:

Definition 76 (LP-Algorithm) An *LP-algorithm* is a procedure that computes for all inputs F, S, where F is a propositional sentence and S is a literal scope[2] a propositional sentence F' as output such that

$$\mathsf{LP}(F, \emptyset, S, F').$$

An LP-algorithm computes the considered task, abstracted from a linear postprocessing operation: If F' is the output of an LP-algorithm applied to inputs F and S, then the sentence obtained from F' by replacing all literals that are not in S with $\top$ precisely meets the requirements corresponding to the considered task, that is, it is *fully linkless* and *equivalent to* $\mathsf{project}(F, S)$. This can be shown as follows: From $\mathsf{LP}(F, \emptyset, S, F')$ it follows by Proposition 122 that also $\mathsf{LP}(F, S, S, F')$; hence by Proposition 121 it holds that $\mathsf{project}(F, S)$ is equivalent to F' with all literals not in S replaced by $\top$. By the definition of the LP relation it holds that F' is fully linkless. This property is clearly preserved by replacing literals with $\top$.

A further approach to the considered task would be the computation of an intermediate sentence F' that is equivalent to the input sentence F and linkless *outside the scope* S of the projection, that is, it holds that

$$\mathsf{LP}(F, S, \mathsf{GLITS}, F').$$

From $\mathsf{LP}(F, S, \mathsf{GLITS}, F')$ follows by Proposition 122 that also $\mathsf{LP}(F, S, S, F')$ holds. Thus, also with this approach F' can serve as basis for the linear projection elimination according to Proposition 121. But we leave further investigation of this approach to future work and turn again to LP-algorithms.

---

[1] In [Dar01a] the considered task is used in a slight variation: Projection in performed just on atom scopes instead of literal scopes, and the compilation target format is DNNF, which is a strengthening of fully linkless form. An atom scope can be expressed as a literal scope S constrained by the condition $S = \widetilde{S}$. Our material in this chapter easily transfers to DNNF instead of fully linkless form.

[2] As input to a procedure, a *literal scope* is understood as a data structure representing the literal scope such that size and membership test are linear in cardinality for finite sets, and constant for GLITS.

A straightforward way to realize an LP-algorithm is to compile F to a fully linkless equivalent, which, as outlined in the introduction to this chapter, is the proposed method of [Dar01a] and [MR03]. We call LP-algorithms that proceed in this way *EQ-constrained*, the prefix *EQ* suggesting "fully linkless *EQ*uivalent".

Definition 77 (EQ-Constrained LP-Algorithm) An LP-algorithm is called *EQ-constrained* if and only if it relates its input sentence F and its output F' by

$$\mathsf{LP}(F, \emptyset, \mathsf{GLITS}, F').$$

The second input to LP-algorithms, the literal scope S, is ignored by EQ-constrained LP-algorithms. The *EQ-constrained* condition strengthens the input-output relation of LP-algorithms, since $\mathsf{LP}(F, \emptyset, \mathsf{GLITS}, F')$ implies $\mathsf{LP}(F, \emptyset, S, F')$, which follows from Proposition 122.

An LP-algorithm that is not E-constrained is permitted to perform projection elimination already during compilation on intermediately resulting subformulas. Performing elimination on occasions where this is cheaply possible can effect that subformulas which do not contribute to the final result get deleted, instead of having to be expensively compiled. With EQ-constrained algorithms, such irrelevant subformulas can be deleted only after compilation in a postprocessing step by truth value simplification,[3] after the linear projection elimination by replacing literals not in the scope with $\top$. Although EQ-constrained LP-algorithms are then not distinguished with respect to the final results, the involved construction of a fully linkless equivalent to the input sentence as an intermediate can essentially worsen the *efficiency of the compilation procedure.*

In the rest of this section, we work out a precise argument for this, stated below as Theorem 7, which is based on a family of classes of sentences, *disjoin-sentences* that exemplify the different behavior of EQ-constrained LP-algorithms and unconstrained LP-algorithms:

Definition 78 (Disjoin-Sentence) If A is a ground atom and $F = (C_1 \land \ldots \land C_n)$ is a propositional CNF sentence such that $A \notin \mathcal{A}(F)$, then the *disjoin-sentence over F upon A* is the propositional CNF sentence

$$(C_1 \lor A) \land \ldots \land (C_n \lor A).$$

The disjoin-sentence over F upon A is equivalent to $(F \lor A)$. Disjoin-sentences have two key properties, which will be made precise as Propositions 124

[3] A propositional sentence is said to be obtained by *truth value simplification* from a given propositional sentence if it is obtained from the given sentence by exhaustive rewriting according to the following equivalences oriented from left to right (modulo commutativity of $\land, \lor$ and $\leftrightarrow$): $(\top \land F) \equiv F$, $(\bot \land F) \equiv \bot$, $(\top \lor F) \equiv \top$, $(\bot \lor F) \equiv F$, $(\top \leftrightarrow F) \equiv F$, $(\bot \leftrightarrow F) \equiv \neg F$, $(\top \rightarrow F) \equiv F$, $(\bot \rightarrow F) \equiv \top$, $(F \rightarrow \top) \equiv \top$, $(F \rightarrow \bot) \equiv \neg F$, $(\neg\top) \equiv \bot$, $(\neg\bot) \equiv \top$.

and 125 below: On the one hand, projection elimination in $\mathsf{project}(F, S)$ can be performed in polynomial time for disjoin-sentences F upon A, where $+A$ is not in S. On the other hand, the size of fully linkless equivalents of disjoin-sentences upon any given atom is not polynomially bounded, under the assumption $\mathsf{NP} \not\subseteq \mathsf{P/poly}$.[4]

These two properties of disjoin-sentence are combined in Theorem 7 below to show that for any EQ-constrained LP-algorithm K there exists an LP-algorithm K' that is not EQ-constrained and essentially improves on K, in that neither time nor space requirements of K are polynomially bounded by the respective requirements of K' (under the assumption $\mathsf{NP} \not\subseteq \mathsf{P/poly}$). The proof of the theorem gives a way to construct such a procedure K' for given K. We let the statement of Theorem 7 precede the two lemmas about disjoin-sentences, Propositions 124 and 125.

To show that LP-algorithms which are EQ-constrained, as in current approaches to combine knowledge compilation with projection elimination, are in principle essentially less efficient than unconstrained LP-algorithms, it suffices to consider just the efficiency for disjoin-sentences. In practice, disjoin-sentences are not expected to be important as global inputs to reasoning tasks, but it is quite plausible that they (or other types of sentences that analogously allow efficient elimination of projection) are constructed during reasoning, such that the principal improvements of unconstrained LP-algorithms can take effect on many occasions during a typical compilation task.

Theorem 7 (Weaving Projection into Compilation) *If K is an EQ-constrained LP-algorithm, then there exists an LP-algorithm K', which is not EQ-constrained, such that there does not exist a polynomial p such that for all propositional formulas F and literal scopes S it holds that the time (space resp.) required by $K(F, S)$ is less than or equal to p applied to the time (space resp.) required by $K'(F, S)$, unless $\mathsf{NP} \subseteq \mathsf{P/poly}$.*

Proof. Let K be an EQ-constrained LP-algorithm. An LP-algorithm K' that satisfies the conditions in the theorem statement can then be defined as follows: Let F and S be the inputs. If F is a disjoin-sentence upon some atom in S, then return $\top$, else return the result of invoking $K(F, S)$.

It is easy to see that the if-condition, the check whether F is a disjoin formula, can be performed in time polynomial in the sum of $|F|$ and the

[4] $\mathsf{P/poly}$ is a non-uniform complexity class. Its relationship to knowledge compilation has been brought to attention by Kautz and Selman [KS92]. Cadoli et al. have generalized their results in [CDS96]. Details and further references can be found in that work in the context of Theorem 6, which has the assumption $\mathsf{NP} \not\subseteq \mathsf{P/poly}$ as a precondition. Failure of this assumption would imply the collapse of the polynomial hierarchy. Our proof of Proposition 125 is based on that theorem, as actually are many complexity results about knowledge compilation formats [DM02].

cardinality of S (or just in $|F|$ if $S = \mathsf{GLITS}$). For inputs that do not satisfy the if-condition, K' proceeds in the same way as K. For inputs that satisfy the if-condition, K' and K differ: The time (and thus space) required by K' is trivially polynomially bounded by the size of the inputs, and correctness is ensured by Proposition 124. However, the space (and thus time) required by K is not polynomially bounded by $|F|$, which follows from Proposition 125.

□

Proposition 124 *If A is a ground atom, F is a disjoin-sentence upon A, and S is literal scope such that $+A \notin S$, then*

$$\mathsf{LP}(F, \emptyset, S, \top).$$

Proof. It has to be shown that the three conditions of the LP relation, LP-L, LP-U and LP-D, are satisfied for the given values. For LP-L and LP-D this is easy to see. It remains to show condition LP-U, that is, $\top \models_S F$. This is implied by $\mathsf{project}(F, S) \equiv \top$, which can be shown as follows:

$$\begin{array}{lll}
(1) & \mathsf{project}(F, S) & \equiv \\
(2) & \mathsf{project}(F, \overline{\{+A\}} \cap S) & \equiv \\
(3) & \mathsf{project}(\mathsf{project}(F, \overline{\{+A\}}), S) & \equiv \\
(4) & \mathsf{project}(\top, S) & \equiv \\
(5) & \top. &
\end{array}$$

Equivalence of (2) to (1) holds since the precondition $+A \notin S$ implies $S = \overline{\{+A\}} \cap S$. Equivalence of (3) to (2) follows from Proposition 34. By the definition of *disjoin-sentence*, the atom A can occur in F only in positive literals, thus F is linkless outside $\overline{\{+A\}}$, from which it follows that $\mathsf{LP}(F, \overline{\{+A\}}, \overline{\{+A\}}, F)$ is satisfied. Hence by Proposition 121 it holds that $\mathsf{project}(F, \overline{\{+A\}}) \equiv F[\![+A \backslash \top]\!]$. From the definition of *disjoin-sentence*, it is easy to see that each clause in $F[\![+A \backslash \top]\!]$ contains $\top$. Thus $F_A[\![+A \backslash \top]\!]$ can be reduced by truth value simplification to $\top$; hence $\mathsf{project}(F, \overline{\{+A\}}) \equiv \top$. Along with Proposition 32, this justifies the equivalence of (4) to (3). Equivalence of (5) to (4) follows from Proposition 45.

□

Proposition 125 *Under the assumption* $\mathsf{NP} \not\subseteq \mathsf{P/poly}$, *if A is a ground atom, then there does not exist a polynomial p such that for all sentences F that are disjoin-sentences upon A there exists a propositional sentence F' such that*

$$\mathsf{LP}(F, \emptyset, \mathsf{GLITS}, F') \textit{ and } |F'| \le p(|F|).$$

Proof. We first give an outline of the proof: Theorem 6 in [CDS96] by Cadoli et al. states that – under the assumption $\mathsf{NP} \not\subseteq \mathsf{P/poly}$, which is considered as very likely in complexity theory – for a knowledge compiler that takes propositional CNF sentences as input and computes results which permit linear clausal entailment, the size of these results can not be polynomially bounded. We show that for all propositional CNF sentences F there exists a compilation target F' which permits linear clausal entailment and also satisfies $\mathsf{LP}(G, \emptyset, \mathsf{GLITS}, F')$ for some disjoin-sentence G whose size is polynomially bounded by the size of F. If the size of F' would be polynomially bounded by the size of G, then it would also be bounded by the size of F, contradicting the theorem by Cadoli et al., unless $\mathsf{NP} \subseteq \mathsf{P/poly}$.

We now work out the proof in detail. All sentences, clauses and atoms considered in the proof are understood as *propositional*, or *ground*, respectively. We make the assumption $\mathsf{NP} \not\subseteq \mathsf{P/poly}$. Under this assumption, Theorem 6 in [CDS96] by Cadoli et al., states the following:

(1) There do not exist polynomials p_1, p_2
and an algorithm CE such that
for all CNF sentences F
there exists a data structure D with size $|D|$ such that
(a) $|D| \leq p_1(|F|)$,
(b) for all clauses C it holds that
$CE(D, C)$ returns yes if and only if $F \models C$, and
(c) for all clauses C it holds that
$CE(D, C)$ requires time $\leq p_2(|D| + |C|)$.

Assuming an infinite number of atoms, it is not hard to derive (2) from (1), a variant of the theorem by Cadoli et al., where F is restricted by $A \notin \mathcal{A}(F)$.

(2) For all atoms A
there do not exist polynomials p_1, p_2
and an algorithm CE such that
for all CNF sentences F such that $A \notin \mathcal{A}(F)$
there exists a data structure D with size $|D|$ such that
(1a), (1b) and (1c) hold.

We now prove the proposition by showing that the assumption of its negation, step (3), leads to a contradiction with (2). Variable F in the proposition statement has been renamed to G in (3), to facilitate the presentation of subsequent proof steps.

(3) There exists an atom A
and a polynomial p such that
for all sentences G that are disjoin-sentences upon A
there exists a sentence F' such that
$\mathsf{LP}(G, \emptyset, \mathsf{GLITS}, F')$ and $|F'| \leq p(|G|)$.

(4) There exists an atom A,
polynomials p, p_1, p_2
and an algorithm CE such that
for all CNF sentences F such that $A \notin \mathcal{A}(F)$
there exist sentences G and F' such that
(a) G is the disjoin sentence over F upon A,
(b) $\mathsf{LP}(G, \emptyset, \mathsf{GLITS}, F')$,
(c) $|F'| \leq p(|G|)$,

(d) $G \equiv F \vee A$,
(e) $|G| \leq 2 * |F|$,
(f) $F' \equiv G$,

(g) F' is fully linkless,
(h) $F' \equiv F \vee A$,

(i) $|F'| \leq p_1(|F|)$,
(j) for all clauses C it holds that
$CE(F', C)$ returns yes iff $F \models C$, and
(k) for all clauses C it holds that
$CE(F', C)$ requires time $\leq p_2(|F'| + |C|)$.

Assume (3), the negation of the proposition to be proven. Step (4) with items (4a)–(4c) follows from (3) since the disjoin-sentence G over F upon A does exist for all atoms A and CNF sentences F such that $A \notin \mathcal{A}(F)$. Items (4d) and (4e) follow from (4a) and the definition of *disjoin-sentence*; items (4f) and (4g) from (4b) and the definition of the LP relation. Item (4h) follows from (4f) and (4d); item (4i) from (4e) and (4c).

For all atoms A there exists an algorithm CE with the following properties: The inputs of CE are a fully linkless sentence F' and a clause C. If C contains complementary literals, then CE returns yes. Otherwise it returns the result of an invocation of some algorithm that linearly decides clausal entailment for fully linkless sentences, applied to F' and $(C' \vee A)$, where C' is the clause obtained from C by removing all literals whose atom is A. More precisely, the invoked algorithm returns yes if and only if $F' \models (C' \vee A)$, and operates in time linear in $|F'| + |C' \vee A|$. That such linear algorithms exist has been shown above in Section 5.12, p. 79.

Item (4k) then straightforwardly follows from the specification of CE. Item (4j) can be shown as follows: If C contains the complementary literals A and $\neg A$, then C is tautological; thus $F \models C$ and CE correctly returns yes. Otherwise C contains A either only positively, in which case $C \equiv (C' \vee A)$, only negatively, in which case $C \equiv (C' \vee \neg A)$, or not at all, in which case $C \equiv C'$. Item (4j) then follows, since these three cases correspond to items (ii)–(iv) in the following general property of sentences: For all atoms A, sentences F and clauses C' such that $A \notin \mathcal{A}(F)$ and $A \notin \mathcal{A}(C')$ the following statements are equivalent:

(i) $F \vee A \models C' \vee A$.
(ii) $F \models C' \vee A$.
(iii) $F \models C' \vee \neg A$.
(iv) $F \models C'$.

Step (4) flatly contradicts with (2), the sentence F' in the role of the data structure D and items (4i), (4j), (4k) matching (1a), (1b), (1c), respectively. Hence our assumption (3), that the proposition to be shown is false, leads to a contradiction, which concludes the proof.

□

9 A Tableau Framework for Formula Transformation

We investigate the application of tableau methods to "compute LP", which means to compute for a given sentence F and literal scopes S_l, S_p, where $S_l \subseteq S_p$, a sentence F' such that it holds that

$$\mathsf{LP}(F, S_l, S_p, F').$$

The main motivation for turning to tableau methods is that many of the automated deduction systems for which successful applications have been shown in recent years proceed by constructing a tree data structure that can be regarded as a *tableau* in the sense of [DGHP99, Häh01]. This includes theorem provers and model generators for first-order logic that implement calculi like hypertableau and model evolution [MB88, Wer03, Bau00, BFT04, LS01], specialized reasoners for modal and description logics [Hor98, HM01], propositional satisfiability solvers and model counters [MSS96, BS97] as well as answer set programming systems for non-monotonic propositional logics [NS97]. Techniques employed in such systems should transfer to projection elimination. Typically these systems are space efficient, since they construct the tree in such a way that at any point of time only a single branch is in memory. Since a branch represents a partial interpretation of the input sentence, such methods can be considered as trying to construct a model and are also termed *model-based.* For satisfiable inputs, some of the systems output such model representations.

We now illustrate the principal idea of applying tableau methods to compute LP. We make simplifications to show the intuitions more clearly: Abstracting from the tree shape of tableaux, we identify a tableau with the disjunction of its branches and do not take into account that only a single branch needs to be stored in memory. Let F be a propositional sentence. We consider computing a propositional sentence F' such that $\mathsf{LP}(F, \emptyset, \mathsf{GLITS}, F')$ holds.

A clausal tableau method typically maintains a disjunction $(B_1 \lor \ldots \lor B_n)$ of non-complementary conjunctions of literals, called *branches*, that usually varies over time and satisfies the invariant

$$\text{(i)} \qquad F \models B_1 \lor \ldots \lor B_n,$$

which is clearly equivalent to

(ii) $$F \equiv F \land (B_1 \lor \ldots \lor B_n),$$

and to the following statement, where each branch "has its own copy" of F:

(iii) $$F \equiv (B_1 \land F) \lor \ldots \lor (B_n \land F).$$

If B is a branch, let $F[B\backslash\top]$ denote the result of substituting in F the atoms A that also occur in B by $\top$ ($\bot$, resp.) if $+A$ ($-A$, resp.) is in B, followed by eliminating the truth value constants with truth value simplification. Clearly (iii) is then equivalent to

(iv) $$F \equiv (B_1 \land F[B_1\backslash\top]) \lor \ldots \lor (B_n \land F[B_n\backslash\top]).$$

A sentence F' such that it holds that

$$\mathsf{LP}(F, \emptyset, \mathsf{GLITS}, F')$$

can be computed by a tableau method which ensures that for all branches B of a terminal state it holds that $(B \land (F[B\backslash\top]))$ is fully linkless. This must be the case if each branch is "large enough", at least if it contains all atoms in F. If $(B_1 \lor \ldots \lor B_n)$ is the disjunction of branches at such a terminal state, then let F' be defined like the right side of (iv). It is easy to see that F' is fully linkless and thus meets condition LP-L of the definition of LP. From (iv) it is easy to see that F' is equivalent to F, and thus also meets the two other conditions, LP-U and LP-D.

Many aspects of utilizing tableau methods to the computation of LP as just sketched are independent of the way in which tableaux are constructed and hold for different variants of tableau structures. These aspects have been isolated and worked out in this chapter, resulting in a formal framework that provides a set of constraints on tableaux that can be applied to different construction methods. Later on, in Chapter 11, a variant of DPLL for propositional logic is worked out in an exemplary way as an instance of this framework.

Various refinements of tableau methods are essential for practical applicability. Some, which seem particularly useful for computing LP, are explicitly considered in the framework:

- Support for space-efficient operation with only a single tableau branch in memory;
- Support for dependency directed backjumping, formally modeled with techniques similar to *Abstract DPLL* [NOT05, NOT06];
- Support for and-or trees as tableau structures, as introduced to DPLL-based model counters [BP00] and used in a DNNF compiler derived from these [HD05].

A suitable tableau structure, *fwd-tableau*, is defined in Section 9.1. In Sections 9.2–9.4 constraints on tableaux are specified in a "local" manner, in terms of relationships of a single tableau node with its children or a single branch with a leaf node. This facilitates their verification for tableau construction methods that are specified by means of rules that relate nodes locally in a similar way. These local properties imply global properties of tableaux that make them suitable for the computation of sentences satisfying the LP-L, LP-U and LP-D conditions, respectively, which is formally proven. In Section 9.5 these results are combined to a single set of constraints that ensures that a tableau construction method can be applied to compute LP. A tabular overview on this "interface" of the framework to construction methods is given at the end of the chapter in Table 9.5 (p. 151).

9.1 Fwd-Tableaux and Leafy Sentences

In this section a tableau structure, *fwd-tableau*, short for *tableau with forward labels*, is defined. It is the tableau structure of the framework developed in the subsequent sections. Before we describe fwd-tableaux concretely, we indicate their place within the many existing variations of tableaux and outline how we use their particular features. As noted for example in [Fit99], there are two different basic ways of thinking about tableau methods: as refutation procedures and as search procedures for models. Our *fwd-tableaux* are based on the latter view, where each branch of a tableau is considered as partial description of a model. We generalize this approach to thinking about tableau methods as procedures for *formula transformation* by taking into account *all branches* of a tableau. A tableau then corresponds to a formula with a particular syntactic form: The disjunction of the formulas corresponding to branches, conjunctions of the formulas labeling their nodes. If nodes are not labeled with complex formulas, but just with literals, the tableau corresponds to a formula in disjunctive normal form. The tree structure of the tableau provides a structure sharing representation for this formula. Our fwd-tableaux further extend this formula view by the inclusion of and-nodes.

Considered as a refutation procedure, a tableau construction method records each proof step by attaching a new node to the tableau, proceeding until each branch is *closed*, that is, contains contradicting formulas that are cheap to detect. In the model-based tableau view, there is no need to preserve a closed branch – which would just represent a failed attempt to construct a model. Accordingly, our variation of tableaux does not include the concept *closed*. If a situation arises where a branch would be closed, our methods destructively modify the tableau or, if this is not possible, terminate.

As common in highly efficient methods for automated tableau construction, node labels in fwd-tableaux must be literals, in contrast to complex formulas. In methods that construct such tableaux, the – complex – input formula must be represented in some special way, external to the tableau. Fwd-tableaux provide a means to avoid such external structures, and, moreover, to incorporate formula simplifications that are useful for transformation tasks but can not be straightforwardly expressed as tableau manipulations: Nodes are decorated with a second label, the *forward label*, a complex formula that is a copy of the input formula on which simplifications with respect to the branch to the node have been performed. In implementations, forward labels not necessarily have to be fully materialized.

We now turn to the concrete description of fwd-tableaux. Similar to a clausal tableaux [Let98], a fwd-tableau is basically a tree whose nodes are labeled with a literal or $\top$; siblings are however not constrained to be the literals of an input clause. Fwd-tableaux extend clausal tableaux in two respects that are relevant for computing LP:

- *Forward labels.* Aside from the labeling by a literal, a fwd-tableau node has a second label, the *forward label*, which is a sentence. Intuitively, the forward label represents a part of the computation problem that is associated with the node while being in the focus of computation and remains to be solved (will possibly be solved at a future "*forward*" point in time) when another node gets into the focus in computation. For computing LP, the forward labels of leaf nodes at the terminal state of a computation are included into the output.
- *And-nodes.* Along with nodes in the standard sense for clausal tableaux, fwd-tableaux can contain nodes of a second type, called *a-nodes*, short for *and-nodes*. A fwd-tableau can then be considered as an and-or tree. And-nodes have been introduced to DPLL-based model counters [BP00], where they make it possible just to multiply the numbers of models counted for subformulas that are independent from each other in a certain way. And-nodes have subsequently been used in a DNNF compiler based on such a model counter [HD05].

Similar to a clausal tableau, a fwd-tableau can be considered as representing a sentence. We use two ways of mapping fwd-tableaux to sentences, both specified formally in Definition 82: The *associated sentence* of a fwd-tableau T, in symbols $\mathsf{sentence}(T)$, is the "standard way" – forward labels are not considered. For a fwd-tableau T without a-nodes, $\mathsf{sentence}(T)$ is equivalent to the disjunction of the conjunctions of the literal labels of its branches. The second way, the *leafy sentence* of a fwd-tableau T, in symbols $\mathsf{leafy}(T)$, incorporates forward labels of leaf nodes. It is defined by an identical induction as $\mathsf{sentence}$, except that leaf nodes are mapped to their literal label *conjoined with their forward label.* As shown in the subsequent sections, a tableau procedure can be applied to compute LP by computing a fwd-tableau that meets certain constraints and returning its leafy sentence. Example 18 shows the associated and leafy sentence of the example fwd-tableau displayed in Fig. 9.1.

Definition 79 (Terminology for Trees) We use the following terms with their conventional meaning [Knu97, Section 2.3]: *root*, *leaf*, *child*, *parent*, *descendant*, *ancestor*, *sibling*, *subtree*. The *outdegree* of a node is the number of its children. A node in an ordered tree is *left of* (*right of*, resp.) a sibling if, in the ordering associated with the tree, the subtree rooted at the node precedes (succeeds, resp.) the subtree rooted at the sibling.

Definition 80 (Fwd-Tableau) An *fwd-tableau* (short for *forward labeled tableau*) is an ordered tree with three node labeling functions: If N is a node in a fwd-tableau, then

- Its *literal label*, in symbols L_N, is a sentence that is either a ground literal, a literal prefixed with universal quantifiers that bind all variables in the literal, or the truth value constant $\top$.[1]
- Its *forward label*, in symbols F_N, is a sentence, and
- If N is a non-leaf node, then it is either an *o-node* (short for *or-node*) or *a-node* (short for *and-node*). A leaf node is neither an o-node nor an a-node.

Unless especially noted, we only consider fwd-tableaux with a finite number of nodes.

Definition 81 (Root, Branch) If T is a fwd-tableau and N is a node in T, then

(i) $\mathsf{root}(T)$ denotes the root of T.

(ii) The *branch in T to N*, in symbols B_N, is the sequence of nodes defined as:

$$B_N \stackrel{\text{def}}{=} N_1 \ldots N_n,$$

where $N_1 = \mathsf{root}(T)$, $N_n = N$, and for all N_i, N_{i+1} such that $i \in \{1, \ldots, n-1\}$ it holds that N_i is the parent of N_{i+1}. For the symbolic notation "B_N" it is assumed that T is clear from the context.[2]

(iii) We overload notation for branches: If $B_N = N_1 \ldots N_n$ is the branch in T to N, then B_N is also used to denote the sentence defined as:

$$B_N \stackrel{\text{def}}{=} L_{N_1} \land \ldots \land L_{N_n}.$$

(iv) A *branch of T* is a branch in T to a leaf node.

[1] This restriction of literal labels is in accordance with clausal tableaux with non-rigid [Häh01] variables and suffices as a basis for refinements and instantiations of the fwd-tableau framework developed in subsequent chapters. The material in this chapter, however, technically does not depend on this restriction and also applies if arbitrary sentences are permitted as literal labels.

[2] A related notation that explicitly takes into account the first node of a *branch segment* is specified in Definition 129.

Definition 82 (Associated and Leafy Sentence)

(i) If N is a node in a fwd-tableau, then the *associated sentence* of N, in symbols $\mathsf{sentence}(N)$, is a sentence defined as: If N is a leaf node, then

$$\mathsf{sentence}(N) \stackrel{\text{def}}{=} L_N;$$

If N is an o-node whose children are $N_1, \ldots, N_n$, then

$$\mathsf{sentence}(N) \stackrel{\text{def}}{=} L_N \wedge \bigvee_{i \in \{1,\ldots,n\}} \mathsf{sentence}(N_i);$$

If N is an a-node whose children are $N_1, \ldots, N_n$, then

$$\mathsf{sentence}(N) \stackrel{\text{def}}{=} L_N \wedge \bigwedge_{i \in \{1,\ldots,n\}} \mathsf{sentence}(N_i).$$

(ii) If N is a node in a fwd-tableau, then the *leafy sentence* of N, in symbols $\mathsf{leafy}(N)$, is a sentence defined as: If N is a leaf node, then

$$\mathsf{leafy}(N) \stackrel{\text{def}}{=} L_N \wedge F_N;$$

If N is an o-node whose children are $N_1, \ldots, N_n$, then

$$\mathsf{leafy}(N) \stackrel{\text{def}}{=} L_N \wedge \bigvee_{i \in \{1,\ldots,n\}} \mathsf{leafy}(N_i);$$

If N is an a-node whose children are $N_1, \ldots, N_n$, then

$$\mathsf{leafy}(N) \stackrel{\text{def}}{=} L_N \wedge \bigwedge_{i \in \{1,\ldots,n\}} \mathsf{leafy}(N_i).$$

(iii) If T is a fwd-tableau, then the *associated sentence* of T, in symbols $\mathsf{sentence}(T)$, and the *leafy sentence* of T, in symbols $\mathsf{leafy}(T)$, are sentences defined as:

$$\mathsf{sentence}(T) \stackrel{\text{def}}{=} \mathsf{sentence}(\mathsf{root}(T));$$

$$\mathsf{leafy}(T) \stackrel{\text{def}}{=} \mathsf{leafy}(\mathsf{root}(T)).$$

Example 18 (Fwd-Tableau and Leafy Sentence) Consider the fwd-tableau in Fig. 9.1. Nodes are identified by numbers. For each node N in the tableau, the literal label L_N and forward label F_N is shown; F_N framed in a box. The boxes for leaf nodes are bold to emphasize that their forward labels are constituents of the leafy sentence. Node 1 is an a-node, which is indicated by the arc connecting its outgoing edges. Let T be the fwd-tableau; its associated sentence, $\mathsf{sentence}(T)$, and leafy sentence, $\mathsf{leafy}(T)$, are shown in Fig. 9.2.

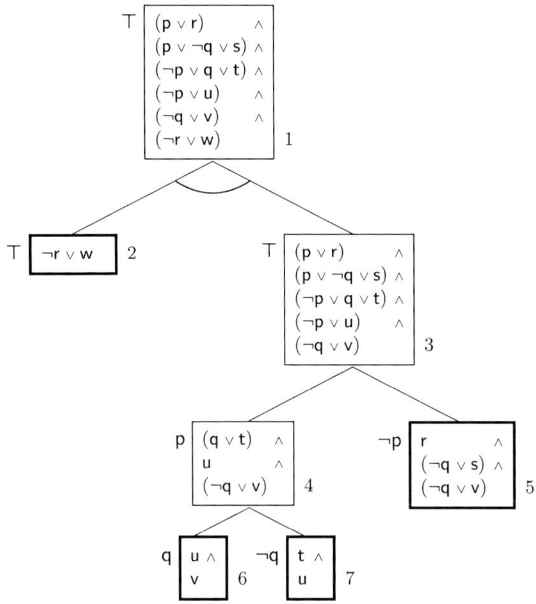

Figure 9.1. A Fwd-Tableau

$$
\begin{aligned}
\mathsf{sentence}(T) = {} & \top \wedge \\
& (\top \wedge \\
& \quad (\top \wedge \\
& \qquad ((\mathsf{p} \wedge (\mathsf{q} \vee \\
& \qquad\qquad\qquad \neg\mathsf{q})) \vee \\
& \qquad\quad \neg\mathsf{p}))).
\end{aligned}
$$

$$
\begin{aligned}
\mathsf{leafy}(T) = {} & \top \wedge \\
& ((\top \wedge (\neg\mathsf{r} \vee \mathsf{w})) \wedge \\
& \quad (\top \wedge \\
& \qquad ((\mathsf{p} \wedge ((\mathsf{q} \wedge (\mathsf{u} \wedge \mathsf{v})) \vee \\
& \qquad\qquad\qquad (\neg\mathsf{q} \wedge (\mathsf{t} \wedge \mathsf{u})))) \vee \\
& \qquad\; (\neg\mathsf{p} \wedge (\mathsf{r} \wedge ((\neg\mathsf{q} \vee \mathsf{s}) \wedge (\neg\mathsf{q} \vee \mathsf{v}))))))).
\end{aligned}
$$

Figure 9.2. Associated and Leafy Sentence of the Fwd-Tableau in Fig. 9.1

9.2 Ensuring LP-L

A constraint, *linklessness-preserving*, and a property, PB-L, for determining that the construction of branch of a tableau is complete are defined in Sections 9.2.1 and 9.2.2. As then shown in Section 9.2.3, if a fwd-tableau T is linklessness-preserving for a literal scope S_l, and each of its leaf nodes satisfies PB-L with respect to S_l, then its leafy sentence satisfies the LP-L condition: $\mathsf{leafy}(T)$ *is polar and linkless outside* S_l.

9.2.1 Linklessness-Preserving Fwd-Tableaux

Linklessness-preserving, specified in the following definition, is a constraint that is parameterized with a literal scope S. Nodes of a fwd-tableau without a-nodes trivially satisfy this constraint. It is used as a requirement on fwd-tableaux to ensure that their leafy sentences satisfy the LP-L condition. The first condition of *linklessness-preserving* states that the literal and forward labels of different children of an a-node are pairwise linkless outside S. The second condition ensures that the literal base of literal labels and forward labels of descendants of such a child is a subset of that of the child's forward label. This implies that also the leafy sentences of different children of an a-node are pairwise linkless outside S, as stated in Proposition 126.

Definition 83 (Linklessness-Preserving) A fwd-tableau is called *linklessness-preserving* for a literal scope S if and only if for all nodes N in the fwd-tableau it holds that

(i) If N is an a-node whose children are $N_1, \ldots, N_n$, then for all $i, j \in \{1, \ldots, n\}$ such that $i \neq j$ it holds that

$$\langle (L_{N_i} \wedge F_{N_i}), (L_{N_j} \wedge F_{N_j}) \rangle \textit{ is linkless outside } S;$$

(ii) If N is a node that has an a-node as ancestor and N' is a child of N, then

$$\mathcal{L}(L_{N'} \wedge F_{N'}) \subseteq \mathcal{L}(F_N) \cup (S \cap \widetilde{S}).$$

Example 19 (Linklessness-Preserving) Consider the fwd-tableau in Fig. 9.3. Node 1 is the only a-node. Its two children, nodes 2 and 3, have $\top$ as literal label. The pair of the forward labels of nodes 2 and 3 is linkless outside $S \stackrel{\text{def}}{=} \overline{\{\mathsf{p}, \neg\mathsf{p}, \mathsf{q}, \neg\mathsf{q}\}}$, implying the condition of Definition 83.i. The condition of Definition 83.ii follows, since all literals appearing in literal and forward labels of the children of node 3 also appear in the forward label of node 3.

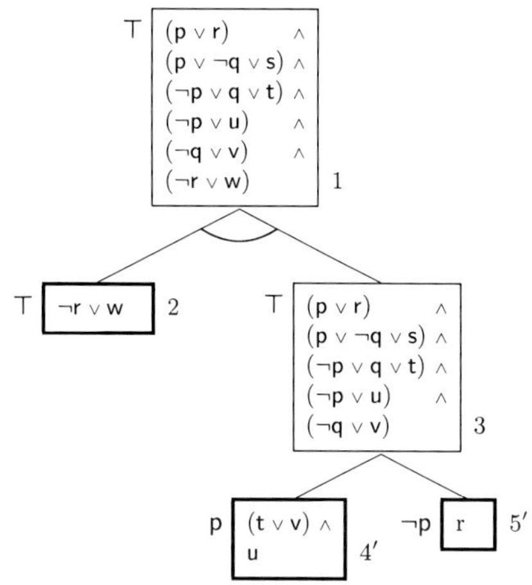

Figure 9.3. A Fwd-Tableau for Computing $\mathsf{LP}(F, S, S, F')$, where $S = \overline{\{\mathsf{p}, \neg\mathsf{p}, \mathsf{q}, \neg\mathsf{q}\}}$ (For the Legend, see Example 18 on p. 134)

Proposition 126 *If N is an a-node in a fwd-tableau that is linklessness-preserving for a literal scope S, and $N_1, \ldots, N_n$ are the children of N, then for all $i, j \in \{1, \ldots, n\}$ such that $i \neq j$ it holds that*

$$\langle \mathsf{leafy}(N_i), \mathsf{leafy}(N_j) \rangle \text{ is linkless outside } S.$$

Proof.

(1) For $i \in \{1, \ldots, n\}$: if N'' is a descendant of N_i with parent N', then $\mathcal{L}(L_{N''} \wedge F_{N''}) \subseteq \mathcal{L}(F_{N'}) \cup (S \cap \widetilde{S})$.

(2) For $i \in \{1, \ldots, n\}$: if N' is a descendant of N_i, then $\mathcal{L}(L_{N'} \wedge F_{N'}) \subseteq \mathcal{L}(F_{N_i}) \cup (S \cap \widetilde{S})$.

(3) For $i \in \{1, \ldots, n\}$: $\mathcal{L}(\mathsf{leafy}(N_i)) \subseteq \mathcal{L}(L_{N_i} \wedge F_{N_i}) \cup (S \cap \widetilde{S})$.

(4) For $i, j \in \{1, \ldots, n\}$ such that $i \neq j$: $\langle \mathsf{leafy}(N_i), \mathsf{leafy}(N_j) \rangle$ is linkless outside S.

(1) follows from the *linklessness-preserving* property (Definition 83.ii). (2) follows from (1) by straightforward induction. (3) follows from (2) and the definition of leafy. (4) follows from (3) and the *linklessness-preserving* property (Definition 83.i).

□

The condition of Definition 83.ii does not constrain the literal base of forward labels and literal labels with respect to literals in $S \cap \widetilde{S}$. Thus, if $S = \mathsf{GLITS}$, this condition is trivially satisfied. A further aspect of the phrase $S \cap \widetilde{S}$ in Definition 83.ii is discussed in Section 11.2.4.

Proposition 127 *If T is a fwd-tableau and S, S' are literal scopes, then*

if T is linklessness-preserving for S and $S \subseteq S'$, then
T is linklessness-preserving for S'.

Proof. Follows easily from the definitions of *linklessness-preserving* (Definition 83) and *linkless outside* (Definition 64).

□

9.2.2 The Branch Completeness Property PB-L

PB-L, specified in the following definition, is a property that applies to a node and is parameterized with a literal scope. As Proposition 129 shows, the PB-L condition is used as criterion for determining that the construction of a branch of a tableau that should satisfy LP-L is complete. Thus PB-L is called a *branch completeness property*.

Definition 84 (Branch Completeness Property PB-L) If N is a node in a fwd-tableau and S is a literal scope, then N satisfies the property $\mathsf{PB\text{-}L}_S$ if and only if

$$(B_N \land F_N) \text{ is polar and linkless outside } S.$$

Example 20 (Branch Completeness Property $\mathsf{PB\text{-}L}_S$) Consider the fwd-tableau in Fig. 9.3. Let $S \overset{\text{def}}{=} \overline{\{\mathsf{p}, \neg\mathsf{p}, \mathsf{q}, \neg\mathsf{q}\}}$. Node 3 does not satisfy $\mathsf{PB\text{-}L}_S$ since F_3 contains for example p and $\neg\mathsf{p}$ in different clauses. Node 4′ satisfies $\mathsf{PB\text{-}L}_S$ since $(\mathsf{p} \land ((\mathsf{t} \lor \mathsf{v}) \land \mathsf{u}))$ is clearly linkless outside S.

9.2.3 Leafy Sentences that Satisfy LP-L

Proposition 129 shows conditions under which leafy sentences associated with fwd-tableaux satisfy the LP-L condition, that is, are linkless outside some scope. The auxiliary Proposition 128 is used to prove Proposition 129.

Proposition 128 *If N is a node in a fwd-tableau and L is a ground literal such that $L \in \mathcal{L}(\mathsf{leafy}(N))$, then there exists a node N' that is identical to N or a descendant of N such that*

$$L \in \mathcal{L}(L_{N'}), \text{ or}$$
$$L \in \mathcal{L}(F_{N'}) \text{ and } N' \text{ is a leaf node.}$$

Proof. Easy to see from the definition of leafy.

□

Proposition 129 *If T is a fwd-tableau that is linklessness-preserving for a literal scope S and all leaf nodes of T satisfy* $\mathsf{PB\text{-}L}_S$, *then*

$$\mathsf{leafy}(T) \textit{ is polar and linkless outside } S.$$

Proof. We show that if N is a node in a fwd-tableau that is linklessness-preserving for a literal scope S and all descendants of N that are leaf nodes satisfy $\mathsf{PB\text{-}L}_S$ with respect to the branch starting from N, then

$$\mathsf{leafy}(N) \textit{ is polar and linkless outside } S.$$

The proposition immediately follows from this fact. The *polar* property easily follows from the definition of PB-L, since the construction of the leafy sentence only involves the $\wedge$ and $\vee$ operators. The proof of the *linkless* property proceeds by induction on the structure of the tableau, bottom-up from leaf nodes to the root. In the base case, where N is a leaf node, it holds that $\mathsf{leafy}(N) = (L_N \wedge F_N)$. The branch to N that starts from N, considered as a sentence, equals L_N. Thus, if N satisfies the $\mathsf{PB\text{-}L}_S$ property as stated in the preconditions of the proposition, then $(L_N \wedge F_N)$ is linkless outside S; hence $\mathsf{leafy}(N)$ is linkless outside S. The induction step for an o-node N whose children are $N_1, \ldots, N_n$ can be shown as follows:

(1) $\mathsf{leafy}(N) = L_N \wedge \bigvee_{i\in\{1,\ldots,n\}} \mathsf{leafy}(N_i)$.
(2) L_N is linkless outside S.
(3) For $i \in \{1,\ldots,n\}$: $\mathsf{leafy}(N_i)$ is linkless outside S.
(4) $\bigvee_{i\in\{1,\ldots,n\}} \mathsf{leafy}(N_i)$ is linkless outside S.
(5) $\widetilde{\mathcal{L}(L_N)} \cap \mathcal{L}(\bigvee_{i\in\{1,\ldots,n\}} \mathsf{leafy}(N_i)) \subseteq S \cap \widetilde{S}$.
(6) $\mathsf{leafy}(N)$ is linkless outside S.

(1) follows from the definition of leafy. (2) follows from the PB-L precondition. (Step (2) also holds trivially if literal labels are restricted as in Definition 80.) (3) holds by the induction assumption. (4) follows from (3) and the definition of *linkless formula*. (5) follows from the $\mathsf{PB\text{-}L}_S$ precondition and Proposition 128: If (5) were false, by Proposition 128 there would exist a descendant N' of N such that $\widetilde{\mathcal{L}(L_N)} \cap \mathcal{L}(L'_N) \not\subseteq S \cap \widetilde{S}$, or N' is a leaf node and $\widetilde{\mathcal{L}(L_N)} \cap \mathcal{L}(F'_N) \not\subseteq S \cap \widetilde{S}$. The PB-L precondition would fail in both cases, either for N' itself if it is a leaf node, or for the leaf descendants of N'. (6) follows from (5) and (4).

The induction step for an a-node N whose children are $N_1, \ldots, N_n$ follows in the same way as the induction step for an o-node, with the $\bigwedge$ connective in place of $\bigvee$. Step (4) follows from Proposition 126, since T is linklessness-preserving for S.

□

9.3 Ensuring LP-U

In Section 9.3.1 *upward-preserving*, a constraint on fwd-tableaux, which is parameterized with a literal scope, is specified. It is shown that the leafy sentence of a fwd-tableau T that is upward preserving for a literal scope S satisfies the LP-U condition with respect to the forward label of its root node: $\mathsf{leafy}(T) \models_S F_{\mathsf{root}(T)}$.

9.3.1 Upward-Preserving Fwd-Tableaux

Definition 85 (Upward-Preserving) A fwd-tableau is called *upward-preserving for* a literal scope S if and only if for all nodes N in the fwd-tableau whose children are $N_1, \ldots, N_n$ it holds that

(i) If N is an o-node, then

$$\bigvee_{i \in \{1,\ldots,n\}} (B_{N_i} \land \mathsf{project}(F_{N_i}, S)) \models \mathsf{project}(F_N, S);$$

(ii) If N is an a-node, then

$$\bigwedge_{i \in \{1,\ldots,n\}} (B_{N_i} \land \mathsf{project}(F_{N_i}, S)) \models \mathsf{project}(F_N, S).$$

Example 21 (Upward-Preserving for GLITS) The fwd-tableau in Fig. 9.1 (p. 135) is upward-preserving for GLITS. Since for all sentences F it holds that $\mathsf{project}(F, \mathsf{GLITS}) \equiv F$ (Proposition 44), the project operator in the conditions for *upward-preserving* can be dropped. Consider for example node 4. The sentence B_4 is p. The forward labels F_4 and F_3 are the boxed formulas at nodes 4 and 3, respectively. It is easy to see that

$$\mathsf{p} \land F_4 \models F_3.$$

As a second example, consider node 1, an a-node. $B_1 = \top$. The forward label F_2 is just the last clause of F_1. The forward label F_3 is the conjunction of the other clauses of F_1. It is easy to see that

$$F_2 \land F_3 \models F_1.$$

Example 22 (Upward-Preserving for an Atom Scope) Let S be defined as $\overline{\{\mathsf{p}, \neg\mathsf{p}, \mathsf{q}, \neg\mathsf{q}\}}$. S represents an atom scope, since $S = \widetilde{S}$. The fwd-tableau in Fig. 9.3 (p. 137) is upward-preserving for S. We show exemplarily that the condition of Definition 85.i of the definition of *upward-preserving* is satisfied for node $4'$ in relation to 3, i. e., that it holds that:

$$\text{(v)} \qquad \mathsf{p} \land \mathsf{project}(F_{4'}, S) \models \mathsf{project}(F_3, S).$$

Nodes 1 to 3 are the same as in Fig. 9.1. In Example 21 we have seen that for the tableau of Fig. 9.1 it holds that

(vi) $$\mathsf{p} \land F_4 \models F_3.$$

The forward label $F_{4'}$ in Fig. 9.3 can be considered as being obtained from F_4 by applying the *isol* simplification (see Section 7.4.2) upon q. Thus

(vii) $$\mathsf{project}(F_4, S) \equiv \mathsf{project}(F_{4'}, S).$$

That statements (vi) and (vii) imply (v) can be shown as follows:

(1) $\mathsf{project}(\mathsf{p} \land F_4, S) \models \mathsf{project}(F_3, S)$.
(2) $\mathsf{project}(\mathsf{p}, S) \land \mathsf{project}(F_4, S) \models \mathsf{project}(F_3, S)$.
(3) $\mathsf{p} \land \mathsf{project}(F_4, S) \models \mathsf{project}(F_3, S)$.

(1) follows from (vi) by Proposition 31. (2) follows from (1) and Theorem 2, since $\langle \mathsf{p}, F_4 \rangle$ is linkless outside S. (3) follows from (2) and Proposition 30. (v) follows from (3) and (vii).

Example 23 (Upward-Preserving for a Literal Scope) The fwd-tableau in Fig. 9.4 is identical to the fwd-tableau in Fig. 9.3, except for node 4″. It is upward-preserving for $\overline{\{\neg \mathsf{p}, \neg \mathsf{q}\}}$, a scope that contains p and q just positively.

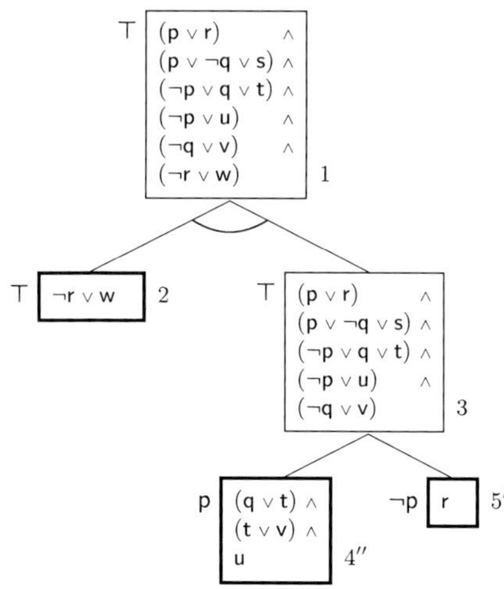

Figure 9.4. A Fwd-Tableau for Computing $\mathsf{LP}(F, S, S, F')$, where $S = \overline{\{\neg \mathsf{p}, \neg \mathsf{q}\}}$ (For the Legend, see Example 18 on p. 134)

9.3.2 Leafy Sentences that Satisfy LP-U

Proposition 130 *If T is a fwd-tableau that is upward-preserving for a literal scope S, then*

$$\mathsf{leafy}(T) \models_S F_{\mathsf{root}(T)}.$$

Proof. We show that if N is a node in a fwd-tableau that is upward-preserving for a literal scope S, then

$$\mathsf{leafy}(N) \models \mathsf{project}(F_N, S).$$

The proposition follows from this fact, since $\mathsf{leafy}(T) = \mathsf{leafy}(\mathsf{root}(T))$ and from $\mathsf{leafy}(T) \models \mathsf{project}(F_{\mathsf{root}(T)}, S)$ follows by Proposition 36 that $\mathsf{leafy}(T) \models_S F_{\mathsf{root}(T)}$. The proof proceeds by induction on the structure of the tableau, bottom-up from leaf nodes to the root. In the base case, where N is a leaf node, $\mathsf{leafy}(N) = (L_N \land F_N)$; thus $\mathsf{leafy}(N) \models F_N$. From Proposition 30 then follows $\mathsf{leafy}(N) \models \mathsf{project}(F_N, S)$. The induction step for an o-node N whose children are $N_1, \ldots, N_n$ can be shown as follows:

(1) $\mathsf{leafy}(N) = L_N \land \bigvee_{i \in \{1,\ldots,n\}} \mathsf{leafy}(N_i)$.
(2) $\mathsf{leafy}(N) \models L_N \land \bigvee_{i \in \{1,\ldots,n\}} (L_{N_i} \land \mathsf{leafy}(N_i))$.
(3) $\mathsf{leafy}(N) \models L_N \land \bigvee_{i \in \{1,\ldots,n\}} (L_{N_i} \land \mathsf{project}(F_{N_i}, S))$.
(4) $\mathsf{leafy}(N) \models \bigvee_{i \in \{1,\ldots,n\}} (B_{N_i} \land \mathsf{project}(F_{N_i}, S))$.
(5) $\mathsf{leafy}(N) \models \mathsf{project}(F_N, S)$.

(1) follows from the definition of leafy. (2) follows from (1), since by the definition of leafy for $i \in \{1, \ldots, n\}$ it holds that $\mathsf{leafy}(N_i) \models L_{N_i}$. (3) follows from (2), since by the induction assumption for $i \in \{1, \ldots, n\}$ it holds that $\mathsf{leafy}(N_i) \models \mathsf{project}(F_{N_i}, S)$. (4) follows from (3), since for $i \in \{1, \ldots, n\}$ it holds that $B_{N_i} \equiv B_N \land L_{N_i}$. (5) follows from (4) and the *upward-preserving* property (Definition 85.i).

The induction step for an a-node N whose children are $N_1, \ldots, N_n$ follows in the same way as the induction step for an o-node, with the $\bigwedge$ connective in place of $\bigvee$ and Definition 85.ii in the role of Definition 85.i.

□

9.3.3 A Further Possibility to Specify *Upward-Preserving*

With additional assumptions, the two conditions of *upward-preserving* are equivalent to simpler conditions. The first of these assumptions is that for all nodes N it holds that

(viii) $$B_N \land \mathsf{project}(F_N, S) \models \mathsf{project}(B_N \land F_N, S).$$

This assumption follows from Theorem 2 if for all nodes N it holds that $\langle B_N, F_N \rangle$ is linkless outside S. In variants of the DPLL method for propositional logic, the forward label F_N of a node N is considered as obtained from the forward label of the parent node by substituting all atoms that appear in B_N with truth values. Since F_N and B_N then obviously have disjoint atom bases, their pair $\langle B_N, F_N\rangle$ is linkless outside S, implying assumption (viii).

Under assumption (viii), the condition of Definition 85.i is equivalent to

$$\bigvee_{i\in\{1,\ldots,n\}} (B_{N_i} \land F_{N_i}) \models \mathsf{project}(F_N, S).$$

The left-to-right direction of this equivalence follows from Proposition 30, which implies $\bigvee_{i\in\{1,\ldots,n\}}(B_{N_i} \land F_{N_i}) \models \bigvee_{i\in\{1,\ldots,n\}}(B_{N_i} \land \mathsf{project}(F_{N_i}, S))$. The right-to-left direction can be shown as follows:

(1) $\bigvee_{i\in\{1,\ldots,n\}}(B_{N_i} \land F_{N_i}) \models \mathsf{project}(F_N, S)$.
(2) $\mathsf{project}(\bigvee_{i\in\{1,\ldots,n\}}(B_{N_i} \land F_{N_i}), S) \models \mathsf{project}(F_N, S)$.
(3) $\bigvee_{i\in\{1,\ldots,n\}} \mathsf{project}(B_{N_i} \land F_{N_i}, S) \models \mathsf{project}(F_N, S)$.
(4) $\bigvee_{i\in\{1,\ldots,n\}}(\mathsf{project}(B_{N_i}, S) \land \mathsf{project}(F_{N_i}, S)) \models \mathsf{project}(F_N, S)$.
(5) $\bigvee_{i\in\{1,\ldots,n\}}(B_{N_i} \land \mathsf{project}(F_{N_i}, S)) \models \mathsf{project}(F_N, S)$.

(2) follows from (1) and Proposition 36. (3) follows from (2) and Proposition 74. (4) follows from (3) and assumption (viii). (5), the condition of Definition 85.i, follows from (4) and Proposition 30. Equivalence of the condition of Definition 85.ii to

$$\bigwedge_{i\in\{1,\ldots,n\}} (B_{N_i} \land F_{N_i}) \models \mathsf{project}(F_N, S)$$

can be shown in a similar way, with the $\bigwedge$ connective in place of $\bigvee$. However, deriving the analogs of step (3) from (2) requires the additional assumption

(ix) $$\bigwedge_{i\in\{1,\ldots,n\}} \mathsf{project}(B_{N_i} \land F_{N_i}, S) \models \mathsf{project}(\bigwedge_{i\in\{1,\ldots,n\}} (B_{N_i} \land F_{N_i}), S).$$

This assumption follows from Theorem 2 if for all a-nodes whose children are $N_1, \ldots, N_n$ it holds that if $i, j \in \{1, \ldots, n\}$ and $j \neq i$, then $\langle (B_{N_i} \land F_{N_i}), (B_{N_j} \land F_{N_j})\rangle$ is linkless outside S. A sufficient condition for this is that 1. for all nodes N it holds that $\langle B_N, F_N\rangle$ is linkless outside S; 2. for all branches B it holds that $\langle B, B\rangle$ is linkless outside S (if only ground literals are used besides $\top$ as literal labels, this holds if branches are non-complementary, i. e., do never contain two nodes with a literal and its complement as literal labels); and 3. the tableau satisfies the linklessness-preserving condition of Definition 83.i for S.

9.4 Ensuring LP-D

That the leafy sentence of a fwd-tableaux T satisfies the LP-D condition, $F \models \mathsf{leafy}(T)$, follows from the interplay of two constraints:

- The *extensional* property, which affects the *literal labels* of the tableau in relation to the forward label of the root node. *Extensional* is defined in Section 9.4.1. Its application to verify LP-D is shown in Section 9.4.3. As we will see in Section 9.4.4, many familiar tableau methods for theorem proving construct tableaux with the *extensional* property for the input sentence. In Section 9.4.5 the *extensional* property is related to associated sentences of tableaux.
- The second property, *branch implied forward labels*, constrains the forward labels of nodes such that they have to be implied by the branch to the node and the forward label of the parent node. This property is defined in Section 9.4.2. Its application to verify LP-D in combination with the *extensional* property is shown in Section 9.4.3. Like *extensional*, this is also a property of tableaux constructed by many familiar methods. This is particularly straightforward to see for variants of the DPLL method for propositional logic, where the forward label F_N of a node N is considered as obtained from the forward label of the parent node by substituting all atoms that appear in B_N with truth values according to their polarity in B_N. A rule that is not compatible with branch implied forward labels is Disjoint, which, along with a compatible substitute, is discussed in Section 14.3.

9.4.1 Extensional Fwd-Tableaux

Definition 86 (Extensional) A fwd-tableau T is called *extensional* if and only if for all nodes N in T whose children are $N_1, \ldots, N_n$ it holds that

(i) If N is an o-node, then

$$F_{\mathsf{root}(T)} \land B_N \models \bigvee_{i \in \{1,\ldots,n\}} L_{N_i};$$

(ii) If N is an a-node, then

$$F_{\mathsf{root}(T)} \land B_N \models \bigwedge_{i \in \{1,\ldots,n\}} L_{N_i}.$$

Example 24 (Extensional) It is easy to see that the fwd-tableau in Fig. 9.3 (p. 137) is extensional: O-nodes have two children with complementary ground literals as literal labels. Their disjunction is a tautology, such that the condition of Definition 86.i of *extensional* is trivially satisfied. Also the condition of Definition 86.ii is trivially satisfied, since children of a-nodes have $\top$ as literal label.

9.4.2 Branch Implied Forward Labels

The definition of *branch implied forward labels* is succeeded by Proposition 131, which states that this property entails a similar property: The formula labels of nodes are implied by the branch to the node and the formula label of the *root node*. While the definition of *branch implied forward labels* seems more straightforward to verify for the rules of a calculus, since it only relates nodes with their parents, in the proof of the LP-D condition (Proposition 132) the property of Proposition 131 is used.

Definition 87 (Branch Implied Forward Labels) A fwd-tableau is said to have *branch implied forward labels* if and only if for all nodes N, N' in the tableau such that N' is a child of N it holds that

$$F_N \land B_{N'} \models F_{N'}.$$

Example 25 (Branch Implied Forward Labels) It is easy to verify that the fwd-tableaux in Fig. 9.3 (p. 137) has branch implied forward labels. An example instantiation of the condition of Definition 87 where N is an o-node is $(F_3 \land \mathsf{p}) \models F_{4'}$. An example where N is an a-node is $F_1 \models F_3$.

Proposition 131 *If N is a node in a fwd-tableau T with branch implied forward labels, then*

$$F_{\mathsf{root}(T)} \land B_N \models F_N.$$

Proof. We show that if $N_1 \ldots N_n$ is a branch in a fwd-tableau with branch implied forward labels and $i \in \{1, \ldots, n\}$, then

$$F_{N_i} \land B_{N_n} \models F_{N_n}.$$

The proposition immediately follows from this fact. The proof proceeds by induction on the length of the sequence $N_i \ldots N_n$. In the base case, where $n = i$, it is evident that $(F_{N_i} \land B_{N_n}) \models F_{N_n}$. The induction step for $n > i$ can be shown as follows:

(IA) $F_{N_i} \land B_{N_{n-1}} \models F_{N_{n-1}}$.
(1) $F_{N_{n-1}} \land B_{N_n} \models F_{N_n}$.
(IC) $F_{N_i} \land B_{N_n} \models F_{N_n}$.

(IA) is the induction assumption. (1) follows from the definition of *branch implied forward labels* (Definition 87). (IC), the induction conclusion, follows from (1) and (IA).

□

9.4.3 Leafy Sentences that Satisfy LP-D

Proposition 132 *If T is a fwd-tableau such that*

- *T is extensional,*
- *$L_{\mathsf{root}(T)} = \top$, and*
- *T has branch implied forward labels,*

then

$$F_{\mathsf{root}(T)} \models \mathsf{leafy}(T).$$

Proof. We show that if N is a node in T, then

$$F_{\mathsf{root}(T)} \wedge B_N \models \mathsf{leafy}(N).$$

The proposition easily follows from this fact, since $B_{\mathsf{root(T)}} \equiv \top$ and $\mathsf{leafy}(T) = \mathsf{leafy}(\mathsf{root}(T))$. The proof proceeds by induction on the structure of T, bottom-up from leaf nodes to the root. In the base case, where N is a leaf node, since T has branch implied forward labels, it follows from Proposition 131 that $(F_{\mathsf{root}(T)} \wedge B_N) \models F_N$. Since $B_N \models L_N$ and $\mathsf{leafy}(N) = (L_N \wedge F_N)$ it follows that $(F_{\mathsf{root}(T)} \wedge B_N) \models \mathsf{leafy}(N)$. The induction step where N is an o-node whose children are $N_1, \ldots, N_n$ can be shown as follows:

(IA) For $i \in \{1, \ldots, n\}$: $F_{\mathsf{root}(T)} \wedge B_{N_i} \models \mathsf{leafy}(N_i)$.
(1) $F_{\mathsf{root}(T)} \wedge B_N \models \bigvee_{i \in \{1,\ldots,n\}} L_{N_i}$.
(2) $F_{\mathsf{root}(T)} \wedge B_N \models \bigvee_{i \in \{1,\ldots,n\}} B_{N_i}$.
(3) $F_{\mathsf{root}(T)} \wedge B_N \models \bigvee_{i \in \{1,\ldots,n\}} \mathsf{leafy}_{N_i}$.
(4) $F_{\mathsf{root}(T)} \wedge B_N \models L_N \wedge \bigvee_{i \in \{1,\ldots,n\}} \mathsf{leafy}_{N_i}$.
(IC) $F_{\mathsf{root}(T)} \wedge B_N \models \mathsf{leafy}(N)$.

(IA) is the induction assumption. (1) follows from the definition of *extensional* (Definition 86.i). (2) follows from (1), since for $i \in \{1, \ldots, n\}$ it holds that $B_{N_i} \equiv (B_N \wedge L_{N_i})$. (3) follows from (2) and (IA). (4) follows from (3), since $B_N \models L_N$. (IC), the induction conclusion, follows from (4) and the definition of leafy. The induction step for an a-node N whose children are $N_1, \ldots, N_n$ follows in the same way as the induction step for an o-node, with the $\bigwedge$ connective in place of $\bigvee$ and Definition 86.ii in the role of Definition 86.i.

□

9.4.4 Construction of Extensional Fwd-Tableaux

It is easy to see that many of the familiar rules for the construction of clausal tableaux to show unsatisfiability of an input sentence preserve the *extensional* property for the input sentence. Examples include attaching to a leaf node a "cut" (two children with complementary literal labels), a clause from the input sentence (for each literal in the clause a child labeled with that literal), or a single child that has been inferred by unit propagation from the input sentence and the branch to the leaf node.

We specify in Definition 88 abstract tableau construction operations, *Extension*, *A-Extension* and *Truncation*, which, as stated in Proposition 133, preserve the *extensional* property. A concrete method then can be shown to construct extensional tableaux by proving that each of its rules performs instances of these abstract operations. It is easy to see that the familiar rules just mentioned are instances of *Extension*. *Truncation* can be used to model tableau construction techniques that involve destructive operations. In particular, certain kinds of dependency directed backtracking can be understood as a *Truncation* step followed by an *Extension* step, which is shown in Section 10.2.

The *A-Extension* operation is included mainly to allow handling of a-nodes analogously to o-nodes. An example for *A-Extension* is the Disconnect rule (Section 11.2.6, p. 176), which only attaches children with literal label $\top$, such that the condition of Definition 88.ii is trivially satisfied.

In Definition 88 we make use of operational metaphors and describe tableau construction operations as tree modifications. These operations can obviously be understood declaratively as specifications of mappings between fwd-tableaux.

Definition 88 (Extension and Truncation) A fwd-tableau T' is obtained from a fwd-tableau T by

(i) *Extension* if and only if T' is obtained from T by labeling a leaf node N in T as an o-node and attaching children $N_1, \ldots, N_n$, where $n \geq 1$, to N such that

$$F_{\mathsf{root}(T)} \wedge B_N \models \bigvee_{i \in \{1,\ldots,n\}} L_{N_i};$$

(ii) *A-Extension* if and only if T' is obtained from T by labeling a leaf node N in T as an a-node and attaching children $N_1, \ldots, N_n$, where $n \geq 1$, to N such that

$$F_{\mathsf{root}(T)} \wedge B_N \models \bigwedge_{i \in \{1,\ldots,n\}} L_{N_i};$$

(iii) *Truncation* if and only if T' is obtained from T by removing all children from some node (this node is then no longer labeled as o-node or a-node, respectively).

Proposition 133 *If T, T' are fwd-tableaux, T is extensional and T' is obtained from T by applying* Extension, A-Extension *or* Truncation, *then*

$$T' \textit{ is extensional.}$$

Proof. Follows easily from the definitions of *Extension*, *A-Extension*, *Truncation* (Definition 88) and the *extensional* property (Definition 86).

□

In specifications of rule preconditions it can be convenient to refer to the "local" forward label of a leaf node, instead of "globally" to the forward label of the root node. The specification of the *Extension* operation refers to the forward label of the root node. Proposition 134 shows, however, that for fwd-tableaux with branch implied formula labels also operations that instead refer to the forward label of a leaf node are instances of *Extension*.

Proposition 134 *If T is a fwd-tableau with branch implied forward labels and T' is obtained from T by labeling a leaf node N in T as an o-node and attaching children $N_1, \ldots, N_n$, where $n \geq 1$, to N such that*

$$B_N \wedge F_N \models \bigvee_{i \in \{1,\ldots,n\}} L_{N_i},$$

then T' is obtained from T by Extension.

Proof.

(1) $F_{\mathsf{root}(T)} \wedge B_N \models F_N$.
(2) $F_N \wedge B_N \models \bigvee_{i \in \{1,\ldots,n\}} L_{N_i}$.
(3) $F_{\mathsf{root}(T)} \wedge B_N \models \bigvee_{i \in \{1,\ldots,n\}} L_{N_i}$.

(1) follows from the assumption that T has branch implied forward labels. Assume (2). (3), which matches the specification of *Extension* (Definition 88.i), follows from (2) and (1). □

The analog of Proposition 134 for a-nodes can be shown in a similar way. We omit this, since later on we will only consider concrete calculi in which children of a-nodes always get $\top$ as literal labels, such that the construction of a-nodes trivially corresponds to *A-Extension*.

9.4.5 Extensional Fwd-Tableaux and Associated Sentences

Proposition 135 and its corollary Proposition 136 show the relationship between the *extensional* property and associated sentences of tableaux.

Proposition 135 *If T is a fwd-tableau, then the following statements are equivalent:*

T is extensional;

For all nodes N in T it holds that $F_{\mathsf{root}(T)} \wedge B_N \models \mathsf{sentence}(N)$.

Proof.
Left to Right. By induction on the structure of the tableau rooted at N, proceeding bottom-up from leaf nodes to the root. In the base case, where N is a leaf node, $\mathsf{sentence}(N) = L_N$. Since $B_N \models L_N$ it follows that $(F_{\mathsf{root}(T)} \wedge B_N) \models \mathsf{sentence}(N)$. The induction step for the case that N is an o-node whose children are $N_1, \ldots, N_n$ can be shown as follows:

(IA) For $i \in \{1, \ldots, n\}$: $F_{\mathsf{root}(T)} \wedge B_{N_i} \models \mathsf{sentence}(N_i)$.
(1) For $i \in \{1, \ldots, n\}$: $F_{\mathsf{root}(T)} \wedge B_N \wedge L_{N_i} \models \mathsf{sentence}(N_i)$.
(2) $F_{\mathsf{root}(T)} \wedge B_N \models \bigvee_{i\in\{1,\ldots,n\}} L_{N_i}$.
(3) $F_{\mathsf{root}(T)} \wedge B_N \models \bigvee_{i\in\{1,\ldots,n\}} \mathsf{sentence}(N_i)$.
(4) $F_{\mathsf{root}(T)} \wedge B_N \models L_N \wedge \bigvee_{i\in\{1,\ldots,n\}} \mathsf{sentence}(N_i)$.
(IC) $F_{\mathsf{root}(T)} \wedge B_N \models \mathsf{sentence}(N)$.

(IA) is the induction assumption. (1) follows from (IA), since for $i \in \{1, \ldots, n\}$ it holds that $B_{N_i} \equiv (B_N \wedge L_{N_i})$. (2) follows from the assumption that the tableau containing N is extensional (Definition 86.i). (3) follows from (2) and (1). (4) follows from (3), since $B_N \models L_N$. (IC), the induction conclusion, follows from (4) and the definition of sentence. The induction step for the case that N is an a-node with children $N_1, \ldots, N_n$ can be shown in the same way, with the $\bigwedge$ connective in place of $\bigvee$ and Definition 86.ii in the role of Definition 86.i.

Right to Left.

(1) $F_{\mathsf{root}(T)} \wedge B_N \models \mathsf{sentence}(N)$.
(2) $F_{\mathsf{root}(T)} \wedge B_N \models \bigvee_{i\in\{1,\ldots,n\}} \mathsf{sentence}(N_i)$.
(3) $F_{\mathsf{root}(T)} \wedge B_N \models \bigvee_{i\in\{1,\ldots,n\}} L_{N_i}$.

In case N is an o-node in the tableau whose children are $N_1, \ldots, N_n$, the *extensional* property can be derived as follows: Assume (1). (2) follows from (1) and the definition of sentence. (3), the condition for *extensional* of Definition 86.i, follows from (2) and the definition of sentence. In case N is an a-node in the tableau whose children are $N_1, \ldots, N_n$, the condition of Definition 86.ii follows in the same way, with the $\bigwedge$ connective in place of $\bigvee$.

□

Proposition 136 *If T is a fwd-tableau that is extensional and $L_{\mathsf{root}(T)} = \top$, then*

$$F_{\mathsf{root}(T)} \models \mathsf{sentence}(T).$$

Proof. Follows from Proposition 135, since $B_{\mathsf{root}(T)} \equiv \top$ and $\mathsf{sentence}(T) = \mathsf{sentence}(\mathsf{root}(T))$.

□

9.5 Tableau Methods to Compute LP

In Sections 9.2–9.4 conditions on fwd-tableaux have been developed that ensure that their leafy sentences satisfy the LP-L, LP-U and LP-D relations, respectively. Theorem 8 combines them to a single list of conditions on fwd-tableau that ensures that their leafy sentence satisfies the LP relation.

Table 9.5 (p. 151) summarizes these conditions along with their definitions and thus shows the "interface" of the framework developed in Sections 9.2–9.4 to concrete tableau construction methods: If F is a sentence, S_l, S_p are literal scopes such that $S_l \subseteq S_p$, and T is a fwd-tableau such that for all nodes $N, N', N_1, \ldots, N_n$ in T it holds that the properties in the *Condition* column are satisfied, then it follows that $\mathsf{LP}(F, S_l, S_p, \mathsf{leafy}(T))$.

Theorem 8 (Tableaux for Computing LP) *If F is a sentence, S_l, S_p are literal scopes such that $S_l \subseteq S_p$, and T is a fwd-tableau such that*

1. *T is linklessness-preserving for S_l,*
2. *All leaf nodes of T satisfy $\mathsf{PB\text{-}L}_{S_l}$,*
3. *T is upward-preserving for S_p,*
4. *$F_{\mathsf{root}(T)} \models_{S_p} F$,*
5. *T is extensional,*
6. *$L_{\mathsf{root}(T)} = \top$,*
7. *T has branch implied forward labels,*
8. *$F \models F_{\mathsf{root}(T)}$,*

then

$$\mathsf{LP}(F, S_l, S_p, \mathsf{leafy}(T)).$$

Proof.

(1)	$\mathsf{leafy}(T)$ is polar and linkless outside S_l.	LP-L
(2)	$\mathsf{leafy}(T) \models_{S_p} F_{\mathsf{root}(T)}$.	
(3)	$\mathsf{leafy}(T) \models_{S_p} F$.	LP-U
(4)	$F_{\mathsf{root}(T)} \models \mathsf{leafy}(T)$.	
(5)	$F \models \mathsf{leafy}(T)$.	LP-D
(6)	$\mathsf{LP}(F, S_l, S_p, \mathsf{leafy}(T))$.	

(1) follows from preconditions 1. and 2. and Proposition 129. (2) follows from precondition 3. and Proposition 130. (3) follows from (2) and precondition 4. (4) follows from preconditions 5.–7. and Proposition 132. (5) follows from (4) and precondition 8. (6) follows from (5), (3), (1) and the definition of LP.

□

With respect to a tableau construction method, conditions 4., 6. and 8. typically concern the initialization phase: For a given input sentence F and specification of a literal scope S_p, an initial tableau consisting of a single root node with literal label $\top$ and a forward label that satisfies 4. and 6. complies with the framework. The remaining conditions with exception of 2., i.e., conditions 1., 3., 5., and 7., are typically invariants of the method, holding in all stages of the tableau construction. Condition 2. indicates when the construction of a branch is complete. Additional tools to ensure condition 5. are provided with the abstract operations *Extension* and *Truncation*. An example instantiation of this framework for a variant of the DPLL method will be developed in Chapter 11.

<table>
<tr><th></th><th>Condition</th><th>Used to Ensure</th></tr>
<tr><td>1.</td><td>T is linklessness-preserving for S_l
– If N, N' are different children of an a-node, then $\langle(L_N \wedge F_N), (L_{N'} \wedge F_{N'})\rangle$ is linkless outside S_l
– If N' is a child of N and an ancestor of N is an a-node, then $\mathcal{L}(L_{N'} \wedge F_{N'}) \subseteq \mathcal{L}(F_N) \cup (S_l \cap \widetilde{S_l})$</td><td rowspan="2">LP-L:
$\mathsf{leafy}(T)$ is polar and linkless outside S_l</td></tr>
<tr><td>2.</td><td>Leaf nodes of T satisfy $\mathsf{PB}\text{-}\mathsf{L}_{S_l}$
– If N is a leaf node, then $(B_N \wedge F_N)$ is polar and linkless outside S_l</td></tr>
<tr><td>3.</td><td>T is upward-preserving for S_p
if $N_1, \ldots, N_n$ are the children of N, then
– If N is an o-node, then $\bigvee_{i \in \{1,\ldots,n\}} (B_{N_i} \wedge \mathsf{project}(F_{N_i}, S)) \models \mathsf{project}(F_N, S)$
– If N is an a-node, then $\bigwedge_{i \in \{1,\ldots,n\}} (B_{N_i} \wedge \mathsf{project}(F_{N_i}, S)) \models \mathsf{project}(F_N, S)$</td><td rowspan="2">LP-U:
$\mathsf{leafy}(T) \models_{S_p} F$</td></tr>
<tr><td>4.</td><td>$F_{\mathsf{root}(T)} \models_{S_p} F$</td></tr>
<tr><td>5.</td><td>T is extensional
if $N_1, \ldots, N_n$ are the children of N, then
– If N is an o-node, then $F_{\mathsf{root}(T)} \wedge B_N \models \bigvee_{i \in \{1,\ldots,n\}} L_{N_i}$
– If N is an a-node, then $F_{\mathsf{root}(T)} \wedge B_N \models \bigwedge_{i \in \{1,\ldots,n\}} L_{N_i}$</td><td rowspan="4">LP-D:
$F \models \mathsf{leafy}(T)$</td></tr>
<tr><td>6.</td><td>$L_{\mathsf{root}(T)} = \top$</td></tr>
<tr><td>7.</td><td>T has branch implied forward labels
– If N' is a child of N, then $F_N \wedge B_{N'} \models F_{N'}$</td></tr>
<tr><td>8.</td><td>$F \models F_{\mathsf{root}(T)}$</td></tr>
</table>

Table 9.1. The Tableau Framework to Compute LP (See Section 9.5)

10 Dependency Directed Backtracking

Techniques for dependency directed backtracking belong to the key refinements of modern deduction systems based on DPLL and other tableau methods. We develop such a technique, *backjumping*, in the context of our tableau framework. It is based on the specification of backjumping for *Abstract DPLL* [NOT05, NOT06], which formally models the main technique used in modern DPLL-based SAT solvers [BS97, MSS96, ZM02] for backtracking in conjunction with the generation of context related unit lemmas. In the literature on satisfiability solving systems, such techniques are commonly specified in less accessible ways by means of pseudocode. Based on the notions of extensional tableaux and branch implied forward labels, backjumping fits smoothly with our framework and thus indicates that this framework covers systems efficient enough for practical application.

On top of the concept of *decision nodes*, defined in Section 10.1, the *Backjumping* operation is introduced in Section 10.2. Its is shown that it corresponds to a step of the *Truncation* abstract operation, followed by *Extension*. The *Backjumping* operation is not restricted to DPLL-like calculi, which construct variants of semantic trees, but more generally applies also to other methods that construct extensional tableaux, such as clausal tableau methods. This is a consequence of our definitions and is made explicit by means of an example. In Section 10.3 it is shown that chronological backtracking is a special case of backjumping, where the preconditions for application are particular easy to verify. In Section 10.4 a structural measure of tableaux is defined that is strictly reduced by the *Backjumping* operation, and thus can be employed in termination proofs. In Section 10.5 some subtleties are discussed that concern alternate possibilities of preconditions for backjumping: The preconditions can refer either "globally" to the forward label of the tableau root (or the input sentence), or "locally" to forward labels of nodes within the tableau. In Section 10.6 some features of backjumping particular to its use for formula transformation tasks, in contrast to theorem proving, are shown by means of examples.

10.1 Decision Nodes

The notion of *decision node* straightforwardly generalizes the concept of *decision literal* as defined for ADPLL [NOT06]. Proposition 137 shows the key property of decision nodes: The literal labels of all nodes of a branch are implied by the literal labels of just the decision nodes on the branch, along with the forward label of the root node.

Definition 89 (Decision Node)

(i) A node in a fwd-tableau that is the child of an o-node and has siblings is called *decision node.*

(ii) If N is a node of a fwd-tableau, then D_N is the sequence of decision nodes in B_N, in order as they appear in B_N. Similar as with B_N, we overload this notation and use D_N also for the conjunction of the literal labels of the nodes in the sequence.

Proposition 137 *If N is a node in an extensional fwd-tableau, then*

$$F_{\mathsf{root}(T)} \wedge L_{\mathsf{root}(T)} \wedge D_N \models B_N.$$

Proof. By induction on the length of B_N. In the base case, where $N = \mathsf{root}(T)$ it holds that $B_N \equiv L_N \equiv L_{\mathsf{root}(T)}$, which immediately implies $(F_{\mathsf{root}(T)} \wedge L_{\mathsf{root}(T)} \wedge D_N) \models B_N$. We now show the induction step.

(IA) $F_{\mathsf{root}(T)} \wedge L_{\mathsf{root}(T)} \wedge D_{N'} \models B_{N'}$.
(1) $D_N \equiv D_{N'} \wedge L_N$.
(IC) $F_{\mathsf{root}(T)} \wedge L_{\mathsf{root}(T)} \wedge D_N \models B_N$.

Let N' be the parent of N. (IA) is then induction assumption. Consider the case that N is a decision node. (1) follows from the definition of D_N. (IC), the induction conclusion, follows from (1) and (IA) since $B_N \equiv (B_{N'} \wedge L_N)$. In the case that N is not a decision node, the induction step can be shown as follows:

(2) $D_N \equiv D_{N'}$.
(3) $F_{\mathsf{root}(T)} \wedge B_{N'} \models L_N$.

(2) then follows from the definition of D_N. In case N' is an o-node, N is its only child. Thus the definition of *extensional* (Definition 86.i) implies (3). In case N' is an a-node, (3) follows immediately from the definition of *extensional* (Definition 86.ii). (IC), the induction conclusion, follows from (3), (2) and (IA), since $B_N \equiv (B_{N'} \wedge L_N)$.

□

10.2 Backjumping Preconditions and Operation

In Definition 91 *Backjumping*, an abstract operation, similar to *Extension* and *Truncation* (Definition 88), is specified. It is preceded by the specification of *backjumping preconditions* (Definition 90), which collects the conditions that a branch must match for *Backjumping* to be applicable. Theorem 9 then shows how the *Backjumping* operation can be modeled as *Truncation* followed by *Extension*. This modeling allows to conclude from Proposition 133 that *Backjumping* preserves the *extensional* property and thus can be safely included into methods that construct extensional tableaux.

Definition 90 (Backjumping Preconditions) A branch of a fwd-tableau T is said to match the *backjumping preconditions* if and only if it has the form

$$B_a N_a B_b N_b B_c,$$

where B_a, B_b, B_c are possibly empty sequences of nodes and N_a, N_b are nodes such that

1. The children of N_a are decision nodes,
2. N_b is a decision node, and
3. $F_{\mathsf{root}(T)} \wedge B_{N_a} \wedge L_{N_b} \models \bot$.

We use the parameter names in Proposition 90 $(B_a, N_a, B_b, N_b, B_c)$ to refer to the respective match components of given branches.

Definition 91 (Backjumping Operation) A fwd-tableau T' is obtained from a fwd-tableau T by *Backjumping* if and only if T' is obtained by replacing in a branch that matches *backjumping preconditions* the children of N_a with a single child with literal label $\widetilde{L_{N_b}}$.

Backjumping takes effect in situations where a tableau construction method has detected that for a leaf node N it holds that $(F_{\mathsf{root}(T)} \wedge B_N) \models \bot$, and thus tableau construction should not proceed below N. If additional information is available that the derivation of $\bot$ actually not depends on the full branch B_N, but just on some portions of it – the initial fragment B_{N_a} and the literal label L_{N_b} of a subsequent decision node – then the *Backjumping* operation can be performed. The more close to the root N_a is, the smaller is the tableau resulting from the *Backjumping* operation. Since N_b is added as the single child to N_a, its literal label L_{N_b} can be considered as a unit clause that becomes available as a lemma in the part of the tableau rooted at N_a, a so-called *context unit lemma* [LMG94].

As said above, this formalization is based on Abstract DPLL [NOT06], where its relation to concepts found in the literature on DPLL-based methods, such as *decision levels*, is shown in more detail. Our framework does not include an explicit representation of the dependency information used to determine B_{N_a} and N_b.

Theorem 9 (Backjumping as Truncation and Extension) *The* Backjumping *operation corresponds to a* Truncation *step (removing the children from N_a) followed by an* Extension *step (attaching the single child to N_a).*

Proof. N_a must be an o-node, since its children are decision nodes. Thus, removing the children from N_a is a *Truncation* step. From Precondition 3. of *backjumping preconditions* follows immediately that

$$F_{root}(T) \wedge B_{N_a} \models \widetilde{L_{N_b}}.$$

Thus, attaching a node with literal label $\widetilde{L_{N_b}}$ as single child to N_a is an *Extension* step.

□

Example 26 (Backjumping) Consider the left side of Figure 10.1. The figure shows a fwd-tableaux with its literal labels, which we also use to identify nodes in the example description. Assume

$$\begin{aligned} F_\top = (\neg \mathsf{p} \vee \neg \mathsf{r} \vee \mathsf{s}) \quad \wedge \\ (\neg \mathsf{p} \vee \neg \mathsf{r} \vee \neg \mathsf{s}). \end{aligned}$$

The branch to node s, which is displayed in bold, then matches *backjumping preconditions* with

$$B_a \equiv \top,\ N_a = \mathsf{p},\ B_b \equiv \mathsf{q},\ N_b = \mathsf{r},\ B_c \equiv \mathsf{s}.$$

Precondition 3., which is $(F_\top \wedge \mathsf{p} \wedge \mathsf{r}) \models \bot$, can be established, since the branch to s contradicts with the second clause of $F_\top$ and s is not a decision node (from Proposition 137 it follows that s is entailed by $F_\top$ and the decision nodes preceding s). The fwd-tableau that results from performing the *Backjumping* operation with respect to this matching is shown on the right side of Figure 10.1.

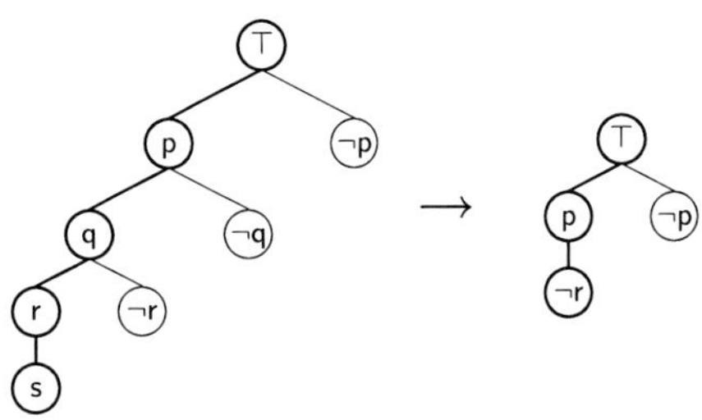

Figure 10.1. Backjumping Example

The fwd-tableau in Example 26 has the form of a semantic tree, as generated by DPLL methods: A node has at most two children, and siblings are labeled with complementary literals. Backjumping, as specified above, is however not restricted to fwd-tableaux of this form, but also applies to clausal tableaux in general.

Example 27 (Backjumping in a Clausal Tableau) Consider the fwd-tableau on the left side of Figure 10.2. As in Example 26, we use the displayed literal labels to identify nodes. Assume

$$\begin{aligned} F_{\top} = \ & (\mathsf{p} \lor \mathsf{t}) \land \\ & (\neg\mathsf{p} \lor \mathsf{q} \lor \mathsf{u}) \land \\ & (\neg\mathsf{q} \lor \mathsf{r} \lor \mathsf{v}) \land \\ & (\neg\mathsf{r} \lor \neg\mathsf{p}). \end{aligned}$$

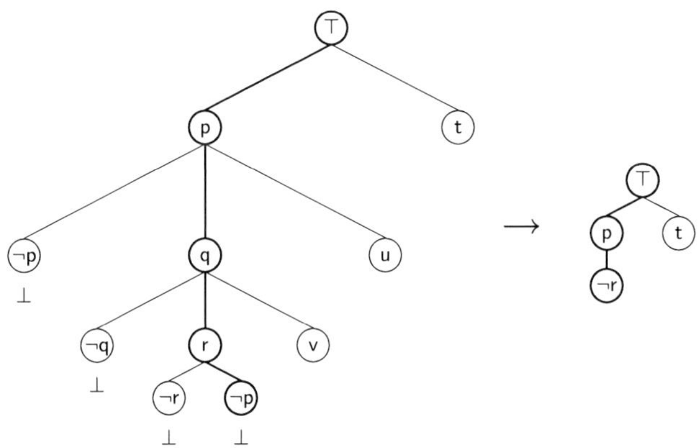

Figure 10.2. Backjumping in a Clausal Tableau

The tableau is a clausal tableau for $F_{\top}$, since for all nodes with children it holds that the disjunction of the literal labels of the children is a clause in $F_{\top}$. Branches which are *closed*, which means that they contain nodes with complementary literal labels, are indicated by $\bot$ in the figure. The branch displayed in bold matches *backjumping preconditions* with

$$B_a \equiv \top,\ N_a = \mathsf{p},\ B_b \equiv \mathsf{q},\ N_b = \mathsf{r},\ B_c \equiv \neg\mathsf{p}.$$

Precondition 3., which is $(F_{\top} \land \mathsf{p} \land \mathsf{r}) \models \bot$, can be established based on the fact that all branches through node r are closed, and p is the only ancestor of r on which this depends. The fwd-tableau resulting from performing the *Backjumping* operation with respect to this matching is shown on the right side of Figure 10.2. Of course, as can be seen from the example, the resulting tableau is not necessarily a clausal tableau anymore, but, as follows from Theorem 9, the *extensional* property is preserved by backjumping.

Folding up [LMG94] is a technique that has been developed for clausal tableau calculi and is closely related to related to our notion of backjumping. The clausal tableau structure is preserved by folding up, since the derived unit lemmas, such as $\neg\mathsf{r}$ in the example, are not incorporated into the tableau, but are associated as a special label type with edges. In our example the edge leading to p would receive $\neg\mathsf{r}$ as such a label. Unlike backjumping, folding up does not effect the destruction of already constructed parts of the tableau. Thus it corresponds to backjumping followed by further operations that reconstruct the tableau.

The example could be modified by omitting the leaf nodes marked with $\bot$. The tableau is then no longer a clausal tableau in the strict sense with disjunctions of siblings corresponding to clauses in $F_\top$, but it is still extensional. Precondition 3., which is $(F_\top \land \mathsf{p} \land \mathsf{r}) \models \bot$, can then be established in a similar way as in Example 26, since B_r contradicts with the clause $(\neg\mathsf{r} \lor \neg\mathsf{p})$ in $F_\top$.

10.3 Applicability of Chronological Backtracking

In Theorem 10 it is shown that whenever N is a node in an *extensional* fwd-tableau T such that

$$F_{\mathsf{root}(T)} \land B_N \models \bot,$$

then B_N matches *backjumping preconditions* with the last decision node in B_N as N_b. The backjumping step then just corresponds to chronological backtracking. This holds in general, also if no dependency information of how exactly $(F_{\mathsf{root}(T)} \land B_N) \models \bot$ has been derived is available. This property can be used for proving soundness of theorem proving methods, since it shows that in any situation where it has been established that $(F_{\mathsf{root}(T)} \land B_N) \models \bot$ (for example, by detecting that there is a clause in $F_{\mathsf{root}(T)}$ such that the complements of all of its literals are in B_N) backjumping is applicable, ensuring that alternative branches to B_N can not remain unexplored.

Theorem 10 (Applicability of Chronological Backtracking) *If N is a node in a fwd-tableau T that is extensional, $L_{\mathsf{root}(T)} = \top$,*

$$F_{\mathsf{root}(T)} \land B_N \models \bot,$$

and B_N contains a decision node, then B_N matches backjumping preconditions *such that*

- *N_b is the last decision node in B_N, and*
- *N_a is the parent of N_b.*

Proof. If B_N contains a decision node, then it also contains a last decision node. Precondition 1.–2. of *backjumping preconditions* are clearly satisfied for N_a and N_b as specified in the proposition. It remains to show precondition 3.:

(1) $F_{\mathsf{root}(T)} \wedge B_N \models \bot$.
(2) $F_{\mathsf{root}(T)} \wedge D_N \models \bot$.
(3) $F_{\mathsf{root}(T)} \wedge D_{N_b} \models \bot$.
(4) $F_{\mathsf{root}(T)} \wedge B_{N_b} \models \bot$.
(5) $F_{\mathsf{root}(T)} \wedge B_{N_a} \wedge L_{N_b} \models \bot$.

Assume (1), which is a precondition of the proposition. (2) follows from (1) and Proposition 137, since T is extensional and $L_{\mathsf{root}(T)} = \top$. Since N_b is the last decision node in B_N, it holds that $D_N \equiv D_{N_b}$. Thus (3) follows from (2). (4) follows from (3) and the definition of D_{N_b}. (5), which is precondition 3. of *backjumping preconditions*, follows from (4), since N_a is the parent of N_b. □

10.4 Reduction of the Outdegrees Along a Branch

Since N_a in *backjumping preconditions* is required to be the parent of a decision node, N_a must have more than a single child. After application of the *Backjumping* operation, it has just a single child. Thus the outdegree of N_a is strictly smaller after performing *Backjumping*. The ancestors of N_a are unchanged by *Backjumping*. Thus, with respect to lexical comparison of the sequence of outdegrees of their nodes, all branches through N_a in the tableau after application of *Backjumping* are strictly smaller than all branches through N_a in the tableau before. In Section 11.5 this property is used to show termination of a tableau construction method for propositional logic.

10.5 Preconditions that Refer to Non-Root Forward Labels

Precondition 3. of *backjumping preconditions* (Definition 90) and Theorem 10 "globally" refer to the forward label of the *root node* of a given fwd-tableau. We compare this with analogs where instead the forward label of other nodes are referenced, more "locally" related to the branch matched against *backjumping preconditions*. As Theorems 11 and 12 below show, for fwd-tableaux with branch implied forward labels the "local" variants are subsumed by the "global" ones. The reference to a "global" sentence in *backjumping preconditions* is reflected in the *extensional* property (Definition 86) and the *Extension* operation (Definition 88). It has already been shown in Proposition 134 that *Extension* subsumes for fwd-tableaux with branch implied forward labels an analogous "local" operation. Due to a-nodes and the involvement of projection in the upward-preserving precondition, a "local" variant of *backjumping preconditions* would be properly stronger than the "global" variant, as discussed following Theorem 12. However, it is open whether this additional freedom of the "global" backjumping can be utilized for any essential improvement towards the "local" variant.

In certain tableau construction methods it invariantly holds for all nodes N of the tableau T under construction that

$$\text{(i)} \qquad F_N \wedge B_N \equiv F_{\mathsf{root}(T)} \wedge B_N.$$

Abstract DPLL [NOT06], viewed in the fwd-tableau framework, is for example such a method. In Abstract DPLL forward labels F_N are only implicitly represented by B_N and $F_{\mathsf{root}(T)}$: The forward label F_N is $F_{\mathsf{root}(T)}$ with atoms occurring in B_N replaced by truth values according to their polarity in B_N. If (i) holds, then evidently conditions that "globally" refer to $F_{\mathsf{root}(T)}$ are equivalent to conditions that instead "locally" refer to F_N instead. For fwd-tableau with branch implied forward labels, the right-to-left direction of (i) follows from Proposition 131:

$$\text{(ii)} \qquad F_{\mathsf{root}(T)} \wedge B_N \models F_N \wedge B_N.$$

The "local" analog to Theorem 10, that a branch B_N matches *backjumping preconditions* for a chronological backtracking step whenever $(F_N \wedge B_N) \models \bot$, is stated for fwd-tableaux with branch implied forward labels as the following theorem:

Theorem 11 (Local Applicability of Chronological Backtracking) *If N is a node in a fwd-tableau T that is extensional and has branch implied forward labels, $L_{\mathsf{root}(T)} = \top$, and*

$$F_N \wedge B_N \models \bot,$$

and B_N contains a decision node, then B_N matches backjumping preconditions *such that*

- *N_b is the last decision node in B_N, and*
- *N_a is the parent of N_b.*

Proof. Follows easily from Theorem 10 and Proposition 131.

□

Theorem 12, which follows, shows that for fwd-tableaux with branch implied forward labels the third of *backjumping preconditions*, that is, $(F_{\mathsf{root}(T)} \wedge B_{N_a} \wedge L_{N_b}) \models \bot$, also is satisfied if it can be established that for some node N on the branch it holds that $(F_N \wedge B_{N_a} \wedge L_{N_b}) \models \bot$. Instead of the forward label of the root node, the forward label of node N is then referred.

Theorem 12 (Local Matching of Backjumping Preconditions) *If B is a branch of a fwd-tableau T with branch implied forward labels and B has the form*

$$B_a N_a B_b N_b B_c,$$

where B_a, B_b, B_c are possibly empty sequences of nodes and N_a, N_b are nodes such that

1. *The children of N_a are decision nodes,*
2. *N_b is a decision node, and*
3. *$F_N \wedge B_{N_a} \wedge L_{N_b} \models \bot$ for some node N in B_{N_a},*

then B matches backjumping preconditions *for B_a, N_a, B_b, N_b, B_c.*

Proof. Preconditions 1.–2. of *backjumping preconditions* (Definition 90) hold immediately. It remains to show precondition 3.:

(1) $F_N \wedge B_{N_a} \wedge L_{N_b} \models \bot$.
(2) $F_{\mathsf{root}(T)} \wedge B_N \models F_N$.
(3) $F_{\mathsf{root}(T)} \wedge B_N \wedge B_{N_a} \wedge L_{N_b} \models \bot$.
(4) $F_{\mathsf{root}(T)} \wedge B_{N_a} \wedge L_{N_b} \models \bot$.

Assume (1), item 3. of the preconditions of the proposition. (2) follows from Proposition 131, since T has branch implied forward labels. (3) follows from (2) and (1). (4), which is precondition 3. of *backjumping preconditions*, follows from (3), since N is in B_{N_a}.

□

Theorems 11 and 12 show that checks for backjumping preconditions can refer "locally" to forward labels of nodes on the active branch more close to its leaf, instead of just "globally" to the forward label of the root node. This might be more convenient for an implementation. However, these theorems also show that in all cases where the backjumping preconditions are satisfied with referencing to such a "local" forward label, they are also satisfied with referencing to the "global" root label. That is, with the "local" variant there do not arise additional situations in which backjumping is found to be applicable that could not also be detected by the "global" variant.

One might ask whether, conversely, with the "global" variant there arise situations in which backjumping is found to be applicable that could not be detected by a "local" variant. In principle this is indeed the case since the left-to-right direction of (i) is not implied by the conditions for fwd-tableau to compute LP presupposed in Theorem 8. One of the reasons is the mismatch with a-nodes: According to the clause for a-nodes of the definition of *upward-preserving* (Definition 85.ii), the conjunction of the forward labels of *all children* of an a-node is required for entailment of the forward label of the a-node. A second reason, which is independent of the presence of a-nodes, is that the *upward-preserving* conditions state that the forward label of parent nodes are entailed *only relative to a scope S_p* by the forward label of children and the branches to them. For fwd-tableaux T without a-nodes, from the clause for o-nodes of the definition of *upward-preserving* (Definition 85.i) it can be derived that

$$\text{(iii)} \qquad F_N \wedge B_N \models \mathsf{project}(F_{\mathsf{root}(T)}, S_p) \wedge B_N,$$

which is weaker than the left-to-right direction of (i). Entailment (iii) indicates that in situations where backjumping is found to be applicable with the "global" variant but not a "local" variant it holds that $F \wedge B_N \models \bot$ but not $\mathsf{project}(F_{\mathsf{root}(T)}, S_p) \wedge B_N \models \bot$. It remains an issue for future research to investigate under which conditions such situations actually might arise and whether methods can benefit from these additional possibilities to apply backjumping.

10.6 Backjumping in Transformation Tasks

For theorem proving or model computation tasks, backjumping is commonly applied with respect to a branch in which siblings to the right represent possibilities to explore in future computation and siblings to the left are either not present or can be ignored, since they correspond to parts of the problem that already have been solved. For transformation tasks this is different. Although siblings to the left might correspond to already transformed parts of the input formula, a backjumping step can effect that these are deleted and an improved transformation, in which more unit lemmas are available below some nodes, is computed.

We illustrate effects of backjumping for transformation tasks by means of some examples. They use tableaux in the form of semantic trees, such as constructed by DPLL methods: A node has at most two children and siblings are labeled with complementary literals. The figures show fwd-tableaux with their literal labels, which are also used to identify nodes in the example descriptions. The branches that are matched against *backjumping preconditions* are indicated by bold arcs and nodes.

Example 28 (Backjumping with N_b Having a Right Sibling) Consider the tableau fragment on the left side of Figure 10.3. Nodes p_5 and p_7 are the roots of subtrees T_5 and T_7. The branch to p_8 contains nodes with siblings to their left. Let F be the forward label of the root of the tableau and assume that it had been established that

$$\text{(iv)} \qquad F \wedge \mathsf{p}_2 \wedge \mathsf{p}_6 \models \bot.$$

The branch to p_8 then matches *backjumping preconditions* with $N_a = \mathsf{p}_3$, since the children of p_3 are decision nodes (precondition 1.), and $N_b = \mathsf{p}_6$, since p_6 is a decision node (precondition 2.). Precondition 3. is satisfied since (iv) entails

$$F \wedge B_{\mathsf{p}_3} \wedge \mathsf{p}_6 \models \bot.$$

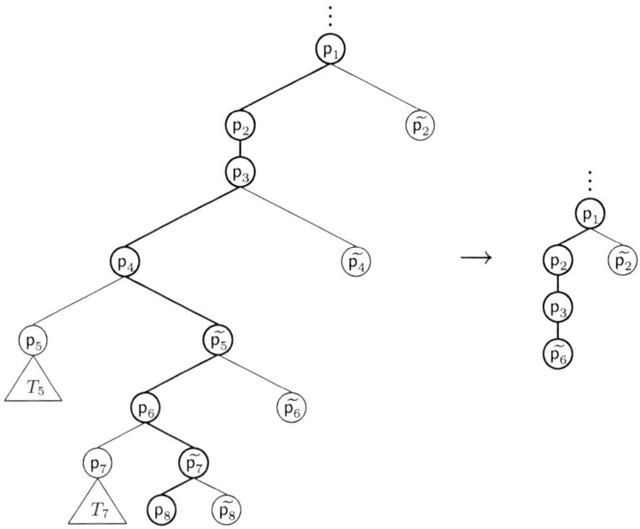

Figure 10.3. Backjumping with $N_b = \mathsf{p}_6$ Having a Right Sibling – See Example 28

The right side of Figure 10.3 shows the result of the applying the *Backjumping* operation with respect to this match. Node p_3 is retained in the result, since N_a is required to be the parent of a decision node. The subtree T_5 is not present in the result, which intuitively makes sense for two reasons: First, T_5 might depend on p_4 and thus can not be straightforwardly attached to the new active branch, which does not contain p_4. Second, after backjumping with the additional ancestor $\widetilde{\mathsf{p}_6}$, a simpler subtree than T_5 can possibly be constructed. Also the subtree T_7 is not present in the result. Actually, once $(F \wedge \mathsf{p}_2 \wedge \mathsf{p}_6) \models \bot$ has been established, the whole subtree rooted at p_6, including T_7, becomes void.

Example 29 (Backjumping with N_b Having a Left Sibling) Consider the tableau fragment displayed on the left side of Figure 10.4. It is identical to the left side of Figure 10.3 (p. 163) , except that the ordering of the siblings p_6 and $\widetilde{\mathsf{p}_6}$ is switched and $\widetilde{\mathsf{p}_6}$ is the root of a subtree T_6. If, as in Example 28, it is assumed that

$$F \wedge \mathsf{p}_2 \wedge \mathsf{p}_6 \models \bot,$$

then the branch to p_8 matches *backjumping preconditions* similarly as in Example 28, also with $N_a = \mathsf{p}_3$ and $N_b = \mathsf{p}_6$. The difference is that N_b now

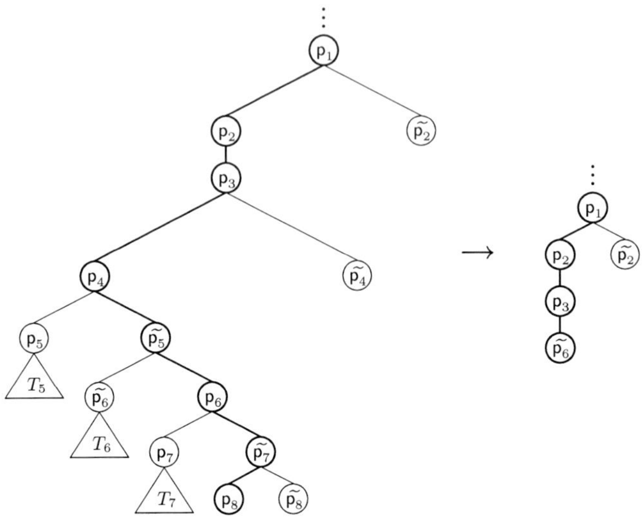

Figure 10.4. Backjumping with $N_b = \mathsf{p}_6$ Having a Left Sibling – See Example 29

has a left sibling. Thus, with a left-to-right tableau construction method, an already constructed tableau part can be below $\widetilde{\mathsf{p}_6}$, the subtree T_6.

Like T_5 and T_7, also T_6 is not present in the result of backjumping, which is shown on the right side of Figure 10.4. This intuitively makes sense for the same reason that was given as first reason for the deletion of T_5 in Example 28: T_6 might depend on p_4 or p_5, and thus can not be straightforwardly attached to the new active branch.

Example 30 (Backjumping where the Deletion is not Useful) This example shows a case where the deletion of a subtree by backjumping on a node N_b with a left sibling is not useful, and some refinement should be employed. The tableau fragment on the left side of Figure 10.5 is similar to the left side of Figure 10.4 (p. 164), except that p_4 and $\widetilde{\mathsf{p}_5}$ have no siblings. Given, as in Example 29, that

$$F \wedge \mathsf{p}_2 \wedge \mathsf{p}_6 \models \bot,$$

the branch to p_8 matches *backjumping preconditions* with $N_a = \widetilde{\mathsf{p}_5}$ and $N_b = \mathsf{p}_6$. The right side of Figure 10.5 shows the result of backjumping with respect to this matching. Subtree T_7 is not present in the result, similar to Example 28. But T_6 clearly could be attached to $\widetilde{\mathsf{p}_6}$ also in the result state, since $\widetilde{\mathsf{p}_6}$ has in both states the same ancestors.

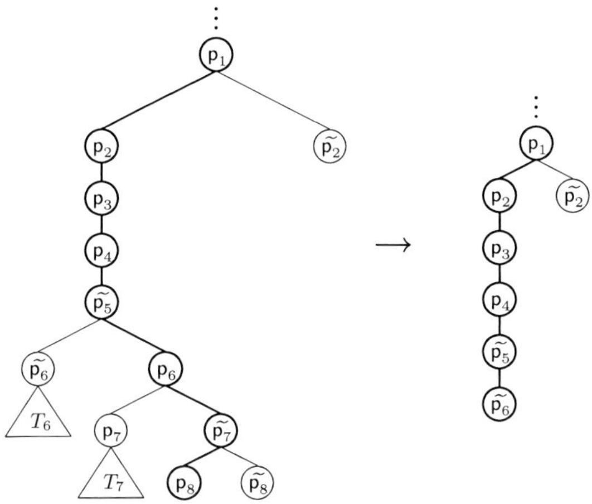

Figure 10.5. The Deletion of T_6 by Backjump is not Useful – See Example 30

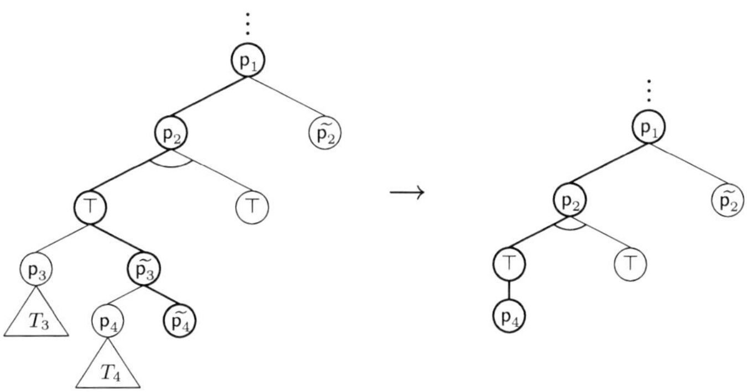

Figure 10.6. Modifications Below A-Node p_2 – See Example 31

Example 31 (Backjumping with A-Nodes) This example illustrates a further situation where backjumping is possible since a node on the active branch that has siblings *to its left*. Consider the tableau fragment on the left side of Figure 10.6. Let F be the forward label of the root of the tableau, and assume that it has been established that

$$F \wedge \mathsf{p}_2 \wedge \widetilde{\mathsf{p}_4} \models \bot.$$

The branch to $\widetilde{\mathsf{p}_4}$ then matches *backjumping preconditions* with the left child of p_2 as N_a and $N_b = \widetilde{\mathsf{p}_4}$. The right side of Figure 10.6 shows the result of backjumping with respect to this matching. This backjumping step, which preserves the a-node p_2 and its children, is possible since $\widetilde{\mathsf{p}_4}$ is a decision node, that is, it is child of an o-node and it has a sibling – also if the sibling is to its left, which can occur specifically in tableaux for transformation tasks, in contrast to theorem proving.

11 DPLL-Like Methods for Formula Transformation

As an exemplary instance of the tableau framework for computing LP that has been developed in Chapter 9, we work out a family of methods for propositional logic that are variations of the DPLL calculus [DLL62]. To compute for a sentence F and representations of literal scopes S_l, S_p as inputs a sentence F' such that $\mathsf{LP}(F, S_l, S_p, F')$ is satisfied, these methods basically construct a tableau from atomic cuts upon those atoms in F which are not permitted to occur in "links" in F'. These are the atoms that are not contained positively as well as negatively in the link scope S_l. For projection elimination, where the literal scope S_p is the same as S_l, this corresponds to the atoms of the literals that are to be forgotten. The examples of fwd-tableau shown in Figs. 9.1, 9.3 and 9.4 (pp. 135, 137 and 141, resp.) are in accord with these methods.

We specify the family of DPLL-like methods by means of state transition rules. In this chapter, these rules are incompletely specified by referring to semantic concepts, thus permitting different syntactic realizations depending on the class of sentences used as forward labels, especially clausal sentences or propositional sentences in general.

Current state-of-the-art systems for processing propositional sentences are based on the DPLL method, enhanced by important refinements such as varieties of dependency directed backtracking and lemma generation. In the literature on SAT solving systems, such refinements are conventionally described by means of pseudocode, which complicates analysis, comparison with other methods and the design of variations and extensions. Our goal is to develop an abstract formal specification that covers important refinements. *Abstract DPLL* [NOT06] is a recent formalization of DPLL with backjumping and lemma generation. Our formalization of backjumping in Chapter 10 is based on Abstract DPLL. Since this form of dependency directed backtracking with context unit lemmas actually is independent of DPLL, characterized as based on atomic cuts, we introduced it already at the level of the framework for computing LP.

The instantiation of our formula transformation framework with DPLL-like methods is related to recent DNNF compilers that are based on DPLL methods [Dar04, HD05]. In tradition of the literature on SAT solving, they are described by means of pseudocode. The method of [HD05] uses the *trace* of a

DPLL-based model counter [BP00] as compilation result. Our formalization with the explicit use of tableau structures provides a formal account and more systematic understanding of essential features of these methods. In [HMR05] a knowledge compilation method is specified by means of tableau construction rules, but it is not clear if this method permits refinements like dependency directed backtracking, which seem essential for practical success.

Notions of *state*, *rule*, *calculus* and *derivation*, as required for our formalization of tableau construction methods are specified in Section 11.1. *Sem-Fwd-Tableaux*, fwd-tableaux with a restricted form that complies with the construction by atomic cuts and thus corresponds to a semantic tree, are specified in Section 11.2. Rules for the construction of such tableaux are then introduced, and bundled as *DPLL-Fwd calculi*. In Section 11.3 it is shown that these calculi instantiate the framework for computing LP of Chapter 9, including the backjumping refinements described in Chapter 10. In Section 11.4 a bound on the length of branches of tableaux constructed by DPLL-Fwd calculi is shown, which is applied in Section 11.5 to prove termination, and in Chapter 12 to show efficiency properties.

11.1 Preliminaries

The methods to compute LP that we investigate are quite similar to calculi for theorem proving, which are conveniently expressed by means of inference rules. Such a rule-based specification provides a formalization of the computation method that facilitates analyzing it, proving properties of it, relating it to other methods, and getting aware of possible refinements. So we express methods for computing LP by means of inference rules. As in theorem proving, we call a set of such rules a *calculus*. A calculus establishes mappings between objects called *states*. After discussing such state objects in the following subsection, we provide formal characterizations of *calculus*, *rule* and related notions.

11.1.1 State Objects

A rule is a mapping between objects called *states*. Since the structure of a state object can be very different, depending on the particular calculus, we do not define or constrain state objects at this place. An example for a concrete specification is given in Definition 100 in the context of a calculus.

We understand a state object as representing the *complete* "state" of a derivation. This contrasts with another understanding, which also is useful and can sometimes be found in the literature on automated deduction, where a rule is considered as mapping a *substructure* of a complete state to other substructures that extend or replace them. An example for that other understanding is binary resolution considered as a rule that maps two parent clauses (substructures of a clause set) to a resolvent clause (that extends the clause set). In our understanding, binary resolution would map a clause set that includes the parent clauses to this set extended by the resolvent.

A state object, as we understand it here, does not necessarily correspond to a data structure that is explicitly present in main memory. For example, the rules defined in Section 11.2.6 work on states as defined in Definition 100, which include a tableau, and require only a particular branch of the tableau to be explicitly represented in main memory, while other parts of it can be stored offline. *Rule* and *derivation*, as defined here, do not distinguish substructures that have to be represented explicitly in main memory. Extra means are required for that, as for example the specification of a so-called *working data structure* in Section 12.1. This understanding facilitates to show properties of complete states, for example correctness properties of complete states that represent the result of a formula transformation. It also facilitates the inclusion of techniques that explicitly control which components of a state are represented in main memory and which are offline, as described for example in Chapter 13.

11.1.2 Rule, Calculus, Derivation and Related Notions

Definition 92 (Rule) A *rule* is a binary relation between states.

Definition 93 (Rule Specification) A way to specify a rule is by

- *Preconditions*, a set of conditions on a state, and
- *Effects*, a description of a state as obtained from a given state, in terms of operational metaphors.

The preconditions and effects of a rule may involve parameters, which can be shared between them. A parameter of the effects must also be present in the preconditions. A rule specified in this way consists of the pairs of states $\langle S, S' \rangle$ such that for some parameter instantiation it holds that S satisfies the preconditions and is related to S' as described by the effects.

The following condition is additionally imposed on a rule specified in this way: If a state S satisfies the preconditions for some parameter instantiation, then there exists a state S' such that S is related to S' as described by the effects with respect to this parameter instantiation.

Definition 94 (Applicable) A rule that is specified according to Definition 93 is called *applicable* to a state S if and only if there exists a state S' such that $\langle S, S' \rangle$ is an element of the rule.

Definition 95 (Calculus) A *calculus* is a triple $\langle S^*, S_0^*, R^* \rangle$ of a set of states S^*, a subset S_0^* of S^*, called *initial states*, and a set of rules over elements of S^*.

Definition 96 (Derivation) If $\langle S^*, S_0^*, R^* \rangle$ is a calculus, then any finite sequence of states $S_1 \ldots S_n$, where $n \geq 1$, such that $S_1 \in S^*$ and for all $i \in \{2, \ldots, n\}$ there exists a rule $R \in R^*$ such that $\langle S_{i-1}, S_i \rangle \in R$ is called a *derivation from* S_1 *to* S_n *with* the calculus.

A derivation from a state $S_0 \in S_0^*$ to a state S with a calculus is called a *derivation of* S *with* the calculus.

Definition 97 (State Derivable with a Calculus) A state is called *derivable with* a calculus if and only if there exists a derivation of the state with the calculus.

Definition 98 (Terminal State) A state S derivable with a calculus is called *terminal* if and only there does not exist a rule R of the calculus and a state S' such that $\langle S, S' \rangle \in R$.

11.2 DPLL-Fwd Calculi

11.2.1 Sem-Fwd-Tableaux

The DPLL calculus [DLL62] constructs a *semantic tree* [Rob68, KH69, CL73], which can be considered as a tableau that is restricted in a certain way. In the following definition of *sem-fwd-tableaux* this restriction is adapted to fwd-tableaux.

Definition 99 (Sem-Fwd-Tableau) A *sem-fwd-tableau* (short for *semantic tree shaped tableau with forward labels*) is a fwd-tableau (as specified in Definition 80) that satisfies the following additional conditions:

1. Literal labels are ground literals or $\top$.
2. An o-node has at most two children.
3. The literal labels of the children of an o-node with two children are complementary literals.

11.2.2 State Objects of DPLL-Fwd

DPLL-Fwd calculi operate on state objects (as discussed in Section 11.1.1) that combine a sem-fwd-tableau with one of its leaf nodes, the *active leaf*, which indicates the *active branch* on which computation is focused.

Definition 100 (TN-State, Active Leaf, Active Branch) A *tn-state* is a pair $\langle T, N \rangle$ of a sem-fwd-tableau T and a leaf node N, the *active leaf*. B_N is called the *active branch*.

11.2.3 DPLL-Fwd Calculi and their Global Parameters

DPLL-Fwd is a family of calculi, whose members differ in that they apply to different classes of sentences, such as propositional sentences in general or in CNF, and that certain "global" parameters in the rule specifications are instantiated differently, depending on the task to be performed, for example projection elimination, compilation to linkless form or satisfiability solving.

The "global" parameters in the specification of DPLL-Fwd have to be distinguished from the "rule local" parameters of rule specifications in the sense of Definition 93. It is assumed that for a DPLL-Fwd calculus the global parameters are instantiated to specific values. They are shared across different rules and their values in all states of a derivation are the same. The rule local parameters, in contrast, are instantiated differently for each rule application.

To get an overview on the global parameters of DPLL-Fwd, we let the definition of DPLL-Fwd precede the definitions of its initial states, rules and some of the parameter types:

Definition 101 (DPLL-Fwd Calculus) If

- F is a propositional polar[1] sentence
- S_l, S_p are literal scopes such that $S_l \subseteq S_p \subseteq \mathcal{L}(F)$,
- PB is a branch completeness property,
- PD is a decision property,
- fb is a fwd-bounding function, and
- *Simplify-Fwd* is a fwd-simplification algorithm for S_p and fb,

then a DPLL-Fwd *calculus for sentence F, link scope S_l, projection scope S_p, branch completeness property PB, decision property PD, fwd-bounding function fb*, and *fwd-simplification algorithm Simplify-Fwd* is a calculus $\langle S^*, S_0^*, R^* \rangle$ such that

- S^* is the set of tn-states,
- S_0^* is Init, and
- R^* is a subset of

{ Unit,
Decide(PD),
Backjump,
Disconnect(S_l),
Next(PB),
True-Up(S_p) }.

[1] We consider in Chapters 11–13 only propositional sentences which are *polar*, which means that they are in NNF, modulo some "syntactic sugar" – see Section 2.6. To apply the material in these chapters to sentences with the $\leftrightarrow$ operator, the notion of *linkless formula* (Definition 67) has to be adapted, and efficiency properties might need revision.

Only parameters that are referenced in the precondition specifications of rules are explicitly written as rule arguments. An example for a branch completeness property is PB-L, specified in Definition 84, p. 138. An example for a decision property is PD-L, specified in Definition 114, p. 185. *Fwd-bounding function* and *fwd-simplification algorithm* will be defined in Section 11.2.5. Init and the rules will be defined in Section 11.2.6.

11.2.4 Restrictions of the Scope Parameters of DPLL-Fwd

The two global parameters of DPLL-Fwd which are literal scopes, the link scope S_l and the projection scope S_p, are restricted by $S_l \subseteq S_p \subseteq \mathcal{L}(F)$. The restriction $S_l \subseteq S_p$ corresponds to the precondition in the definition of the LP relation. The restrictions $S_l \subseteq \mathcal{L}(F)$ and $S_p \subseteq \mathcal{L}(F)$ allow to assume that S_l and S_p can be represented in space polynomially bounded by $|F|$, such that in the complexity considerations in Chapter 12 representations of S_l and S_p have not to be taken explicitly into account.

Although the definition of *linklessness-preserving* would permit that the forward label and literal label of a node contain literals not occurring in the forward label of the parent node, but in $S_l \cap \widetilde{S_l}$ (see Definition 83.ii), the rules of DPLL-Fwd do not utilize this possibility. A consequence is that if a DPLL-Fwd calculus is used – as shown later in Theorem 13 – to compute for given sentence F and literal scopes S_l, S_p a sentence F' such that $\mathsf{LP}(F, S_l, S_p, F')$ holds, then $\mathcal{L}(F')$ is a subset of $\mathcal{L}(F)$. This implies that $\mathsf{LP}(F, S_l, S_p, F')$ holds if and only if it holds that $\mathsf{LP}(F, (S_l \cap \mathcal{L}(F)), (S_p \cap \mathcal{L}(F)), F')$, as shown now in Proposition 138. In this sense the restriction by $S_l \subseteq \mathcal{L}(F)$ and $S_p \subseteq \mathcal{L}(F)$ is without loss of generality.

Proposition 138 *If* F, F' *are propositional sentences such that* $\mathcal{L}(F') \subseteq \mathcal{L}(F)$ *and* S_l, S_p *are literal scopes such that* $S_l \subseteq S_p$*, then*

$$\mathsf{LP}(F, S_l, S_p, F') \text{ if and only if } \mathsf{LP}(F, (S_l \cap \mathcal{L}(F)), (S_p \cap \mathcal{L}(F)), F').$$

Proof. Relation LP is defined by three conditions, LP-L, LP-U and LP-D. Literal scope S_l appears only in condition LP-L. Condition LP-L for the left side of the equivalence stated in the proposition is equivalent to LP-L for the right side, since from the definition of *linkless formula* it follows that if $\mathcal{L}(F') \subseteq \mathcal{L}(F)$, then

$$F' \text{ is linkless outside } S_l \text{ if and only if } F' \text{ is linkless outside } S_l \cap \mathcal{L}(F).$$

The second literal scope argument appears only in condition LP-U. Like condition LP-L, also LP-U is equivalent for both sides of the equivalence stated in the proposition: Since F is a propositional sentence, from Proposition 70 it follows that $\mathsf{project}(F, S_p)$ is an $\mathcal{E}$-sentence; thus from Proposition 92 follows

$$F' \models_{S_p} F \text{ if and only if } F' \models_{S_p \cap \mathcal{L}(F)} F.$$

□

11.2.5 Construction of Forward Labels

Init and the effects of most of the rules of DPLL-Fwd calculi involve that forward labels are assigned to newly constructed nodes (the exceptions are rules Next and True-Up). These forward labels are specified in rule definitions as result of a so-called *fwd-simplification algorithm* (Definition 106) applied to the branch to the new node and the forward label of the parent node (or a subformula of this parent label in case of rule Disconnect, or an externally given sentence in case of Init, respectively). The notion *fwd-simplification algorithm* combines a requirement on time complexity with properties that relate its in- and outputs, which are bundled as the property *fwd-admissible* (Definition 104).

Viewed operationally, a fwd-simplification algorithm is based on substituting in the given sentence all atoms that appear in the given branch with $\top$ or $\bot$, depending on whether they occur in the branch with polarity 1 or -1. Definition 102.ii introduces the symbolic notation $F[B]$ for the result of this substitution. The specification of *fwd-simplification algorithm* generalizes this: it does not require its output to be exactly the result of the substitution, but abstractly characterizes properties of further operations that can be applied to simplify it. Such simplification operations interact with the *fwd-bounding function* (Definition 103) supplied to the DPLL-Fwd calculus. Examples for simplification operations and fwd-bounding functions are given in Section 12.2.2.

In implementations, the explicit construction of forward labels can often be avoided. For example, in SAT solvers forward labels usually correspond to sentences implicitly represented by the input sentence and a branch. Since SAT solvers require only access to a single forward label at a time, dynamically maintained auxiliary data structures like watch literals [MMZ+01, TBW04] can be used to provide efficient access to this implicitly represented forward label.

Definition 102 (Ground Branch, Branch Substitution)

(i) A branch is called *ground* if and only if its nodes have as literal labels only ground literals or $\top$.

(ii) If F is a propositional sentence and B is a ground branch such that $A_1, \ldots, A_m$ are the atoms of nodes on B with positive and $A_{m+1}, \ldots, A_n$ with negative literals as literal labels, then

$$F[B] \stackrel{\text{def}}{=} F[A_1 \backslash \top] \ldots [A_m \backslash \top][A_{m+1} \backslash \bot] \ldots [A_n \backslash \bot].$$

Definition 103 (Fwd-Bounding Function) A *fwd-bounding function* is a function fb from propositional sentences to natural numbers such that if F is a propositional sentence, then

(i) If B is a ground branch, then

$$\mathit{fb}(F) \geq \mathit{fb}(F[B]);$$

(ii)

$$\mathit{fb}(F) \geq \mathit{fb}(\top);$$

(iii) If F' is a proper subformula of F, then

$$\mathit{fb}(F) > \mathit{fb}(F');$$

(iv) There exist a polynomial p_1 such that for all propositional sentences F it holds that

$$p_1(|F|) \geq \mathit{fb}(F);$$

(v) There exist a polynomial p_2 such that for all propositional sentences F it holds that

$$p_2(\mathit{fb}(F)) \geq |F|.$$

Definition 104 (Fwd-Admissible) A propositional sentence F' is called *fwd-admissible* for sentence F, literal scope S_p and fwd-bounding function fb if and only if

(i) $F' \models_{S_p} F$;

(ii) $F \models F'$;

(iii) $\mathcal{L}(F') \subseteq \mathcal{L}(F)$;

(iv) $\mathit{fb}(F) \geq \mathit{fb}(F')$.

Definition 105 (Length of a Branch) If B is a ground branch, then

$|B|$ is the length of B.[2]

Definition 106 (Fwd-Simplification Algorithm) A *fwd-simplification algorithm* for literal scope S_p and fwd-bounding function fb is an algorithm with a propositional sentence F and a ground branch B as inputs that constructs in time polynomial in $|F| + |B|$ a propositional sentence F' such that

F' is fwd-admissible for $F[B], S_p$ and fb.

[2] The length of a branch B is linearly related to the formula size of B considered as propositional sentence according to Definition 81.iii. Thus in contexts of complexity considerations modulo polynomials, $|B|$ can also be read as the formula size of B considered as a sentence.

11.2.6 The Rules of DPLL-Fwd

In this section the set of initial states and the rules of DPLL-Fwd calculi are specified. These characterizations are "incomplete" in that they involve semantic relationships, which are sufficient to show many properties related to formula transformation tasks. Concrete syntactic realizations are for clausal sentences either well known or straightforward to see. The more abstract characterizations give room for different realizations, also for sentences not in clausal form. Nevertheless, we consider later on in Section 12.3 in some depth aspects concerning the efficiency by which the matching and verification of the rule preconditions as well as computation of initial and successor states can be performed.

The specifications of Init and the rules (Definitions 107–112) are to be read in the context of the global parameters F, S_l, S_p, PB, PD, fb and *Simplify-Fwd* as introduced in the specification of DPLL-Fwd (Definition 101).

Definition 107 (Initial States Init) Init is the set of all tn-states $\langle T, N\rangle$, where T is a fwd-tableau containing a single node N such that $L_N = \top$ and $F_N = \mathit{Simplify\text{-}Fwd}(F, \top)$.

The rules Unit and Decide express the "standard operations" of DPLL, unit propagation and splitting. Decide is parameterized with a "decision property" that constrains the choice of literals on which the splitting is performed.

Definition 108 (Rule Unit)

PRECONDITIONS: Let N be the active leaf. There exists a literal $L \in \mathcal{L}(F_N)$ such that $(B_N \wedge F_N) \models L$ and $\mathsf{atom}(L) \notin \mathcal{A}(B_N)$.

EFFECTS: Attach to N a child N' with $L_{N'} = L$. Label N as o-node. Assign N' as active leaf. Assign $F_{N'}$ to $\mathit{Simplify\text{-}Fwd}(F_N, B'_N)$.

Definition 109 (Rule Decide(PD))

PRECONDITIONS: Let N be the active leaf. There exists a literal $L \in \mathcal{L}(F_N) \cap \widetilde{\mathcal{L}(F_N)}$ such that $PD(L, N)$ is satisfied and $\mathsf{atom}(L) \notin \mathcal{A}(B_N)$.

EFFECTS: Attach to N two children; the left one labeled with L, the right one with $\widetilde{L}$. Label N as o-node. Assign the left child as active leaf. For each child N', assign $F_{N'}$ to $\mathit{Simplify\text{-}Fwd}(F_N, B'_N)$.

The rule Backjump corresponds to the *Backjumping* operation specified in Chapter 10.

Definition 110 (Rule Backjump)

PRECONDITIONS: The active branch B_N matches *backjumping preconditions* (Definition 90, p. 155).

EFFECTS: Apply *Backjumping* (Definition 91, p. 155) with respect to the matching of the preconditions. Assign $F_{N'}$ to $\mathit{Simplify\text{-}Fwd}(F_{N_a}, B_{N'})$ and assign N' as active leaf, where N' is the newly attached child of N_a with literal label $\widetilde{L_{N_b}}$.

Disconnect is the rule that effects construction of a-nodes. It expresses as a rule a dynamic problem decomposition as developed by Bayardo and Pehousek [BP00] for DPLL-based model counting and used by Huang and Darwiche for DNNF compilation [HD05]. For model counting and DNNF compilation the components $F_1, \ldots, F_n$ not only have to be pairwise linkless, but are required to have pairwise disjoint atom bases.

Definition 111 (Rule Disconnect(S_l))

PRECONDITIONS: Let N be the active leaf. Its forward label F_N is equal (modulo associativity and commutativity of the $\wedge$ operator) to a propositional sentence $(F_1 \wedge \ldots \wedge F_n)$, where $n > 1$ and for all $i, j \in \{1, \ldots, n\}$ such that $i \neq j$ it holds that $\langle F_i, F_j \rangle$ is linkless outside S_l.

EFFECTS: For each of the F_i, where $i \in \{1, \ldots, n\}$, attach to N – from left to right – a child N_i with $L_{N_i} = \top$ and F_{N_i} assigned to *Simplify-Fwd*(F_i, B_{N_i}). Label N as a-node. Assign N_1 as active leaf.

Next is a backtracking rule particular for transformation tasks. It effects that if the active branch satisfies the branch completeness property PB, and hence is completely constructed, then another branch gets explored. For deciding satisfiability, it is just necessary to backtrack if the active branch contradicts with the input sentence. While this could also be handled by Next(PB), parameterized with a suitable PB, it can be performed more efficiently by Backjump, making Next dispensable for satisfiability checking.

Definition 112 (Rule Next(PB))

PRECONDITIONS: The active leaf satisfies PB and the active branch has the form $B_1 N B_2$, where B_1, B_2 are sequences of nodes (B_2 is possibly empty) and N is the last node in the active branch that has an open sibling to the right.

EFFECTS: Assign the next right sibling of N as active leaf.

The rule True-Up(S_p) integrates special cases of projection elimination that are computable at low cost into the tableau construction.

Definition 113 (Rule True-Up(S_p))

PRECONDITIONS: Let N be the active leaf. $F_N = \top$, and N is the child of a node $N^{\backprime}$ such that

– If $N^{\backprime}$ is an o-node, then $L_N \notin S_p$;

– If $N^{\backprime}$ is an a-node, then for all siblings N' of N it holds that $F_{N'} = \top$.

In case $N^{\backprime}$ is an a-node, it is further assumed that $L_{N'} = \top$ and $L_N = \top$, which needs no explicit verification since it always holds for children of a-nodes constructed by Disconnect, and can not be affected by any other rule of DPLL-Fwd.

EFFECTS: Remove the children of $N^{\backprime}$. Assign $F_{N^{\backprime}}$ to $\top$. Assign $N^{\backprime}$ as active leaf.

An intuitive argument for the correctness of True-Up is that it preserves equivalence *relative to* S_p of the leafy sentence of the parent of the active node. For example, if N, N' are nodes matching the preconditions of True-Up with N' being an o-node, then the preservation of relative equivalence can be shown as follows, where M' is the node corresponding to N' in the tableau resulting from the rule application (in operational metaphors "M' is N' after application of True-Up"):

$$
\begin{array}{lll}
(1) & \mathsf{project}(\mathsf{leafy}(N'), S_p) & \equiv \\
(2) & \mathsf{project}(L_{N'} \land ((L_N \land \top) \lor G), S_p) & \equiv \\
(3) & \mathsf{project}((L_{N'} \land L_N) \lor (L_{N'} \land G), S_p) & \equiv \\
(4) & \mathsf{project}(L_{N'} \land L_N, S_p) \lor \mathsf{project}(L_{N'} \land G, S_p) & \equiv \\
(5) & (\mathsf{project}(L_{N'}, S_p) \land \mathsf{project}(L_N, S_p)) \lor \mathsf{project}(L_{N'} \land G, S_p) & \equiv \\
(6) & \mathsf{project}(L_{N'}, S_p) \lor \mathsf{project}(L_{N'} \land G, S_p) & \equiv \\
(7) & \mathsf{project}(L_{N'}, S_p) & \equiv \\
(8) & \mathsf{project}(L_{N'} \land \top, S_p) & \equiv \\
(9) & \mathsf{project}(\mathsf{leafy}(M'), S_p) &
\end{array}
$$

Equivalence of (2) to (1), where G is some sentence, follows from the definition of leafy. Clearly, the formula arguments of the project operator in (3) and (2) are equivalent. Equivalence of (4) to (3) holds since projection distributes over disjunction (Proposition 74). As shown below (Proposition 152), a branch of an fwd-tableau constructed by DPLL-Fwd does not contain nodes with complementary literals as literal labels. Thus $\langle L_{N'}, L_N \rangle$ is fully linkless and Proposition 80 justifies distributing the leftmost projection operator in (4) over the conjunction in its argument, yielding (5). Since $L_N \notin S_p$ is a precondition of True-Up, it follows from the semantic definition of projection that $\mathsf{project}(L_N, S_p) \equiv \top$. Hence (6) is equivalent to (5). Equivalence of (7) to (6) follows from Proposition 30. The formula arguments of (8) and (7) are equivalent. Equivalence of (9) to (8) again follows from the definition of leafy.

The equivalence of (1)–(9) permits to view the effect of True-Up as a *formula simplification of a leafy sentence* – which corresponds to a destructive modification of the tableau structure. Thus True-Up can be considered as a simplification at the "tableau level" [HMR05]. This is in contrast to simplifications at the "formula level", discussed in Section 12.2 below, which are performed in the construction of forward labels and also integrate special cases of projection elimination, but without altering the tableau structure.

An application of True-Up can trigger another one if, for example, the parent of the active node before rule application is an o-node whose literal label is like that of the active node not in S_p. If S_p is empty, in this way, when (by a calculus that does not construct a-nodes) a model has been found – indicated by the forward label of the active node being $\top$ – the True-Up rule can be repeatedly applied until the fwd-tableau consists of just a single node with $\top$ as literal as well as forward label. This single-node tableau indicates satisfiability of the input sentence. Thus, the method terminates "inherently" after finding the first model; it has not to be stopped extraneously from backtracking and searching for alternative models.

If the active node is a child of an o-node and has a sibling to its left, then True-Up can effect, similar to Backjump, that a part of the tableau under construction is thrown away. Unlike the other rules introduced this section, True-Up effects that an existing node, the parent of the active node, gets assigned a new forward label (speaking in operational metaphors, of course). Although True-Up is presented here as a rule specifically for DPLL-Fwd, it is not restricted to sem-fwd-tableau, but does work on fwd-tableau in general.

11.3 Computing LP with DPLL-Fwd Calculi

We show that DPLL-Fwd calculi match the framework for computing LP developed in Chapter 9. After stating some auxiliary propositions in Section 11.3.1, we show in Sections 11.3.2–11.3.5 that sem-fwd-tableaux constructed by DPLL-Fwd calculi satisfy as invariants the *linklessness-preserving*, *upward-preserving*, *extensional*, and *branch implied forward labels* constraints. In Section 11.3.6 it is shown that, with certain provisions, in the tableau of a terminal state derivable with a DPLL-Fwd calculus for link scope S_l, all leaf nodes satisfy the branch completeness property $\mathsf{PB\text{-}L}_{S_l}$. These results are combined in Section 11.3.7 to show that all the preconditions of Theorem 8 are satisfied by DPLL-Fwd calculi, and thus the framework is matched.

11.3.1 Fwd-Admissibility of Forward Labels

Propositions 139 and 140 make precise in which sense the forward labels of "all" nodes of fwd-tableaux constructed by DPLL-Fwd calculi are fwd-admissible for the forward labels of their parents. These propositions are subsequently used as lemmas in the proofs of further invariants. Two such invariants are included in this section: Proposition 141, which states that the branch to any node has no atoms in common with the forward label of the node, and Proposition 142, which states that for a non-root node the literal bases of literal and forward labels are included in the literal base of the forward label of the parent node.

Proposition 139 *If T is the tableau of a tn-stated derivable with a* DPLL-Fwd *calculus for projection scope S_p and fwd-bounding function fb, then*

$$F_{\mathsf{root}(T)} \text{ is fwd-admissible for } F.$$

Proof. Follows easily from the definitions *fwd-simplification algorithm* and Init.

□

Proposition 140 *If N is a node in the tableau of a tn-state derivable with a* DPLL-Fwd *calculus for for link scope S_l, projection scope S_p and fwd-bounding function fb, then*

(i) *If N is an o-node with a child N', then*

$$F_{N'} \text{ is fwd-admissible for } F_N[B_{N'}],\ S_p \text{ and } \mathit{fb};$$

(ii) *If N is an a-node whose children are $N_1, \ldots, N_n$, then there exist propositional sentences $F_1, \ldots, F_n$ such that*

(a)

$$F_N \equiv \bigwedge_{i \in \{1,\ldots,n\}} F_i;$$

(b) *For all $i \in \{1, \ldots, n\}$ it holds that*

$$F_i \text{ is a proper subformula of } F_N;$$

(c) *For all $i \in \{1, \ldots, n\}$ it holds that*

$$F_{N_i} \text{ is fwd-admissible for } F_i[B_{N_i}], S_p \text{ and } \mathit{fb};$$

(d) *For all $i, j \in \{1, \ldots, n\}$ such that $i \neq j$ it holds that*

$$\langle F_i, F_j \rangle \text{ is linkless outside } S_l;$$

(e) *For all $i, j \in \{1, \ldots, n\}$ such that $i \neq j$ it holds that*

$$\langle F_i, F_j \rangle \text{ is linkless outside } S_p.$$

Proof. By induction on the structure of the fwd-tableau as constructed by the rules of DPLL-Fwd. (140.i) follows easily from the definition of *fwd-simplification algorithm* if $F_{N'}$ is a forward label assigned by Unit, Decide or Backjump to a child of an o-node. Similarly, (140.ii.a)–(140.ii.d) follow easily from the definition of *fwd-simplification algorithm* if forward labels F_{N_i} for $i \in \{1, \ldots, n\}$ have been assigned by Disconnect. (140.ii.e) follows from (140.ii.d) and the definition of *linkless*, since by the definition of DPLL-Fwd it holds that $S_l \subseteq S_p$.

For forward labels assigned by True-Up we explicitly show the induction step. Let N be an node, N' be a child of N, and N'' be a child of N' such that the preconditions for True-Up are matched for active node N''.

In case N is an o-node, by the induction assumption it holds that $F_{N'}$ is fwd-admissible for $F_N[B_{N'}]$, S_p and *fb*. The induction step follows if $\top$ is fwd-admissible for $F_N[B_{N'}]$, S_p and *fb*. In case N is an a-node whose children are $N_1, \ldots, N_n$, where $N' = N_k$ for some $k \in \{1, \ldots, i\}$, by the induction assumption there exist sentences $F_1, \ldots, F_n$ that satisfy (140.ii.b)–(140.ii.e), which includes that $F_{N'}$ is fwd-admissible for $F_k[B_{N'}]$, S_p and *fb*.

The induction step follows if $\top$ is fwd-admissible for $F_k[B_{N'}]$, S_p and *fb*. These two cases can be generalized to a single one by defining the sentence G as F_N in case N is an o-node, and as F_k in case N is an a-node. The following statement, (1), then holds by the induction assumption, and the induction step follows if $\top$ is fwd-admissible for $G[B_{N'}]$, S_p and *fb*.

(1) $F_{N'}$ is fwd-admissible for $G[B_{N'}]$, S_p and *fb*.

Definitions 104.ii–104.iv of the definition of *fwd-admissible* immediately apply to $\top$ in the role of F'. It remains to verify the property of Definition 104.i, which is $\top \models_{S_p} G[B_{N'}]$:

(2) $\{L_{N''}\} \cap S_p = \emptyset$.
(3) $\top \models \mathsf{project}(F_{N'}[B_{N''}], S_p)$.
(4) $\top \models \mathsf{project}(F_{N'}[B_{N''}], S_p - S_B)$.
(5) $\top \models \mathsf{project}(B_{N''} \land F_{N'}[B_{N''}], S_p - S_B)$.
(6) $\top \models \mathsf{project}(B_{N''} \land F_{N'}, S_p - S_B)$.
(7) $\top \models \mathsf{project}(F_{N'}, S_p - S_B)$.
(8) $\mathsf{project}(F_{N'}, S_p) \models \mathsf{project}(G[B_{N'}], S_p)$.
(9) $\top \models \mathsf{project}(G[B_{N'}], S_p)$.
(10) $\top \models_{S_p} G[B_{N'}]$.

(2) holds, since True-Up is applicable. In case N' is an o-node, by the induction assumption and the applicability of True-Up it holds that $\top$ is fwd-admissible for $F_{N'}[B_{N''}]$, S_p and *fb*, which by the definition of *fwd-admissible* (Definition 104.i) entails (3). In case N' is an a-node, (3) can be derived from the induction assumption and the applicability of True-Up. Let S_B be the set of literals whose atoms are in $B_{N'}$. (4) follows from (3) and Proposition 88. $B_{N''} = (B_{N'} \land L_{N''})$. Thus (5) follows from (2) and properties of projection, for example Propositions 80 and 87. (6) follows from (5), since the formula arguments of the projection operator are equivalent. (7) follows from (6) and Proposition 31. (8) follows from (1) and the definition of *fwd-admissible* (Definition 104.i). (9) follows from (8), (7) and Proposition 60. (10), the property of Definition 104.i, follows from (9) and Proposition 36. □

Proposition 141 *If N is a node in the tableau of a tn-state derivable with a* DPLL-Fwd *calculus, then*

$$\mathcal{A}(B_N) \cap \mathcal{A}(F_N) = \emptyset.$$

Proof. If N is the root node, the proposition follows from the definition of Init, which includes $L_N = \top$. If N is not the root node, then from Propositions 140.i and 140.ii it follows that there exists a formula F' such that F_N is fwd-admissible for $F'[B_N]$. *Fwd-admissible* then includes $\mathcal{L}(F_N) \subseteq \mathcal{L}(F'[B_N])$ (Definition 104.iii). The proposition then follows since it holds clearly that $\mathcal{A}(F'[B_N]) \cap \mathcal{A}(B_N) = \emptyset$.

□

Proposition 142 *If N, N' are nodes in the tableau of a tn-state derivable with a* DPLL-Fwd *calculus and N' is a child of N, then*

(i)
$$\mathcal{L}(F_{N'}) \subseteq \mathcal{L}(F_N);$$

(ii)
$$\mathcal{L}(L_{N'}) \subseteq \mathcal{L}(F_N).$$

Proof.

(142.i) If N is an o-node, by Proposition 140.i it holds that $F_{N'}$ is fwd-admissible for $F_N[B_{N'}]$. *Fwd-admissible* includes $\mathcal{L}(F_{N'}) \subseteq \mathcal{L}(F_N[B_{N'}])$ (Definition 104.iii), which implies $\mathcal{L}(F_{N'}) \subseteq \mathcal{L}(F_N)$. If N is an a-node, from Proposition 140.ii it follows that there exists a formula F' such that $\mathcal{L}(F') \subseteq \mathcal{L}(F_N)$ and $F_{N'}$ is fwd-admissible for $F'[B_{N'}]$. *Fwd-admissible* includes $\mathcal{L}(F_{N'}) \subseteq \mathcal{L}(F'[B_{N'}])$ (Definition 104.iii), which implies that $\mathcal{L}(F_{N'}) \subseteq \mathcal{L}(F')$. Then $\mathcal{L}(F') \subseteq \mathcal{L}(F_N)$ implies $\mathcal{L}(F_{N'}) \subseteq \mathcal{L}(F_N)$.

(142.ii) By induction on the structure of the sem-fwd-tableau as constructed by the rules. The base case, where the tableau is just a single node, holds trivially. The induction step for nodes N' attached as child to N by Unit or Decide holds, since the preconditions of these rules ensure that $L_{N'} \in \mathcal{L}(F_N)$. The induction step for nodes N' attached by Disconnect holds, since $L_N = \top$. The induction step for nodes N' attached as child to N by Backjump can be shown as follows: By the definition of Backjump, in the state before application, a descendant of N must have $L_{N'}$ as literal label. Let $N^{\backprime}$ be the parent of this descendant. By straightforward induction on the structure of fwd-tableaux it follows from Proposition 142 that $\mathcal{L}(F_{N^{\backprime}}) \subseteq \mathcal{L}(F_N)$. The induction step for Backjump then follows from the induction assumption $\mathcal{L}(L_{N'}) \subseteq \mathcal{L}(F_{N^{\backprime}})$.

□

11.3.2 DPLL-Fwd Tableaux are Linklessness-Preserving

Proposition 143 *If T is the tableau of a tn-state derivable with a* DPLL-Fwd *calculus for link scope S_l, then*

$$T \text{ is linklessness-preserving for } S_l.$$

Proof. We show that T satisfies the two conditions of *linklessness-preserving*.

1. Let N be an a-node in T, let $N_1, \ldots, N_n$ be the children of N and let i, j be different numbers in $1, \ldots, n$. It has to be shown that the pair $\langle (L_{N_i} \wedge F_{N_i}), (L_{N_j} \wedge F_{N_j}) \rangle$ is linkless outside S_l (Definition 83.i).

   By Proposition 140.ii there exist sentences F_i and F_j such that $\langle F_i, F_j \rangle$ is linkless outside S_l and for $k \in \{i, j\}$ it holds that F_{N_k} is fwd-admissible for $F_k[B_{N_k}]$. *Fwd-admissible* includes $\mathcal{L}(F_{N_k}) \subseteq \mathcal{L}(F_k[B_{N_k}])$ (Definition 104.iii), which implies $\mathcal{L}(F_{N_k}) \subseteq \mathcal{L}(F_k)$. Thus $\langle F_{N_i}, F_{N_j} \rangle$ is also linkless outside S_l. By the definition of Disconnect, which is the only rule that effects construction of a-nodes, it holds that $L_{N_i} = L_{N_j} = \top$. Thus $\langle (L_{N_i} \wedge F_{N_i}), (L_{N_j} \wedge F_{N_j}) \rangle$ is linkless outside S_l.

2. Let N, N' be nodes of T such that N' is a child of N. It has to be shown that if N has an a-node as ancestor, then $\mathcal{L}(L_{N'} \wedge F_{N'}) \subseteq \mathcal{L}(F_N) \cup (S_l \cap \widetilde{S_l})$ (Definition 83.ii). The more general fact that $\mathcal{L}(L_{N'} \wedge F_{N'})$ is implied by Proposition 142.

□

Proposition 144 *If T is the tableau of a tn-state derivable with a* DPLL-Fwd *calculus for projection scope S_p, then*

$$T \text{ is linklessness-preserving for } S_p.$$

Proof. By the definition of DPLL-Fwd it holds that $S_l \subseteq S_p$. The proposition then follows from Propositions 143 and 127.

□

11.3.3 DPLL-Fwd Tableaux are Upward-Preserving

Proposition 145 *If F, F' are propositional sentences, B is a ground branch and S_p is a literal scope such that F' is fwd-admissible for $F[B]$ and S_p, then*

$$B \wedge \mathsf{project}(F', S_p) \models \mathsf{project}(F, S_p).$$

Proof.

(1) F' is fwd-admissible for $F[B]$ and S_p.
(2) $\mathsf{project}(F', S_p) \models \mathsf{project}(F[B], S_p)$.
(3) $B \wedge \mathsf{project}(F', S_p) \models B \wedge \mathsf{project}(F[B], S_p)$.
(4) $B \wedge \mathsf{project}(F', S_p) \models \mathsf{project}(B, S_p) \wedge \mathsf{project}(F[B], S_p)$.
(5) $B \wedge \mathsf{project}(F', S_p) \models \mathsf{project}(B \wedge F[B], S_p)$.
(6) $B \wedge F[B] \models F$.
(7) $B \wedge \mathsf{project}(F', S_p) \models \mathsf{project}(F, S_p)$.

Assume (1). (2) follows from (1), the definition of *fwd-admissible* (Definition 104.i) and the definition of $\models_{S_p}$. (3) follows from (2). (4) follows from (3) and Proposition 30. From the definition of branch substitution it follows that $\mathcal{A}(B) \cap \mathcal{A}(F[B]) = \emptyset$; thus $\langle B, F[B] \rangle$ is linkless outside S_p. Hence (5) follows from (4) and Theorem 2. (6) follows easily from the definition of branch substitution. (7) follows from (6), (5) and Proposition 31.

□

Proposition 146 *If T is the tableau of a tn-state derivable with a* DPLL-Fwd *calculus for projection scope S_p, then*

$$T \text{ is upward-preserving for } S_p.$$

Proof. We show that T satisfies the two conditions of *upward-preserving*.

1. Let N be an o-node in T and $N_1, \ldots, N_n$ be the children of N. It has to be shown that $\bigvee_{i\in\{1,\ldots,n\}}(B_{N_i} \wedge \mathsf{project}(F_{N_i}, S)) \models \mathsf{project}(F_N, S)$ (Definition 85.i).

   (1) For $i \in \{1, \ldots, n\}$: F_{N_i} is fwd-admissible for $F_N[B_{N_i}]$ and S_p.
   (2) For $i \in \{1, \ldots, n\}$: $B_{N_i} \wedge \mathsf{project}(F_{N_i}, S_p) \models \mathsf{project}(F_N, S_p)$.
   (3) $\bigvee_{i\in\{1,\ldots,n\}}(B_{N_i} \wedge \mathsf{project}(F_{N_i}, S_p)) \models \mathsf{project}(F_N, S_p)$.

   (1) follows from Proposition 140.i. (2) follows from (1) and Proposition 145. (3) follows from (2).

2. Let N be an a-node in T and $N_1, \ldots, N_n$ be the children of N. It has to be shown that $\bigwedge_{i\in\{1,\ldots,n\}}(B_{N_i} \wedge \mathsf{project}(F_{N_i}, S)) \models \mathsf{project}(F_N, S)$ (Definition 85.ii).

   (1) $\bigwedge_{i\in\{1,\ldots,n\}} F_i \models F_N$.
   (2) For $i \in \{1, \ldots, n\}$: F_{N_i} is fwd-admissible for $F_i[B_{N_i}]$ and S_p.
   (3) For $i, j \in \{1, \ldots, n\}$, $i \neq j$,: $\langle F_i, F_j\rangle$ is linkless outside S_p.
   (4) For $i \in \{1, \ldots, n\}$: $B_{N_i} \wedge \mathsf{project}(F_{N_i}, S_p) \models \mathsf{project}(F_i, S_p)$.
   (5) $\bigwedge_{i\in\{1,\ldots,n\}}(B_{N_i} \wedge \mathsf{project}(F_{N_i}, S_p)) \models \bigwedge_{i\in\{1,\ldots,n\}} \mathsf{project}(F_i, S_p)$.
   (6) $\bigwedge_{i\in\{1,\ldots,n\}}(B_{N_i} \wedge \mathsf{project}(F_{N_i}, S_p)) \models \mathsf{project}(\bigwedge_{i\in\{1,\ldots,n\}} F_i, S_p)$.
   (7) $\bigwedge_{i\in\{1,\ldots,n\}}(B_{N_i} \wedge \mathsf{project}(F_{N_i}, S_p)) \models \mathsf{project}(F_N, S_p)$.

   From Proposition 140.ii follows the existence of sentences $F_1, \ldots, F_n$ such that (1)–(3) hold. (4) follows from (2) and Proposition 145. (5) follows from (4). (6) follows from (5), (3) and Theorem 2. (7) follows from (6), (1) and Proposition 31.

□

11.3.4 DPLL-Fwd Tableaux Have Branch Implied Forward Labels

Proposition 147 *If F, F' are propositional sentences, B is a ground branch and S_p is a literal scope such that F' is fwd-admissible for $F[B]$, then*

$$F \wedge B \models F'.$$

Proof.

(1) F' is fwd-admissible for $F[B]$.
(2) $F_N[B] \models F'$.
(3) $F \wedge B \models F[B]$.
(4) $F \wedge B \models F'$.

Assume (1). (2) follows from (1) and the definition of *fwd-admissible* (Definition 104.ii). (3) easily follows from the definition of branch substitution. (4) follows from (3) and (2).

□

Proposition 148 *A tableau of a tn-state derivable with a* DPLL-Fwd *calculus has branch implied forward labels.*

Proof. Let N, N' be nodes in the tableau of a tn-state derivable with a DPLL-Fwd calculus such that N' is a child of N. In case N is an o-node, the proposition can be shown as follows: By Proposition 140.i it holds that $F_{N'}$ is fwd-admissible for $F_N[B_{N'}]$. From Proposition 147 then follows $(F_N \wedge B_{N'}) \models F_{N'}$. In case N is an a-node, the proposition can be shown as follows:

(1) $F_N \models F'$.
(2) $F_{N'}$ is fwd-admissible for $F'[B_{N'}]$.
(3) $F' \wedge B_{N'} \models F_{N'}$.
(4) $F_N \wedge B_{N'} \models F_{N'}$.

From Proposition 140.ii it follows that there exist a sentence F' such that (1) and (2) hold. (3) follows from (2) and Proposition 147. (4) follows from (3) and (1).

□

11.3.5 DPLL-Fwd Tableaux are Extensional

Proposition 149 *If T is the tableau of a tn-state derivable with a* DPLL-Fwd *calculus, then*

$$T \textit{ is extensional.}$$

Proof. By induction on the structure of T as constructed by the rules. In the base case, where T is just the single root node, T is trivially extensional, since it does not contain a node with children. The induction step follows from Proposition 133, since all rules of DPLL-Fwd that modify the tableau correspond as far as tableau structure and literal labels are concerned to instances of the abstract operations *Extension*, *A-Extension* and *Truncation*.

This can be shown as follows: From Proposition 148 it follows that T has branch implied forward labels; hence from Proposition 134 and the respective rule definitions it is easy to see that Unit and Decide are instances of the *Extension* operation. The Backjump rule is based on the *Backjumping* operation, for which the correspondence to a *Truncation* step followed by an *Extension* step has been shown in Theorem 9. As can be seen from the definition of Disconnect, children attached by Disconnect have $\top$ as literal label. Thus Disconnect trivially is an instance of *A-Extension*. True-Up does not affect literal labels, it just corresponds to a *Truncation* step.

□

11.3.6 Leaves of Terminal DPLL-Fwd Tableaux Satisfy PB-L

We show that in the tableau of a terminal state derivable with a DPLL-Fwd calculus for link scope S_l and a certain decision property, PD-L_{S_l} (Definition 114), all leaf nodes satisfy the branch completeness property PB-L_{S_l}. The proof of this depends on several auxiliary propositions, which might appear unmotivated by themselves. Thus we present the material in this section in a top down fashion: We let the formal statement of the main result (Proposition 150) precede the propositions that state lemmas used in its proof (Propositions 151–154). Next we define the decision property PD-L_{S_l}. Some alterations of this decision property are discussed later in Section 11.6.

Definition 114 (Decision Property PD-L) If L is a ground literal, N is a node in a fwd-tableau and S is a literal scope, then L and N satisfy the property PD-L_S if and only if

$$L \notin S \cap \widetilde{S}, \text{ and}$$
$$(B_N \wedge F_N) \text{ is not linkless inside } \{L\}.$$

For the PD-L property, actually, only the atom of L, and not its polarity, is relevant: if L satisfies PD-L for some values of N and S, then also $\widetilde{L}$ does.

Definition 115 (Left, Right Branches) If N_1, N_2 are nodes of a fwd-tableau, then B_{N_1} is *left of* (*right of*, resp.) B_{N_2}, if and only if N_1 precedes (succeeds, resp.) N_2 in a left-to-right depth-first traversal of the fwd-tableau.

Proposition 150 *If N is a leaf node in the tableau of a terminal state derivable with a* DPLL-Fwd *calculus that includes as rules at least* Decide(PD-L_{S_l}) *and* Next(PB-L_{S_l}) *for link scope S_l, decision property* PD-L_{S_l} *and branch completeness property* PB-L_{S_l}, *then*

$$N \textit{ satisfies } \text{PB-L}_{S_l}.$$

Proof. It is easy to see that if N is a leaf node in the tableau of a terminal tn-state derived with a calculus and PB is a property of nodes, then

$$N \textit{ satisfies } PB$$

if for all tn-states derivable with the calculus the following three conditions hold:

Cond-Left: All leaf nodes of branches left of the active branch satisfy PB;

Cond-Active: If the active leaf does not satisfy PB, then a rule is applicable;

Cond-Right: If there exists a branch right of the active branch, then a rule is applicable.

Cond-Left is shown for DPLL-Fwd calculi and branch completeness properties in general in Proposition 151. *Cond-Active* and *Cond-Right* are then shown for the branch completeness property $\mathsf{PB\text{-}L}_{S_l}$ in Proposition 153 and 154, respectively.

The precondition of the proposition that $\mathsf{Decide}(\mathsf{PD\text{-}L}_{S_l})$ is included in the rules of the calculus is required by Propositions 153 and 154. That $\mathsf{Next}(\mathsf{PB\text{-}L}_{S_l})$ is included, by Proposition 154.

□

DPLL-Fwd Tableaux Satisfy *Cond-Left.*

Proposition 151 *If* $\langle T, N\rangle$ *is a tn-state derivable with a* DPLL-Fwd *calculus for branch completeness property PB, then*

all leaf nodes of branches left of B_N satisfy *PB.*[3]

Proof. Let $\langle T_0, N_0\rangle \ldots \langle T_n, N_n\rangle$, where $n \geq 0$, be a derivation of $\langle T, N\rangle = \langle T_n, N_n\rangle$ with a DPLL-Fwd calculus for branch completeness property *PB*. Let left_i, where $i \in \{0, \ldots, n\}$, be the set of branches in T_i left of B_{N_i} – where a branch is identified with the sequences of literal and forward labels of its nodes, complying with the remark in footnote 3. We say that a rule effects that a branch B is *added* to left if for some $i \in \{0, \ldots, n-1\}$ it holds that $B \notin \mathsf{left}_i$ and $B \in \mathsf{left}_{i+1}$. Clearly $\mathsf{left}_0 = \emptyset$. The only rule which can effect that a branch is added to left is $\mathsf{Next}(PB)$. It is a precondition of $\mathsf{Next}(PB)$ that the leaf node of the branch added satisfies PB.

□

DPLL-Fwd Tableaux Satisfy *Cond-Active.*

Proposition 152 *A fwd-tableau of a tn-state derivable with a* DPLL-Fwd *calculus is* non-complementary*, i. e., no two nodes on a branch of the fwd-tableau have complementary literals as literal labels.*

Proof. Unit and Decide are the only rules that effect that a node with a literal (in contrast to $\top$) as literal label is newly attached to a branch. These rules have as a precondition that the atom of the literal label of the newly attached node does not yet occur in the literal labels of the branch.

□

[3] It is assumed that whether a given node satisfies a branch completeness property depends on no other properties of the node than the sequences of literal and forward labels of nodes along the branch to it.

Proposition 153 *If* $\langle T, N \rangle$ *is a tn-state derivable with a* DPLL-Fwd *calculus for link scope* S_l *and decision property* PD-L$_{S_l}$*, and* N *does not satisfy* PB-L$_{S_l}$*, then*

$$\text{Decide(PD-L}_{S_l}\text{) is applicable.}$$

Proof. Assume the preconditions of the proposition. Then N does not satisfy PB-L$_{S_l}$; hence $(B_N \wedge F_N)$ is not linkless outside S_l. Thus there exists a ground literal L such that L and N satisfy PD-L$_{S_l}$. From Proposition 152 it follows that B_N does not contain complementary literals. Since $(B_N \wedge F_N)$ is not linkless inside $\{L\}$, the atom of L must be in $\mathcal{A}(F_N)$. The last precondition of Decide, that is, $\mathsf{atom}(L) \notin \mathcal{A}(B_N)$, then follows from Proposition 141, which states that $\mathcal{A}(B_N) \cap \mathcal{A}(F_N) = \emptyset$.

□

DPLL-Fwd Tableaux Satisfy *Cond-Right*.

Proposition 154 *If* $\langle T, N \rangle$ *is a tn-state derivable with a* DPLL-Fwd *calculus for link scope* S_l*, branch completeness property* PB-L$_{S_l}$ *and decision property* PD-L$_{S_l}$*, and there exists a branch right of* B_N*, then*

$$\text{Decide(PD-L}_{S_l}\text{) or Next(PB-L}_{S_l}\text{) is applicable.}$$

Proof. We distinguish two cases:

- If the active leaf does not satisfy PB-L$_{S_l}$, then Decide(PD-L$_{S_l}$) is applicable by Proposition 153.
- If the active leaf satisfies PB-L$_{S_l}$ and the active branch contains a node that has a sibling to its right, then Next(PB-L$_{S_l}$) is applicable, which is easy to see.

□

11.3.7 DPLL-Fwd Calculi Compute LP

In Sections 11.3.2–11.3.6 it has been shown for different parts of the tableau framework for computing LP of Chapter 9 that DPLL-Fwd calculi comply with them. These results are now combined in Theorem 13 to make precise how DPLL-Fwd calculi can be used to compute LP.

Theorem 13 (Computing LP with DPLL-Fwd) *If* T *is the tableau of a terminal tn-state derivable with a* DPLL-Fwd *calculus that includes as rules at least* Decide(PD-L$_{S_l}$) *and* Next(PB-L$_{S_l}$) *for sentence* F*, link scope* S_l*, projection scope* S_p*, branch completeness property* PB-L$_{S_l}$ *and decision property* PD-L$_{S_l}$*, then*

$$\mathsf{LP}(F, S_l, S_p, \mathsf{leafy}(T)).$$

Proof. Follows from Theorem 8, since all eight of its preconditions (see Table 9.5, p. 151) are satisfied:

1. By Proposition 143 it holds that T is linklessness-preserving.
2. Since the calculus includes Decide(PD-L_{S_l}) and Next(PB-L_{S_l}), by Proposition 150, it holds that all leaf nodes of T satisfy PB-L_{S_l}.
3. By Proposition 146 it holds that T is upward-preserving for F and S_p.
4. By Proposition 139 and the definition of *fwd-admissible* it holds that $F_{\mathsf{root}(T)} \models_{S_p} F$.
5. By Proposition 149 it holds that T is extensional for F.
6. From the definition of Init follows immediately that $L_{\mathsf{root}(T)} = \top$.
7. By Proposition 148 it holds that T has branch implied forward labels.
8. By Proposition 139 and the definition of *fwd-admissible* it holds that $F \models F_{\mathsf{root}(T)}$.

□

11.4 Bounded Branch Length of DPLL-Fwd Tableaux

The length of branches of tableaux constructed by a DPLL-Fwd calculus for sentence F and fwd-bounding function *fb* is bounded by the sum of the cardinality of the atom base of F and the value of *fb* applied to F. This is shown in Proposition 157. DPLL-Fwd calculi construct *regular* tableaux (Proposition 155) and all atoms appearing in literal labels stem from F, which follows from Propositions 139 and 142. This alone does not suffice to show a bound on the length of branches, since they can contain nodes with literal label $\top$, which correspond to applications of Disconnect. A bound on the number of Disconnect steps along a branch follows from Proposition 156, which shows that the forward labels of the nodes along a branch are constrained with respect to their value of the fwd-bounding function.

Proposition 155 *A fwd-tableau of a tn-state derivable with a* DPLL-Fwd *calculus is* regular, *i. e., no two nodes on a branch of the fwd-tableau have the same literals as literal labels.*

Proof. Unit and Decide are the only rules that effect that a node with a literal (in contrast to $\top$) as literal label is newly attached to a branch. These rules have as precondition that the literal label of a newly attached node is not the literal label of a node on the branch.

□

Proposition 156 *If N, N' are nodes of the tableau of a tn-state derivable with a* DPLL-Fwd *calculus for fwd-bounding function fb, then*

(i) *If N is the root of the tableau, then*

$$fb(F) \geq fb(F_N);$$

(ii) *If N' is a child of N, then*

$$fb(F_N) \geq fb(F_{N'});$$

(iii) *If N' is a child of N and the literal label of N' is $\top$, then*

$$fb(F_N) > fb(F_{N'}).$$

Proof. If N is the root node of the tableau, then from Proposition 139 it follows that F_N is fwd-admissible for F. From the definition of *f-admissible* then follows $fb(F) \geq fb(F_N)$ (Definition 104.iv).

If N' is a child of an o-node N, then by Proposition 140.i it holds that $F_{N'}$ is fwd-admissible for $F_N[B_{N'}]$. *Fwd-admissible* then includes that $fb(F_N[B_{N'}]) \geq fb(F_{N'})$ (Definition 104.iv). Since the definition of *fwd-bounding function* (Definition 103.i) includes $fb(F_N) \geq fb(F_N[B_{N'}])$ it follows that $fb(F_N) \geq fb(F_{N'})$.

If N' is a child of an a-node N, then from Proposition 140.ii it follows that there exists a proper subformula F' of F_N such that $F_{N'}$ is fwd-admissible for $F'[B_{N'}]$. Similar to the case where N is an o-node, from Definitions 104.iv and 103.i follows $fb(F') \geq fb(F_{N'})$. From the definition of *fwd-bounding function* (Definition 103.iii) follows $fb(F_N) > fb(F')$; thus $fb(F_N) > fb(F_{N'})$.

□

Proposition 157 *If B is a branch of a tableau of a tn-state derivable with a* DPLL-Fwd *calculus for sentence F and fwd-bounding function fb, then*

$$|B| \leq |\mathcal{A}(F)| + 1 + fb(F).$$

Proof. The literal label of a node on B is either a literal or $\top$. If it is a literal, then its atom occurs in the forward label of the tableau root, as follows from Proposition 142. Hence, by Proposition 139 and the definition of *fwd-admissible*, its atom also occurs in F. By regularity (Proposition 155) and non-complementariness (Proposition 152), an atom can occur in the literal label of at most one node on B. By the definition of Init, the first node on B has literal label $\top$. Further nodes on B with literal label $\top$ are only added by the Disconnect rule and thus are children of a-nodes. It then follows from Proposition 156 that at most $fb(F)$ nodes on B besides the root node can have literal label $\top$.

□

11.5 Termination of DPLL-Fwd

DPLL-Fwd calculi terminate, since the active branch after a rule application is strictly smaller than before with respect to a certain ordering relation that is well founded when restricted to branches derivable with a given DPLL-Fwd calculus.

Definition 116 (Ordering Branches by Outdegree-Right Strings)

(i) If $B = N_1 \ldots N_n$ is a branch of a fwd-tableau, then the *outdegree-right string* of B, in symbols $\mathsf{o\text{-}r\text{-}string}(B)$, is the sequence of pairs $\langle o_1, r_1 \rangle \ldots \langle o_n, r_n \rangle$ such that

o_i is the number of children of N_i, if $i \in \{1, \ldots, n-1\}$;
r_i is the number of children of N_i right of N_{i+1}, if $i \in \{1, \ldots, n-1\}$;
o_n is 0, if $F_{N_n} = \top$;
o_n is the symbol ω, if $F_{N_n} \neq \top$;
r_n is 0.

(ii) If B_1, B_2 are branches of ordered trees, then $B_1 >_o B_2$ holds if and only if $\mathsf{o\text{-}r\text{-}string}(B_1)$ is lexicographically greater than $\mathsf{o\text{-}r\text{-}string}(B_2)$, where the elements of B_1 and B_2 are compared lexicographically, and the components of these elements by are compared by numerical value, considering the symbol ω greater than any number.

Proposition 158 *On the set of branches of tableaux of tn-states derivable with a* DPLL-Fwd *calculus*

$$\textit{the ordering relation } >_o \textit{ is well founded.}$$

Proof. By Proposition 157 the length of branches of tableaux of tn-states derivable with a DPLL-Fwd calculus is finitely bounded.

□

Proposition 159 *If $\langle T, N \rangle$ and $\langle T', N' \rangle$ are tn-states that are related by a rule of a* DPLL-Fwd *calculus, then*

$$\mathsf{o\text{-}r\text{-}string}(B_N) >_o \mathsf{o\text{-}r\text{-}string}(B_{N'}).$$

Proof. We show the proposition schematically for each rule of DPLL-Fwd. The variables S, T, U match subsequences of outdegree-right strings. The preconditions of Unit, Decide and Disconnect implicitly exclude that $\top$ is the forward label of the active leaf. Thus, the outdegree-right string of the state before an application of one of these rules must be of the form $S\langle \omega, 0 \rangle$.

Unit:	$S\langle\omega,0\rangle$	$>_o$	$S\langle 1,0\rangle T$;	
Decide:	$S\langle\omega,0\rangle$	$>_o$	$S\langle 2,1\rangle T$	
Backjump:	$S\langle 2,1\rangle T$	$>_o$	$S\langle 1,0\rangle U$,	and
	$S\langle 2,0\rangle T$	$>_o$	$S\langle 1,0\rangle U$;	
Disconnect:	$S\langle\omega,0\rangle$	$>_o$	$S\langle n,n-1\rangle T$,	where $n \geq 1$;
Next:	$S\langle n,m\rangle T$	$>_o$	$S\langle n,m-1\rangle U$,	where $n > m \geq 1$;
True-Up:	$S\langle n,m\rangle T$	$>_o$	$S\langle 0,0\rangle$,	where $n > m \geq 0$.

□

Theorem 14 (Termination of DPLL-Fwd) *A* DPLL-Fwd *calculus terminates.*

Proof. Follows immediately from Propositions 159 and 158.

□

11.6 Loosening the Decision Property PD-L

The decision property PD-L_{S_l} as parameter to Decide is sufficient for computing LP, as shown in Theorem 13 and explicated in Section 11.3.6. This decision property effects that an active leaf is extended with an atomic cut upon an atom A (i. e., two children with literal labels $+A$ and $-A$, respectively), where A is chosen in a way such that:

- It belongs to those atoms that are not permitted to be involved in "links" of the overall result of computation. This is expressed in Definition 114 by the condition $L \notin S_l \cap \widetilde{S_l}$. For projection elimination, where $S_l = S_p$, this means that at least one of the literals $+A$ or $-A$ is "to forget about", i. e., is not in the projection scope S_p.
- There is a "link" involving A in the forward label of the active leaf. This is expressed in Definition 114 by the condition that $(B_N \wedge F_N)$ is not linkless inside $\{L\}$.

Also variants of Decide with a decision property that loosens both of these properties, but at least requires that A is chosen from the forward label of the active leaf, are suitable to compute LP without compromising correctness or termination properties. Such loosened variants of PD-L permit a wider range of choices for the atoms upon which atomic cuts are performed, which can be heuristically beneficial. For example, an atom for an atomic cut can be chosen because it allows to simplify the forward labels of the newly attached node in some particular way.

If, for example, in a projection elimination task with scope $S_p = \{+\mathsf{p}, -\mathsf{p}\}$ the forward label F of the active node is

$$\begin{aligned} F = \;& (\mathsf{p} \lor \mathsf{q}) && \land \\ & (\neg\mathsf{p} \lor \neg\mathsf{s}) && \land \\ & (\neg\mathsf{q} \lor \mathsf{r}) && \land \\ & (\neg\mathsf{r} \lor \mathsf{s}), \end{aligned}$$

then an atomic cut upon p allows to assign $\top$ as forward labels of the two children. This can be justified as follows: Substituting p in F with, say, $\top$ and performing truth value simplification yields

$$\begin{aligned} F' = \;& \neg\mathsf{s} && \land \\ & (\neg\mathsf{q} \lor \mathsf{r}) && \land \\ & (\neg\mathsf{r} \lor \mathsf{s}) && . \end{aligned}$$

It can be efficiently detected that F' is satisfiable, since it does not contain a clause with only positive literals. Furthermore, F' contains only literals "to forget about", i. e., $\mathcal{L}(F') \cap S_p = \emptyset$. From properties of projection, Propositions 52 and 73, it then follows that $\mathsf{project}(F', S_p) \equiv \top$.

Another application of loosened variants of PD-L is the simulation of clausal tableaux. The central construction rule for clausal tableaux [Let98], *clausal expansion*, effects that to a leaf node children corresponding to some clause of the input sentence are attached: For each literal of the clause, there is a child labeled with that literal. *Complement splitting* [MB88], also called *folding down* [LMG94], is a refinement of clausal expansion, which is applicable if the tableau is an *ordered* tree. It effects that with each of the new children, in addition, the complements of the literal labels of its right siblings are associated. The branch to such a child is then regarded as including these complements. Clausal expansion with complement splitting can be simulated with loosened variants of PD-L by choosing atoms for cuts in a suitable way. Fig. 11.1 illustrates this for the clause $(\mathsf{p} \lor \mathsf{q} \lor \neg\mathsf{r})$. (The branch marked with $\bot$ is inconsistent with the clause, and thus would be backtracked by Next or Backjump.)

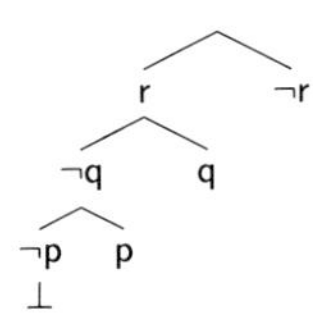

Figure 11.1. Simulation of Clausal Expansion

12 Efficiency Aspects of DPLL-Fwd Calculi

The rules of DPLL-Fwd have been specified in Section 11.2 by referring to semantic relationships, without concern how the matching of their preconditions against a tn-state and the computation of their effects can be performed with an efficiency that is adequate for speaking of a calculus. This adequacy can be ensured in a precise sense, by showing that DPLL-Fwd calculi with certain provisions are *polynomially transparent* [Let93], which means that the time to compute a derivation is bounded by a polynomial in two arguments, the size of the initial state and the length of the derivation. This property allows to use the length of a derivation as a measure of its complexity, abstracted modulo polynomials.

In Section 12.1 we define the *working data structure* of DPLL-Fwd calculi for a sentence F, a representation of the portion of tn-states that is required by the calculus to be explicitly represented in memory. It is shown that its size is polynomially bounded by the size of F.

The specifications of Init and the effects of most rules of DPLL-Fwd involve the construction of forward labels by a fwd-simplification algorithm. In Section 12.2 it is shown that this can be performed efficiently. It can include simplification operations, some of which are specific to projection elimination. We show that DPLL-Fwd calculi that employ such simplifications enjoy the improvements of unconstrained LP-algorithms over EQ-constrained LP-algorithms, as discussed in Section 8.3.

Given that forward labels can be efficiently computed, it is shown in Section 12.3 that a successor state to a given state (i. e., a derivation step) can be computed with DPLL-Fwd (with certain provisions) in time polynomial in the size of the working data structure of the given state. Based on this and the fact that the size of working data structures of DPLL-Fwd calculi for sentence F is polynomially bounded by the size of F, we show in Section 12.4 that those calculi are polynomially transparent.

12.1 The Working Data Structure of DPLL-Fwd

As explained in Section 11.1.1, we use a notion of derivation whose state objects do not necessarily need to be represented fully in main memory. Inspection of the rules of DPLL-Fwd shows that their preconditions, which are matched against tn-states, depend only on some components of the tableau of the tn-state. We call the combination of these components the *working data structure* of the tn-state (Definition 117).

It is shown in Theorem 15 that the size of the working data structure of a DPLL-Fwd calculus for sentence F is polynomially bounded by $|F|$. No effort has been made to further reduce the size of the working data structure. For example, it is conceivable that a working data structure that does not include forward labels in explicitly constructed form (as sketched in the introduction to Section 11.2.5) is also sufficient.

Definition 117 (Working Data Structure of a DPLL-Fwd State) The *working data structure* of a state derivable with a DPLL-Fwd calculus for sentence F, link scope S_l and projection scope S_p is a data structure that comprises representations of

- The active branch with the literal labels of its nodes,
- Siblings of nodes on the active branch, along with their literal labels
- The forward labels of the nodes on the active branch,
- The forward labels of the siblings of the nodes on the active branch,
- F,
- S_l, and S_p that allow to decide membership of a given ground literal in time polynomial in their cardinality.

Theorem 15 (Size of Working Data Structures of DPLL-Fwd) *The space required to represent the working data structure of a state derivable with a* DPLL-Fwd *calculus for sentence F is polynomially bounded $|F|$.*

Proof.

(1) $|B_N|$ is polynomially bounded by $|F|$.

Assume the preconditions of the proposition. Let $\langle T, N\rangle$ be a tn-state derivable from a calculus as specified in the proposition. (1) follows from the definition of *fwd-bounding function* (Definition 103.iv) and Proposition 157.

(2) $|F_{N'}|$ is polynomially bounded by $fb(F_{N'})$.
(3) $fb(F) \geq fb(F_{N'})$.
(4) $|F_{N'}|$ is polynomially bounded by $fb(F)$.
(5) $|F_{N'}|$ is polynomially bounded by $|F|$.

Let N' be a node in T. (2) follows from the definition of *fwd-bounding function* (Definition 103.v). (3) follows from Proposition 156 by straightforward induction. (4) follows from (3) and (2). (5) follows from (4) and the definition of *fwd-bounding function* (Definition 103.iv).

(6) The number of siblings of a node on B_N is polynomially bounded by $|F|$.

(6) holds, since the root of T has no sibling, children of o-nodes have at most one sibling, and the number of children of an a-node N' is polynomially bounded by $|F|$. This bounding of the number of children follows from (5), since, by the definition of Disconnect, the number of children of N' can not exceed $|F_{N'}|$.

(7) F, S_l as well as S_p can be represented in space polynomially bounded by $|F|$.

(7) holds, since by the definition of DPLL-Fwd calculus $S_l \subseteq \mathcal{L}(F)$ and $S_p \subseteq \mathcal{L}(F)$. Assuming that a literal label can be represented in constant space, the proposition follows from (7), (6), (5), (1) and the definition of *working data structure.*

□

12.2 Efficiency Aspects of the Construction of Forward Labels

12.2.1 Efficient Construction of Forward Labels

It is almost inherent in the definition of *fwd-simplification algorithm* that the computation of a forward label involved a in rule application can be performed in time polynomial in the size of the working data structure of the state to which the rule is applied, as shown by the following proposition:

Proposition 160 *A call to Simplify-Fwd in the computation of a successor state to a given state S according to the rule specifications of* DPLL-Fwd *calculi for fwd-simplification algorithm Simplify-Fwd can be performed in time polynomial in the size of the working data structure of S.*

Proof. In the rule specifications *Simplify-Fwd* is used to compute the forward label $F_{N'}$ of a newly attached node N' from $F^{\backslash}$ and $B_{N'}$, where $F^{\backslash}$ is the forward label of the parent of N', or, in the case of Disconnect, a subformula of it. Since $|B_{N'}| \leq |B_N|+1$ and $F^{\backslash}$ is the forward label of a node on B_N or a subformula of such a forward label, where N is the active leaf of the given tn-state S, the proposition then follows from the definitions of *fwd-simplification algorithm* and *working data structure.*

□

12.2.2 Simplifications in the Construction of Forward Labels

A fwd-simplification algorithm invoked on a propositional sentence F and ground branch B can involve the application of simplification operations to $F[B]$. Some of these simplifications are widely used in the context of automated theorem proving for they preserve satisfiability. Their application to the computation of fwd-admissible sentences, however, requires a closer look, since not only satisfiability, but, moreover, equivalence relative to the projection scope S_p has to be preserved. We now give some examples of such simplification operations that can be employed in fwd-simplification algorithms, along with measures that are not increased by them and thus can be used as fwd-bounding functions.

The formula size is an immediate instance of a fwd-bounding function. Simplification operations that are suitable for this fwd-bounding function – which means that they do not increase the formula size – include equivalence preserving simplifications such as truth value simplification. Simplification of a CNF sentence F by unit subsumption and unit resolution upon literals on a branch B can be considered as truth value simplification applied to $F[B]$.

Also operations that just preserve equivalence with respect to the scope argument S_p and reduce the formula size are suitable simplifications for the formula size as fwd-bounding function. Examples for CNF sentences are the *purity* and *isol* simplifications upon literals not in S_p. Both of these operations are special cases of replace-by-resolvents (see Section 7.4). An example operation that also applies to sentences not in CNF is literal substitution with $\top$ of literals not in S_p, according to Proposition 87. Combined with truth value simplification, this operation reduces the formula size and generalizes *purity* simplification.

The *isol** simplification for CNF sentences, another special case of replace-by-resolvents, might increase the formula size, but reduces the number of clauses. The size of a propositional CNF sentence (such that a clause does not contain multiple occurrences of same literal) is bounded by the product of the number of its clauses and the cardinality of its literal signature. Thus the *isol** simplification is suitable for the sum of the number of clauses and the size of the literal base as fwd-bounding function.

12.2.3 Weaving Projection into Compilation

As discussed in Section 8.3, LP-algorithms that are not EQ-constrained permit to perform projection elimination partially already during compilation, avoiding unnecessary blow-ups of formula parts that otherwise would be projected away at later stages. Aside of rule True-Up (Section 11.2.6), in DPLL-Fwd calculi, this partial projection elimination can take place in the construction of forward labels, by including simplification operations that correspond to special cases of projection elimination which can be performed at low cost. The inclusion of such simplification operations is semantically justified by the *upward-preserving* constraint, which is reflected in the *fwd-admissible* property. The forward label of a node, conjoined with the branch to the node, is required to entail the forward label of a parent just *relative to the projection scope*.

We show a concrete example of how an unconstrained LP-algorithm based on a DPLL-Fwd calculus can utilize the possibilities of improvement over EQ-constrained LP-algorithms. Consider the task of computing for a disjoin-sentence F upon some atom A and a representation of a literal scope $S \subseteq \mathcal{L}(F) - \{+A\}$ as inputs a propositional sentence F' such that

$$\mathsf{LP}(F, \emptyset, S, F').$$

It follows from Theorem 13 that F' can be computed by a DPLL-Fwd calculus for sentence F, the empty set as link scope and S as projection scope. As has been shown in Section 8.3, for *EQ-constrained* LP-algorithms, the size of the output formula F' is not polynomially bounded by the size of the input sentence, unless $\mathsf{NP} \subseteq \mathsf{P/poly}$, which is considered as very unlikely in complexity theory; if however the *EQ-constrained* condition is dropped, the task can be performed in polynomial time. A DPLL-Fwd calculus has this polynomial behavior, if its fwd-simplification algorithm applies *purity* and truth value simplification upon literals not in S on inputs that happen to be in CNF. Such a fwd-simplification algorithm returns $\top$ if it is applied to a disjoin-sentence upon an atom A where $+A \notin S$. It follows from the definition of Init it that the DPLL-Fwd calculus for such a disjoin-sentence proceeds by constructing in the initialization phase a tn-state with a tableau that consists of a single node that has $\top$ as literal label as well as forward label. This tn-state is also a terminal state. By Proposition 161 it can be constructed in time polynomial in $|F|$. Clearly also the final step of the DPLL-Fwd based LP-algorithm, the computation of the leafy sentence $(\top \wedge \top)$ of the single-node tableau, can be performed in time polynomial in $|F|$.

Practical value of the inclusion of such simplification operations is expected less for the extreme case of disjoin-sentences as global inputs to DPLL-Fwd, but for the inclusion of simplifications that preserve equivalence just relative to the projection scope on the many forward labels that are typically constructed during a DPLL-Fwd derivation.

12.3 Efficient Rule Applications

Given that forward labels can be efficiently computed, as shown in Section 12.2, we show for the rules of DPLL-Fwd, with parameters instantiated to compute LP for a propositional polar sentence F according to Theorem 13 that the time required to compute an initial derivation state is polynomial in the size of F and that the time required to compute a derivation step, which means a successor state to a given state, is polynomial in the size of the working data structure of the given state.

A Decide and a Next rule are sufficient for a DPLL-Fwd calculus to compute LP, as follows from Theorem 13. We show the time bound for derivation steps with these two rules in Proposition 162. The remaining rules are optional. Unit and Backjump become useful if they are further restricted, depending on the class of sentences allowed as formula labels and extra information maintained by the system, such that the matching of preconditions and computation of a successor state only takes place in situations when it is sure that the time required is polynomially bounded by the size of the working space.

For True-Up it is apparent from the rule definition that the checking of preconditions and computation of a successor state can be performed efficiently.

Efficient Construction of Initial States with of Init.

Proposition 161 *From a propositional polar sentence F as input, a tn-state in* Init *for a* DPLL-Fwd *calculus for sentence F can be constructed in time polynomial in $|F|$.*

Proof. Follows from the definition of Init. With similar arguments as in the proof of Proposition 160 it can be shown that the time to compute the call of *Simplify-Fwd* according to the specification of Init is polynomial in $|F|$. □

Efficient Application of Decide and Next.

Proposition 162 *Let S_l be a literal scope. From a tn-state S as input, to which* Decide(PD-L$_{S_l}$) *or* Next(PB-L$_{S_l}$) *is applicable, a successor state related by* Decide(PD-L$_{S_l}$) *or* Next(PB-L$_{S_l}$)*, respectively, can be constructed in time polynomial in the size of the working data structure of S.*

Proof. That the matching of preconditions is for both rules polynomial in the size of the working data structure of S can be shown as follows: Let N be the active leaf of S. By Proposition 141 it holds that $\mathcal{A}(B_N) \cap \mathcal{A}(F_N) = \emptyset$ and by Proposition 152 it holds that B_N is non-complementary. Thus if $(B_N \wedge F_N)$ is not linkless outside S_l, then F_N is not linkless outside S_l. The preconditions of Decide and Next are then dual: For Decide(PD-L$_{S_l}$) it is required to find a literal $L \notin S \cap \widetilde{S}$ such that F_N is not linkless inside $\{L\}$. For Next(PB-L$_{S_l}$) it is required to verify that F_N is linkless outside S_l, which is equivalent to the condition that there is no literal $L \notin S \cap \widetilde{S}$ such that F_N is not linkless inside $\{L\}$. Both cases can be computed by traversing F_N and computing for each member $\langle F_1, F_2 \rangle$ of the pairs of conjuncts in F_N a representation of the set $\mathcal{L}(F_1) \cap \widetilde{\mathcal{L}(F_2)} - (S_l \cap \widetilde{S_l})$ that allows to check whether it is empty (for Next), and to choose an element if it is not empty (for Decide). This can obviously be performed in time polynomial in the sum of $|F_N|$ and the size of the representation of S_l included in the working data structure of S.

Performing the effects of Decide(PD-L$_{S_l}$) includes computation of two forward labels. From Proposition 160 it follows that the time required for this is polynomial in the size of the working data structure of S. It is then easy to see that for both of the rules the effects can be computed in time polynomial in the size of the working data structure of S. □

Efficient Application of Disconnect.

Proposition 163 *Let S_l be a literal scope. From a tn-state S as input, to which* Disconnect(S_l) *is applicable, a successor state related by* Disconnect(S_l) *can be constructed in time polynomial in the size of the working data structure of S.*

Proof. That the preconditions of Disconnect can be matched in time polynomial in the size of the working data structure of S can be shown as follows: Let N be the active leaf of S. Let $G_1, \ldots, G_m$ be the sentences that occur as smallest subformulas of F_N that are not in the scope of a logic operator with exception of $\land$ (each of the $G_1, \ldots, G_m$ corresponds to a subformula *occurrence*). Clearly F_N is equal to $(G_1 \land \ldots \land G_m)$ modulo associativity and commutativity of $\land$. The conjuncts $G_1, \ldots, G_m$ have to be partitioned into "connected components", that is formulas $F_1, \ldots, F_n$, each of which is a conjunction of one or more sentences from $G_1, \ldots, G_m$ such that each of the $G_1, \ldots, G_m$ occurs in exactly one of $F_1, \ldots, F_n$, and for all $i, j \in \{1, \ldots, n\}$ such that $i \neq j$ it holds that $\langle F_i, F_j \rangle$ is linkless outside S_l.

In the model counting method of [BP00], a set of clauses is partitioned such that the atom bases of the groups are mutually disjoint. This is performed by constructing the so-called *constraint graph* of the clause set: each atom of the clause set is represented by a node and if two atoms appear in the same clause, they are linked by an edge. The connected components, i. e., maximal subgraphs such that for every pair of nodes n_1, n_2 in the subgraph there is a path from n_1 to n_2 are identified and the clauses are grouped accordingly. The computation of connected components of a graph can be performed in time linear in the size of the graph by a depth-first traversal.

This method can also be applied for the Disconnect rule (generalized to *set of conjuncts* instead of *set of clauses*), with the difference that a smaller constraint graph suffices: Only edges between atoms have to be considered that

1. Do not occur with both polarities in S_l, and
2. Occur in F_N with both polarities.

The time required for this is obviously polynomial in the sum of $|F_N|$ and the size of the representation of S_l included in the working data structure.

That computing the effects of Disconnect is polynomial in the size of the working data structure of S is easy to see from the definition of Disconnect: The number of new nodes attached to the tableau of a state with active leaf N can not exceed $|F_N|$; the computation of the forward labels of the new nodes is polynomially bounded by the size of the working data structure of S, as follows from Proposition 160.

□

Efficient Application of Unit. Unit can for forward labels in CNF be restricted to the case where the forward label of the active leaf contains a unit clause with a literal that is neither directly nor complementary on the active branch. Our formalization also allows to handle unit propagation not by a rule, but instead *within* the computation of a derivation step, as a simplification operation in computation of fwd-admissible forward labels.

Efficient Application of Backjump. Since a fwd-tableau T constructed by DPLL-Fwd has branch implied forward labels (Proposition 148), if N is a node in T such that $F_N = \bot$, then $F_{\mathsf{root}} \wedge B_N \models \bot$. Theorem 10 ensures that in this case B_N matches *backjumping preconditions* for a chronological backjumping step. The matching can obviously be performed in time polynomial in the length of B_N, since it essentially just consists in finding the last decision node in B_N.

Matches for *backjumping preconditions* with nodes N_a and N_b that are closer to the root can be obtained by considering on which of the nodes on B_N the false forward label F_N actually depends. Maintenance of such information is not explicitly modeled in our formalization. Assuming that the overhead with respect to computation time and size to maintain this extra information is polynomially bounded by the size of the working data structure, also in cases where Backjump effects not just chronological backtracking, but actually "jumping back" over irrelevant decisions, the preconditions can be matched in time polynomial in the size the working data structure.

That computing the effects of Backjump is polynomial in the size of the working data structure of the state to which Backjump is applied is easy to see from the definition of Backjump, given that the included computation of the forward label is polynomial in the size of the working data structure, which follows from Proposition 160.

12.4 Polynomial Transparency

The efficiency properties of the DPLL-Fwd calculi shown in Section 12.3 imply that with certain provisions such calculi are *polynomially transparent*, as defined by Letz [Let93, pp. 77f]. Polynomial transparency allows to use the length of a derivation as a measure of its complexity. A calculus[1] is polynomially transparent if there is a polynomial p in two variables such that for every derivation D with the calculus it holds that the number of machine steps to compute D is smaller than p applied to the size the initial state of D and the length of D.

This definition does not carry over fully literally to derivations with DPLL-Fwd for sentence F, since the initial state of such a derivation might not correspond to the initial state of computation: By the definition of Init, some

[1] The original notion in [Let93] is based on *transition system*; we have adapted it here to our more specific terminology.

preprocessing might be involved to compute an initial state, namely computation of the forward label of the root node with a fwd-simplification algorithm applied to F. It is of course possible to adapt the calculus and consider Init as a rule that is applied to a special initial state that comprises a representation of F, but it seems more straightforward to use as first argument of the polynomial p the size of F instead of the size of the initial state.

Theorem 16 (Polynomial Transparency of DPLL-Fwd) *There exists a polynomial p in two variables such that for all propositional polar sentences F and literal scopes S_l, S_p, where $S_l \subseteq S_p \subseteq \mathcal{L}(F)$, it holds that if D is a derivation with a* DPLL-Fwd *calculus*[2] *for sentence F, link scope S_l, projection scope S_p branch completeness property* $\mathsf{PB\text{-}L}_{S_l}$*, and decision property* $\mathsf{PD\text{-}L}_{S_l}$*, then*

> *the time required to compute D from F and representations of S_l and S_p is smaller than p applied to $|F|$ and the length of D.*

Proof.

(1) The initial state of D can be constructed in time polynomial in $|F|$.
(2) The successor to a state S in D can be constructed in time polynomial in the size of the working data structure of S.
(3) The space required to represent a working data structure of a state in D is polynomially bounded by $|F|$.
(4) The successor to a state in D can be constructed in time polynomial in $|F|$.

(1) follows from Proposition 161. (2) follow from Propositions 162 and 163 (along with the considerations in Sections 12.3 and 12.3 for *Unit* and Backjump). (3) follows from Theorem 15. (4) follows from (3) and (2). The proposition follows from (4) and (1).

□

[2] Assuming that if Unit and Backjump are included in the rules of the calculus, then with restrictions that ensure efficient applicability, as shown in Sections 12.3 and 12.3.

13 DPLL-Fwd with Piecemeal Output

As we have seen in Section 12.1, DPLL-Fwd operates with a working data structure that is polynomially bounded by the size of the input sentence, although the size of the output, the constructed tableau, is not polynomially bounded. Thus at any point of time only a piece of the tableau under construction has to be explicitly represented in memory; the remaining piece can be considered as offline. While the polynomial space requirements are clearly beneficial for theorem proving tasks in which a yes/no answer is computed, they can also be utilized for formula transformation tasks. To this end we investigate variants of DPLL-Fwd that output pieces of their overall output as soon as they are computed, and thus fully operate in polynomial space. Such algorithms can be employed in applications in which output pieces by themselves are useful, can be piped to another program, or it is expected that the first few output pieces provide a solution. Output pieces can for example be piped to a theorem prover: if an overall output sentence F is equivalent to the disjunction of output pieces, then a theorem G follows from F if and only if G follows from each of the pieces.

We confine ourselves here to cases where the overall output corresponds to the *disjunctive* combination of the output pieces. Since this is not straightforward to realize for tableaux with and-nodes, we consider DPLL-Fwd calculi with the restriction that they do not contain Disconnect, the rule that effects construction of and-nodes. DPLL-Fwd (without Disconnect) can be run in a way such that whenever Next is applied to a state with active leaf N, the sentence $(B_N \land F_N)$ is returned as an output piece. Finally, $(B_N \land F_N)$ for the active leaf N of the terminal state is returned as the last output piece. The overall output, a sentence satisfying the LP relation with respect to the input sentence, is the disjunction of those pieces.

For tableau construction methods that do not involve destructive operations such as backjumping, the combination of output pieces, each corresponding to a branch of the final tableau, is trivially equal to the final tableau. For methods that include destructive operations, extra effort is required to show that none of the output pieces are "wrong" and no essential output piece is "missing" at termination. It may be acceptable that output pieces may become redundant in the presence of output pieces delivered at a later point of time. We now formally show how DPLL-Fwd without Disconnect, but with Backjump, can be employed in a piecemeal manner.

13.1 DPLL-Fwd-O and Leafy Pieces

As state objects for the piecemeal variants of DPLL-Fwd we take tn-states (Definition 100), extended by a further component that indicates whether the state has been obtained by the Next rule.

Definition 118 (DPLL-Fwd-O Calculus) A *DPLL-Fwd-O* calculus is an DPLL-Fwd calculus that does not include an instance of rule Disconnect.

The exclusion of Disconnect in DPLL-Fwd-O calculi has the purpose to ensure that there are no a-nodes in the constructed fwd-tableaux.

Definition 119 (Leafy Pieces) If D is a derivation with a DPLL-Fwd-O calculus, then leafy-pieces(D) is the propositional sentence defined as

$$\mathsf{leafy\text{-}pieces}(D) \stackrel{\text{def}}{=} \bigvee_{\langle T,N\rangle \in D'} B_N \wedge F_N,$$

where D' is the set of states in D that

- Have a successor state obtained with the Next rule, or
- Are terminal.

13.2 Leafy Pieces that Satisfy LP-L

Proposition 164 *If D is a derivation with a* DPLL-Fwd-O *calculus that includes as rules at least* Decide(PD-L_{S_l}) *for link scope S_l, then*

$$\mathsf{leafy\text{-}pieces}(D) \textit{ is linkless outside } S_l.$$

Proof. The sentence leafy-pieces(D) is a disjunction. We show that all of its disjuncts are linkless outside S_l, which implies that the sentence itself is linkless outside S_l. Recall that a node N satisfies the property PB-L_{S_l} if and only if $(B_N \wedge F_N)$ is linkless outside S_l (Definition 84, p. 138). If $(B_N \wedge F_N)$ is a disjunct in leafy-pieces(D), then one of the following two cases must hold:

- N is the active leaf of a state in D whose successor state is obtained by Next(PB-L_{S_l}). By the preconditions of Next it holds that N satisfies PB-L_{S_l}.
- N is the active leaf of a terminal state. If N would not satisfy PB-L_{S_l}, then Decide(PD-L_{S_l}) is applicable by Proposition 153, contradicting with N being a terminal state.

□

13.3 Leafy Pieces that Satisfy LP-U

Proposition 165 *If D is a derivation with a* DPLL-Fwd-O *calculus for sentence F and projection scope S_p, then*

$$\mathsf{leafy\text{-}pieces}(D) \models_{S_p} F.$$

Proof. If $\langle T, N\rangle$ is a state in D, then by Proposition 146 it holds that

$$T \text{ is upward-preserving for } S_p.$$

Since T is a tableau without a-nodes, it follows by straightforward induction from the specification of *upward-preserving* (Definition 85, p. 140) that

$$B_N \land \mathsf{project}(F_N, S_p) \models \mathsf{project}(F_{\mathsf{root}(T)}, S_p),$$

which by Proposition 30 implies $(B_N \land F_N) \models \mathsf{project}(F_{\mathsf{root}(T)}, S_p)$. Along with the fact that $\mathsf{project}(F_{\mathsf{root}(T)}, S_p) \models \mathsf{project}(F, S_p)$, which follows from Proposition 139 and the definition of *fwd-admissible*, this implies that $(B_N \land F_N) \models \mathsf{project}(F, S_p)$, which by Proposition 37 is equivalent to

$$B_N \land F_N \models_{S_p} F.$$

Since $\mathsf{leafy\text{-}pieces}(D)$ is a disjunction of sentences $(B_N \land F_N)$, where N is the active leaf of a state in D, the proposition then follows from Proposition 76.

□

13.4 Leafy Pieces that Satisfy LP-D

Definition 120 (Leafy Lefts) If T is a fwd-tableau without a-nodes and $N_1, \ldots, N_k, \ldots, N_n$, where $1 \leq k \leq n$, are the leaf nodes of T in the ordering in which they are visited in a left-to-right depth-first tree traversal, then $\mathsf{leafy\text{-}lefts}(N_k)$ is the propositional sentence defined as

$$\mathsf{leafy\text{-}lefts}(N_k) \stackrel{\text{def}}{=} \bigvee_{i \in \{1,\ldots,k-1\}} B_{N_i} \land F_{N_i}.$$

Proposition 166 *If D is a derivation of a tn-state $\langle T, N\rangle$ with a* DPLL-Fwd-O *calculus, then*

$$\mathsf{leafy\text{-}lefts}(N) \models \mathsf{leafy\text{-}pieces}(D).$$

Proof. By induction on the length of the derivation. In the base case, where the length is 1, it holds that $\langle T, N\rangle$ is a member of Init; thus $T = N$ and $\mathsf{leafy\text{-}lefts}(N) \equiv \bot$, which implies the proposition to be proved. The induction step for derivations of length $n > 1$ can be shown as follows:

(IA) $\mathsf{leafy\text{-}lefts}(N) \models \mathsf{leafy\text{-}pieces}(D)$.
(IC) $\mathsf{leafy\text{-}lefts}(N') \models \mathsf{leafy\text{-}pieces}(D')$.
(1) $\mathsf{leafy\text{-}pieces}(D) \models \mathsf{leafy\text{-}pieces}(D')$.

Let D' be a derivation with length n of a tn-state $\langle T', N' \rangle$, let D be the prefix of D' with length $n-1$, and let $\langle T, N \rangle$ be the last state of D. (IA) is then the induction assumption and (IC) the induction conclusion to be shown. (1) follows from the definition of leafy-pieces. $\langle T', N' \rangle$ is obtained from $\langle T, N \rangle$ by application of a rule of the DPLL-Fwd-O calculus. In case D' is obtained from D by Unit or Decide, it is easy to see that

(2) $\mathsf{leafy\text{-}lefts}(N') = \mathsf{leafy\text{-}lefts}(N)$.

Thus, in this case (IC) follows from (2), (1) and (IA). In case D' is obtained from D by True-Up or Backjump, (IC) can be shown as follows: True-Up and Backjump can be viewed as a *Truncation* step, which for Backjump is followed by Extension (as noted in the proof of Proposition 149 and shown in Section 9). The Truncation step can only "effect that disjuncts are removed from leafy-lefts", while the Extension step has "no effect on leafy-lefts". Thus, for True-Up and Backjump the disjuncts of $\mathsf{leafy\text{-}lefts}(N')$ are a subset of those of $\mathsf{leafy\text{-}lefts}(N)$, which implies

(3) $\mathsf{leafy\text{-}lefts}(N') \models \mathsf{leafy\text{-}lefts}(N)$.

Thus, in this case (IC) follows from (3), (1) and (IA). Finally we have to consider the case where D' is obtained from D by Next.

(4) $\mathsf{leafy\text{-}pieces}(D') = \mathsf{leafy\text{-}pieces}(D) \lor (B_{N'} \land F_{N'})$.
(5) $\mathsf{leafy\text{-}lefts}(N') = \mathsf{leafy\text{-}lefts}(N) \lor (B_{N'} \land F_{N'})$.

(4) follows from the definition of leafy-pieces. (5) is easy to see. In this case (IC) follows from (5), (4) and (IA).

□

Proposition 167 *If D is a derivation of a terminal state with a* DPLL-Fwd-O *calculus that includes as rules at least* $\mathsf{Decide}(\mathsf{PD\text{-}L}_{S_l})$ *and* $\mathsf{Next}(\mathsf{PB\text{-}L}_{S_l})$ *for sentence F and link scope S_l, then*

$$F \models \mathsf{leafy\text{-}pieces}(D).$$

Proof.

(1) $\mathsf{leafy}(T) \equiv \mathsf{leafy\text{-}lefts}(N) \lor (B_N \land F_N)$.
(2) $F \models \mathsf{leafy}(T)$.
(3) $F \models \mathsf{leafy\text{-}lefts}(N) \lor (B_N \land F_N)$.
(4) $F \models \mathsf{leafy\text{-}pieces}(D) \lor (B_N \land F_N)$.
(5) $\mathsf{leafy\text{-}pieces}(D) \lor (B_N \land F_N) \equiv \mathsf{leafy\text{-}pieces}(D)$.
(6) $F \models \mathsf{leafy\text{-}pieces}(D)$.

Let $\langle T, N \rangle$ be the last state in D. It is a terminal state. The branch B_N does not contain a node with a sibling to its right, since otherwise by Proposition 154 a rule would applicable to $\langle T, N \rangle$, contradicting the fact that it is a terminal state. Since B_N does not contain a node with a right sibling, N is the last leaf of T (in the ordering in which leaf nodes are visited in a left-to-right depth-first traversal) and thus (1) holds. (2) follows from Theorem 13. (3) follows from (2) and (1). (4) follows from (3) and Proposition 166. N is the active leaf of a terminal state, the last state in D. (5) then follows from the definition of leafy-pieces. (6) follows from (5) and (4).

The preconditions that $\mathsf{Decide}(\mathsf{PD\text{-}L}_{S_l})$ and $\mathsf{Next}(\mathsf{PB\text{-}L}_{S_l})$ are included in the rules of the calculus are required by Proposition 154.

□

13.5 DPLL-Fwd-O Calculi Compute LP Piecemeal

The following theorem combines the results of the previous Sections 13.2–13.4 to show that DPLL-Fwd calculi used in piecemeal fashion correctly compute LP, analogously to Theorem 13 above, which shows correctness for "non-piecemeal" use. The correctness property for piecemeal use applies to all DPLL-Fwd-O calculi, that is to DPLL-Fwd calculi without the Disconnect rule, which at least include the rules Decide and Next as described in the preconditions of the theorem. Thus also, if the optional destructive rules Backjump and True-Up are present. The explicit consideration of these rules takes place in the proof of Proposition 166, which is used, via Proposition 167, as a lemma to prove the theorem.

Theorem 17 (Computing LP Piecemeal with DPLL-Fwd-O) *If D is a derivation of a terminal state derivable with a* DPLL-Fwd-O *calculus that includes as rules at least* $\mathsf{Decide}(\mathsf{PD\text{-}L}_{S_l})$ *and* $\mathsf{Next}(\mathsf{PB\text{-}L}_{S_l})$ *for sentence F, link scope S_l, projection scope S_p, branch completeness property* $\mathsf{PB\text{-}L}_{S_l}$ *and decision property* $\mathsf{PD\text{-}L}_{S_l}$*, then*

$$\mathsf{LP}(F, S_l, S_p, \mathsf{leafy\text{-}pieces}(D)).$$

Proof. The three conditions, LP-L, LP-U and LP-D, of the specification of LP (Definition 75) are satisfied by $\mathsf{leafy\text{-}pieces}(D)$:

- LP-L, since by Proposition 164 it holds that $\mathsf{leafy\text{-}pieces}(D)$ is linkless outside S_l;
- LP-U, since by Proposition 165 it holds that $\mathsf{leafy\text{-}pieces}(D) \models_{S_p} F$;
- LP-D, since by Proposition 167 it holds that $F \models \mathsf{leafy\text{-}pieces}(D)$.

The precondition of the proposition that $\mathsf{Decide}(\mathsf{PD\text{-}L}_{S_l})$ is included in the rules of the calculus is required by Propositions 164 and 167. That $\mathsf{Next}(\mathsf{PB\text{-}L}_{S_l})$ is included, by Proposition 167.

□

14 Related Work on Formula Transformation Methods

We discuss three groups of methods that have been presented in recent years and are related to our tableau-based methods for knowledge compilation and projection elimination. The first two are based on DPLL and thus implicitly work by constructing a tableau. They adapt DPLL for knowledge compilation into DNNF and for the elimination of Boolean quantifiers, a special case of projection elimination, respectively. The author of the method for quantifier elimination has also developed a method for approximating quantifier elimination by interpolant computation in certain applications of symbolic model checking. We also outline this, introduced by a general overview on the relationship of projection to interpolation. Methods of the third group that we discuss essentially work by rewriting subformulas in non-clausal sentences. For a particular such method, which has been designed for the application to knowledge compilation, we work out in detail a simulation by a variant of our DPLL-based methods.

14.1 DPLL-Based DNNF Compilation

Darwiche [Dar04] and Darwiche and Huang [HD05] present DPLL-based compilers for CNF into some variants of binary decision diagrams and a subclass of DNNF, called *d-DNNF* (for *deterministic decomposable negation normal form*). A propositional formula is in d-DNNF if and only if it is in DNNF and for all of its disjunctive subformulas $(F_1 \lor F_2)$ it holds that F_1 and F_2 contradict. D-DNNF and DNNF have different complexity properties: DNNF is strictly more succinct than d-DNNF, but only for d-DNNF the queries *validity check*, *implicant check*, *model counting* and *model enumeration* are polytime operations [DM02]. The underlying essential difference is that only for sentences in d-DNNF model counting is a polytime operation [Dar01b], since the number of models of a disjunction can be determined by adding together the number of models of each disjunct. In [Dar04, HD05] it is observed that trees generated by DPLL actually correspond to sentences of a subclass of d-DNNF, for which it is currently not known if it has different complexity properties than d-DNNF: All disjunctive subformulas have the form $((L \land F_1) \lor (\widetilde{L} \land F_2))$ for some literal L.

For our tableau framework we adopted two features of the DPLL-based DNNF compilers: the independent compilation of conjuncts, corresponding to and-nodes, and the use of dependency directed backtracking to delete already constructed tableau parts. These features, as present in the DNNF compilers, and their relation to our work are discussed in Sections 14.1.1 and 14.1.2. Further features of the DNNF compilers that are so far not considered in our methods, and features of our methods that are not present in the DNNF compilers are then discussed in Sections 14.1.3 and 14.1.4, respectively.

14.1.1 And-Nodes

If a clause set can be partitioned into disjoint subsets that pairwise to not share any atoms (the *connected components* of the *constraint graph* of the clause set [BP00], see also Section 12.3), then the number of models of the clause set can be determined by multiplying together the number of models of each partition. Based on an earlier work by Birnbaum and Lozinskii [BL99], Bayardo and Pehousek [BP00] extend a DPLL-based SAT solver by integrating the dynamic identification and independent processing of such connected components. The *relsat* system [BS97] is a highly effective SAT solver that has been extended by an implementation of this method for model counting.

Darwiche [HD05] transfers this technique to the application of DPLL to DNNF compilation, where components that do not share atoms can be compiled independently and the transformation results are connected conjunctively, corresponding to *and-nodes* in a tree view.

As discussed in Section 12.3, identifying connected components is a linear operation. Nevertheless it seems to introduce potentially considerable overhead: As remarked in a footnote in [BP00], the implementation of *relsat* determines the component structure lazily while backtracking; Darwiche [Dar04] only permits statically restricted possibilities for decomposition, based on a data structure called *decomposition tree*, which is determined in advance and maintained with respect to the active branch. Our representation with the Disconnect and Disconnect-Dec rules corresponds to the dynamic variant, as presented for model counting in [BP00].

The decomposition tree used by Darwiche [Dar04] is a binary tree whose leaves are labeled with the clauses of the input sentence and whose inner nodes are labeled with the set of atoms that are shared between both subtrees, i. e., occur in a clause on its left subtree as well as in a clause on its right subtree. The DPLL algorithm described in [Dar04] takes this decomposition tree as argument. For certain examples, Darwiche [Dar04] reports superiority of his methods based on decomposition trees to the dynamic methods.

14.1.2 Backtracking for Transformation Tasks

In Section 10.6 examples of backjumping peculiar to formula transformation tasks are illustrated. Differently from SAT solving, siblings to the left of the active branch that correspond to already transformed parts of the input formula can be deleted by dependency directed backtracking.

Like the backjumping mechanism of Section 10, which has been adapted from Abstract DPLL, also the DPLL-like compilation procedure in [Dar04] behaves in that way. This compilation procedure is presented as a recursive algorithm, similar to a DPLL-based SAT algorithm, with added formula construction procedures. Its body contains a sequence of two very similar blocks, the first for the construction of the left subformula of a disjunction, the second for the right. If one of these blocks fails (i. e., the corresponding subformula turns out to be unsatisfiable), then backtracking is effected. Even if the first subformula has been successfully constructed (corresponding to an already transformed output part that is rooted at a left sibling of a node on the active branch), backtracking effects that it is removed from the formula under construction.

The compilation algorithm *cnf2dnnf* is in [Dar04] expressed by means of pseudocode. It involves auxiliary procedures with side effects and six recursive calls of itself, including two calls in an auxiliary procedure *cnf2-aux*. Thus, implications of this kind of backtracking, as shown in our examples in Section 10.6, are not immediately discernible from the specification of *cnf2dnnf*.

14.1.3 Further Features of the DNNF Compilers

Caching and Structure Sharing of Formulas. The DNNF compiler in [Dar04] includes a sophisticated caching scheme, which has been evolved from earlier schemes described in [Dar01a, Dar01b]. Additionally, the system constructs DAG representations of the sentences resulting from compilation, by means of a tabling technique from the OBDD literature.

With exception of the context unit lemmas in connection with backjumping, as described in Chapter 10, we do not consider caching or lemma generation within this work. It is a rich subject in itself and depends crucially on the class of input sentences. On the other hand, it might well be possible that existing techniques, such as the lemma mechanism described for Abstract DPLL [NOT06], can be straightforwardly adapted to DPLL-Fwd.

Caching might compromise space bounds, such as the polynomial bound of the size of the working space of DPLL-Fwd calculi shown in Section 12.1. One might argue that for knowledge compilation a cache whose size does not exceed the size of the compilation result is acceptable, except when a method like the piecemeal compilation, as described in Chapter 13, is used, which explicitly utilizes partial compilation results.

It seems that a possible interaction of the feature of backtracking with transformation tasks, which effects deletion of already compiled subformulas that are potentially no longer needed, has not been considered so far: If the cache size is to be bounded by the size of the compilation result, then it could be useful to reduce the cache by "garbage collecting" entries for subformulas that are deleted by backtracking.

Atom Ordering. Knowledge compilation target languages such as the OBDD representation [Bry92] involve a total ordering on atoms that is reflected in structural constraints. In such target languages, sentences typically have canonical representations, i. e., equivalent sentences compile into identical targets. Variants of DPLL can be employed for compilation into ordered formats by requiring that the atoms upon which atomic cuts are performed are selected in correspondence with the atom ordering. A DPLL-based OBDD compiler that proceeds in this way described by Huang and Darwiche [HD04]. In [HD05] it is presented in parallel with a DPLL-based d-DNNF compiler. For the FNNF compiler described by [HMR05], and discussed in Section 14.3.7, also an adaption for compiling into *OFNNF*, a variant of FNNF with ordering constraints, is presented in [HMR05].

Implementation and Experiments. Three DPLL-based knowledge compilers have been implemented by Huang and Darwiche: An OBDD compiler [HD04] that is based on the ZChaff SAT solver [MMZ$^+$01], an FBDD compiler [HD05], and a d-DNNF compiler [Dar04]. In [HD05] experiments are reported that include random 3-CNF and graph coloring problems from the *SATLIB* library [HS00] and some of the ISCAS89 circuits. In [Dar04] also results for some of the ISCAS85 circuits are shown.[1] As said in [HD05], compilation of the theories modeling the ISCAS circuits is for example practically useful for reachability analysis of the circuits.

These experimental successes of the DPLL-like d-DNNF compilers indicate that also our tableau framework for projection elimination and its instantiation by DPLL-Fwd calculi can be a basis for practically successful systems.

14.1.4 Features not Present in the DNNF Compilers

Interplay of Compilation with Projection Elimination. As already noted in Section 6.2, it seems that the term *projection* has been introduced in [Dar01a] by Darwiche in the context of knowledge compilation into DNNF along with example applications such as circuit diagnosis. In [Dar01a] it is further shown that projection elimination can be performed in linear time on sentences in DNNF, thus projection is introduced in [Dar01a] as an operation that is applied to the result of an equivalence preserving compilation into DNNF. As

[1] For the ISCAS circuits, the precise formulations of the inputs for the knowledge compilation experiments are not referenced. In [Dar04] the Web pages http://www.cbl.ncsu.edu/www/CBL_Docs/iscas85.html and http://www.cbl.ncsu.edu/www/CBL_Docs/iscas89.html are given as reference for the circuit sources. Meanwhile these pages are only accessible as archived copies from http://www.archive.org.

shown in Section 8.3, when the efficiency of the compilation procedure is taken into consideration, this construction of an intermediate equivalent can be an unnecessary step that introduces exponential instead of polynomial time and space requirements. It can be avoided by the partial integration of projection elimination into the compilation process by techniques as shown in Section 12.2.3 and rules like True-Up. The partial integration of projection elimination into knowledge compilation procedures has so far not been considered in the literature on DNNF [Dar01a, Dar04, HD05, MR03].

Compilation to a sentence that is not fully in DNNF, but decomposable *outside* a certain set of atoms S might be considered as a first step towards the integration of projection elimination into knowledge compilation, since it allows linear projection elimination onto atom scopes that are supersets of S, as implied by Theorem 2. In [Dar01a] decomposability *outside* a set of atoms is also defined (called *decomposable except on atoms*), but the above relationship to projection elimination is not stated or utilized.

In [Dar01a] it is observed that for sentences that are decomposable *outside* S, clausal entailment is a linear operation for queries whose signature is a superset of S. Thus, for tasks in which queries are known to be clauses whose signature is a superset of a fixed set of atoms, compilation to a form that is decomposable just outside this set of atoms is suggested as target format in [Dar01a].

Generalization to Various Formula Classes and Tableau Methods. Many of the key aspects of applying DPLL-like procedures to compiling propositional CNF into DNNF or linkless sentences actually are neither tied to propositional CNF as input format nor to tableau construction by means of atomic cuts. With the framework in Chapter 9, we worked out these aspects in isolation and in an abstract manner based on the semantic properties of sentences associated with tableau structures. The main motivation for this generalization is that, as shown in the introduction to Chapter 9, besides SAT solvers, there are other sophisticated tableau-based techniques and systems that are used for practical applications, such as model generators for first-order logic, answer set computation systems and description logic reasoners. Thus the framework can possibly be a bridge to incorporate aspects of projection elimination and knowledge compilation also into those other techniques. Showing this, however, remains future work.

Permitting Non-Exhaustive Application of DPLL. The compilation methods of [Dar04] and [HD05] consider the trace of an *exhaustive* DPLL search as representation of the compilation result. In our framework, this corresponds to a tableau in which the forward labels of all leaf nodes are either $\top$ or $\bot$. The inclusion of forward labels into the leafy sentence allows to express in our framework also methods that do not perform exhaustive search, but, for example, do not extend a branch whose leaf has a forward label in DNNF.

Actually, the method shown in Section 11.3.6, with the $\mathsf{Decide}(\mathsf{PD}\text{-}\mathsf{L}_{S_l})$ rule, works according to this principle (for compilation to linkless formulas).

The result of a DNNF compilation by a DPLL-like method is then not necessarily in d-DNNF. Just in the "top part" of the result, which corresponds to literal labels of the tableau, the disjuncts are contradicting, in the "bottom part", that corresponds to forward labels of leaf nodes, arbitrary DNNF formulas are accepted.

It remains future work, to show whether essential improvements can be gained by permitting such "hybrid" compilation results and whether they can be used also to express compilation into further interesting target formats.

Linklessness Instead of Decomposability. We use linklessness instead of DNNF as a basis for our framework and methods, since linklessness is a strictly weaker property that already allows linear projection elimination, as shown in Proposition 87.

14.2 Projection and Interpolation in Symbolic Model Checking

14.2.1 Image Computation with Quantifier Elimination

Proving invariants of transition systems is an important task in symbolic model checking, which can be performed by so-called *image computation* with Boolean quantifier elimination. Following the presentation in [McM05], we summarize the pattern of the corresponding proof tasks, adapted to our notation.

An invariant of a finite state transition system that is represented with propositional logic can be proven by showing that it is entailed by the semantic fixed point of a certain formula transformation that involves projection elimination. Let I and F be "state formulas", propositional sentences over a signature S_0, and T be a "transition formula", a propositional sentence over the signature $S_0 \cup S_1$, where S_1 is a signature that is disjoint with S_0 and related to S_0 by a one-one correspondence. Let $G[S_1 \backslash S_0]$ stand for the sentence G with each atom from S_1 replaced by the corresponding atom from S_0. For natural numbers $i \geq 0$ let $R^i(F)$ be sentences over S_0 defined as follows:

$$\begin{aligned} R^0(F) &\stackrel{\text{def}}{=} F; \\ R^{i+1}(F) &\stackrel{\text{def}}{=} I \vee \mathsf{project\text{-}atoms}(R^i(F) \wedge T, S_1)[S_1 \backslash S_0] \quad \text{for } i \geq 0. \end{aligned}$$

Let $R(F) \stackrel{\text{def}}{=} R^n(F)$, where n is the smallest number such that $R^n(F) \equiv R^{n+1}(F)$. For finite state systems expressed with propositional logic it can be shown that such an n exists. The sentence F is an invariant of the transition system characterized by I and T if and only if it can be proven that

$$R(F) \models F.$$

14.2.2 DPLL-Based Quantifier Elimination

Motivated by the applications of Boolean quantifier elimination in model checking, McMillan [McM02] developed a variant of DPLL for the elimination of Boolean quantifiers. The procedure can be understood as a DNF translator that eliminates the project-atoms operator in a sentence of the form project-atoms(F, S), where F is a propositional sentence and S specifies a set of atoms.

The method is originally presented in [McM02] as a CNF translator that eliminates universal Boolean quantifiers. To stay in sync with our other material on tableau methods for knowledge compilation and projection elimination, we adopt here the dual understanding as a DNF translator.

The method proceeds as follows: In a preprocessing step, for the input sentence F a standard definitional normal form, the Tseitin encoding [Tse70, TBW04], which is in CNF, is constructed. The signature of the Tseitin encoding extends the signature of F by an additional atom for each subformula of F. We call these extra atoms and literals constructed from them *definitional*. Let $\mathsf{TSE}(F)$ denote the Tseitin encoding of F and d_F be the "top-level" definitional atom of the Tseitin encoding, i. e., the atom corresponding to F itself. The Tseitin encoding has the following property:[2]

(i) $$\textsf{project-atoms}(\mathsf{TSE}(F) \land d_F, \mathcal{A}(F)) \equiv F.$$

The algorithm maintains a clause set F', which is initialized to

$$F' := \mathsf{TSE}(F) \land d_F,$$

and a DNF sentence G, which is initialized to $\bot$. The main loop of the algorithm proceeds by searching an implicant of F, which is then added as a disjunct to G and whose complement is added as an additional clause to F'.

The search for an implicant of F is performed by applying DPLL techniques to first search an implicant M of F' that is total, which means that $\mathcal{A}(M) = \mathcal{A}(\mathsf{TSE}(F))$. Since M entails $(\mathsf{TSE}(F) \land d_F)$ it follows from (i) that M entails F. Thus, also project-atoms$(M, \mathcal{A}(F))$, which is equivalent to the conjunction of the non-definitional literals in M, entails F. The algorithm then attempts to find a subset of these non-definitional literals whose conjunction already entails F. It uses a special type of implication graph, an auxiliary data structure for lemma maintenance [MSS96], for this purpose.

On termination of the main loop it holds that G is a DNF sentence that is equivalent to F. This can be argued as follows: Since each disjunct of G entails F, it holds that

(ii) $$G \models F.$$

It is straightforward to see that the following invariant is maintained by the algorithm:

---

[2] This property is expressed in terms of projection "at the meta-level", unrelated to the projection on S that is going to be eliminated by the procedure.

(iii) $$F' = \mathsf{TSE}(F) \land d_F \land \neg G.$$

If the main loop of the algorithm terminates, then F' has no model, thus $(\mathsf{TSE}(F) \land d_F)$ then entails G. Since $\mathcal{A}(G) \subseteq \mathcal{A}(F)$, it follows that

(iv) $$\mathsf{project\text{-}atoms}(\mathsf{TSE}(F) \land d_F, \mathcal{A}(F)) \models G.$$

Hence, by (i), on termination it holds that

(v) $$F \models G.$$

Projection elimination is incorporated into the algorithm by removing from each implicant of F that is computed in the main loop those literals whose atom is not in S, just before adding it to G and its complement to F'.

On termination it holds that G is a DNF sentence that is equivalent to $\mathsf{project}(F, S)$: If M' is a conjunction of literals, then the conjunction of the literals in M' whose atom is not in S is equivalent to $\mathsf{project}(M', S)$. Thus, if M' is an implicant of F, then M' with literals whose atom is not in S removed is an implicant of $\mathsf{project}(F, S)$. Since then each disjunct of G entails $\mathsf{project}(F, S)$, it holds that

(vi) $$G \models \mathsf{project}(F, S).$$

The invariant (iii) holds unaltered. Since $\mathcal{A}(G) \subseteq S$, it follows from $F \models G$ that

(vii) $$\mathsf{project}(F, S) \models G.$$

The procedure by McMillan, which is called forall (since it is originally described as a procedure for eliminating *universal* Boolean quantifiers), shares some main features with our tableau-based methods: Both approaches perform projection elimination by variations of DPLL procedures that take important refinements from SAT solving systems into account. In both approaches projection elimination is incorporated into a formula transformation procedure and not just performed on the result of an equivalence preserving formula transformation. The methods differ in the following aspects:

- The forall procedure compiles into DNF, while our approach permits outputs with weaker restrictions, such as DNNF, linkless formulas, or also unrestricted outputs that are obtained from requiring linklessness *outside the scope of the projection* as an internal intermediate format. On this intermediate format, projection elimination is a linear operation. No syntactic restriction is then enforced on the output of projection elimination.

  In [McM02] it is observed that if elimination of universal Boolean quantifiers is performed on the result of an equivalence preserving CNF transformation, in the extreme case the CNF can be exponentially large, while the result of quantifier elimination is just $\bot$. Our material in Section 8.3 can be considered as a generalization and systematization of this observation.

- The forall algorithm has no polynomially bounded working space, since implicants are not just added to the output data structure G, but also (as complements) to the internal data structure F'.

  Nevertheless, it might be useful, to add a similar lemma mechanism to our tableau methods, but this remains future work. For the forall algorithm, the adding of implicants to F' is however not an option to improve performance, but an essential ingredient.
- As far as described in [McM02], the forall algorithm constructs the output DNF in a "monotonous" way by just adding implicants to G. Dependency directed backjumping on the other hand can effect deletion of parts of an already constructed tableau, which corresponds to deletion of implicants that have been found at earlier stages of computation and will render as redundant in presence of implicants found later. This suggests that the construction of the output DNF by forall could be improved.
- The forall algorithm involves the Tseitin encoding for handling non-clausal inputs. This affects the inner workings of the algorithm, since definitional literals are distinguished in the implicant computation with the implication graph data structure.

  For our tableau framework we avoided commitment to such a specific format, since also dedicated constraint propagation methods for variants of DPLL with non-clausal input are available, as for example shown in [TBW04].

14.2.3 Projection and Interpolation

Projection is related to *interpolation properties*, which are studied in model theory [Hoo01, GM05]. A logic with an implication operator has the *Craig interpolation property* if for any pair F, G of sentences such that F implies G there exists a *Craig interpolant* of F and G. That is a sentence F' such that

1. F' contains only symbols that occur in both F and G,
2. F implies F', and
3. F' implies G.

This property was proven for first-order logic by Craig [Cra57, Hoo01]. For various first-order calculi it is possible to construct a Craig interpolant from a proof of the inconsistency of F with $\neg G$. For tableau calculi such interpolant constructions are shown in [Smu95] and [Fit95].

A stronger property than Craig interpolation is the *uniform interpolation property.* It holds for a logic if for any sentence F and signature S which is a subset of the signature of F there exists a *uniform interpolant with respect to S*. That is a sentence F' such that

1. The signature of F' is a subset of S,
2. F implies F', and
3. For all sentences G such that
   - The symbols that occur in both F and G are also in S, and
   - F implies G

   it holds that F' implies G.

Classical propositional logic, the modal logic K, and intuitionistic propositional logic are for example known to have the uniform interpolation property, while first-order logic does not have it (see Chapter 2 of [Hoo01] for a survey of the respective results).

For propositional logic, projection elimination can be used to compute uniform interpolants. If F is a propositional sentence and S is a set of atoms, then project-atoms(F, S) satisfies the semantic requirements on a uniform interpolant of F with respect to S. Thus, a uniform interpolant can be computed by eliminating the project-atoms operator in project-atoms(F, S), followed by eliminating any possibly remaining atoms that are not in S by substituting them with truth value constants according to Proposition 20.[3]

The *Lyndon interpolation theorem* [Lyn59, Hoo01] strengthens the Craig interpolation theorem for first-order logic without function and constant symbols by taking the polarity in which predicate symbols appear into account. It shows the existence of Craig interpolants F' in NNF for sentences F and G in NNF such that a predicate symbol that occurs in an atom on F' with polarity 1 (-1, resp.) also occurs with polarity 1 (-1, resp.) in both F and G. With the literal projection operator project, projection elimination can also be used to compute a uniform interpolant in propositional logic with respect to a set of *literals*, such that polarity is considered analogously to the Lyndon theorem.

14.2.4 Interpolation and Approximate Image Computation

Proving invariants as sketched in Section 14.2.1 by means of projection elimination – i. e., computing uniform interpolants – can be very costly. McMillan [McM05] shows that invariants can also be proven by approximating the uniform interpolants with Craig interpolants that are extracted from the proofs of bounded reachability problems. This optimization has been successfully applied to benchmark problems from industrial applications of model checking [McM05].

We outline the principle how Craig interpolants are used in [McM05] to approximate projection elimination. Let I, T, F, S_0, S_1 be defined as in Section 14.2.1. Let $k \geq 0$ be a natural number and let $S_2, \ldots, S_{k+1}$ be further

[3] Typically, methods for projection elimination in propositional logic (for example those based on Proposition 87) also syntactically eliminate atoms not in S, and thus the second step of eliminating inessential atoms is not explicitly necessary.

signatures with a one-one correspondence to S_0 that are mutually disjoint and also disjoint with S_0 and S_1. For $i, j \in \{0, \ldots, k+1\}$, let $F[S_i]$ be F with each atom from S_0 replaced by the corresponding atom from S_i, and let $T[S_i, S_j]$ be T with each atom from S_0 or S_1 replaced by the corresponding atom from S_i or S_j, respectively.

If G is a sentence over S_0, then deciding the following statement corresponds to solving the *bounded* model checking problem that F holds in all states that are reachable in at least one and at most $k+1$ steps from a state satisfying G:

(viii) $$G \wedge T[S_0, S_1] \ldots \wedge T[S_k, S_{k+1}] \models F[S_1] \wedge \ldots \wedge F[S_{k+1}].$$

If the sentence B_k is defined as follows:

$$B_k \stackrel{\text{def}}{=} \neg T[S_1, S_2] \vee \ldots \vee \neg T[S_k, S_{k+1}] \vee (F[S_1] \wedge \ldots \wedge F[S_{k+1}]),$$

then (viii) can be expressed as

(ix) $$G \wedge T \models B_k.$$

For natural numbers $i \geq 0$, let $R^i(F)$ be sentences over S_0 defined as

$$\begin{aligned} \overline{R}^0(F) &\stackrel{\text{def}}{=} F; \\ \overline{R}^{i+1}(F) &\stackrel{\text{def}}{=} I \vee \mathsf{interpolant}(\overline{R}^i(F) \wedge T, B_k)[S_1 \backslash S_0] \quad \text{for } i \geq 0, \end{aligned}$$

where $\mathsf{interpolant}(\overline{R}^i(F) \wedge T, B_k)$ is some Craig interpolant of $(\overline{R}^i(F) \wedge T)$ and B_k. Such an interpolant can be extracted from a proof of the bounded model checking problem $(\overline{R}^i(F) \wedge T) \models B_k$. Let $\overline{R}(F) \stackrel{\text{def}}{=} R^n(F)$, where n is the smallest number such that $\overline{R}^n(F) \equiv \overline{R}^{n+1}(F)$. The task of proving an invariant F of the transition system characterized by I and T then can be approximated by trying to prove

(x) $$\overline{R}(F) \models F.$$

Since only symbols in S_1 are shared by $(R^i(F) \wedge T)$ and B_k, for all sentences G over the signature S_0 it holds that

(xi) $$\mathsf{project\text{-}atoms}(G \wedge T, S_1) \models \mathsf{interpolant}(G \wedge T, B_k).$$

Based on this fact it can be shown that

(xii) $$R(F) \models \overline{R}(F).$$

Thus, if $\overline{R}(F) \models F$ has been proven, then F is indeed an invariant, since also $R(F) \models F$ must hold. The computation of $\overline{R}(F)$ fails if one of the bounded model checking tasks of the form $(\overline{R}^i(F) \wedge T) \models B_k$, used to obtain an interpolant, fails. The approximation is then tried again with a larger value for k. Termination is ensured for finite state systems, since for them the value of k that has to be considered in this way is bound [McM05].

14.3 Tableau Simulation of Shannon Expansion of Subformulas

We show that any sentence obtained from a given propositional NNF sentence by successive rewriting of subformulas with the Shannon expansion (which has been described on p. 61) can also be obtained as leafy sentence of a fwd-tableau constructed with a certain variant of a DPLL-Fwd calculus, applied to an initial node with the given sentence as forward label.

The rewriting of subformulas with the Shannon expansion as a method for knowledge compilation was recently proposed under the name *semantic factoring* by Murray and Rosenthal [MR03] for compilation into DNNF.[4] They describe it in terms of their framework of *semantic graphs* and *dissolution* [MR87, MR93, MR03], inference methods that are based on equivalence preserving transformation of formulas in negation normal form. The central idea of semantic factoring is that by applying the Shannon expansion whenever possible *just to subformulas*, the exponential behavior of repeated expansion can be avoided in many cases. As an example, it is shown in [MR03] for the class of sentences C_n^n that it can be compiled in linear time and space to DNNF by semantic factoring, whereas an earlier method by Darwiche [Dar01a] constructs exponentially large outputs.

While the correspondence of applying the Shannon expansion to a propositional sentence with a Decide step of a DPLL calculus is obvious, relating a DPLL calculus to the successive Shannon expansion of *subformulas* of a non-clausal sentence is not immediate. Benefits of the tableau method in contrast to subformula expansion are the following features:

- Dependency directed backtracking
- Efficient integration of simplifications such as unit propagation
- Space efficiency, for example by polynomially bounded working data structure requirements
- Efficient integration of simplifications that just preserve equivalence relative to the target scope of a projection.

The first three are key features of modern tableau-based automated deduction systems, such as those referred to on p. 129, that are successfully used in practical applications. Impacts of the fourth point are discussed in Section 8.3. Of course, in principle it might be possible to express these features also in terms of subformula rewriting.[5] The correspondence to subformula

[4] In the work that introduces semantic factoring [MR03], it is also shown that (the associated formula of) a fully developed regular clausal tableau for a given formula is an equivalent to the formula and in DNNF; thus any method for computing such a tableau can be considered as a DNNF compiler. However, this is developed in [MR03] just in parallel to semantic factoring, without making relationships between the two approaches explicit.

[5] In [MR94] it is for example shown that a tableau method, the construction of analytic tableaux as described Smullyan [Smu95], can be expressed as dissolution.

rewriting indicates refinements of tableau methods that are useful for formula transformation tasks. An example is the handling of disjunctions in non-clausal sentences described in Section 14.3.2.

The simulation of rewriting with the Shannon expansion by a tableau method is made precise with Theorem 18 in Section 14.3.6. This theorem refers to a mapping between sentences, called SF, which formally expresses the rewriting with the Shannon expansion, and is defined in Section 14.3.1. If F is a NNF sentence and A is a ground atom, then $\mathsf{SF}(A, F)$ is a NNF sentence obtained from F by rewriting subformulas with their Shannon expansion upon A as the atom that is substituted by truth value constants. This is done in such a way that the result is "decomposable inside A", meaning that in all conjunctive subformulas of the result at most a single conjunct contains an occurrence of A. The notation $\mathsf{SF}^{A_1 \ldots A_n}$ stands for the successive application of SF for atoms $A_1, \ldots, A_n$. By Theorem 18, the value of any such successive application of the Shannon expansion of subformulas to a given NNF sentence can also be obtained as the (roughly) leafy sentence of a fwd-tableau constructed by a variant of DPLL-Fwd, applied to an initial node with (roughly) F as forward label. Moreover, the length of such a tableau derivation is linearly bounded by the size of the result sentence.

Rewriting of a subformula with the Shannon expansion can make it possible that simplification operations can be applied to the rewritten subformula and also to its "context", the formula that contains it as a proper subformula. These issues are not taken into account for Theorem 18. They are also not considered in [MR03], but in a subsequent work by in part the same authors [HMR05]. We discuss some aspects of such simplifications in Section 14.3.7.

The proof given for Theorem 18 is based on a mapping between sem-fwd-tableaux, called TSF, that is defined in Section 14.3.3. On one hand, the sentence represented by the fwd-tableau resulting from successive application of TSF corresponds to the sentence obtained from SF, applied successively in the same way, which is shown in Section 14.3.4. On the other hand, fwd-tableaux obtained as values of a successive application of TSF can be constructed by a certain variant of a DPLL-Fwd calculus, which is shown in Section 14.3.5. This calculus does not in general construct intermediate tableaux corresponding to each of the nested applications of SF or TSF, respectively, thus the way in which the tableau construction proceeds does not reflect the successive rewriting with the Shannon expansion.

14.3.1 Semantic Factoring

We define a mapping between sentences, SF (Definition 122), that makes precise the *semantic factoring* method as proposed in [MR03], i. e., the Shannon expansion of subformulas for the purpose of compilation into DNNF. In [MR03] some criteria for identifying the subformulas which are to be rewritten by the Shannon expansion are hinted, but not made precise. Our definition attempts to take these hints into account. The definition of semantic factoring is preceded by the definition of *decomposable formula*, the analog to *linkless formula* for compilation into DNNF.

Definition 121 (Decomposable Formula) A plain formula F is called *decomposable outside* an atom scope S if and only if for all elements $\langle F_1, F_2 \rangle$ of the pairs of conjuncts of F it holds that

$$\mathcal{A}(F_1) \cap \mathcal{A}(F_2) \subseteq S.$$

A plain formula F is called *decomposable inside* an atom scope S if and only if it is decomposable outside $\overline{S}$.

Definition 122 (Semantic Factoring)

(i) If A is a ground atom and F is a propositional NNF sentence, then $\mathsf{SF}(A, F)$ is also a propositional NNF sentence, defined inductively by the following clauses, to be matched in the order listed:

$$\begin{array}{lrcll}
1. & \mathsf{SF}(A,F) & \stackrel{\text{def}}{=} & F, & \text{if } F \text{ is decomposable inside } \{A\}; \\
2. & \mathsf{SF}(A,F_1 \lor F_2) & \stackrel{\text{def}}{=} & \mathsf{SF}(A,F_1) \lor \mathsf{SF}(A,F_2), & \text{if } A \in \mathcal{A}(F_1 \lor F_2); \\
3. & \mathsf{SF}(A,F_1 \land F_2) & \stackrel{\text{def}}{=} & \mathsf{SF}(A,F_1) \land \mathsf{SF}(A,F_2), & \text{if } A \notin \mathcal{A}(F_1) \cap \mathcal{A}(F_2); \\
4. & \mathsf{SF}(A,F) & \stackrel{\text{def}}{=} & (A \land F[A \backslash \top]) \lor (\neg A \land F[A \backslash \bot]). &
\end{array}$$

(ii) If $A_1 \ldots A_n$, where $n \geq 0$, is a sequence of different ground atoms and F is a propositional NNF sentence, then $\mathsf{SF}^{A_1 \ldots A_n}(F)$ denotes the result of the successive application for the members of $A_1 \ldots A_n$ of semantic factoring to F, formally:

$$\begin{array}{rcll}
\mathsf{SF}^{\emptyset}(F) & \stackrel{\text{def}}{=} & F; & \\
\mathsf{SF}^{A_1 \ldots A_n}(F) & \stackrel{\text{def}}{=} & \mathsf{SF}(A_n, \mathsf{SF}^{A_1 \ldots A_{n-1}}(F)), & \text{if } n > 0.
\end{array}$$

14.3.2 Mimicking Navigation into Subformulas by Tableaux

In simulating the Shannon expansion, the tableau calculus has to mimic the "navigation" to the subformula that is rewritten. Navigation into the subformulas of a conjunction $(F_1 \land F_2)$ corresponds to an application of the Disconnect rule, which effects that F_1 and F_2 are attached as forward labels of the two children of an a-node. Navigation into the subformulas of a disjunction could be achieved with a special rule Disjoint, analogous to Disconnect:

Definition 123 (Rule Disjoint)
PRECONDITIONS: Let N be the active leaf. F_N is equal modulo associativity and commutativity of the $\lor$ operator to a propositional sentence $(F_1 \lor \ldots \lor F_n)$, where $n > 1$.

EFFECTS: For each of the F_i, where $i \in \{1, \ldots, n\}$, attach to N – from left to right – a child N_i with $L_{N_i} = \top$ and F_{N_i} assigned to *Simplify-Fwd*(F_i, B_{N_i}). Label N as o-node. Assign N_1 as active leaf.

However, Disjoint does not fit smoothly into our tableau framework, since it does not preserve the property of *branch implied forward labels*: For Disconnect, preservation of this property is a consequence of the fact that for all sentences F_1, F_2 it holds that $(F_1 \land F_2) \models F_1$. But it is not in general the case that $(F_1 \lor F_2) \models F_1$. A remedy is the following transformation, which allows the construction of child nodes that effectively have as forward labels the disjuncts of the forward label of their parent, just by means of the Decide rule, and thus in a manner that preserves the *branch implied forward labels* property.

Definition 124 (D-Labeled Sentences)

(i) Define d-labels as a reserved set of ground atoms that are not used in formula construction, except when introduced by the add-d-labels transformation defined below.

(ii) If F is a propositional NNF sentence with n occurrences of the $\lor$ connective, then add-d-labels(F) is the sentence obtained from F by successively replacing for $i \in \{1, \ldots, n\}$ the i-th subformula occurrence (with respect to some arbitrary ordering) of the form $(F_1 \lor F_2)$ by

$$(D_i \land F_1) \lor (\neg D_i \land F_2),$$

where $D_i \in$ d-labels, and if $i \neq j$, then $D_i \neq D_j$.

(iii) A propositional NNF sentence F such that F is decomposable inside d-labels, and all subformulas of F with the $\lor$ connective as main operator have the form $((D \land F_1) \lor (\neg D \land F_2))$ for some atom $D \in$ d-labels is called *d-labeled.*

(iv) If F is a propositional NNF sentence, then rem-d-labels(F) is F with subformulas of the form $((D \land F_1) \lor (\neg D \land F_2))$, where $D \in$ d-labels, exhaustively replaced by

$$F_1 \lor F_2.$$

If F is a propositional NNF sentence whose atom base is disjoint with d-labels, then clearly

(xiii) $$\text{rem-d-labels}(\text{add-d-labels}(F)) = F.$$

Let d-label-literals be the set of literals whose atom is in d-labels. It is easy to see that add-d-labels(F) is decomposable inside d-labels and thus also linkless inside d-label-literals. From Proposition 87 it then easily follows that the add-d-labels transformation preserves equivalence relative to the complement of d-label-literals, which is formally expressed by

(xiv) $$F \equiv_{\overline{\text{d-label-literals}}} \text{add-d-labels}(F).$$

If N is a node with a forward label of the form $((D \land F_1) \lor (\neg D \land F_2))$, where $D \in$ d-labels, then a Decide step on D can effect that two children N_1, N_2 are attached to N such that $L_{N_1} = D$, $L_{N_2} = \neg D$, $F_{N_1} = F_1$, and $F_{N_2} = F_2$.

14.3.3 The TSF Mapping Between Tableaux

We define a mapping between sem-fwd-tableaux, TSF (Definition 128), whose two key properties are a correspondence to application of the Shannon expansion of subformulas, applied in succession for different atoms (Proposition 171), and a correspondence to tableau construction with a variant of DPLL-Fwd (Proposition 177).

To get syntactic equality to the Shannon expansion, the fwd-tableaux obtained as values of TSF are mapped to sentences with a slightly modified version of the leafy mapping, leafy′ (Definition 125), that has built-in a trivial truth value simplification of literal labels which are ⊤, as well as elimination of atoms from d-labels. To show correspondence to the Shannon expansion, it suffices to consider only Sem-Fwd-Tableaux of a restricted form, called *d-labeled binary sem-fwd-tableaux* (Definition 126). TSF is specified by reference to a further mapping, FSF (Definition 127), which maps propositional NNF sentences that occur as forward labels to sem-fwd-tableaux. Notation to express successive application of TSF is defined analogously to SF (Definition 128.ii). This section is concluded by the definition of *branch segment* (Definition 129) and some formally stated properties of TSF (Proposition 168), which will be later used in proofs.

Definition 125 (Leafy′ Sentence)

(i)

If N is a node in a fwd-tableau, then the *leafy′ sentence* of N, in symbols $\mathsf{leafy}'(N)$, is a sentence defined as:

– If $L_N = \top$ or $\mathsf{atom}(L_N) \in \mathsf{d\text{-}labels}$, then
  If N is a leaf node, then

$$\mathsf{leafy}'(N) \stackrel{\text{def}}{=} \mathsf{rem\text{-}d\text{-}labels}(F_N);$$

  If N is an o-node whose children are $N_1, \ldots, N_n$, then

$$\mathsf{leafy}'(N) \stackrel{\text{def}}{=} \bigvee_{i \in \{1,\ldots,n\}} \mathsf{leafy}'(N_i);$$

  If N is an a-node whose children are $N_1, \ldots, N_n$, then

$$\mathsf{leafy}'(N) \stackrel{\text{def}}{=} \bigwedge_{i \in \{1,\ldots,n\}} \mathsf{leafy}'(N_i);$$

– Otherwise, i. e., if $L_N \neq \top$ and $\mathsf{atom}(L_N) \notin \mathsf{d\text{-}labels}$, then
  If N is a leaf node, then

$$\mathsf{leafy}'(N) \stackrel{\text{def}}{=} \mathsf{rem\text{-}d\text{-}labels}(L_N \wedge F_N);$$

  If N is an o-node whose children are $N_1, \ldots, N_n$, then

$$\mathsf{leafy}'(N) \stackrel{\text{def}}{=} L_N \wedge \bigvee_{i \in \{1,\ldots,n\}} \mathsf{leafy}'(N_i);$$

If N is an a-node whose children are $N_1, \ldots, N_n$, then

$$\mathsf{leafy}'(N) \stackrel{\text{def}}{=} L_N \wedge \bigwedge_{i \in \{1,\ldots,n\}} \mathsf{leafy}'(N_i).$$

(ii) If T is a fwd-tableau, then the *leafy ′ sentence* of T, in symbols $\mathsf{leafy}'(T)$, is a sentence defined as:

$$\mathsf{leafy}'(T) \stackrel{\text{def}}{=} \mathsf{leafy}'(\mathsf{root}(T)).$$

Definition 126 (D-Labeled and Binary Sem-Fwd-Tableaux) A sem-fwd-tableau such that the forward labels of all of its nodes are d-labeled propositional NNF sentences is called a *d-labeled* sem-fwd-tableau. A sem-fwd-tableau in which all o-nodes and a-nodes have exactly two children is called a *binary* sem-fwd-tableau.

The definitions of FSF and TSF, which follow, involve "constructor" and "copying" mappings that map their arguments to "fresh" tableaux, whose nodes so far have not been used. We now sketch their definitions. A *copy of* a node is a second node such that the sub-tableaux rooted at both nodes have the same structure, and corresponding nodes in both sub-tableaux have the same literal and forward label. If L is a literal or $\top$, F is a sentence, N, N_1, N_2 are nodes, A is a ground atom and W is a truth value constant, then

- $\mathsf{leaf}(L, F)$ is a fresh leaf node with literal label L and forward label F;
- $\mathsf{o\text{-}node}(L, F, N_1, N_2)$ ($\mathsf{a\text{-}node}(L, F, N_1, N_2)$, resp.) is a fresh o-node (a-node, resp.) with literal label N and forward label F whose children are fresh copies of N_1 and N_2;
- $\mathsf{copy}(N)$ is a fresh copy of N;
- $\mathsf{subst\text{-}copy}(N, A\backslash W)$ is like a fresh copy of N, except that in all forward labels the atom A is replaced by the truth value constant W.

Definition 127 (FSF Mapping) If A is a ground atom not in d-labels, L is a ground literal or $\top$, and F is a d-labeled propositional NNF sentence, then $\mathsf{FSF}(A, L, F)$ is the root of a d-labeled binary fwd-tableau, defined inductively by the following clauses, to be matched in the order listed:

1. $\mathsf{FSF}(A, L, F) \stackrel{\text{def}}{=} \mathsf{leaf}(L, F)$, if F is decomposable inside $\{A\}$;
2. $\stackrel{\text{def}}{=} \mathsf{o\text{-}node}(L, F, \mathsf{FSF}(A, D, F_1), \mathsf{FSF}(A, \neg D, F_2))$, if $F = ((D \wedge F_1) \vee (\neg D \wedge F_2))$;
3. $\stackrel{\text{def}}{=} \mathsf{a\text{-}node}(L, F, \mathsf{FSF}(A, \top, F_1), \mathsf{FSF}(A, \top, F_2))$, if $F = F_1 \wedge F_2$ and $A \notin \mathcal{A}(F_1) \cap \mathcal{A}(F_2)$;
4. $\stackrel{\text{def}}{=} \mathsf{o\text{-}node}(L, F, \mathsf{leaf}(A, F[A\backslash\top]), \mathsf{leaf}(\neg A, F[A\backslash\bot]))$.

Definition 128 (TSF Mapping)

(i) If A is a ground atom not in d-labels and N is a node of a d-labeled binary sem-fwd-tableau, then $\mathsf{TSF}(A, N)$ is the root of a sem-fwd-tableau that also is d-labeled and binary, defined inductively by the following clauses, to be matched in the order listed:

1. $\mathsf{TSF}(A, N) \stackrel{\text{def}}{=} \mathsf{copy}(N)$,
   if $\mathsf{leafy}'(N)$ is decomposable inside $\{A\}$;
2. $\stackrel{\text{def}}{=} \mathsf{o\text{-}node}(L_N, F_N, \mathsf{TSF}(A, N_1), \mathsf{TSF}(A, N_2))$,
   if N is an o-node whose children are N_1 and N_2;
3. $\stackrel{\text{def}}{=} \mathsf{a\text{-}node}(L_N, F_N, \mathsf{TSF}(A, N_1), \mathsf{TSF}(A, N_2))$,
   if N is an a-node whose children are N_1 and N_2 and $A \notin \mathcal{A}(\mathsf{leafy}'(N_1)) \cap \mathcal{A}(\mathsf{leafy}'(N_2))$;
4. $\stackrel{\text{def}}{=} \mathsf{o\text{-}node}(L_N, F_N,$
   $\mathsf{a\text{-}node}(A, F_N[A\backslash\top], \mathsf{subst\text{-}copy}(N_1, A\backslash\top),$
   $\mathsf{subst\text{-}copy}(N_2, A\backslash\top)),$
   $\mathsf{a\text{-}node}(\neg A, F_N[A\backslash\bot], \mathsf{subst\text{-}copy}(N_1, A\backslash\bot),$
   $\mathsf{subst\text{-}copy}(N_2, A\backslash\bot)))$,
   if N is an a-node whose children are N_1 and N_2;
5. $\stackrel{\text{def}}{=} \mathsf{FSF}(A, L_N, F_N)$,
   if N is a leaf node.

(ii) If $A_1 \ldots A_n$, where $n \geq 0$, is a sequence of different ground atoms not in d-labels and N is a node of a d-labeled binary sem-fwd-tableau such that $\mathcal{A}(\mathsf{sentence}(N)) \cap \{A_1, \ldots, A_n\} = \emptyset$, then $\mathsf{TSF}^{A_1 \ldots A_n}(N)$ denotes the result of the successive application for the members of $A_1 \ldots A_n$ of the TSF operator to N, formally:

$$\begin{aligned} \mathsf{TSF}^{\emptyset}(N) &\stackrel{\text{def}}{=} N; \\ \mathsf{TSF}^{A_1 \ldots A_n}(N) &\stackrel{\text{def}}{=} \mathsf{TSF}(A_n, \mathsf{TSF}^{A_1 \ldots A_{n-1}}(N)), \qquad \text{if } n > 0. \end{aligned}$$

The following definition extends the notation B_N for *branch in T to N*, where the first node of B_N is the root of an implicitly given tableau T, by the notation B_N^M, which explicitly includes the first node and thus allows to refer to subsequences of branches, called *branch segments.*

Definition 129 (Branch Segment)

(i) If $B_N = N_1 \ldots N_n$ is a branch of a fwd-tableau and $M = N_k$ for some $k \in \{1, \ldots, n\}$, then the *branch segment from M to N*, in symbols B_N^M, is the sequence of nodes defined as

$$B_N^M \stackrel{\text{def}}{=} N_k \ldots N_n.$$

(ii) We overload notation for branch segments: If $B_N^M = N_k \ldots N_n$ is the branch segment from M to N, then B_N^M is also used to denote the sentence defined as

$$B_N^M \stackrel{\text{def}}{=} L_{N_k} \wedge \ldots \wedge L_{N_n}.$$

Proposition 168 collects some straightforward properties of the TSF mapping, which will be referenced in proofs of subsequent propositions. Note that $\mathcal{A}(\mathsf{sentence}(N))$ is set of atoms that appear in literal labels on the fwd-tableau with root node N. This expression is used in Proposition 168.iv and in preconditions of propositions in later sections. Proposition 168.iv thus states that A is the only atom that can appear in a literal label of the tableau rooted at $\mathsf{TSF}(A, N)$, besides atoms that appear already as literal labels in the tableau rooted at N and atoms in d-labels.

Proposition 168 *If A is a ground atom not in* d-labels *and N is a node of a d-labeled binary sem-fwd-tableau, then it holds that*

(i)

$$L_{\mathsf{TSF}(A,N)} = L_N;$$

(ii)

$$F_{\mathsf{TSF}(A,N)} = F_N;$$

(iii)

$$B_{\mathsf{TSF}(A,N)}^{\mathsf{TSF}(A,N_0)} = B_N^{N_0};$$ [6]

(iv)

$$\mathcal{A}(\mathsf{sentence}(\mathsf{TSF}(A, N))) \subseteq \{A\} \cup \mathcal{A}(\mathsf{sentence}(N)) \cup \text{d-labels}.$$

Proof. Follows easily from the definitions of TSF and FSF.

□

14.3.4 TSF and Semantic Factoring

We show that, with certain provisions, the leafy′ sentence of the fwd-tableau resulting from successive application of the TSF mapping is identical to the result of application of the SF mapping in analogous succession (Proposition 171). The proof of this is based on two lemmas that relate the SF mapping to the FSF mapping and to a single step of the TSF mapping (Propositions 169 and 170).

[6] The branch segments are considered as sentences in this equation.

Proposition 169 *If A is a ground atom not in* d-labels *and F is a d-labeled propositional NNF sentence, then*

– *If L is a literal such that* $\mathsf{atom}(L) \neq A$ *and* $\mathsf{atom}(L) \notin \mathsf{d\text{-}labels}$, *then*

$$\mathsf{leafy}'(\mathsf{FSF}(A, L, F)) = \mathsf{SF}(A, \mathsf{rem\text{-}d\text{-}labels}(L \wedge F));$$

– *If $L = \top$, or L is a literal such that* $\mathsf{atom}(L) \neq A$ *and* $\mathsf{atom}(L) \in \mathsf{d\text{-}labels}$, *then*

$$\mathsf{leafy}'(\mathsf{FSF}(A, L, F)) = \mathsf{SF}(A, \mathsf{rem\text{-}d\text{-}labels}(F)).$$

Proof. We only show the case where L is a literal and $\mathsf{atom}(L) \notin \mathsf{d\text{-}labels}$. The other case, where $L = \top$ or $\mathsf{atom}(L) \in \mathsf{d\text{-}labels}$, can be shown analogously, in general just by dropping the "$L \wedge$" prefix from the affected formulas in the equations. The proof proceeds by induction on the structure of F, corresponding to the match cases of the definition of FSF (Definition 127). There are two base cases, corresponding to clauses (1.) and (4.) of the definition of FSF.

Base Case if Clause (1.) of the Definition of FSF *is Matched.*

$$\begin{array}{lll}
(1) & \mathsf{leafy}'(\mathsf{FSF}(A, L, F)) & = \\
(2) & \mathsf{rem\text{-}d\text{-}labels}(L \wedge F) & = \\
(3) & L \wedge \mathsf{rem\text{-}d\text{-}labels}(F) & = \\
(4) & L \wedge \mathsf{SF}(\mathsf{rem\text{-}d\text{-}labels}(F)) & = \\
(5) & \mathsf{SF}(L \wedge \mathsf{rem\text{-}d\text{-}labels}(F)) & = \\
(6) & \mathsf{SF}(\mathsf{rem\text{-}d\text{-}labels}(L \wedge F)). &
\end{array}$$

Sentence F is decomposable inside $\{A\}$. Equivalence of (2) to (1) follows since the value of FSF is a leaf node. Equivalence of (3) to (2) follows from the definition of rem-d-labels. Equivalence of (4) to (3) follows from clause (1.) of the definition of SF, since $\mathsf{rem\text{-}d\text{-}labels}(F)$ is decomposable inside $\{A\}$ if F is so. Equivalence of (5) to (4) follows from clauses (3.) and (1.) of the definition of SF, since $A \notin \mathcal{A}(L)$. Equivalence of (6) to (5) follows from the equivalence of (3) to (2).

Base Case if Clause (4.) of the Definition of FSF *is Matched.*

$$\begin{array}{lll}
(1) & \mathsf{leafy}'(\mathsf{FSF}(A, L, F)) & = \\
(2) & \mathsf{rem\text{-}d\text{-}labels}(L \wedge (A \wedge F[A\backslash\top]) \vee (\neg A \wedge F[A\backslash\bot])) & = \\
(3) & L \wedge (A \wedge \mathsf{rem\text{-}d\text{-}labels}(F)[A\backslash\top]) \vee (\neg A \wedge \mathsf{rem\text{-}d\text{-}labels}(F)[A\backslash\bot])) & = \\
(4) & L \wedge \mathsf{SF}(\mathsf{rem\text{-}d\text{-}labels}(F)) & = \\
(5) & \mathsf{SF}(A, \mathsf{rem\text{-}d\text{-}labels}(L \wedge F)). &
\end{array}$$

Equivalence of (2) to (1) follows from the definitions of FSF and leafy$'$. Equivalence of (3) to (2) follows from the definition of rem-d-labels, since $A \notin \mathsf{d\text{-}labels}$. Equivalence of (4) to (3) follows from clause (4.) of the definition of SF, which is matched by $\mathsf{rem\text{-}d\text{-}labels}(F)$. Equivalence of (5) to (4) follows analogously to the equivalence of (6) to (5) for the base case that clause (1.) of the definition of FSF is matched.

Induction Step if Clause (2.) of the Definition of FSF *is Matched.*

$$\begin{array}{lll} (1) & \mathsf{leafy}'(\mathsf{FSF}(A, L, F)) & = \\ (2) & L \wedge (\mathsf{leafy}'(\mathsf{FSF}(A, D, F_1)) \vee \mathsf{leafy}'(\mathsf{FSF}(A, \neg D, F_2))) & = \\ (3) & L \wedge (\mathsf{SF}(A, \mathsf{rem\text{-}d\text{-}labels}(D \wedge F_1)) \vee & \\ & \quad \mathsf{SF}(A, \mathsf{rem\text{-}d\text{-}labels}(\neg D \wedge F_2))) & = \\ (4) & L \wedge \mathsf{SF}(A, \mathsf{rem\text{-}d\text{-}labels}((D \wedge F_1) \vee (\neg D \wedge F_2))) & = \\ (5) & \mathsf{SF}(A, \mathsf{rem\text{-}d\text{-}labels}(L \wedge F)). & \end{array}$$

Sentence F has the form $((D \wedge F_1) \vee (\neg D \wedge F_2))$. Equivalence of (2) to (1) follows from the definitions of FSF and leafy′. By the induction assumption it holds that $\mathsf{leafy}'(\mathsf{FSF}(A, D, F_1)) = \mathsf{SF}(A, \mathsf{rem\text{-}d\text{-}labels}(D \wedge F_1))$ and $\mathsf{leafy}'(\mathsf{FSF}(A, D, F_2)) = \mathsf{SF}(A, \mathsf{rem\text{-}d\text{-}labels}(\neg D \wedge F_2))$. Thus equivalence of (3) to (2) follows from the induction assumption. Equivalence of (4) to (3) follows from clause (2.) of the definition of SF, which is matched by $\mathsf{rem\text{-}d\text{-}labels}(F)$. Equivalence of (5) to (4) follows from clauses (3.) and (1.) of the definition of SF, since $A \notin \mathcal{A}(L)$, and from the definition of rem-d-labels.

Induction Step if Clause (3.) of the Definition of FSF *is Matched.*

$$\begin{array}{lll} (1) & \mathsf{leafy}'(\mathsf{FSF}(A, L, F)) & = \\ (2) & L \wedge \mathsf{leafy}'(\mathsf{FSF}(A, \top, F_1)) \wedge \mathsf{rem\text{-}d\text{-}labels}(F_2) & = \\ (3) & L \wedge \mathsf{SF}(A, \mathsf{rem\text{-}d\text{-}labels}(F_1)) \wedge \mathsf{rem\text{-}d\text{-}labels}(F_2) & = \\ (4) & L \wedge \mathsf{SF}(A, \mathsf{rem\text{-}d\text{-}labels}(F_1 \wedge F_2)) & = \\ (5) & \mathsf{SF}(A, \mathsf{rem\text{-}d\text{-}labels}(L \wedge F)) & \end{array}$$

We assume that $A \notin \mathcal{A}(F_2)$. The case where $A \notin \mathcal{A}(F_1)$ can be shown analogously. Sentence F has the form $(F_1 \wedge F_2)$. Equivalence of (2) to (1) follows from the definitions of FSF and leafy′. By the induction assumption it holds that $\mathsf{leafy}'(\mathsf{FSF}(A, \top, F_1)) = \mathsf{SF}(A, \mathsf{rem\text{-}d\text{-}labels}(F_1))$. The remaining equivalences follow analogously to equivalences of (2)–(5) for the induction step for clause (2.) of the definition of FSF, with clause (3.) of the definition of SF in the role of clause (2.)

□

Proposition 170 *If A is a ground atom not in* d-labels *and N is a node of a d-labeled binary sem-fwd-tableau such that $A \notin \mathcal{A}(\mathsf{sentence}(N))$, then*

$$\mathsf{leafy}'(\mathsf{TSF}(A, N)) = \mathsf{SF}(A, \mathsf{leafy}'(N)).$$

Proof. Similar as in the proof of Proposition 169, we only show the case where L_N is a literal and $\mathsf{atom}(L_N) \notin \mathsf{d\text{-}labels}$, and thus L_N appears in $\mathsf{leafy}'(N)$ as first conjunct. The other case, where $L = \top$ or $\mathsf{atom}(L) \in \mathsf{d\text{-}labels}$, and thus L_N does not appear in $\mathsf{leafy}'(N)$, can be shown analogously, in general just by dropping the "$L\ \wedge$" prefix from the affected formulas in the equations.

The proof proceeds by induction on the structure of the tableau with root N, corresponding to the match cases of the definition of TSF (Definition 128.i). There are three base cases, corresponding to clauses (1.), (4.) and (5.) of the definition of TSF.

Base Case if Clause (1.) of the Definition of TSF *is Matched.*

$$\begin{array}{lll}
(1) & \mathsf{leafy}'(\mathsf{TSF}(A, N)) & = \\
(2) & \mathsf{leafy}'(N) & = \\
(3) & \mathsf{SF}(A, \mathsf{leafy}'(N)). &
\end{array}$$

Sentence $\mathsf{leafy}'(N)$ is decomposable inside $\{A\}$. Thus equivalence of (2) to (1) follows from the definition of TSF and equivalence of (3) to (2) follows from clause (1.) of the definition of SF.

Base Case if Clause (4.) of the Definition of TSF *is Matched.*

$$\begin{array}{lll}
(1) & \mathsf{leafy}'(\mathsf{TSF}(A, N)) & = \\
(2) & L_N \land ((A \land (\mathsf{leafy}'(N_1) \land \mathsf{leafy}'(N_2))[A\backslash\top]) \lor & \\
 & \qquad (\neg A \land (\mathsf{leafy}'(N_1) \land \mathsf{leafy}'(N_2))[A\backslash\bot])) & = \\
(3) & L_N \land \mathsf{SF}(A, \mathsf{leafy}'(N_1) \land \mathsf{leafy}'(N_2)) & = \\
(4) & \mathsf{SF}(A, L_N \land \mathsf{leafy}'(N_1) \land \mathsf{leafy}'(N_2)) & = \\
(5) & \mathsf{SF}(A, \mathsf{leafy}'(N)). &
\end{array}$$

Node N is an a-node whose children are N_1 and N_2. The precondition $A \notin \mathcal{A}(\mathsf{sentence}(N))$ implies that for $i \in \{1, 2\}$ and $W \in \{\top, \bot\}$ it holds that $\mathsf{leafy}'(N_i)[A\backslash W] = \mathsf{leafy}'(\mathsf{subst\text{-}copy}(N_i, A\backslash W))$. Equivalence of (2) to (1) then follows from the definitions of TSF and leafy'. Equivalence of (3) to (2) follows from clause (4.) of the definition of SF. Equivalence of (4) to (3) follows from clauses (3.) and (1.) of the definition of SF, since $A \notin \mathcal{A}(L_N)$. Equivalence of (5) to (4) follows from the definition of leafy'.

Base Case if Clause (5.) of the Definition of TSF *is Matched.*

$$\begin{array}{lll}
(1) & \mathsf{leafy}'(\mathsf{TSF}(A, N)) & = \\
(2) & \mathsf{leafy}'(\mathsf{FSF}(A, L_N, F_N)) & = \\
(3) & \mathsf{SF}(A, \mathsf{rem\text{-}d\text{-}labels}(L_N \land F_N)) & = \\
(4) & \mathsf{SF}(A, \mathsf{leafy}'(N)). &
\end{array}$$

Equivalence of (2) to (1) follows from the definition of TSF. Equivalence of (3) to (2) follows from Proposition 169. Equivalence of (4) to (3) follows from the definition of leafy'.

Induction Step if Clause (2.) of the Definition of TSF *is Matched.*

$$
\begin{array}{lll}
(1) & \mathsf{leafy}'(\mathsf{TSF}(A, N)) & = \\
(2) & L_N \wedge (\mathsf{leafy}'(\mathsf{TSF}(A, N_1)) \vee \mathsf{leafy}'(\mathsf{TSF}(A, N_2))) & = \\
(3) & L_N \wedge (\mathsf{SF}(A, \mathsf{leafy}'(N_1)) \vee \mathsf{SF}(A, \mathsf{leafy}'(N_2))) & = \\
(4) & L_N \wedge \mathsf{SF}(A, \mathsf{leafy}'(N_1) \vee \mathsf{leafy}'(N_2)) & = \\
(5) & \mathsf{SF}(A, L_N \wedge (\mathsf{leafy}'(N_1) \vee \mathsf{leafy}'(N_2))) & = \\
(6) & \mathsf{SF}(A, \mathsf{leafy}'(N)). &
\end{array}
$$

Node N is an o-node whose children are N_1 and N_2. Equivalence of (2) to (1) follows from the definitions of TSF and leafy'. By the induction assumption it holds that $\mathsf{leafy}'(\mathsf{TSF}(A, N_1)) = \mathsf{SF}(A, \mathsf{leafy}'(N_1))$ and that $\mathsf{leafy}'(\mathsf{TSF}(A, N_2)) = \mathsf{SF}(A, \mathsf{leafy}'(N_2))$. Thus equivalence of (3) to (2) follows from the induction assumption.

Equivalence of (4) to (3) follows from clause (2.) of the definition of SF, which is matched by $(\mathsf{leafy}'(N_1) \vee \mathsf{leafy}'(N_2))$: That $(\mathsf{leafy}'(N_1) \vee \mathsf{leafy}'(N_2))$ is not decomposable inside $\{A\}$ follows, since $A \notin \mathcal{A}(L_N)$ and the match condition for clause (2.) of the definition of TSF includes that clause (1.) fails, i. e., that $(L_N \wedge (\mathsf{leafy}'(N_1) \vee \mathsf{leafy}'(N_2)))$ is not decomposable inside $\{A\}$. Equivalence of (5) to (4) follows from clauses (3.) and (1.) of SF, since $A \notin \mathcal{A}(L_N)$. Equivalence of (6) to (5) follows from the definition of leafy'.

Induction Step if Clause (3.) of the Definition of TSF *is Matched.*

$$
\begin{array}{lll}
(1) & \mathsf{leafy}'(\mathsf{TSF}(A, N)) & = \\
(2) & L_N \wedge (\mathsf{leafy}'(\mathsf{TSF}(A, N_1)) \wedge \mathsf{leafy}'(N_2)) & = \\
(3) & L_N \wedge (\mathsf{SF}(A, \mathsf{leafy}'(N_1)) \wedge \mathsf{leafy}'(N_2)) & = \\
(4) & L_N \wedge \mathsf{SF}(A, \mathsf{leafy}'(N_1) \wedge \mathsf{leafy}'(N_2)) & = \\
(5) & \mathsf{SF}(A, L_N \wedge \mathsf{leafy}'(N_1) \wedge \mathsf{leafy}'(N_2)) & = \\
(6) & \mathsf{SF}(A, \mathsf{leafy}'(N)). &
\end{array}
$$

We assume that $A \notin \mathcal{A}(\mathsf{leafy}'(F_2))$. The case where $A \notin \mathcal{A}(\mathsf{leafy}'(F_1))$ can be shown analogously. Node N is an a-node whose children are N_1 and N_2. Equivalence of (2) to (1) follows from the definitions of TSF and leafy'. By the induction assumption it holds that $\mathsf{leafy}'(\mathsf{TSF}(A, N_1)) = \mathsf{SF}(A, \mathsf{leafy}'(N_1))$. Thus equivalence of (3) to (2) follows from the induction assumption. Equivalence of (4) to (3) follows from clause (3.) of the definition of SF, which is matched by $(\mathsf{leafy}'(N_1) \wedge \mathsf{leafy}'(N_2))$: That $(\mathsf{leafy}'(N_1) \wedge \mathsf{leafy}'(N_2))$ is not decomposable inside $\{A\}$ follows, since $A \notin \mathcal{A}(L_N)$ analogously as shown for $(\mathsf{leafy}'(N_1) \vee \mathsf{leafy}'(N_2))$ in the induction step for clause (2.) of the definition of TSF. Equivalences (5) and (6) follow analogously to equivalences of (5) and (6) for the induction step for clause (2.) of the definition of TSF. □

Proposition 171 *If* $A_1 \ldots A_n$*, where* $n \geq 0$*, is a sequence of different ground atoms not in* d-labels *and* N *is a node of a d-labeled binary sem-fwd-tableau such that* $\mathcal{A}(\mathsf{sentence}(N)) \cap \{A_1, \ldots, A_n\} = \emptyset$*, then*

$$\mathsf{leafy}'(\mathsf{TSF}^{A_1 \ldots A_n}(N)) = \mathsf{SF}^{A_1 \ldots A_n}(\mathsf{leafy}'(N)).$$

Proof. By induction on n. In the base case, where $n = 0$, it holds that $\mathsf{TSF}^{\emptyset}(N) = N$ and $S^{\emptyset}(\mathsf{leafy}'(N)) = \mathsf{leafy}'(N)$. Hence

$$\mathsf{leafy}'(\mathsf{TSF}^{\emptyset}(N)) = S^{\emptyset}(\mathsf{leafy}'(N)).$$

The induction step for $n > 0$ can be shown as follows:

$$\begin{array}{rl} (1) & \mathsf{leafy}'(\mathsf{TSF}(A_n, \mathsf{TSF}^{A_1 \ldots A_{n-1}}(N))) = \mathsf{SF}(A_n, \mathsf{leafy}'(\mathsf{TSF}^{A_1 \ldots A_{n-1}}(N))). \\ (\text{IA}) & \mathsf{leafy}'(\mathsf{TSF}^{A_1 \ldots A_{n-1}}(N)) = \mathsf{SF}^{A_1 \ldots A_{n-1}}(\mathsf{leafy}'(N)). \\ (2) & \mathsf{leafy}'(\mathsf{TSF}(A_n, \mathsf{TSF}^{A_1 \ldots A_{n-1}}(N))) = \mathsf{SF}(A_n, \mathsf{SF}^{A_1 \ldots A_{n-1}}(\mathsf{leafy}'(N)). \\ (\text{IC}) & \mathsf{leafy}'(\mathsf{TSF}^{A_1 \ldots A_n}(N)) = \mathsf{SF}^{A_1 \ldots A_n}(\mathsf{leafy}'(N)). \end{array}$$

From the precondition $\mathcal{A}(\mathsf{sentence}(N)) \cap \{A_1, \ldots, A_n\} = \emptyset$ and Proposition 168.iv it follows that $A_n \notin \mathcal{A}(\mathsf{sentence}(\mathsf{TSF}^{A_1 \ldots A_{n-1}}(N)))$. Thus the preconditions of Proposition 170 to infer (1) are satisfied. (2) follows from the induction assumption (IA) and (1). (IC), the induction conclusion, follows from (2) and the definitions of $\mathsf{TSF}^{A_1 \ldots A_n}$ and $\mathsf{SF}^{A_1 \ldots A_n}$. □

14.3.5 Deriving Values of TSF with a Tableau Method

We show that a fwd-tableau obtained as value a of successive application of the TSF mapping can be constructed by a variant of a DPLL-Fwd calculus, where the length of the derivation is linearly bounded by the size of the leafy′ sentence of the resulting fwd-tableau (Proposition 177).

To document precisely the correspondence with semantic factoring, as described in [MR03], we use the calculus DPLL-Fwd-Dec-Mini. It is similar to DPLL-Fwd, but constructs DNNF sentences (therefore the *Dec* in its name) instead of linkless sentences and only includes three rules necessary to show the correspondence to semantic factoring (thus called *Mini*).

The construction of a decomposable equivalent to a given sentence F by means of semantic factoring proceeds in correspondence with the inductive definition of $\mathsf{SF}^{A_1 \ldots A_n}(F)$, i.e., by performing the SF transformation in succession for $A_1, \ldots, A_n$, starting from F. The inductive definition of $\mathsf{TSF}^{A_1 \ldots A_n}$, however, is a just a "theoretic" device that bears no direct correspondence to tableau construction by the DPLL-Fwd-Dec-Mini calculus; the calculus does not in general construct for a given node N the tableaux $\mathsf{TSF}^{A_1 \ldots A_m}(N)$ with $m < n$ as intermediate results.

The specification of the DPLL-Fwd-Dec-Mini calculus (Definition 133) is based on some auxiliary concepts that are analogs for decomposability to related concepts for linklessness. *Decomposable formula*, the analog to *linkless formula* (Definition 67) has already been defined above (Definition 121). The decision and branch completeness properties PD-DEC and PB-DEC (Definitions 130 and 131) are analogs to PD-L and PB-L (Definitions 114 and 84). Rule Disconnect-Dec (Definition 132) is analog to Disconnect (Definition 111).

The notion *dec-mini-derivable* (Definition 134) gathers structural constraints on fwd-tableaux such that any given fwd-tableau which satisfies them can be constructed with DPLL-Fwd-Dec-Mini. This is shown in Proposition 174, along with the fact that the length of such a derivation with DPLL-Fwd-Dec-Mini is linearly bounded by the size of the leafy′ sentence of the constructed tableau.

Proposition 177, the main result of this section, is based on two lemmas that show correspondence of derivations with DPLL-Fwd-Mini to the FSF mapping and to a single step of the TSF mapping (Propositions 175 and 176).

Definition 130 (Decision Property PD-DEC) If L is a ground literal, N is a node in a fwd-tableau and S is an atom scope, then L and N satisfy the property $\mathsf{PD\text{-}DEC}_S$ if and only if

$A \in$ d-labels,

or

$A \notin S$, and $(B_N \land F_N)$ is not decomposable inside $\{\mathsf{atom}(L)\}$.

Definition 131 (Branch Completeness Property PB-DEC) If N is a node in a fwd-tableau and S is an atom scope, then N satisfies the property $\mathsf{PB\text{-}DEC}_S$ if and only if

$$(B_N \land F_N) \text{ is decomposable outside } S.$$

Definition 132 (Rule Disconnect-Dec(S)) The rule Disconnect-Dec(S) is identical to Disconnect(S), except that the scope parameter S is an atom scope instead of a literal scope, and

$$\mathcal{A}(F_i) \cap \mathcal{A}(F_j) \subseteq S$$

is used in the precondition instead of $\langle F_i, F_j \rangle$ *is linkless outside* S.[7]

Definition 133 (DPLL-Fwd-Dec-Mini Calculus) If S is an atom scope, then the DPLL-Fwd-Dec-Mini *calculus* for scope S is the calculus $\langle S^*, S_0^*, R^* \rangle$ such that S^* is the set of tn-states, S_0^* is the set of tn-states $\langle T, N \rangle$ such that T is a fwd-tableau containing a single node N, and R^* is

$$\{\mathsf{Decide}(\mathsf{PD\text{-}DEC}_S),\ \mathsf{Disconnect\text{-}Dec}(S),\ \mathsf{Next}(\mathsf{PB\text{-}DEC}_S)\},$$

where *Simplify-Fwd* in the specification of these rules is an algorithm that in general returns $F[B]$ for a sentence F and branch B as inputs, but additionally applies certain truth value simplification steps if F has the form

$$((D \land F_1) \lor (\neg D \land F_2)),\ \textit{where}\ D \in \text{d-labels},$$

and D ($\neg D$, resp.) occurs as literal label in B : For F of this form, it returns the sentence $F_1[B]$ ($F_2[B]$, resp.).[8]

[7] The scope parameter is called differently, S_l, in the original definition of Disconnect (Definition 111).

[8] For the Disconnect-Dec(S) rule, the *Simplify-Fwd* algorithm specified in this way just returns its input sentence F. Thus, actually, Decide($\mathsf{PD\text{-}DEC}_S$) is the only rule in which *Simplify-Fwd* takes effect.

Definition 134 (Dec-Mini-Derivable Sem-Fwd-Tableaux)

(i) If N is a node of a d-labeled binary fwd-tableau, S is an atom scope, and N_0 is a node that is either identical to N or is an ancestor of N, then N is called *dec-mini-derivable for* a S *relative to* N_0 if and only if

1. If N is a leaf node, then N satisfies $\mathsf{PB\text{-}DEC}_S$, i. e.,

$$F_N \text{ is decomposable outside } S;$$

2. If N is an o-node whose children are N_1, N_2, then these children could have been attached by a $\mathsf{Decide}(\mathsf{PD\text{-}DEC}_S)$ step with respect to the branch segment starting from N_0, i. e.,
   a) $L_{N_1} \in \mathcal{A}(F_N)$,
   b) $L_{N_1} \notin \mathcal{A}(B_N^{N_0})$,
   c) If $L_{N_1} \notin \mathsf{d\text{-}labels}$, then $L_{N_1} \notin S$,
   d) If $L_{N_1} \notin \mathsf{d\text{-}labels}$, then F_N is not decomposable inside $\{L_{N_1}\}$,
   e) $L_{N_2} = \neg L_{N_1}$, and
   f) If $L_{N_1} \in \mathsf{d\text{-}labels}$ and $F = ((L_{N_1} \wedge F_1) \vee (\neg L_{N_1} \wedge F_2))$, then $F_{N_1} = F_1$ and $F_{N_2} = F_2$, otherwise $F_{N_1} = F_N[L_{N_1} \backslash \top]$ and $F_{N_2} = F_N[L_{N_1} \backslash \bot]$;
3. If N is an a-node whose children are N_1, N_2, then these children could have been attached by a $\mathsf{Disconnect\text{-}Dec}(S)$ step, i. e.,
   a) $F_N = F_{N_1} \wedge F_{N_2}$,
   b) $\mathcal{A}(F_{N_1}) \cap \mathcal{A}(F_{N_2}) \subseteq S$, and
   c) $L_{N_1} = L_{N_2} = \top$.

(ii) A binary sem-fwd-tableau T is called *dec-mini-derivable for* an atom scope S if and only if all nodes in T are dec-mini-derivable for S relative to the root of T.

In conditions (1) and (2d) of the definition of *dec-mini-derivable*, the preconditions of $\mathsf{Next}(\mathsf{PD\text{-}DEC}_S)$ and $\mathsf{Decide}(\mathsf{PD\text{-}DEC}_S)$ appear in a simplified form, where the branch is dropped. In condition (2f) the forward labels are just specified by referring to L_{N_1} and L_{N_2}, instead of B_{N_1} and B_{N_2}, as in Definition 133. These simplified forms facilitate to prove that certain fwd-tableaux are dec-mini-derivable. Their equivalence to the original forms is justified by the following Proposition 172.

Proposition 172 *If N is a node in a d-labeled binary fwd-tableau T that is dec-mini-derivable, then*

(i) *If $L_{\mathsf{root}(T)} = \top$, then*

$$\mathcal{A}(B_N) \cap \mathcal{A}(F_N) = \emptyset;$$

(ii) *If N' is a child of N, then*

$$\mathcal{A}(B_N) \cap \mathcal{A}(L_{N'}) = \emptyset.$$

Proof. Follows easily from the definition of *dec-mini-derivable*.

□

Propositions 173.i and 173.ii, which follow, are used as lemmas in the proof of Proposition 176. They mediate between decomposability/non-decomposability of leafy sentences and forward labels of inner tableau nodes. If DPLL-Fwd-Dec-Mini would be extended to permit further simplifications in the construction of forward labels, Proposition 173.i might no longer hold.

Proposition 173 *If N is a node in a fwd-tableau that is dec-mini-derivable and A is a ground atom such that $A \notin$ d-labels, then*

(i) *If N is an a-node with children N_1, N_2 and $\mathsf{leafy}'(N)$ is decomposable inside $\{A\}$, then*

$$A \notin \mathcal{A}(F_{N_1}) \cap \mathcal{A}(F_{N_2});$$

(ii) *If $A \notin \mathsf{sentence}(N)$ and $\mathsf{leafy}'(N)$ is not decomposable inside $\{A\}$, then*

$$F_N \text{ is not decomposable inside } A.$$

Proof. (173.i) Follows from the definition of *dec-mini-derivable*. It can be shown that if N is node in a dec-mini-derivable fwd-tableau, then

$$\mathcal{A}(L_N) \cup \mathcal{A}(F_N) \subseteq \mathcal{A}(\mathsf{leafy}'(N)) \cup \mathsf{d\text{-}labels}.$$

The proposition follows, since this holds in particular for N_1 and N_2 in the role of N.

(173.ii) Follows from the definition of *dec-mini-derivable*.

□

Proposition 174 *If T_0 is a d-labeled fwd-tableau containing a single node N such that $L_N = \top$, S is an atom scope, and T is a d-labeled binary fwd-tableau that is dec-mini-derivable for S, where $L_{\mathsf{root}(T)} = \top$ and $F_{\mathsf{root}(T)} = F_N$, then there exists a derivation D with the* DPLL-Fwd-Mini *calculus for scope S such that*

1. *The initial state of D is $\langle T_0, N \rangle$,*
2. *The tableau component of the last state of D is T,*
3. *The length of D is less than or equal to $2 * \mathsf{leafy}'(T)$.*

Proof. That there exists a derivation with the DPLL-Fwd-Mini calculus with initial and last states as specified in the proposition, and with a length that is less than or equal to the number of nodes in T, straightforwardly follows from the definition of *dec-mini-derivable*. From the definition of leafy' it follows that the number of nodes in T is less than or equal to $2 * \mathsf{leafy}'(T)$: Each non-leaf node corresponds to a different occurrence of a binary operator in $\mathsf{leafy}'(T)$, each leaf node corresponds to a different subformula of $\mathsf{leafy}'(T)$.

□

Proposition 175 *If A is a ground atom, L is a ground literal or* $\top$, *and F is a d-labeled propositional NNF sentence such that* $A \notin \mathsf{d\text{-}labels}$, $A \notin \mathcal{A}(L)$ *and* $\mathcal{A}(L) \cap \mathcal{A}(F) = \emptyset$, *then*

all nodes in the tableau with root $\mathsf{FSF}(A, L, F)$ *are dec-mini-derivable for* $\overline{\{A\}}$ *relative to* $\mathsf{FSF}(A, L, F)$.

Proof. Let N be a node in the tableau with root $\mathsf{FSF}(A, L, F)$. We show that N is dec-mini-derivable relative to $\mathsf{FSF}(A, L, F)$.

- If N is a leaf node, then condition (1) of *dec-mini-derivable* has to be shown, i.e.: F_N *is decomposable inside* $\{A\}$.

  If N is obtained by a match with clause (1.) of the definition of FSF, it follows immediately from the definition of FSF that F_N is decomposable inside $\{A\}$. If N is obtained by a match with clause (4.) of the definition of FSF, then in F_N the atom A is substituted by a truth value constant. Thus $A \notin \mathcal{A}(F_N)$; hence F_N is decomposable inside $\{A\}$.
- If N is an o-node, then, if it is obtained by a match with clause (4.) of the definition of FSF, the conditions for *dec-mini-derivable* follow easily from the definition of FSF. We consider the case where N is obtained by a match with clause (2.). Let $((D \wedge F_1) \vee (\neg D \wedge F_2))$ be the matching subformula of F. The atom D does not occur in F_1 since this would violate the precondition that F is d-labeled, which includes decomposability inside d-labels. Generalizing this observation, since F is d-labeled and thus decomposable inside d-labels, the definition of FSF implies that an atom in d-labels can occur in a branch that starts from $\mathsf{FSF}(A, L, F)$ at most a single time in the literal label of a descendant of $\mathsf{FSF}(A, L, F)$. The possibility that D occurs in the literal label of $\mathsf{FSF}(A, L, F)$ itself is excluded by the precondition of the proposition $\mathcal{A}(L) \cap \mathcal{A}(F) = \emptyset$. Thus $D \notin \mathcal{A}(B_N^{\mathsf{FSF}(A,L,F)})$, that is, condition (2b) of *dec-mini-derivable*, is satisfied. Since $D \in \mathsf{d\text{-}labels}$, the requirements by *dec-mini-derivable* on the forward labels of the children of N are met by F_1 and F_2. The remaining conditions of *dec-mini-derivable* are easy to see.
- If N is an a-node, then it follows immediately from the definition of FSF that N is dec-mini-derivable for $\overline{\{A\}}$.

□

Proposition 176 *If A is a ground atom and T is a d-labeled binary sem-fwd-tableau that is dec-mini-derivable for an atom scope $\overline{S}$ such that $A \notin$ d-labels, $A \notin \mathcal{A}(\mathsf{sentence}(T))$ and $L_{\mathsf{root}(T)} = \top$, then*

the tableau with root $\mathsf{TSF}(A, \mathsf{root}(T))$
is dec-mini-derivable for $\overline{\{A\} \cup S}$.

Proof. By induction on the structure of the tableau with root $\mathsf{TSF}(A,\mathsf{root}(T))$, corresponding to the match cases of the definition of TSF. The induction property, which is shown for all nodes N in the tableau with root $\mathsf{TSF}(A, \mathsf{root}(T))$, is the following:

For all nodes N' that are identical to N or descendants of N it holds that N' is dec-mini-derivable for $\overline{\{A\} \cup S}$ relative to $\mathsf{TSF}(A, \mathsf{root}(T))$.

There are three base cases, corresponding to clauses (1.), (4.) and (5.) of the definition of TSF.

Base Case if Clause (1.) of the Definition of TSF *is Matched.* Let N' be either $\mathsf{TSF}(A, M)$ or a descendant of $\mathsf{TSF}(A, M)$, where M is a node in T that matches clause (1.) of the definition of TSF. From Propositions 168.i and 168.ii it follows that there exists a node M' in T that is equal to N' as far as literal and forward labels of the node and its children are concerned. More precisely: $L'_N = L'_M$, $F'_N = F'_M$, and if N' has children N_1, N_2, then M' also has children M_1, M_2 such that $L_{N_1} = L_{M_1}$, $F_{N_1} = F_{M_1}$, $L_{N_2} = L_{M_2}$ and $F_{N_2} = F_{M_2}$. In addition, from Proposition 168.iii it follows that the branches (considered as sentences) to N' and M' are equal, i. e. $B_{N'}^{\mathsf{TSF}(A,\mathsf{root}(T))} = B_{M'}^{\mathsf{root}(T)}$. These correspondences of literal labels, forward labels and branches allow to conclude from the fact that M' is dec-mini-derivable for $\overline{S}$ relative to $\mathsf{root}(T)$ that

(xv) N' is dec-mini-derivable for $\overline{S}$ relative to $\mathsf{TSF}(A, \mathsf{root}(T))$.

It remains to show that

(xvi) N' is dec-mini-derivable for $\overline{\{A\} \cup S}$ relative to $\mathsf{TSF}(A, \mathsf{root}(T))$.

We show (xvi) for the three possible node types of N':

– If N' is a leaf node that is dec-mini-derivable for $\overline{S}$, then $F_{N'}$ is decomposable outside $\overline{S}$. From this and the fact that $F_{N'}$ is decomposable outside $\overline{\{A\}}$, which is implied by clause (1.) of the definition of TSF, follows the condition (1) of *dec-mini-derivable*: $F_{N'}$ is decomposable outside $\overline{\{A\} \cup S}$.

- If N' is an o-node, then the only condition of *dec-mini-derivable* affected by the atom scope parameter is (2c). Let N_1, N_2 be the children of N'. Condition (2c) transfers from $\overline{S}$ to $\overline{\{A\} \cup S}$, since $L_{N_1} \notin \overline{S}$ entails $L_{N_1} \notin \overline{\{A\} \cup S}$.
- If N' is an a-node, then the only condition of *dec-mini-derivable* affected by the atom scope parameter is (3b). Let N_1, N_2 be the children of N'. Since N' is dec-mini-derivable for $\overline{S}$ it holds that $F_{N'} = (F_{N_1} \land F_{N_2})$ and

  (xvii) $$\mathcal{A}(F_{N_1}) \cap \mathcal{A}(F_{N_2}) \subseteq \overline{S}.$$

  Clause (1.) of the definition of TSF implies that $\mathsf{leafy}'(F_{N'})$ is decomposable inside $\{A\}$. By Proposition 173.i it then holds that $A \notin \mathcal{A}(F_{N_1}) \cap \mathcal{A}(F_{N_2})$. From (xvii) then follows the condition (3b) of *dec-mini-derivable* for the atom scope $\overline{\{A\} \cup S}$:

  (xviii) $$\mathcal{A}(F_{N_1}) \cap \mathcal{A}(F_{N_2}) \subseteq \overline{\{A\} \cup S}.$$

Induction Step if Clause (2.) or (3.) of the definition of TSF *is Matched.* Let N' be either $\mathsf{TSF}(A, M)$ or a descendant of $\mathsf{TSF}(A, M)$, where M is a node in T that matches clause (2.) or (3.) of the definition of TSF. If N' is a descendant of $\mathsf{TSF}(A, M)$, it holds by the induction assumption that N' is dec-mini-derivable for $\overline{\{A\} \cup S}$ relative to $\mathsf{TSF}(A, \mathsf{root}(T))$. If N' is identical to $\mathsf{TSF}(A, M)$, this fact – that N' is dec-mini-derivable for $\overline{\{A\} \cup S}$ relative to $\mathsf{TSF}(A, \mathsf{root}(T))$ – follows analogously as shown for o-nodes and a-nodes N', respectively, in the base case where clause (1.) of the definition of TSF is matched.

Base Case if Clause (4.) of the Definition of TSF *is Matched.* Let N' be either $\mathsf{TSF}(A, M)$ or a descendant of $\mathsf{TSF}(A, M)$, where M is a node in T that matches clause (4.) of the definition of TSF.

- If N' is identical to $\mathsf{TSF}(A, M)$, then N' is an o-node. N' satisfies condition (2b) of *dec-mini-derivable*, since from precondition $A \notin \mathcal{A}(\mathsf{sentence}(T))$ it follows that $A \notin \mathcal{A}(B_M^{\mathsf{root}(T)})$; hence also $A \notin \mathcal{A}(B_{N'}^{\mathsf{TSF}(A,\mathsf{root}(T))})$. Condition (2c) for N' is $A \notin \overline{\{A\} \cup S}$, which holds trivially. Since M fails to match clause (1.) of the definition of TSF, it holds that $\mathsf{leafy}'(M)$ is not decomposable inside $\{A\}$. From Proposition 173.ii then follows that F_M is not decomposable inside $\{A\}$. By Proposition 168.ii it holds that $F_{N'} = F_M$, which implies condition (2d) of *dec-mini-derivable*: $F_{N'}$ is not decomposable inside $\{A\}$. The remaining conditions of *dec-mini-derivable* for N' are easy to see.

- If N' is a descendant of $\mathsf{TSF}(A, M)$ that is an o-node with children N_1, N_2, then, by the definition of $\mathsf{subst\text{-}copy}$, there exists a corresponding o-node M' in T that is a descendant of M and has children M_1, M_2 such that $L_{N_1} = L_{M_1}$, $L_{N_2} = L_{M_2}$, and $F_{N'} = F_{M'}[A\backslash W]$ for some truth value constant W. By condition (2a) of *dec-mini-derivable* for M' it holds that $L_{M_1} \in \mathcal{A}(F_{M'})$. From the precondition $A \notin \mathcal{A}(\mathsf{sentence}(T))$ follows $L_{M_1} \neq A$. Thus $L_{M_1} \in \mathcal{A}(F_{N'})$. Since $L_{N_1} = L_{M_1}$, this implies condition (2a) of *dec-mini-derivable* for N': $L_{N_1} \in \mathcal{A}(F_{N'})$. By condition (2b) of *dec-mini-derivable* for M' it holds that $L_{M_1} \notin \mathcal{A}(B_{M'}^{\mathsf{root}(T)})$. From the definition of TSF it follows that $\mathcal{A}(B_{N'}^{\mathsf{TSF}(A,\mathsf{root}(T))}) = \mathcal{A}(B_{M'}^{\mathsf{root}(T)}) \cup \{A\}$. Since $L_{M_1} \neq A$ and $L_{N_1} = L_{M_1}$, this implies condition (2b) of *dec-mini-derivable* for N': $L_{N_1} \notin \mathcal{A}(B_{N'}^{\mathsf{TSF}(A,\mathsf{root}(T))})$. It is easy to see that the remaining conditions of *dec-mini-derivable* for o-nodes transfer from M' to N'.
- If N' is a descendant of $\mathsf{TSF}(A, M)$ that is an a-node with children N_1, N_2, then, by the definitions of TSF and $\mathsf{subst\text{-}copy}$, there exists a corresponding a-node M' in T that is a descendant of M (or is M itself, in case N' is a child of $\mathsf{TSF}(A, M)$) and has children M_1, M_2 such that for some truth value constant W it holds that $F_{N_1} = F_{M_1}[A\backslash W]$ and $F_{N_2} = F_{M_2}[A\backslash W]$. The presupposed condition (3b) of *dec-mini-derivable* for M', that $\mathcal{A}(F_{M_1}) \cap \mathcal{A}(F_{M_2}) \subseteq \overline{S}$, then implies condition (3b) for N': $\mathcal{A}(F_{N_1}) \cap \mathcal{A}(F_{N_2}) \subseteq \overline{\{A\} \cup S}$. It is easy to see that the remaining conditions of *dec-mini-derivable* for a-nodes transfer from M' to N'.
- If N' is a descendant of $\mathsf{TSF}(A, M)$ that is a leaf node, then, by the definition of $\mathsf{subst\text{-}copy}$, there exists a corresponding leaf node M' in T that is a descendant of M such that $F_{N'} = F_{M'}[A\backslash W]$ for some truth value constant W. The presupposed condition (1) of *dec-mini-derivable* for M', that $F_{M'}$ is decomposable outside $\overline{S}$, then implies condition (1) for N': $F_{N'}$ is decomposable outside $\overline{\{A\} \cup S}$.

Base Case if Clause (5.) of the Definition of TSF *is Matched.* Let N' be either $\mathsf{TSF}(A, M)$ or a descendant of $\mathsf{TSF}(A, M)$, where M is a node in T that matches clause (5.) of the definition of TSF. That the preconditions of Proposition 175 are satisfied for A, L_M and F_M is immediate, except for the following: $A \notin \mathcal{A}(L_M)$ follows from $A \notin \mathcal{A}(\mathsf{sentence}(T))$, which is a precondition of the proposition to be proven; $\mathcal{A}(L_M) \cap \mathcal{A}(F_M) = \emptyset$ follows from Proposition 172.i, since $\mathsf{root}(T) = \top$, which also is a precondition of the proposition to be proven. It then follows from Proposition 175 that

(xix) N' is dec-mini-derivable for $\overline{\{A\}}$ relative to $\mathsf{FSF}(A, L_M, F_M)$.

It has to be shown that

(xx) N' is dec-mini-derivable for $\overline{\{A\} \cup S}$ relative to $\mathsf{TSF}(A, \mathsf{root}(T))$.

We show (xx) for the three possible node types of N':

– If N' is a leaf node, from (xix) it follows that

(xxi) $F_{N'}$ is decomposable outside $\overline{\{A\}}$.

Since M is a leaf node that is dec-mini-derivable for $\overline{S}$, it holds that F_M is decomposable outside S. It then follows from the definition of FSF that also

(xxii) $F_{N'}$ is decomposable outside $\overline{S}$.

From (xxii) and (xxi) follows the condition (1) of *dec-mini-derivable* for $\overline{\{A\} \cup S}$ relative to $\mathsf{TSF}(A, \mathsf{root}(T))$:

(xxiii) $F_{N'}$ is decomposable outside $\overline{\{A\} \cup S}$.

– If N' is an o-node with children N_1, N_2, there are two conditions of *dec-mini-derivable* that are not immediate, and have to be verified under the assumption (xix):
  – Condition (2b) can be shown as follows: The branch $B_{N'}^{\mathsf{TSF}(A,\mathsf{root}(T))}$ can be considered as composed of two parts, a prefix B_0 succeeded by a postfix B_1: Let
  $$B_0 \stackrel{\text{def}}{=} B_{\mathsf{FSF}(A,L_M,F_M)}^{\mathsf{TSF}(A,\mathsf{root}(T))}.$$
  Let B_1 be the conjunction of the literal labels of nodes on $B_{N'}^{\mathsf{TSF}(A,\mathsf{root}(T))}$ that follow B_0 (if $N' = \mathsf{FSF}(A, L_M, F_M)$, then $B_1 = \top$). From Proposition 168.iii it follows that $B_0 = B_M^{\mathsf{root}(T)}$. From the definition of FSF it follows that $\mathcal{A}(B_1) \subseteq F_M$. By Proposition 172.i, since $L_{\mathsf{root}(T)} = \top$, it holds that $B_0 \cap F_M = \emptyset$. Thus

  (xxiv) $\mathcal{A}(B_0) \cap \mathcal{A}(B_1) = \emptyset.$

  From (xxiv) and the fact that $L_{N_1} \in \mathcal{A}(B_1)$ follows $L_{N_1} \notin \mathcal{A}(B_0)$. This, along with the fact that N' satisfies condition (2b) of *dec-mini-derivable relative to* $\mathsf{FSF}(A, L_M, F_M)$, implies that N' satisfies condition (2b) also relative to $\mathsf{TSF}(A, \mathsf{root}(T))$.
  – Condition (2c) for $\overline{\{A\} \cup S}$ follows from condition (2c) for $\overline{S}$, since $\overline{\{A\} \cup S} \subseteq \overline{S}$.

– If N' is an a-node with children N_1, N_2, then these children are descendants of $\mathsf{FSF}(A, L_M, F_M)$, where M is a leaf node that is dec-mini-derivable for $\overline{S}$. From this it follows that $\mathcal{A}(F_{N_1}) \cap \mathcal{A}(F_{N_2}) \subseteq \overline{S}$. It then follows from (xix) that $\mathcal{A}(F_{N_1}) \cap \mathcal{A}(F_{N_2}) \subseteq \overline{\{A\} \cup S}$, which is condition (3b) of *dec-mini-derivable* for $\overline{\{A\} \cup S}$. The remaining conditions of *dec-mini-derivable* are immediate.

□

Proposition 177 *If T_0 is a d-labeled fwd-tableau containing a single node N such that $L_N = \top$, and $A_1 \ldots A_n$, where $n \geq 0$, is a sequence of different ground atoms not in* d-labels, *then there exists a derivation D with the* DPLL-Fwd-Mini *calculus for scope $\{A_1, \ldots, A_n\}$ such that*

1. *The initial state of D is $\langle T_0, N \rangle$,*
2. *The root of tableau component of the last state of D is $\mathsf{TSF}^{A_1 \ldots A_n}(N)$,*
3. *The length of D is less than or equal to $2 * |\mathsf{leafy}'(\mathsf{TSF}^{A_1 \ldots A_n}(N))|$.*

Proof. Follows from Proposition 174, where the three preconditions of that proposition are matched by the following facts (1)–(3):

(1) The tableau with root $\mathsf{TSF}^{A_1 \ldots A_n}(N)$ is dec-mini-derivable for $\overline{\{A_1, \ldots, A_n\}}$.
(2) $L_{\mathsf{TSF}^{A_1 \ldots A_n}(N)} = \top$.
(3) $F_{\mathsf{TSF}^{A_1 \ldots A_n}(N)} = F_N$.

(2) and (3) follow from the precondition $L_N = \top$ and Propositions 168.i and 168.ii by straightforward induction. (1) follows from Propositions 176 and 168.iv by induction on n, which we now show in detail.

It is easy to see that in the first base case where $n = 0$ the derivation consisting of the single step $\langle T_0, N \rangle$ satisfies all three items of the proposition statement. In the second base case where $n = 1$, the single node tableau T_0 satisfies the preconditions on T stated in Proposition 176, which can be shown as follows: $L_N = \top$ is a precondition of the proposition to be proved. Since N is a leaf and $L_N = \top$, it holds that $A \notin \mathcal{A}(\mathsf{sentence}(N))$. That N is dec-mini-derivable for $\overline{\emptyset}$ follows, since the requirement for *dec-mini-derivable* applying to N as leaf node is that $(B_N \wedge F_N)$ is decomposable outside GLITS, which holds trivially. Proposition 176 then implies that the tableau with root $\mathsf{TSF}(A, N)$ is dec-mini-derivable for $\{A\}$. The induction step for $n > 1$ can be shown as follows:

(IA) The tableau with root $\mathsf{TSF}^{A_1 \ldots A_{n-1}}(N)$ is dec-mini-derivable for $\overline{\{A_1, \ldots, A_{n-1}\}}$.
(4) $\mathcal{A}(\mathsf{sentence}(\mathsf{TSF}^{A_1 \ldots A_{n-1}}(N))) \subseteq \{A_1, \ldots, A_{n-1}\} \cup \text{d-labels}$.
(5) $A_n \notin \mathcal{A}(\mathsf{sentence}(\mathsf{TSF}^{A_1 \ldots A_{n-1}}(N)))$.
(6) $L_{\mathsf{TSF}^{A_1 \ldots A_{n-1}}(N)} = \top$.

(IA) holds by the induction assumption. The precondition $L_N = \top$ implies $\mathcal{A}(\mathsf{sentence}(N)) = \emptyset$; thus (4) follows by straightforward induction from Proposition 168.iv. (5) follows from (4), since $A_1 \ldots A_n$ is a sequence of different ground atoms not in d-labels. (6) follows from the precondition $L_N = \top$ and Proposition 168.i by straightforward induction. With (6), (5) and (IA), the preconditions of Proposition 177 are matched. Proposition 177 then implies (1) as induction conclusion.

□

14.3.6 Tableau Simulation of Semantic Factoring

Propositions 177 and 171 are now combined to a theorem about the simulation of semantic factoring – the successive rewriting subformulas with the Shannon expansion – by DPLL-based tableau construction, as explained informally in the introduction to Section 14.3.

Theorem 18 (Simulation of Semantic Factoring by DPLL-Fwd) *If F is a propositional NNF sentence, $\{A_1, \ldots, A_n\}$ is a set of ground atoms not in* d-labels, *and N is a node such that $L_N = \top$ and $F_N = \mathsf{add\text{-}d\text{-}labels}(F)$, then there exists a derivation D with the* DPLL-Fwd-Dec-Mini *calculus for scope $\{A_1, \ldots, A_n\}$ such that*

1. *The initial state of D is $\langle T_0, N\rangle$, where T_0 is the fwd-tableau that contains N as a single node,*
2. *For the tableau component T of the last state of D it holds that*

$$\mathsf{leafy}'(T) = \mathsf{SF}^{A_1 \ldots A_n}(F),$$

3. *The length of D is less than or equal than $2 * |\mathsf{SF}^{A_1 \ldots A_n}(F)|$.*

Proof. Follows from Propositions 177 and 171. More detailed:

(1) The initial state of D is $\langle T_0, N\rangle$.
(2) The tableau component of the last state of D is T.
(3) The length of D is less than or equal to $2 * |\mathsf{leafy}'(T)|$.
(4) $\mathsf{leafy}'(T) = \mathsf{SF}^{A_1 \ldots A_n}(\mathsf{leafy}'(N))$.
(5) $\mathsf{leafy}'(N) = F$.
(6) $\mathsf{leafy}'(T) = \mathsf{SF}^{A_1 \ldots A_n}(F)$.
(7) The length of D is less than or equal to $2 * |\mathsf{SF}^{A_1 \ldots A_n}(F)|$.

From Proposition 177 it follows that there exists a derivation D such that (1),(2) and (3) hold, where

$$T \textit{ is the tableau with root } \mathsf{TSF}^{A_1 \ldots A_n}(N).$$

(4) follows from Proposition 171. (5) follows from the definition of leafy′. (6) follows from (5) and (4). (7) follows from (6) and (3). Item (1.) of the proposition statement corresponds to (1), item (2.) to (2) in combination with (6), and item (3.) to (7).

□

14.3.7 Comparison with a Tableau Based FNNF Compiler

Hähnle, Murray and Rosenthal [HMR05] describe a tableau procedure for knowledge compilation into a normal form called *factored negation normal form (FNNF)*. Their method is closely related to Shannon expansion. A tableau is constructed by means of the atomic cut rule and simplification rules, both at the level of formulas and at the level of the tableau itself. With a standard depth-first backtracking strategy, the tableau construction can, like the methods based on DPLL-Fwd, be performed with a polynomially bounded working data structure.[9]

The compilation method in [HMR05] does not include and-nodes, nor a technique comparable to the Disjoin rule. It thus fails to simulate independent application of the Shannon expansion to subformulas, of conjunctions as well as disjunctions. Consider for example Fig. 14.1. Compilation of the sentence on the left with respect to $\{\mathsf{q}, \mathsf{t}\}$ can with DPLL-Fwd-Dec-Mini be based on the tableau shown in the center, while the method of [HMR05] would require a duplication of one of the atomic cuts, as shown on the right tableau.

$$(\neg \mathsf{p} \lor \mathsf{q}) \land$$
$$(\neg \mathsf{q} \lor \mathsf{r}) \land$$
$$(\neg \mathsf{s} \lor \mathsf{t}) \land$$
$$(\neg \mathsf{t} \lor \mathsf{u})$$

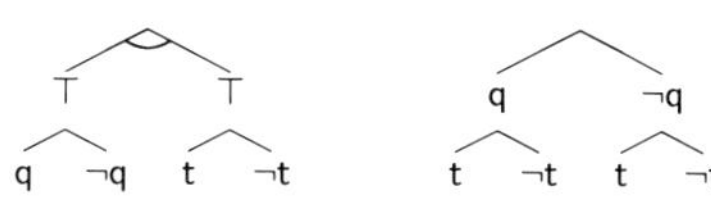

Figure 14.1. And-Nodes for the Independent Compilation of Subformulas

The method in [HMR05] includes simplification rules, at both, the formula and the tableau levels. The systematic study of the integration of such simplifications into DPLL-Fwd remains future work. Roughly, it seems that simplifications at the formula level correspond to simplifications in the construction of forward labels, and tableau level simplifications involving $\bot$ correspond to backjumping. One of the tableau level simplification rules, the rightmost of Fig. 1 in [HMR05], seems useful for DPLL-Fwd, especially since it can effect that True-Up becomes applicable. It can straightforwardly be adapted:

Definition 135 (Rule True-Below-Cut-Up)

PRECONDITIONS: Let N be the active leaf. N is the right child of an o-node $N^{\backprime}$. $F_N = \top$ and $F_{N'} = \top$, where N' is the sibling of N.

EFFECTS: Remove the children of $N^{\backprime}$. Assign $F_{N^{\backprime}}$ to $\top$. Assign $N^{\backprime}$ as active leaf.

In [HMR05] only compilation that preserves full equivalence is taken into account. Thus, simplifications that just preserve equivalence with respect to a scope – such as, at the formula level, the simplifications in the construction of forward labels described in Section 12.2.2, or, at the tableau level, the True-Up rule – are not considered.

[9] Lacking a concept such as *working data structure*, this is expressed in [HMR05] as "the compilation procedure requires only PSPACE for the construction of the tree".

15 Conclusion

We specified a logic operation, *projection*, which is a generalization of second-order quantification and can be used to express in a semantically founded way a variety of tasks in knowledge representation that in some way involve the removal of knowledge about given concepts. Based on techniques employed in recent automated deduction systems that are successful in practice, we developed methods to automate *projection elimination*, the processing of the projection operation.

Starting from a semantic characterization of projection as an add-on to first-order logic, we have shown various properties of projection and indicated how they can be applied. We have proven a property concerning the interplay of projection with conjunction, which can serve as a basis of methods for projection elimination. Our semantic characterization allows to precisely relate projection with similar concepts from the literature, most of which are, however, confined to propositional logic.

Projection elimination cannot straightforwardly be expressed as a theorem proving task, but as a special mode of reasoning, related to model generation and knowledge compilation, which can be performed by adapted theorem provers. We have shown two different approaches to projection elimination, derived from different approaches to theorem proving: resolvent generation and tableau construction, where the latter was our main focus.

Our method based on resolvent generation extends SCAN, an algorithm for second-order quantifier elimination in two respects: It permits not only quantification of "all literals with" given predicates, but also, so to speak, quantification of subsets of literals characterized as instances of given patterns. Furthermore, it is independent of equality. This facilitates its application with semantics in which denoted objects are symbols, as frequently used in knowledge representation – for example, semantics based on Herbrand interpretations. We remarked that special cases of the method correspond to well known simplification operations used in propositional theorem proving, which thus can also be considered as methods that efficiently perform projection elimination for special cases of inputs.

Many of the practically successful automated deduction systems, for different logics and developed in different communities, are based on methods that can be considered as constructing a tableau, a representation of a sentence that satisfies certain syntactic conditions in correspondence to a tree structure. We developed a framework that specifies constraints on tableaux, in accord with the construction methods of such systems, and expressing that tableaux represent results of projection elimination and knowledge compilation tasks. The framework realizes abstractions in two respects: First, it shows projection elimination, certain kinds of knowledge compilation and propositional satisfiability solving as differently parameterized instances of a single task. Second, it abstracts from differences in tableau construction methods that are inessential for the adaption to tasks like projection elimination and knowledge compilation. As a prototypical instantiation of the framework, we have worked out in detail an adaption of the Davis-Putnam-Logemann-Loveland procedure (DPLL) for propositional logic, which is underlying state-of-the-art satisfiability solvers.

Techniques that seem essential for practical success, such as dependency directed backtracking, and techniques that have been proven useful in recent knowledge compilers, such as tableaux corresponding to and-or trees, are explicitly considered in the framework. Various aspects of the combined use of these techniques for formula transformation tasks are clarified by means of the framework, with its abstractly specified constraints and the explicit consideration of tableau structures – in contrast to specifications by means of pseudocode, as common in the literature on related practically successful methods.

Many tableau methods are space efficient because they represent at any point of time just a portion of the constructed tableau in memory. We have shown that this feature can be utilized for formula transformation tasks by methods that deliver output in a piecemeal fashion. Due to destructive tableau construction rules, such as dependency directed backtracking, the combined output pieces are not trivially identical to the implicitly constructed tableau.

If just queries with a restricted vocabulary are posed against a compiled knowledge base, projection elimination might reduce the size of the compiled knowledge base considerably. The current practice for constructing such a reduced knowledge base is to perform projection elimination as a linear operation on the compilation result. We have shown that, under an assumption considered as very likely in complexity theory, the efficiency of the compilation process can be essentially improved by partially weaving in projection elimination. Our tableau framework supports this and the DPLL instantiation realizes it by the integration of appropriate formula simplification operations (such as the special cases of the resolvent generation method mentioned above) and a dedicated destructive tableau construction rule.

An issue for future research is the transfer of the tableau framework to various logics that are important in knowledge representation and are known to be efficiently processable by tableau methods. Such logics include in particular modal and description logics, as well as logics with non-classical semantics, for example minimal model semantics as used for model computation. Our tableau framework directly applies to propositional logic and to first-order logic, with the restriction that, as in hypertableaux [BFN96], the literals associated with tableau nodes must represent *sentences* – meaning that variables are not shared between literal labels of different nodes. Thus, a first approach for using the tableau framework with other logics is via first-order embeddings of these, such as the standard translation of modal logics.

A problem with this approach is to ensure that the first-order formulas resulting from formula transformation computed by the tableau method can be translated back into the other logic. A second concern is the range of inputs for which the method successfully terminates. Blocking techniques [BS01, BS06] ensure termination of tableau decision procedures for satisfiable inputs since they effect that a finite branch witnessing satisfiability is completely constructed before the procedure would eventually compute infinite branches. This is in general not sufficient to ensure termination of tableau-based formula transformation methods which require that *all* branches have to be completed in some sense.

There are two prevalent approaches to second-order quantifier elimination: resolvent computation as exemplified by SCAN, which has been discussed in Chapter 7, and *direct methods* [GSS08], which operate by rewriting second-order formulas to a particular shape for which a theorem such as Ackermann's lemma [Ack35, Sza93] states equivalence to a first-order formula. As shown recently [CGV06, GSS08, Sch08], direct methods are quite successful in handling modal logics and terminate on interesting input classes. Projection elimination by tableau construction can be considered as a third approach, where key techniques of many practically successful systems for satisfiability solving, processing of ontologies and model computation that have been developed in the last decade are transferred.

Investigation of relationships and integration possibilities between the different approaches then arises as an issue for future research. The tableau methods permit to integrate restricted variants of other techniques in a straightforward way as formula simplifications, as shown in Section 12.2.2 for resolvent computation. A challenging question is whether there actually is a single method, of which the three approaches are just different variations. As a step in this direction, in [Wer08] it has been shown that a variant of Ackermann's lemma can be derived from an equivalence that is expressed in terms of a syntactic property related to linklessness and thus to the formal basis of the tableau methods.

References

[Ack35] W. Ackermann. Untersuchungen über das Eliminationsproblem der mathematischen Logik. *Mathematische Annalen*, 110:390–413, 1935.

[Bau00] P. Baumgartner. FDPLL – A first-order Davis-Putnam-Logemann-Loveland procedure. In D. McAllester, editor, *Automated Deduction: CADE-17*, volume 1831 of *LNAI*, pages 200–219. Springer, 2000.

[BE93] W. Bibel and E. Eder. Methods and calculi for deduction. In D. M. Gabbay, C. J. Hogger, and J. A. Robinson, editors, *Handbook of Logic in Artificial Intelligence and Logic Programming*, volume 1, chapter 3, pages 67–182. Oxford University Press, 1993.

[BFN96] P. Baumgartner, U. Furbach, and I. Niemelä. Hyper tableaux. In J. J. Alferes, L. M. Pereira, and E. Orlowska, editors, *Logics in Artificial Intelligence: European Workshop, JELIA'96*, volume 1126 of *LNAI*, pages 1–17. Springer, 1996.

[BFT04] P. Baumgartner, A. Fuchs, and C. Tinelli. Darwin: A theorem prover for the model evolution calculus. In S. Schulz, G. Sutcliffe, and T. Tammet, editors, *Proceedings of the 1st Workshop on Empirically Successful First Order Reasoning, ESFOR'04*, Electronic Notes in Theoretical Computer Science. Elsevier, 2004.

[Bib92] W. Bibel. *Deduktion – Automatisierung der Logik.* Oldenbourg, München, 1992.

[BL99] E. Birnbaum and E. L. Lozinskii. The good old Davis-Putnam procedure helps counting models. *Journal of Artificial Intelligence Research*, 10:457–477, 1999.

[BP00] R. J. Bayardo and J. D. Pehoushek. Counting models using connected components. In *Proceedings of the Seventeenth National Conference on Artificial Intelligence and Twelfth Conference on Innovative Applications of Artificial Intelligence*, pages 157–162. AAAI Press / The MIT Press, 2000.

[Bry92] R. E. Bryant. Symbolic Boolean manipulation with ordered binary-decision diagrams. *ACM Computing Surveys*, 24(3):293–318, 1992.

[BS97] R. J. Bayardo and R. C. Schrag. Using CSP look-back techniques to solve real-world SAT instances. In *AAAI-97: Proceedings of the 14th National Conference on Artificial Intelligence*, pages 203–208. AAAI Press, 1997.

[BS01] F. Baader and U. Sattler. An overview of tableau algorithms for description logics. *Studia Logica*, 69:5–40, 2001.

[BS06] P. Baumgartner and R. Schmidt. Blocking and other enhancements for bottom-up model generation methods. In U. Furbach and N. Shankar, editors, *Automated Reasoning – Third International Joint Conference on Automated Reasoning (IJCAR)*, volume 4130 of *LNAI*, pages 125–139. Springer, 2006.

[CDS96] M. Cadoli, F. M. Donini, and M. Schaerf. Is intractability of nonmonotonic reasoning a real drawback? *Artificial Intelligence*, 88(1–2):215–251, 1996.

[CGV06] W. Conradie, V. Goranko, and D. Vakarelov. Algorithmic correspondence and completeness in modal logic. I. the core algorithm SQEMA. *Logical Methods in Computer Science*, 2(1:5):1–26, 2006.

[CL73] C.-L. Chang and R. C.-T. Lee. *Symbolic Logic and Mechanical Theorem Proving.* Academic Press, Boston, Massachusetts, 1973.

[Cra57] W. Craig. Three uses of the Herbrand-Gentzen theorem in relating model theory and proof theory. *Journal of Symbolic Logic*, 22(3):269–285, 1957.

[Dar01a] A. Darwiche. Decomposable negation normal form. *Journal of the ACM*, 48(4):608–647, 2001.

[Dar01b] A. Darwiche. On the tractability of counting theory models and its application to belief revision and truth maintenance. *Journal of Applied Non-Classical Logics*, 11(1–2):11–34, 2001.

[Dar04] A. Darwiche. New advances in compiling CNF to decomposable negation normal form. In R. L. de Mántaras and L. Saitta, editors, *ECAI 2004: Proceedings of the 16th Eureopean Conference on Artificial Intelligence*, pages 328–332. IOS Press, 2004.

[DGHP99] M. D'Agostino, D. M. Gabbay, R. Hähnle, and J. Posegga, editors. *Handbook of Tableau Methods.* Kluwer Academic Publishers, Dordrecht, 1999.

[DLL62] M. Davis, G. Logemann, and D. Loveland. A machine program for theorem proving. *Communications of the ACM*, 5(7), 1962.

[DŁS97] P. Doherty, W. Łukaszewicz, and A. Szałas. Computing circumscription revisited: A reduction algorithm. *Journal of Automated Reasoning*, 18(3):297–338, 1997.

[DM02] A. Darwiche and P. Marquis. A knowledge compilation map. *Journal of Artificial Intelligence Research*, 17:229–264, 2002.

[DP60] M. Davis and H. Putnam. A computing procedure for quantification theory. *JACM*, 7(3):201–215, 1960.

[DS04] P. Doherty and A. Szałas. On the correspondence between approximations and similarity. In *Rough Sets and Current Trends in Computing: 4th International Conference, RSCTC 2004*, volume 3066 of *LNCS*, pages 143–152. Springer, 2004.

[EFT96] H.-D. Ebbinghaus, J. Flum, and W. Thomas. *Einführung in die mathematische Logik.* Spektrum Akademischer Verlag, Heidelberg, 4th edition, 1996.

[Fit95] M. Fitting. *First-order logic and automated theorem proving.* Springer, Berlin, 2nd edition, 1995.

[Fit99] M. Fitting. Introduction. In D'Agostino et al. [DGHP99], pages 1–43.

[GHSV04] V. Goranko, U. Hustadt, R. A. Schmidt, and D. Vakarelov. SCAN is complete for all Sahlqvist formulae. In R. Berghammer, B. Möller, and G. Struth, editors, *Relational and Kleene-Algebraic Methods in Computer Science, RelMiCS 7*, volume 3051 of *LNCS*, pages 149–162. Springer, 2004.

[GLW06] S. Ghilardi, C. Lutz, and F. Wolter. Did I damage my ontology? a case for conservative extensions in description logics. In P. Doherty, J. Mylopoulos, and C. Welty, editors, *Principles of Knowledge Representation and Reasoning: Proceedings of the Tenth International Conference (KR'06)*, pages 187–197. AAAI Press, 2006.

[GM05] D. M. Gabbay and L. Maksimova. *Interpolation and Definability – Modal and Intuitionistic Logic.* Oxford University Press, 2005.

[GO92] D. Gabbay and H. J. Ohlbach. Quantifier elimination in second-order predicate logic. In B. Nebel, C. Rich, and W. Swartout, editors, *Principles of Knowledge Representation and Reasoning: Proceedings of the Third International Conference (KR'92)*, pages 425–435. Morgan Kaufmann, San Mateo, California, 1992.

[GSS08] D. M. Gabbay, R. A. Schmidt, and A. Szałas. *Second-Order Quantifier Elimination: Foundations, Computational Aspects and Applications.* College Publications, London, 2008.

[Häh01] R. Hähnle. Tableaux and related methods. In A. Robinson and A. Voronkov, editors, *Handbook of Automated Reasoning*, volume I, chapter 3, pages 100–178. Elsevier Science, 2001.

[HD04] J. Huang and A. Darwiche. Using DPLL for efficient OBDD construction. In *Theory and Applications of Satisfiability Testing: 7th International Conference, SAT 2004*, volume 3542 of *LNCS*, pages 157–172. Springer, 2004.

[HD05] J. Huang and A. Darwiche. DPLL with a trace: From SAT to knowledge compilation. In L. P. Kaelbling and A. Saffiotti, editors, *Proceedings of the Nineteenth International Joint Conference on Artificial Intelligence, IJCAI-05*, pages 156–162, 2005.

[HM01] V. Haarslev and R. Möller. RACER system description. In R. Gore, A. Leitsch, and T. Nipkow, editors, *Automated Reasoning: First International Joint Conference, IJCAR-2001*, volume 2083 of *LNAI*, pages 701–706. Springer, 2001.

[HMR05] R. Hähnle, N. V. Murray, and E. Rosenthal. Normal forms for knowledge compilation. In M.-S. Hacid, Z. W. Raś, and S. Tsumoto, editors, *Foundations of Intelligent Systems: 15th International Symposium, ISMIS 2005*, volume 3488 of *LNAI*, pages 304–313. Springer, 2005.

[Hoo01] E. Hoogland. *Definability and Interpolation – Model-theoretic Investigations.* PhD thesis, University of Amsterdam, Amsterdam, 2001.

[Hor98] I. Horrocks. The FaCT system. In H. de Swart, editor, *Automated Reasoning with Analytic Tableaux and Related Methods: International Conference, TABLEAUX'98*, volume 1397 of *LNAI*, pages 307–312. Springer, 1998.

[HS00] H. H. Hoos and T. Stützle. SATLIB: an online resource for research on SAT. In I. P. Gent, H. v. Maaren, and T. Walsh, editors, *SAT 2000*, pages 283–292. IOS Press, 2000.

[KH69] R. Kowalski and P. Hayes. Semantic trees in automatic theorem proving. In B. Meltzer and D. Michie, editors, *Machine intelligence 4*, pages 87–101. Edinburgh University Press, Edinburgh, 1969.

[KHM99] J. Kohlas, R. Haenni, and S. Moral. Propositional information systems. *Journal of Logic and Computation*, 9(5):651–681, 1999.

[KM96] J. Kohlas and S. Moral. Propositional information systems. Technical Report 96–01, Institute of Informatics, University of Fribourg, 1996.

[Knu97] D. E. Knuth. *Fundamental Algorithms*, volume 1 of *The Art of Computer Programming*. Addison-Wesley, Boston, Massachusetts, third edition, 1997.

[Koh03] J. Kohlas. *Information Algebras – Generic Structures for Inference.* Springer, Berlin, 2003.

[Kom91] J. Komorowski. Synthesis of programs in the partial deduction framework. In M. R. Lowry and R. McCartney, editors, *Automating Software Design*, chapter 15, pages 377–404. AAAI Press / The MIT Press, Menlo Park, California, 1991.

[KS91] H. Kautz and B. Selman. A General Framework for Knowledge Compilation. In H. Richter and M. Richter, editors, *Proceedings of the International Workshop on Processing Delarative Knowledge: PDK '91*, volume 567 of *LNCS*, pages 287–300. Springer, 1991.

[KS92] H. A. Kautz and B. Selman. Forming concepts for fast inference. In *AAAI-92: Proceedings of the 10th National Conference on Artifical Intelligence*, pages 786–793. AAAI Press, 1992.

[KS96] J. Kohlas and R. Stärk. Information algebras and information systems. Technical Report 96–14, Institute of Informatics, University of Fribourg, 1996.

[Let93] R. Letz. *First-Order Calculi and Proof Procedures for Automated Deduction.* PhD thesis, Technische Hochschule Darmstadt, Darmstadt, 1993.

[Let98] R. Letz. Clausal tableaux. In W. Bibel and P. H. Schmitt, editors, *Automated Deduction – A Basis for Applications*, volume I, pages 43–72. Kluwer Academic Publishers, Dordrecht, 1998.

[LLM03] J. Lang, P. Liberatore, and P. Marquis. Propositional independence – formula-variable independence and forgetting. *Journal of Artificial Intelligence Research*, 18:391–443, 2003.

[LMG94] R. Letz, K. Mayr, and C. Goller. Controlled integration of the cut rule into connection tableau calculi. *Journal of Automated Reasoning*, 13(3):297–337, December 1994.

[LR94] F. Lin and R. Reiter. Forget It! In R. Greiner and D. Subramanian, editors, *Working Notes, AAAI Fall Symposium on Relevance*, pages 154–159. American Association for Artificial Intelligence, Menlo Park, California, 1994.

[LS88] S. Lauritzen and D. Spiegelhalter. Local computations with probabilities on graphical structures and their application to expert systems. *Journal of the Royal Statistical Society*, 50(2):157–224, 1988.

[LS01] R. Letz and G. Stenz. DCTP: A disconnection calculus theorem prover. In R. Gore, A. Leitsch, and T. Nipkow, editors, *Automated Reasoning: First International Joint Conference, IJCAR-2001*, volume 2083 of *LNAI*, pages 381–385. Springer, 2001.

[Lyn59] R. Lyndon. An interpolation theorem in the predicate calculus. *Pacific Journal of Mathematics*, 9:129–142, 1959.

[MB88] R. Manthey and F. Bry. SATCHMO: A theorem prover implemented in Prolog. In E. L. Lusk and R. A. Overbeek, editors, *9th International Conference on Automated Deduction: CADE-9*, volume 310 of *LNCS*, pages 415–434. Springer, 1988.

[McM02] K. L. McMillan. Applying SAT methods in unbounded symbolic model checking. In E. Brinksma and K. G. Larsen, editors, *Computer Aided Verification: 14th International Conference, CAV 2002*, volume 2404 of *LNCS*, pages 250–264. Springer, 2002.

[McM05] K. L. McMillan. Applications of Craig interpolants in model checking. In N. Halbwachs and L. Zuck, editors, *Tools and Algorithms for the Construction and Analysis of Systems: 11th International Conference, TACAS 2005*, volume 3440 of *LNCS*, pages 1–12. Springer, 2005.

[MMZ+01] M. Moskewicz, C. Madigan, Y. Zhao, L. Zhang, and S. Malik. Chaff: Engineering an efficient SAT solver. In *Proceedings of the 38th Design Automation Conference (DAC'01)*, pages 530–535. ACM Press, New York, 2001.

[MR87] N. V. Murray and E. Rosenthal. Inference with path resolution and semantic graphs. *Journal of the ACM*, 34(2):225–254, 1987.

[MR93] N. V. Murray and E. Rosenthal. Dissolution: Making paths vanish. *Journal of the ACM*, 40(3):504–535, 1993.

[MR94] N. V. Murray and E. Rosenthal. On the relative merits of path dissolution and the method of analytic tableaux. *Theoretical Computer Science*, 131:1–28, 1994.

[MR03] N. V. Murray and E. Rosenthal. Tableaux, path dissolution and decomposable negation normal form for knowledge compilation. In M. Cialdea Mayer and F. Pirri, editors, *Automated Reasoning with Analytic Tableaux and Related Methods: International Conference, TABLEAUX 2003*, volume 2796 of *LNAI*, pages 165–180. Springer, 2003.

[MSS96] J. P. Marques-Silva and K. A. Sakallah. GRASP – a new search algorithm for satisfiability. In *Proceedings of the 1996 IEEE/ACM International Conference on Computer-Aided Design, ICCAD'96*, pages 220–227. IEEE Computer Society, 1996.

[Mun84] D. Mundici. Tautologies with a unique Craig interpolant, uniform vs. nonuniform complexity. *Annals of Pure and Applied Logic*, 27:265–273, 1984.

[NOT05] R. Nieuwenhuis, A. Oliveras, and C. Tinelli. Abstract DPLL and Abstract DPLL modulo theories. In F. Baader and A. Voronkov, editors, *Logic for Programming, Artificial Intelligence, and Reasoning: 11th International Workshop, LPAR 2004*, volume 3452 of *LNAI*, pages 36–50. Springer, 2005.

[NOT06] R. Nieuwenhuis, A. Oliveras, and C. Tinelli. Solving SAT and SAT modulo theories: from an abstract Davis-Putnam-Logemann-Loveland procedure to DPLL(T). *Journal of the ACM*, 53(6):937–977, November 2006.

[NS97] I. Niemelä and P. Simons. Smodels – an implementation of the stable model and well-founded semantics for normal logic programs. In J. Dix, U. Furbach, and A. Nerode, editors, *Logic Programming and Nonmonotonic Reasoning: Fourth International Conference, LPNMR'97*, volume 1265 of *LNCS*, pages 420–429. Springer, 1997.

[Rob68] J. Robinson. The generalized resolution principle. In D. Michie, editor, *Machine intelligence 3*, pages 77–94. Edinburgh University Press, Edinburgh, 1968.

[Sch08] R. A. Schmidt. Improved second-order quantifier elimination in modal logic. In S. Hölldobler, C. Lutz, and H. Wansing, editors, *Logics in Artificial Intelligence: 11th European Conference, JELIA 08*, volume 5293 of *LNAI*, pages 375–388. Springer, 2008.

[Smu95] R. M. Smullyan. *First-Order Logic*. Dover Publications, Inc., New York, corrected edition, 1995.

[SS90] P. Shenoy and G. Shafer. Axioms for probability and belief function propagation. In R. Shachter, T. Levitt, J. Lemmer, and L. Kanal, editors, *UAI '88: Proceedings of the Fourth Annual Conference on Uncertainty in Artificial Intelligence*, pages 169–198. North Holland, 1990.

[ST07] U. Schöning and J. Torán. A note on the size of Craig interpolants. In T. Schwentick, D. Thérien, and H. Vollmer, editors, *Circuits, Logic, and Games*, number 06451 in Dagstuhl Seminar Proceedings. Internationales Begegnungs- und Forschungszentrum für Informatik (IBFI), Dagstuhl, Germany, 2007.

[Sza93] A. Szałas. On the correspondence between modal and classical logic: An automated approach. *Journal of Logic and Computation*, 3(6):605–620, 1993.

[TBW04] C. Thiffault, F. Bacchus, and T. Walsh. Solving non-clausal formulas with DPLL search. In M. Wallace, editor, *Principles and Practice of Constraint Programming: 10th International Conference, CP 2004*, volume 3258 of *LNAI*, pages 663–678. Springer, 2004.

[Tse70] G. S. Tseitin. On the complexity of derivation in propositional calculus. In A. O. Slisenko, editor, *Studies in constructive mathematics and mathematical logic, part 2*, pages 115–125. Consultants Bureau, New York, 1970.

[Wer03] C. Wernhard. System Description: KRHyper. Technical Report Fachberichte Informatik 14–2003, Universität Koblenz-Landau, Institut für Informatik, Universitätsstr. 1, D-56070 Koblenz, 2003.

[Wer04] C. Wernhard. Semantic knowledge partitioning. In J. J. Alferes and J. Leite, editors, *Logics in Artificial Intelligence: 9th European Conference, JELIA 04*, volume 3229 of *LNAI*, pages 552–564. Springer, 2004.

[Wer08] C. Wernhard. Literal projection for first order logic. In S. Hölldobler, C. Lutz, and H. Wansing, editors, *Logics in Artificial Intelligence: 11th European Conference, JELIA 08*, volume 5293 of *LNAI*, pages 389–402. Springer, 2008.

[WM97] N. Wilson and J. Mengin. Logical deduction using the local computation framework. In *International Workshop on First-Order Theorem Proving, FTP'97*, RISC-Linz Report Series No. 97–50, pages 135–139. Johannes Kepler Universität, Linz, 1997.

[ZM02] L. Zhang and S. Malik. The quest for efficient Boolean satisfiability solvers. In A. Voronkov, editor, *Automated Deduction: CADE-18*, volume 2392 of *LNAI*, pages 295–313. Springer, 2002.

Index of Definitions

Index of Examples

Index of Theorems

Index of Propositions

Index of Symbols

$$
\begin{array}{lll}
\mathfrak{I} \models_{std} p(t_1, \ldots, t_n) & \text{iff}_{\text{def}} & \langle \mathfrak{I}(t_1), \ldots, \mathfrak{I}(t_n) \rangle \in \mathfrak{a}(p),^4 \\
\mathfrak{I} \models_{std} \forall x F' & \text{iff}_{\text{def}} & \text{for all } a \in A \text{ it holds that } \mathfrak{I}\frac{a}{x} \models_{std} F', \\
\mathfrak{I} \models_{std} \exists x F' & \text{iff}_{\text{def}} & \text{there exists an } a \in A \text{ such that } \mathfrak{I}\frac{a}{x} \models_{std} F'.
\end{array}
$$

$$\begin{array}{lll}
(1) & \mathfrak{I} \models_{std} (\exists Y F_1)\{x \mapsto a\} & \text{iff} \\
(2) & \mathfrak{I} \models_{std} \exists Y(F_1\{x \mapsto a\}) & \text{iff} \\
(3) & \text{There exists an } R \subseteq A^n\text{: } \mathfrak{I}\tfrac{R}{Y} \models_{std} F_1\{x \mapsto a\} & \text{iff} \\
(4) & \text{There exists an } R \subseteq A^n\text{: } \mathfrak{I}\tfrac{R}{Y}\tfrac{a}{x} \models_{std} F_1 & \text{iff} \\
(5) & \text{There exists an } R \subseteq A^n\text{: } \mathfrak{I}\tfrac{a}{x}\tfrac{R}{Y} \models_{std} F_1 & \text{iff} \\
(6) & \mathfrak{I}\tfrac{a}{x} \models_{std} \exists Y F_1. &
\end{array}$$

$$\begin{array}{l}\text{if } \mathcal{L}(F_2) \subseteq S, \text{ then} \\ \qquad F_1 \models F_2 \text{ if and only if } F_1 \models_S F_2.\end{array}$$

(ii) $$F \equiv F \wedge (B_1 \vee \ldots \vee B_n),$$

(vi) $$\mathsf{p} \wedge F_4 \models F_3.$$

$$F_{N_i} \wedge B_{N_n} \models F_{N_n}.$$

Index

Underlined entries refer to the page where a concept is defined or introduced.

Dissertationen zur Künstlichen Intelligenz

Weitere Titel aus dieser Reihe / Available in the same series

DISKI 323	H. Meine / The GeoMap Representation: On Topologically Correct Sub-pixel Image Analysis
DISKI 322	C. Kühn / An Einsatz von Wissen über Zustandsverhalten für die wissensbasierte Konfigurierung technischer Systeme
DISKI 321	I. Seifert / Spatial Planning Assistance
DISKI 320	F. Dylla / An Agent Control Perspective on Qualitative Reasoning
DISKI 319	C. Becker-Asano / WASABI: Affect Simulation for Agents with Believable Interactivity
DISKI 318	M. Ragni / Räumliche Repräsentation, Komplexität und Deduktion: Eine kognitive Komplexitätstheorie
DISKI 317	A. Fexa / Erzeugung mehrsprachlicher Beschreibungen von Verkehrsbildfolgen
DISKI 316	C. Heβ / Trust-Based Recommendations in Multi-Layer Networks
DISKI 315	P.G. Gebhard / Emotionalisierung interaktiver Virtueller Charaktere
DISKI 314	K.-F. Richter / Context-Specific Route Directions: Generation of Cognitively Motivated Wayfinding Instructions
DISKI 313	A. Kranstedt / Situierte Generierung deiktischer Objektreferenz in der multimodalen Mensch-Maschine-Interaktion
DISKI 312	P. Stelldinger / Image Digitization and its Influence on Shape Properties in Finite Dimensions
DISKI 311	A. Schlapbach / Writer Identification and Verification
DISKI 310	C. Gips / Anwendung von Verfahren des Machinellen Lernens und von Evolutionären Algorithmen bei der räumlichen Inferenz
DISKI 309	A.D. Lattner / Temporal Pattern Mining in Dynamic Environments
DISKI 308	Y. Haxhimusa / The structurally Optimal Dual Graph Pyramid and ist Application in Image Partitioning
DISKI 307	M. Atzmüller / Knowledge-Intensive Subgroup Mining - Techniques for Automatic and Interactive Discovery
DISKI 306	M. Huelse / Multifunktionalität rekurrenter neuronaler Netze Synthese und Analyse nichtlinearer Kontrolle autonomer Roboter
DISKI 305	R. Wasinger / Multimodal Interaction with Mobile Devices: Fusing a Broad Spectrum of Modality Combinations
DISKI 304	Oliver Obst / Controlling Physical Multiagent Teams: Getting League-Independent Results from RoboCup Soccer